Praise for *Fasting and Feasting*

"Of all my culinary heroes, Patience Gray was the most magical—and the most remote. I was lucky enough to meet her—just once. Adam Federman's beautifully considered and well-researched biography shines a bright light on Gray's complicated, surprising, and gutsy life."

—Alice Waters, owner, Chez Panisse; author of *The Art of Simple Food*

"Adam Federman's *Fasting and Feasting* is an impressively thorough, absorbing account of the rich life of Patience Gray, one of the last century's finest and least-known writers on food. No one before her or since has written with more first-hand experience or with the blunt, clear-eyed eloquence that she brought to her classic memoir of Mediterranean village life, *Honey from a Weed*. Federman illuminates her unlikely path from the post-war London newspaper world and translating *Larousse Gastronomique* to stone quarries across the northern Mediterranean and the remote, sculpture-studded corner of Apulia where she settled, wrote, and engaged with the growing community of food writers, sometimes contentiously. *Fasting and Feasting* is a timely celebration of a remarkable life."

—Harold McGee, author of *On Food and Cooking: The Science and Lore of the Kitchen*

"Patience Gray cast a spell over everyone she met, with her smoke-husky voice, darting observations, and bottomless erudition. In this marvelously well-researched biography, Adam Federman gives us sorceress and scholar: the postwar-London artistic Bohemia that shaped her and that she, with her stubborn unconventionality in a notably unconventional milieu, helped shape. Only the remote southern Mediterranean was wild enough for her own imagination and curiosity to soar—and her meticulously observed and researched descriptions of its food and life still have the enchanting force Federman makes us feel."

—Corby Kummer, senior editor, *The Atlantic*; author of *The Pleasures of Slow Food*

"Patience Gray's *Honey from a Weed* is an anomaly in the world of cookbooks—an inimitable, passionate, and reader-challenging account of her off-the-grid life in poverty-stricken rural areas of Catalonia, Tuscany, the Cyclades, and, most importantly, Apulia.

"Part acerbic diarist, part gifted ethnobotanist, part fervent environmentalist, part food writer whose recipes still spoke their rustic dialect, Patience Gray wove her life, thoughts, and experiences into an indisputable masterpiece. Now, in Adam Federman, she has found her biographer—astute, empathetic, indefatigable in pursuit of the painterly details that he then deftly works into a portrait of an amazing original — and the remarkable company she kept."

—John Thorne, author of *Outlaw Cook* and *Serious Pig*

"Adam Federman reveals the fascinating life of Patience Gray, whose *Honey from a Weed* may be the best book ever written about food. With admirable clarity, drawing on deep research, Federman has produced a strong portrait of a compelling personality who chose a way of life far outside the norm."

—Edward Behr, editor and publisher, *The Art of Eating*

"Patience Gray was probably the least-known great food writer the English-speaking world has ever produced. Her influence has been pervasive, even as she herself has resisted easy definition. With grace and impeccable understanding, Adam Federman in *Fasting and Feasting* undertakes the difficult task of explaining Gray's contrary enigma as well as her considerable charm. His book is fascinating in itself and should introduce one of our most important food writers to a much wider audience."

—Nancy Harmon Jenkins, author of
The Four Seasons of Pasta and *Flavors of Puglia*

"A close look at any life is bound to be interesting, but the life of Patience Gray is unusually large and deep. If you know her only from her seminal book, *Honey from a Weed*—which may well be true for many readers—you will possibly be surprised and certainly delighted by *Fasting and Feasting*. What a well-articulated and inspiring life, and how fortunate we are to learn of it in such detail."

—Deborah Madison, author of *Vegetable Literacy* and *In My Kitchen*

"Patience Gray trail-blazed untrammeled ground as she explored the more literary, naturalistic, cultural, and ethnobotanical dimensions of food writing that many of us have come to appreciate today. As this captivating biography reveals, Gray's inimitable style and idiosyncratic choice of subject matter were organically grounded in a life as unique and refreshing as her writing. This book allows us to fully appreciate how Gray became a major but often cryptic force directing the very trajectory of food writing, as it aspired to be literature of the highest order. She would remain without peer, except for the fact that M. F. K. Fisher, Alan Davidson, Robert Capon, Betty Fussell, and Jim Harrison all seemed to have absorbed something of her legacy. Savor this feast."

—Gary Paul Nabhan, author of *Growing Food in a Hotter, Drier Land*

"Being given a behind-the-scenes view of *Honey from a Weed* is a true eye-opener. Federman's elegant, detailed, and insightful account fleshes out one's appreciation of Gray's writing and turns this famous author into a familiar friend. Now it seems clear what the next step in Patience Gray's legacy is for us today: making an environmentally pure lifestyle a choice accessible to everyone, not only those with financially generous family and well-placed connections. Federman brings Patience to life so clearly, I can hear her cautioning and encouraging us with her wisdom."

—Tamara Griffiths, author of *Oaks and the Apennines*

FASTING AND FEASTING

FASTING AND FEASTING

The Life of Visionary Food Writer
PATIENCE GRAY

ADAM FEDERMAN

Chelsea Green Publishing
White River Junction, Vermont
London, UK

Project Manager: Alexander Bullett
Project Editor: Benjamin Watson
Copy Editor: Angela Boyle
Proofreader: Rachel Shields
Indexer: Shana Milkie
Designer: Melissa Jacobson

Printed in the United States of America.
First printing August 2017.
10 9 8 7 6 5 4 3   18 19 20 21

Our Commitment to Green Publishing

Chelsea Green sees publishing as a tool for cultural change and ecological stewardship. We strive to
align our book manufacturing practices with our editorial mission and to reduce the impact of our
business enterprise in the environment. We print our books and catalogs on chlorine-free recycled
paper, using vegetable-based inks whenever possible. This book may cost slightly more because it
was printed on paper that contains recycled fiber, and we hope you'll agree that it's worth it. Chelsea
Green is a member of the Green Press Initiative (www.greenpressinitiative.org), a nonprofit coali-
tion of publishers, manufacturers, and authors working to protect the world's endangered forests
and conserve natural resources. *Fasting and Feasting* was printed on paper supplied by Thomson-
Shore that contains 100% postconsumer recycled fiber.

Library of Congress Cataloging-in-Publication Data
Names: Federman, Adam, 1979– author.
Title: Fasting and feasting : the life of visionary food writer Patience Gray / Adam Federman.
Description: White River Junction, Vermont : Chelsea Green Publishing, [2017]
   | Includes bibliographical references and index.
Identifiers: LCCN 2017001558| ISBN 9781603586085 (hardcover) | ISBN 9781603588232 (pbk.)
   | ISBN 9781603586092 (ebook) | ISBN 9781603587723 (audiobook)
Subjects: LCSH: Gray, Patience. | Food writers—Great Britain—Biography.
Classification: LCC TX649.G73 F43 2017 | DDC 641.5092 [B] —dc23
LC record available at https://lccn.loc.gov/2017001558

Chelsea Green Publishing
85 North Main Street, Suite 120
White River Junction, VT 05001
(802) 295-6300
www.chelseagreen.com

For my parents

Contents

Introduction

Patience Gray's *Honey from a Weed* is one of the most important and best-loved cookbooks of the twentieth century, yet its author remains little known beyond a small circle of food writers and critics. Such is the fate, perhaps, of a woman who lived for more than thirty years in a remote corner of southern Italy—without electricity, modern plumbing, or telephone—and liked to say, deliberately misquoting Gertrude Stein, that she wrote only for herself and friends. As her publisher Alan Davidson once observed, "She simply wished her accumulated knowledge to be preserved in a permanent, beautiful form for the benefit of her grandchildren."[1]

Alan rescued the typescript from oblivion, and when *Honey from a Weed* was published in 1986, it was immediately hailed as a classic. *Gourmet* described it as "magically idiosyncratic" and placed Patience alongside Patrick Leigh Fermor, Freya Stark, and Elizabeth David. In an early review of *Honey from a Weed*, John Thorne wrote that only D. H. Lawrence was her equal "in conveying the rich physical sensuality of Mediterranean life."[2] Cookbook editor Judith Jones, who reviewed the manuscript for Knopf but knew that they would never dare publish it, said she fell in love with it and copied several pages "to read again when I needed that kind of refreshment."[3] In an essay titled "Eat or Die", the late novelist Jim Harrison called Patience "a wandering Bruce Chatwin of food."[4] In other words, she was much more than just a food writer. *Honey from a Weed*—part recipe book, part travelogue, and part memoir—offered a singularly evocative portrait of a remote and fast-disappearing way of life. Following the publication of *Honey from a Weed*, food writers sought Patience out and many made the pilgrimage to Puglia to see her, a testament to the power of her work. She was profiled by Paul Levy, appeared on the BBC's *Food Programme* with Derek Cooper, and was featured along with her partner, the Belgian sculptor Norman Mommens, in the Italian magazine *Casa Vogue*.

Although she enjoyed the attention, Patience was rather guarded about her own life. This applied not only to visiting journalists and food writers but to friends and family as well. There was "an aura of secrecy about her," a sense that her past was somehow shuttered, which Patience did little to dispel.[5] "Patience loved secrets, secret rooms, dark corners, mysteries and so on," her friend Ulrike Voswinckel recalled.[6] This aura of secrecy was enhanced by her interest in astrology and mysticism and her vast folkloric knowledge of edible plants and mushrooms. She shared her workspace in Puglia—to which others were rarely admitted—with a large black snake and often ruminated on the symbolic meaning of the scorpion, which happened to be Patience's astrological sign. She was born on Halloween. It is perhaps not surprising then that several people, including Paul Levy in his profile for the *Observer* and the *Wall Street Journal*, described Patience as a modern-day witch.

Yet in the few interviews she gave, she proffered tantalizing clues to her earlier life: a great-grandfather who was a Polish rabbi; surviving the war years in a primitive cottage in rural Sussex, where she first learned to forage; raising two children out of wedlock in postwar London. Before she embarked on her Mediterranean odyssey in 1962, Patience worked closely with some of the leading designers and landscape architects of her day. She edited a book on indoor plants and gardens in 1952, was assistant to the head of the school of graphic design at the Royal College of Art until 1955, and in the late 1950s and early 1960s, designed textiles for Edinburgh Weavers and wallpapers for Wallpaper Manufacturers Limited. She was also the first editor of the "woman's page" at the *Observer* from 1958 to 1962, and her weekly column reflected her background in art and design.

Of course I knew none of this when I happened upon Patience's obituary in the quarterly food journal *The Art of Eating* in 2005. In the reminiscence, the magazine's editor, Ed Behr, who visited Patience on two occasions at her farmhouse in Puglia, called *Honey from a Weed* "one of the best books that will ever be written about food."[7] It was unusually high praise from a discerning and often unsparing critic. Soon after, I discovered a copy of *Honey from a Weed* on a shelf in my parents' kitchen. A single recipe was marked: "Catalan veal stew with prunes and potatoes," described in a note scribbled in the margin as "fabulous, rich, full, and simple to make." I read the book from cover to cover and was swept away by its originality, its sense of urgency—the introduction is a powerful argument in favor of eating seasonally—and its vivid descriptions of fasting and feasting. It was unlike anything I'd ever read before. Yet despite the book's intensely personal nature, it revealed little of its author's past, with the exception of a fleeting and somewhat cryptic reference to gathering fungi in a wood in Sussex during wartime. Naturally I wanted to know more.

I soon learned that not only had Patience written one of the best-selling British cookbooks of the 1950s, *Plats du Jour*, but she had also had a major hand in translating *Larousse Gastronomique*—the first English-language edition was published in 1961. In addition, she had written a collection of autobiographical essays (*Work Adventures Childhood Dreams*), a travelogue of a year spent on the Greek island of Naxos (*Ring Doves and Snakes*), and had edited a collection of Catalan recipes recorded by her friend Irving Davis. I found the little I knew of Patience tremendously compelling and sent a letter to her daughter, Miranda, who had illustrated her posthumously published book, *The Centaur's Kitchen*. I was told that all Patience's letters, unpublished work, and other papers were still in Puglia, where Patience's son, Nicolas, now lives. In 2006 I made my first visit.

The long drive from the train station in Lecce, a city famous for its baroque architecture and equally refined pastries, takes you through austere and monotonously flat agricultural land dominated by centuries-old olive trees, ancient ruins, and newly built solar arrays. Apart from the glimpses to the south of pale blue sparkling sea, one feels dropped in the middle of a somewhat forsaken and otherworldly landscape. The old farmhouse where Patience and Norman lived, Masseria Spigolizzi, sits atop a high point overlooking the Mediterranean, not far from the villages of Presicce and Salve, at the very southern tip of the heel of Italy. On clear evenings one can see the sun set over Calabria. From the nearby eastern shore of the peninsula, Albania and the island of Corfu are visible on clear days. Now a popular summer venue for European tourists, the region still seems thinly populated. When Patience and Norman settled here in 1970, the countryside was largely empty, owing to decades of rural flight. Few outsiders had heard of the Salento or bothered to visit, let alone make the area their home. In his magisterial wartime picture of life in nearby Basilicata, *Christ Stopped at Eboli*, Carlo Levi noted, "No one has come to this land except as an enemy, a conqueror, or a visitor devoid of understanding."[8]

Patience and Norman's friends in Carrara, the heart of Tuscany's once thriving marble industry and where they had lived for five years, considered the move a "descent into Africa." Even Patience, who would grow to love the wildness of the Mediterranean scrubland (the *macchia*) and the *masseria's* solitary aspect, had her doubts. In a letter to her mother Olive, after a visit in 1968, she wrote, "Puglia is a very intoxicating place but probably altogether too remote to settle in. It really is the *fin du monde*."

During the previous decade Patience and Norman had traveled throughout the Mediterranean, living on Naxos, in Catalonia, Carrara, and the Veneto, searching for a place to live and work. *Honey from a Weed* was the product of those travels and is as much a tribute to the people they befriended—peasants, farmers, and laborers—as it is a book of recipes. Indeed the recipes, often recounted as part of a larger narrative, are inseparable from the way of life that gave rise to and sustained them. It was this relationship that Patience sought to illuminate.

Ed Behr is not alone in his assessment of Patience's work. *Honey from a Weed* has continued to captivate readers and, arguably, appeals to an even wider audience today than it did when it was first published. In the late 1990s Nigel Slater praised it in an essay on the art of recipe writing; a few years later April Bloomfield named it one of her favorite cookbooks; in 2016 Jeremy Lee, head chef of London's *Quo Vadis*, described *Honey from a Weed* as "remarkably ahead of its time." In the mid 1980s there were few people truly interested in foraging for edible plants or raising a pig and making their own *coppa*. Much has changed since then, and the case Patience made for eating locally, observing seasonal rhythms, and growing one's own food has become commonplace. Articles on foraging and wild foods, now de rigueur in such magazines as *Food and Wine* and *Bon Appétit*, have also appeared in mainstream nonculinary publications. In 2006 the *New Yorker's* Bill Buford wrote about the pleasures and perils of butchering a pig in his New York City apartment. Urban gardens and rooftop farms are flourishing. Not surprisingly, some of the world's top restaurants now devote significant resources both to foraging and to cultivating a bit of land. "Perhaps this very old approach is beginning once again to inspire those who cook in more complex urban situations," Patience observed in *Honey from a Weed*.[9] Indeed, her hope that a more traditional approach to food and cooking would take root, even amongst city dwellers, has exceeded the most optimistic expectations. *Honey from a Weed* lives on, a source of inspiration to many, but Patience herself remains an "almost forgotten culinary star."[10] A full account of her remarkable life is long overdue.

CHAPTER ONE

Beginnings

P atience was fifty-two when she and Norman left for the south of
Italy, and they both liked to say that life began at Spigolizzi. Indeed
Patience's life was composed of a series of new beginnings, but there is
some truth to the fact that the move to Puglia marked a more decisive
break with her past and with England. The very southern tip of the Salentine peninsula is about as far from London as one can possibly venture
without actually leaving Europe. The dialects spoken there are unintelligible even to many native Italian speakers. In some villages, Griko, a
language whose origins can be traced back to Homeric Greek, is still in
use. As Patience wrote in *Honey from a Weed*, there is a sense of "being
marooned in an older kind of time."

The arid, unforgiving landscape may have seemed all too remote when
they first visited in 1968, but Patience was immediately drawn to the
rich diversity of plant life, trees, shrubs, and flowers. On that first journey
she encountered the "barbed seeds of minute leguminous plants," "tiny
scented narcissi, fragile starlike crocuses and little cyclamen." It was October, and the ground was covered with the large bulbs of the sea squill—a
plant described at length by Pliny—"bearing their succulent crowns of
virid lily leaves."[1] The rocky outcroppings were covered in orange lichen
and the fossilized imprints of shells, which revealed that millions of years
ago the peninsula had been submerged. Searching for wild asparagus in
early spring, Patience observed pear trees crowned with white blossoms,
rosemary covered in blue flowers, and "asphodels stand[ing] out like
candelabra lit with stars."[2] By mid-April there were purple thistles, yellow
dandelions, the blue and pink flowers of borage, wild garlic (at least eight
varieties), and bright red poppies—a wilderness of flowers that made even
the sea, in all its shades of blue and green, look rather unexceptional.

There are at least 450 species of edible wild plants in the Salento, and Patience gathered many of them. There are so many types of dandelion greens that Patience said they picked them "without mumbling their botanical names." There are all manner of fungi, which Patience considered "the most delicate feast the wild has to offer," usually emerging in early autumn, lasting through January, and reappearing in spring.[3] Well into her eighties Patience continued to forage and identify new species, consulting the sixteenth-century herbals she'd relied on for much of her life.

Patience once described the macchia as "nature unimpaired by human hand" and as the cradle of nearly every valuable wild herb.[4] She inhabited this landscape and was often seen with her basket, wandering alone along the hillside dressed in a long flowing skirt and sandals. Nowhere was she more at home.

Though she returned to England less and less often after the move to Puglia—her last visit was in 1990, fifteen years before her death—Patience never let go of her past, as the thousands of letters to friends and family left behind at Spigolizzi and elsewhere attest. She was a dutiful reader of the *Observer* and later the *Weekly Guardian*, which her mother, Olive, sent by post. It took about three weeks for the papers to arrive, so by the time Patience and Norman received them, it was old copy, ancient by today's standards. But Patience enjoyed reading the work of "a few friends," her old colleagues Peter Heyworth and Philip Toynbee. Plus the papers were useful for starting fires during the long winter months.

This was likely a satisfying exercise for Patience—using the pages of the *Observer*, her old employer and a pillar of British society, to kick-start an incandescent olive-wood fire. Patience often invoked fire as a metaphor, and once told a friend who had experienced a particularly tragic event to "set fire to the past" as she had done with certain episodes in her own life, including to some extent her childhood.[5] Indeed Patience liked to say that her own life could be divided into two periods: the first being postwar London, and the second her travels throughout the Mediterranean beginning in 1962, with emphasis on the latter. This essentially left out the first thirty years of her life, which Patience expressed little interest in revisiting. In her memoir the brief section on childhood is found on page 300 and begins with a quote describing autobiography itself as nothing more than "suppressions" and "lies."

It is perhaps fitting then that *Honey from a Weed* begins and ends with a meditation on fire, its fundamental role in cooking, and its powers of destruction and regeneration. In the book's opening chapter, Patience identifies the properties associated with different types of wood, including a variety of fruit trees, fig wood, tamarisk, olive wood, and ilex. She noted that the Mediterranean scrub and withered shrubs of the macchia "burn with the violence of a blow-torch."[6]

One summer, not long after Patience and Norman had settled in Puglia, the hillside was consumed by just such a fire, the work of an itinerant shepherd hoping to spur the growth of new grass for his impoverished flock. It was a terrifying prospect to watch the flames advance across the wide-open landscape.

But once the fire had dissipated and the fine layer of black ash covering the earth had blown away, Patience and Norman discovered that the neighboring fields were strewn with "jewel-like fragments"—flint, obsidian, splinters of bone, and shards of pottery.

"Picking them up," Patience wrote, "we began to realise that the deserted hill overlooking the Ionian had for millennia been inhabited, if sporadically, by craftsmen and that at our door lay 40,000 years of prehistory, unwritten and unread."[7]

⊰⊰⊰⊱⊱

Patience viewed her own family history as similarly obscured, both by her father's suppression of his Jewish ancestry and her mother's mannered, upper-middle-class, Edwardian background. Her mother, Olive, came from a well-known mercantile family, the Jollys of Bath, whose department stores specialized in women's wear, particularly silk and lace. The Jollys were not only distinguished in the fields of business and politics—Olive's grandfather served as mayor of Bath—but also as writers, critics, and painters.

Patience's grandmother Ethel Dobell Jolly (born March 31, 1856) had a drawing room and salon frequented by artists like the cartoonist George du Maurier, portraitist Hugh Rivière (who was also a cousin), John Collier, and Henry Justice Ford, best known for illustrating Andrew Lang's popular Fairy Books. Ethel's three children all played instruments, and Olive's sister Dorothy ("Dodo"), a towering and influential figure in

Patience's early years, would become a well-regarded violinist who had her own amateur string quartet in London. (She was well known for her musical soirees with artists like Pablo Casals, Alfred Cortot, and Felix Salmond.) They were fluent in Italian and French, could read German, and traveled frequently. Indeed their father, Dr. Henry Colgate (born December 1, 1850), a surgeon in Eastbourne, made it a habit of sending his wife and daughters to Europe during the winter to save on heating costs and focus on his own work and research. Colgate, who attended University College Hospital and was himself the son of a physician, was deeply absorbed in his work and was known to "live and sleep" in his study. As children Patience and her sisters visited him often on Sundays, a "white haired gentleman" who wore the "stiff winged collar, starched cuffs, cutaway coat, [and] grey topper of late Victorians."[8] Patience would inherit another Victorian-era artifact from him, a marble mortar and pestle—used to prepare his various pills and potions (herbs, minerals, and roots)—which she later used regularly in her own cooking.

It was on one of the winter trips abroad that Olive met Hermann Stanham, an athlete and military officer who maintained a sort of double life as a portrait photographer under his given name, Warschawski. His father, Paul Isidor Johann Warschawski, a Hebrew scholar and the son of a Polish rabbi, had emigrated from Warsaw and converted to Christianity in 1865. (He later became a missionary to the Jews, and then a minister.) He was a man of various talents, apparently, and worked as a professional magician who notably eschewed "all mechanical apparatus or assistants," was a fellow of the Royal Asiatic Society, and authored several books on "the music of the bible" and the Hebrew language.[9] In 1872 he married Harriet Stanham, his second wife, a former governess and the daughter of a prominent Lincolnshire farmer. Hermann, the eldest of two children, was born in Brighton three years later, and by the age of fifteen was serving as a photographer's apprentice. He eventually opened his own studio at St. Leonards-on-Sea, the name Warschawski emblazoned above the storefront window. His Polish origins were, however, shrouded in mystery after he adopted his mother's maiden name in 1903 in order to advance his career in the military.

Though Hermann continued to sign his photographs, even self-portraits, with his Polish name, by the time he married Olive in March

1915, the name Warschawksi was mostly a thing of the past. In the marriage announcement published in the *Sussex Express*, he identified himself as Captain H. S. Stanham, Royal Field Artillery.

Patience Jean Stanham was born in Shackleford, Surrey, two years later on October 31, 1917, the second of three daughters. Her older sister, Tania, was born in January 1916, and Helen ("Tiny") in June 1919. Until Patience was six the family lived near Godalming, Surrey, in a two-story seventeenth-century red-brick and sandstone house—"the house I like to remember," she wrote—called Mitchen Hall.[10] Its spacious oak-paneled rooms, filled with sun, looked out onto leafy gardens, rose bushes, and fruit trees. In Patience's early years, up until the financial crisis of 1929, the family had a succession of governesses, one of whom was French. On afternoon walks with the children, the governess would gather dande-lion greens, sorrel, and wild chicory for salad. They had a gardener, Mr. Balchin, who helped Olive "rediscover" the Jacobean garden—peonies, poppies, columbines, and delphiniums—walled in by rows of carefully sculpted yew trees. At the center of the garden was a small stone pool surrounded by lavender beds and hedges where "a child was completely hidden." The well-known landscape architect and gardener Gertrude Jekyll lived in nearby Munstead and designed the gardens at Hall Place, which was just down the road from Mitchen Hall.

Hermann, who had served with several artillery units during the war and commanded a brigade in Mesopotamia in 1919, seemed to struggle upon returning to civilian life. He raised pigs for a time and eventually, when they moved to Bexhill in East Sussex in the early 1920s, took up photography again. They survived largely on Olive's inheritance—a legacy of the Jolly fortune—and were able to keep up middle-class appearances.

In Bexhill the Stanhams lived in the village of Little Common, which Patience later told classmates was easy to remember because she was herself "neither little nor common."[11] Patience was indeed exceptionally tall, with dark-brown shoulder-length hair and brown eyes. Evidently at a young age she had already come to see herself as something of an outsider. Like the vast majority of young girls born into upper-middle-class or even middle-class families at that time, Patience and her sisters were primarily educated at home by visiting governesses from France or Sweden. In her memoir Patience recalled the oppressive atmosphere that prevailed at home and in the evening, being "forced to appear in the drawing-room in identical little velvet dresses with lace collars."[12] For at least one year, in 1929–30, however, Patience attended the Thornbank School in Bexhill, whose aim, according to a brochure from the time, was "to provide a good sound general education on modern lines, to build up character, and to inculcate a spirit of self-reliance and independence." From there she received a scholarship to Queen's College. Perhaps more important though, it was in Bexhill that they came to know the Barnardos—Violet and Frederick (known as "Barny"), who had settled there in about 1923. Barny had been dean of the medical faculty at Calcutta University in India, where two of their children were born, but had returned to England in 1921 to set up a practice in London. They eventually had five children, who sometimes shared a governess with Patience and her two sisters and were closely involved in each other's lives. "We became a group of children," Patience wrote, "doing so many things together that we were a kind of troupe."[13] Indeed the families would remain close, and Patience's daughter, Miranda, eventually married one of Violet and Frederick's grandsons, Ashlyn Armour-Brown.

Patience was especially drawn to Betty, the oldest of the Barnardo children, who shared a similarly strong independent streak, intellectual precocity, and sense of adventure. (She was six years older than Patience.) In 1937 Patience and Betty traveled to Hungary together, hitchhiking through Belgium, Germany, and Austria and then down the Danube to Budapest. Patience later wrote that among their adventures they "traversed the Hungarian *puzsta* [plains] at three miles an hour in an ox wagon."[14]

In 1938 Betty married the Austrian anthropologist Christoph von Fürer-Haimendorf—who studied under Bronisław Malinowski—and with whom she spent nearly forty years among the tribes of northeast India and Nepal.[15] Although Patience would see Betty only infrequently after that, she always held her in high regard. "I don't think I know anyone whose spirit is woven from finer threads," she wrote to her mother in 1939.

They were close in a way that only childhood friendships, forged in the intimate surroundings of family, can be. And by all accounts Patience was closer to Betty than she was to either of her own sisters, a bond solidified during Patience's years at the London School of Economics, when she lived with the Barnardos. "You were always there as this wonderful mythical person in my mother's life—almost but not quite a relative," Betty's son, Nicholas, wrote to Patience several years after his mother's death in 1987.

Although the house at Little Common was not the one Patience preferred to remember, it was the site of one of her most important childhood friendships. This was in some ways overshadowed, though, by her deteriorating relationship with her parents, the result of what Patience described as having been "brought up in the midst of hypocrisy."[16] Patience did little to mask the contempt she felt for her parents, the rigid world of manners they inhabited, and the appearances they struggled to maintain. She described her childhood as one governed by fear, stripped of any sort of creative freedom, and an unhappy one. In her own account Patience explained that as a teenager she "decided that it was not her role to suffer" and began the long and painful process of extricating herself from the bonds of family, a lifelong endeavor; implicit in this statement is the notion that her sisters assumed such submissive roles.[17] Patience rarely acknowledged the fact that among her sisters she was the only one sent off to a competitive boarding school in London, encouraged to attend university, and given the freedom to travel abroad—even hitchhiking across Europe in the late 1930s. Her older sister, Tania, on the other hand, was sent to finishing school in Switzerland to learn the rudiments of home economics. That Patience's parents, especially her mother, might have played more of an active role in her education and intellectual growth never seemed to occur to her. "I have always found it uphill work to read Patience's description of her parents in her memoir," says her daughter, Miranda. "It may make a good story, but there is no resemblance to the person I knew as my grandmother."[18]

Over time England itself would come to stand for some of the shortcomings of her childhood, what she saw as a series of deceptions, however small, and "things unsaid." The subjects that mattered—life, death, beauty, and love—were not spoken of. If her father's own Jewish ancestry had been concealed, one of many "forbidden subjects" that Patience felt typified the repressive undercurrent of Edwardian society and that she spent a lifetime railing against, what else was being kept from them? As she put it, "Why were we always being conjured to tell the truth, when they were concealing it?"[19]

Hermann, who was diagnosed with cancer in the early 1930s, eventually gave up photography and farming, and resumed his military career, commanding artillery units in Bexhill and Eastbourne. He was reportedly "very popular with the local gunners" and credited with leading the 58th Home Counties Brigade to the final of the King's Cup artillery competition.[20]

To his daughters, though, he was a remote figure, uncommunicative and volatile. What Patience was able to learn of his inner world she did by sneaking into his dressing room and study, smelling of leather and tobacco, with its drawers of pinioned butterflies, an "excellent engraving" of Dürer's *Knight, Death and the Devil*, and most of all his books, neatly arranged behind glass-paneled doors, which were locked. Patience eventually found the key and treated herself to Borrow's *Lavengro*, Joseph Conrad, Robert Louis Stevenson, Shakespeare, Dickens, Thackeray, Cervantes, and others. "I can still, in my mind's eye, place individual books in their stations on the shelves," she wrote many years later.[21]

If Patience felt she had to begin her education in a somewhat surreptitious way, it flourished more openly at Queen's College, London. In 1930 just before turning thirteen, she was sent to live with her aunt Dorothy and her husband, the obstetrician Eardley Holland, an experience that "[unlocked] doors that hitherto were closed."[22] (Eardley was eventually honored with a knighthood for services to gynecology.) Patience lived with the Hollands for part of her time at Queen's College—their house on Queen Anne Street was literally around the corner from the school—and was drawn to the intellectual and artistic circles they moved in, though appalled by the conventions of the English upper class. Not to mention the rather unrestrained enmity that existed between Sir Eardley and his wife. "She spat at him at breakfast," begins a poem Patience wrote about life at her aunt's. By all accounts Eardley was an imperious figure—"upright and grand, almost haughty," according to one description—and everyone breathed a great sigh of relief when he left the house every morning.[23]

Despite the rather stifling domestic atmosphere, Dodo opened many doors for Patience. She introduced Patience to the paintings in the Italian rooms of the National Gallery, "which in time became part of my private landscape." Patience compared the impact of viewing these paintings—"the explosion of light, color and form"—to her mother's drab collection of "sepia photographs" of places like Ponte Vecchio, Santa Croce, and Santa Maria Novella.[24] Patience admired Dodo, an exacting and intimidating woman, who encouraged her to study German and economics. Tall and stately, Dodo often wore a fox fur around her shoulders and a close-fitting hat with a net pulled over her face. From Dodo Patience inherited a somewhat high-minded sense of her own intellectual capabilities. "She did feel she was superior to most people," says Miranda. "And if it came from anybody I feel it came from Dodo who was intelligent, well educated, and interested in foreign languages."[25] Dodo was of course also deeply committed to music and every day before school gave her youngest daughter, Jan, who was attending Queen's College with Patience, a violin lesson and sometimes exhorted all the children to sing something from the song cycles of Schumann or Mendelssohn's "Hear My Prayer."

Queen's College itself was a well-known all-girls school—the first of its kind—established in 1848 by the liberal theologian F. D. Maurice. Though it was progressive in many ways, the school did not appoint its first female principal, Miss Holloway, until 1931, the year after Patience enrolled. It had a reputation for high academic standards—all qualified students were encouraged to attend university—small classes (usually fewer than fifteen students), and openness (unlike most girls' schools, students were not required to wear uniforms). The majority of the students were over the age of fourteen, so Patience would have been among the youngest when she started. But she excelled, finishing her coursework in just three years, and later said she was grateful for having gone there (too young to go to university, Patience stayed on at Queen's College for an additional year). Stephanie Fierz, a classmate of Patience's who went on to be principal of the college from 1964 to 1983, described her as a gifted artist and recalled her skillfully drawing a map of the world in great detail for intermediate geography.[26] During her final year, she boarded at the college and shared a room with Edith Goeritz, a German-Jewish émigré, and Ann Stephen, Virginia Woolf's niece, who Patience described as "large, handsome, tangled and untidy."[27] It was a lively place, and in addition to being exposed to life in London, Patience admired the college's "brilliant teachers," full of passion and energy.

It was her French professor, Maurice Thiery, who made a particularly strong impression. He had written a biography of Louis Antoine de Bougainville, the eighteenth-century French explorer famous for his circumnavigation of the globe. It was not lost on Patience that the American climbing plant, bougainvillea, "with its papery magenta flowers," was named after him.[28] Maurice spoke "exquisite French," delivered radio addresses to occupied France during the war, and was remembered for his love of literature and devotion to teaching.[29] His students sat at one large table instead of desks, and his class, according to Patience, was "an adventure in which he explored with passion and vivacity the rhythms of French verse, illustrated by Racine and Corneille. While rooted at the table, this witty man helped me to dart across the Channel and confront his deities."[30] Some of whom would also become her own.

There was also a strong interest in natural history at the school. Miss Holloway, who sought to improve instruction in the sciences, was a proponent of nature study and an avid walker. With a botanist from Kew, Miss M. L. Green, they took students on nature rambles during the summer term, "with Miss Holloway always leading the way."[31] There were also mushroom foraging trips undertaken by Miss Green and others, to places like Bexhill.

Throughout her time at Queen's College, Patience kept a photograph of her father from his army days close at hand. He had been diagnosed with cancer soon after she enrolled and sought what was then experimental radiography treatment in Sweden. She described him at that time as "a mass of cancerous sores apologizing for being too 'untouchable' to kiss."[32] Patience completed her studies in July 1934, and Miss Holloway, in a letter of recommendation to the London School of Economics, described her as "above average in ability, but inclined to be superficial." She also noted that Patience had "mixed with cultured people," most likely a nod to the Hollands and the company they kept.[33] Given that Patience was away during term time and traveled to Germany for a gap year before beginning her studies at the London School of Economics in the autumn of 1935, she would have seen her father only infrequently during his final years.

"I discovered that I loved my father when it was, so soon, too late to tell him," she wrote.[34]

He died in late September 1935, one month before her eighteenth birthday.

It was probably a blessing that Patience did not have to return home, amid her mother's grief and loneliness, after Hermann's death. She began her studies at the London School of Economics in October 1935 and took courses in economics, political science, geography, and German. One of her tutors was the future Labor Party leader Hugh Gaitskell. "It was naturally my fault," she wrote, "that his subject was so completely abstract that I was unable to profit from his disquisitions."[35] Another important teacher was the Canadian economist and mountaineer Campbell Secord, who introduced Patience to one of the many books that would have a lasting impact on her. *Art Forms in Nature* (*Urformen der Kunst*), a photographic study of plant forms by German artist Karl Blossfeldt, first published in 1928, is considered a pioneering work of early twentieth-century photography. Blossfeldt, a sculptor and teacher in Berlin, built his own camera—it had a bellows more than a meter long—in order to pursue his interest in the underlying structure of various botanical specimens. The more than one hundred plants he photographed, what Blossfeldt called "a treasure trove of forms," are presented against a plain white background and greatly magnified, in some cases as much as thirty times.[36] It is as if a new world has suddenly been revealed in the form of flowers, ferns, and common plants such as milkweed and thistles. The book even includes astonishing and unlikely images of the stems and tendrils of a pumpkin, which are evocative of finely sculpted metal. Patience used to pore over the book at the Victoria and Albert Museum and wrote, "Each page is imprinted in me."[37]

Though she may have been easily diverted from her studies and had little passion for economics, Patience was a perfectly capable student. She failed one class, higher senior economics, required for an honors degree, but passed her exams in the British constitution, French, German, and economics.

Perhaps more important than her coursework was the fact that, during the first two years of her time at University, she stayed with the Barnardos in their elegant five-story house near Hyde Park. Barny, a "brilliant racon-teur," was known for his somewhat extravagant lifestyle and fondness for gambling.[38] According to family lore he was relieved of his post at Calcutta

University for throwing lavish parties and not keeping track of expenses. He cultivated a similar atmosphere of bonhomie in London and even kept a key available for anyone "who might be coming, or who would want to stay overnight."[39] Betty, then working as a secretary, would often hold late-night gatherings—what Patience described as "an animated *luogo* for intellectuals"—that were capped by meals prepared in the early hours of the morning when Barny arrived home with vegetables and fish, his last call of the evening being Covent Garden or Billingsgate Fish Market.[40]

Patience also had a lively group of friends at University, including Mary Best and Barbara Kuczynski, whose father, the noted German economist Robert René Kuczynski, was a lecturer at the London School of Economics. Years later Patience and Barbara worked on the translation of *Larousse Gastronomique,* published in 1961. Kuczynski's sister, Ursula, was a key spy for the Soviet Union, and Barbara herself was swept up in MI5's investigation of the family and its ties to Klaus Fuchs. Ursula served as a conduit for secrets obtained by Fuchs while working on the British atomic bomb project after the war. Interestingly Patience's name appears frequently in Barbara's MI5 file during the years 1947 to 1951.[41] During her final year of college, Patience shared an attic flat with Mary Best in West London; it was rather spare containing a single gas ring, toilet on the landing, and a "horrible square stone sink."[42] Best, who had grown up among the landed aristocracy of Dorset and later married a radical trade unionist, introduced Patience to the journalist and writer Nicholas Davenport, and they frequently spent weekends at his estate, Hinton Manor, near Oxford. Davenport was best known for his popular column on politics and economics—he was a good friend of John Maynard Keynes—in the *New Statesman* and then the *Spectator*. It was at Hinton Manor that Patience met the filmmaker Alexander Korda and *Vogue* editor Lesley Blanch, among others.

By the end of her time at the London School of Economics, Patience was no closer to settling on a profession and remained "puzzled" as to why she had chosen to study economics and sociology. She was restless, too. There had been the trip to Hungary with Betty in 1937. And in the summer after graduating in 1938, Patience and Tania traveled to Romania with a grant from the Society of Quakers. They were based in Bucharest but spent several weeks traveling around the country, "even to the point of surveying the Russian border, the banks of the Dniester, and the armed guards on the far side."[43] Years later Patience liked to say, anachronistically, of her trip to Romania that she'd gone "behind the iron curtain."

Indeed by 1938 Romania's relations with the Soviet Union and Germany had become increasingly fraught. Both countries had been seeking to ally themselves with the strategically located eastern European nation, whose modern borders were formed out of the ashes of the First World War. The Soviets wanted the assurance that their troops could pass through Romanian territory and that negotiations would be reopened over Bessarabia; the Germans were eyeing the country's resources, especially its oil and grain. In 1937 the first skirmishes in years between Romanian and Soviet troops occurred along the Dneister. Still Romania sought to remain neutral in the hope that the British or French would come to their defense if necessary. In March 1938 Germany invaded Austria, stoking fears of a wider conflict. That summer, as the rest of Europe failed to rise to the challenge, Romania entered into an arms agreement with Germany in exchange for fuel. On the eve of their arrival, Patience and Tania, it seems, had little sense of the rapidly destabilizing geopolitical situation. Their hosts were mostly well-to-do landowners, and Patience recalled eating lavish meals of caviar, sturgeon, and iced puddings washed down with liberal amounts of champagne.[44]

By the time Patience returned to England in September 1938, the British were involved in negotiations with the Germans in an attempt to avoid a military confrontation. Indeed they had declined to send a high-profile delegation to Romania that summer out of fear of appearing to encourage an anti-German alliance. On September 30 the Munich Agreement was signed, ceding the Sudetenland, a German-speaking region of Czechoslovakia, to Nazi Germany. The agreement also gave Hitler a "free hand" to expand eastward in exchange for assurance that the two countries, along with the other signatories, France and Italy, would not go to war with one another. One year later, however, Hitler annexed the rest of Czechoslovakia and invaded Poland, exposing the fallacy that appeasement would somehow maintain the balance of power in Europe. Patience, who had little interest in foreign affairs and was not politically engaged, was none-theless troubled by what she viewed as her country's shortsightedness.

This was in part because she'd spent time in Germany from 1934 to 1935 and again in December 1937, and had witnessed firsthand the "horrific pageantry" of Hitler's brownshirts parading down the tree-lined streets. The fervor and enthusiasm of the German people, she wrote, shocked and astounded her. These scenes were hard to reconcile with her own intellectual awakening as she abandoned the study of economics for courses on art and architecture during her gap year in Bonn. She attended lectures by the art historian Paul Clemen, best known for his fifty-six-volume series on monuments of the Rhine province, which she found revelatory. "The old-world town, gothic and baroque, came alive," she wrote. Though she tried to make sense of Hitler's appeal, his ominous rise was largely overshadowed by her own youthful optimism and what appears to have been her first romantic relationship, with a twenty-five-year-old diplomat by the name of Wolf-Horst von der Leye. "He would drop by the Observatory and sweep me off in a little black coupé, open to the wind, beyond the reach of parental observation," Patience wrote.[45]

It was only when she returned to Berlin in 1937 for a brief visit that Hitler's true intentions were impressed upon her. She had gone to see the mother of her Queen's College schoolmate and friend, Edith Goeritz, who lived "on the northern edge of the city … in a spacious apartment with paint-ings by [Max] Liebermann."[46] It was this "beautiful dark Jewish lady" who, Patience later recounted, informed her of the gravity of Hitler's plans not only to occupy more of Eastern Europe but also to establish camps for Jews and other minorities. Patience agreed to help her and her younger daughter by having Olive serve as a guarantor so they could join Edith in London. After she returned to London, Patience made good her promise and several months later the family was settled in a modest flat in Notting Hill.

Thus Patience always maintained that she cut her trip to Romania short, leaving Tania behind, in order to see firsthand how her country would respond to the German advance. Years later, in a letter to Kazuo Ishiguro, whose novel *The Remains of the Day*, paints a chilling portrait of British upper-class society in the years leading up to Munich, Patience said that, when she returned home from Romania in 1938, she was ashamed to find her "relations crouching round the radio, weeping with joy and echoing Chamberlain's 'Peace in our Time!'"[47] She was especially shocked to discover her Aunt Dodo's "inexplicable enthusiasm" for Adolf Hitler.[48]

Despite her relative lack of interest in politics, Patience soon found employment as a transcriptionist in the Foreign Office. It was a low-level position—records of her employment have not survived—but Patience was responsible for furnishing the press with the weekly Foreign Office report, which she did in "thirteen carbon copies on an antique machine."[49] The rest of the time was spent drafting obscure letters and shorthand notes of "doubtful importance," all for the trifling sum of 25 shillings a week.

In a letter to her mother on Foreign Office letterhead in July 1939, just two months before England and France declared war on Germany, Patience described the "sweet lassitude which is the core of England," accurately foreshadowing the sense of aimlessness that characterized the so-called phony war.[50] She was filling her time reading books, in French, on the ancient Greek city of Byzantium, attending lectures by the art historian Nikolaus Pevsner, which she described as having "affinities with the finest chamber music," and going to the cinema.[51]

Patience, who was only twenty-one, had a hard time imagining herself staying at the Foreign Office for very long—"they have at least not shown me the door," she wrote—but was equally at a loss about what she might do instead. She lamented Whitehall's stress on efficiency and the "sacrifices made in her name," and wondered if she would ever be expected to "do something on my own initiative."[52] Of course she'd studied economics and German but she had little interest in either subject; she was drawn to literature and art. In a letter one month later, she said, "I am going to write my book at last—to counteract the donkey work."[53]

Late that summer Patience, Mary Best, and Nicholas Davenport traveled to Normandy and toured the abbeys and villas along the Seine near Les Andelys. According to Patience they were rather oblivious of the looming threat of hostilities and were forced to cut their trip short and return home just before the allied countries declared war on Germany on September 3, 1939. Upon returning, Patience was finally sacked from her post at the Foreign Office, in part, she was told, because of her extensive travel and foreign contacts. Later, Davenport, who had a close friend in MI5, told Patience she was a "suspected person."[54]

But there was no love lost. "I was so happy to leave," Patience later wrote.[55]

She was happy to leave, in part, because she was now deeply involved with Thomas Gray, whose circle of friends—émigré intellectuals, Communists, and veterans of the Spanish Civil War—Patience found far more intriguing. Eight years older than Patience, Thomas had taken part in the Spanish Civil War, was a card-carrying Communist, and fancied himself an artist. He was also a bit of a drifter, charming and seductive on the one hand, devilish and unreliable on the other. For Patience, who had come to believe that through study, travel, and foreign languages "one could inherit the earth," he was everything she had been taught to avoid.[56]

CHAPTER TWO

Thomas Gray

It is unclear precisely how Patience and Thomas Gray met, though he inhabited the fringes of the same left-wing and artistic circles that she was drawn to. In the years leading up to the war, he worked for his older brother Milner's design firm and would later refer to himself as an "artist designer" despite having no formal training in the field. He was more of an artist manqué with great powers of persuasion, especially when it came to women. (According to his naval records, he claimed expertise in a variety of disciplines from stage design to munitions work and, as a superior officer noted, "will convince people that he has a knowledge of all these subjects."[1]) Patience, in her early twenties when they met and highly impressionable, was evidently taken in. Nan Youngman, a left-wing artist and educator who knew Thomas, remembered them as having a passionate affair.[2]

Yet throughout their ill-fated relationship, he remained an elusive figure. His younger sister, Margaret, who was closest to him in age and probably knew him better than anyone, said that he drifted in and out of people's lives and had a tendency to disappear for long periods without explanation. Added to that, he was adept at modifying his persona depending on the company he kept. "We are all I suppose to some extent more than one person and Tom was rather too many, too often," his brother Milner recalled in a letter to Patience's daughter, Miranda.[3] A cousin of Thomas's, who was a psychiatrist, once speculated that he perhaps suffered from schizophrenia, but there is little evidence to support such a conclusion. Yet there's little doubt that he lived a life of extremes and, according to Patience, "rushed about the gutters à la Henry Miller."[4]

Born Thomas Archibald Campbell Gray in January 1909 in Greenwich, he was one of five children, having two sisters and two brothers. At age nine he was sent to boarding school at Eltham College and like so many boys his age found it distressing, telling his mother he felt "homesick and persecuted."[5] He eventually settled in, though, and befriended Mervyn Peake, the future novelist and illustrator, with whom he shared a dark and richly imaginative sense of humor. He was a member of the Music Society Committee, participated in the school's debate club, and was a reasonably good student, achieving his General School Certificate and Matriculation in 1926. During holidays, his sister Margaret, who was one year younger, remembered devouring together the serialized novels and pulp fiction of Edgar Wallace and H. C. McNeile, creator of the Bulldog Drummond character, a somewhat damaged veteran of the First World War who seeks out adventure to offset the inevitable boredom of his postwar life. Although they had a "secure and loving childhood," according to Margaret, she also suggested that her brother may have been "deprived emotionally."[6]

He was torn between pursuing a career in medicine, art, or writing, and eventually chose the former, attending St. Thomas's Medical School. This was a great delight to his father, an accountant who had once harbored ambitions of studying medicine himself and who thus felt even greater disappointment when Thomas abandoned his studies after three years. The reasons aren't entirely clear. Margaret suggested that he had been encouraged to leave by his first wife, Alicia Cooper-Wickens, with whom he had two children, in order to focus on his art and writing. It may have simply been because she was pregnant with their first child, they had to marry, and Thomas no longer felt able to continue his studies. (They married in 1932.) As his artistic ambitions never amounted to much, Thomas found himself without a profession, moving from one scheme to the next. "He was always going to write or paint," Margaret wrote, "but it seldom materialized."[7]

From 1933 to 1934 he spent time on the Isle of Sark, where Peake, a founding member of an artists colony, also lived. He was a laborer on coastal boats, and from 1935 to 1940 was a designer in his brother Milner's firm, the Industrial Design Partnership. His first marriage did not last long and, though they never divorced, Thomas was no longer living with his wife and children when he met Patience, most likely sometime in early 1939. By the fall of that year, Thomas had already enlisted Patience in his latest activity with the Art and Entertainment Emergency Council, whose mission was to employ artists in an effort to bring art and culture to the masses. As the group's chairman put it, "In war time the need for Art and Entertainment is far greater than it is in peace time."[8]

The Council was formed shortly after war was declared in September 1939 and boasted the support of such illustrious figures as G. B. Shaw, art critic Sir Kenneth Clark, and the conductor Sir Thomas Beecham. Milner Gray—one of the country's most highly regarded typographers and industrial designers—was also involved and presumably helped in securing his younger brother's appointment as honorary secretary. (If nothing else, the Council's pamphlets and promotional material reflect a highly polished modernist aesthetic.) Patience herself was named secretary and was one of the few members to receive a salary—indeed she seems to have been paid more than anyone else. She described an early committee meeting, in which she "doodled the minutes," as rather amusing and "full of dissension."[9]

As honorary secretary, Thomas was given the unenviable task of making the case for the Council, the very existence of which would depend on government support. In November 1939 he wrote to the president of the Board of Education seeking an appointment to discuss financing. His appeal was met with great skepticism, but nevertheless he did manage to secure a meeting with members of the Home Office on November 16, 1939. Even though he was told, "There was no likelihood whatsoever of financial support being forthcoming from the government," Thomas pushed ahead with the application.[10] "I think the whole thing perilously near nonsense," an official who attended the meeting with Thomas wrote, "and I cannot conceive why various people of some eminence have given their names to it."[11] Throughout his short-lived tenure as honorary secretary, Thomas seems to have done himself few favors. A secretary in the Home Office described him as "extremely tiresome and ignorant," and suggested that the organization "probably suffered from him—as we did."[12]

Still, Thomas continued to appeal to private donors and government agencies to support the Council's pilot project in the city of Bath scheduled for May and June 1940. The "Bath Test Scheme," as they called it, was composed of exhibitions of contemporary art, lectures by the likes of Nikolaus Pevsner and art critic Eric Newton, dance and orchestral performances, and a film series produced by the Ministry of Information. Patience and Thomas traveled around the countryside—"a couple of waifs and strays," as Thomas put it—meeting theater managers and arts organizations.[13] In April they stayed at a bed and breakfast in Bristol where their son, Nicolas, was conceived. Inauspiciously, just as the Bath Test Scheme got underway, the phony war came to an end when German forces invaded France and the Low Countries on May 10, 1940. A few weeks later British and allied troops were evacuated from Dunkirk, and on June 25 France surrendered to Germany. "If there weren't a war, how happy we should be," Patience had written to her mother several months before. "I'm sure this is a *zwischenzeit*, a nightmare, and we shall wake up. . . . I still see things as black and white, good and bad, beautiful and ugly, and the pure in heart are not of today or tomorrow but for always."[14]

⤛⤛⤛ ⤜⤜⤜

Patience was now several months pregnant and living with Thomas in a small flat in Chelsea, arranged through a friend from Thomas's Spanish Civil War days. Thomas had been let go from his post as honorary secretary of the Art and Entertainment Emergency Council, which didn't survive much longer anyway, and was now employed as an explosives instructor at a Home Guard training school in Fulham. "By then London was alight with flares, fires, swept by anti-aircraft beams, sounds of explosions," Patience wrote.[15] Indeed the city was under siege as German warplanes launched air raids every night for two months. London was bombed heavily during the early phase of the Blitz, which lasted from September 1940 to May 1941. During that time more than one million homes were destroyed or damaged—40 percent of the city's housing stock—and nearly thirty thousand civilians were killed.

The prospect of having a child and starting a family under these conditions was, to say the least, a kind of psychological and emotional balancing act. The fear and anxiety alone could be crippling. As early as 1938 a team of doctors submitted a report to the Ministry of Health warning of the potential psychological impact—hysteria, nervous break-downs, and so on—of a sustained air campaign in a densely populated city like London. Air raid sirens were so unnerving, deemed by many to be worse than the raids themselves, that the government soon distributed free rubber earplugs. Gas masks were issued to everybody. The city was often shrouded in a pall of dust and smoke, the streets littered with the wreckage of the previous night's bombing. "For Londoners, there are no longer such things as good nights; there are only bad nights, worse nights, and better nights," wrote the *New Yorker's* London correspondent Mollie Panter-Downes at the onset of the bombing.[16] Throughout the Blitz there was always the expectation that things would get worse. Meanwhile young men were being sent to the front. Women and their children were being evacuated—London's population alone was reduced by almost 25 percent. On top of it all, there was the blackout and food rationing, which began in January 1941. The future, it seemed, was fast diminishing. Patience later described having "an end of world feeling" that contributed to her willingness to attach herself to Thomas in the first place.[17] For his part Thomas said that he never expected to survive the war.

In his diary George Orwell captured the sense of disbelief and fatal-ism that prevailed at the time. "Everyone [is] quite happy in the daytime," he wrote, "never seeming to think about the coming night, like animals which are unable to foresee the future so long as they have a bit of food and a place in the sun."[18]

If nothing else the war brought out a certain heroism and courage on Thomas's part. He was able to act, even thrive, under extreme pressure and received accolades for his service on more than one occasion. In October 1940 he led a team that defused two delayed-action bombs, designed to detonate up to 48 hours after landing, that had fallen in nearby resi-dential neighborhoods. One had burrowed 11 feet below ground, and it took nearly four hours of digging through mud and debris to reach the unexploded ordnance. For both episodes Thomas was highly praised and recommended for the George Cross medal, the country's highest civilian decoration. A captain in the Officer Candidate School wrote that Thomas "was an inspiration in calmness and efficiency to the volunteers of the Home Guard" and that he could not "speak too highly of the example Mr. Gray set on both occasions."[19] Later, in the navy, Thomas was awarded the MBE for his mine recovery work and lauded for his courage. But he could also be careless. It was during a rather routine Home Guard lecture that Thomas somehow mishandled an explosive and badly burned his face and hands. He ended up in Bethnal Green Hospital where, according to Patience, they were ill equipped to treat such severe burns. Patience had to change the bandages daily and apply a mixture of zinc and castor oil to the wounds. "Touching these ghastly burns was excruciating to him, and doing it also was excruciating to me," she wrote. "Anyway he bore it."[20]

Referring to these moments of bravery, Patience later described Thomas as having a certain kind of courage that "perfectly ordinary Englishmen" exhibit under great duress. "Thomas Gray had this quality to a very great extent," she wrote.[21] In her few descriptions of Thomas, she often recounted his wartime exploits and disregarded other features of his personality. She had no interest in defending him, or even invoking him at all, and perhaps it was easier simply to describe him as "heroic" than it was to try to come to terms with who he was and why she'd taken up with him. Nevertheless it does appear that the exigencies of war gave Thomas's life a sense of purpose that it previously lacked and that he would never regain. His sister Margaret said, "The only time he really seemed to do well was in his war service—perhaps there he got both the discipline and encouragement that he needed."[22]

Patience too was seeking encouragement and perhaps approval when, several months before Nicolas's birth in January 1941, she traveled to Shiplake near Henley-on-Thames to visit Violet Barnardo, who had been relocated there with her two youngest children at the onset of war. (Patience's childhood friend Betty had already left for India with Christoph, who was just beginning his anthropological fieldwork.) Violet was living in a "grand but lonely" house—Barny had stayed behind in London—and Patience was hoping to be embraced as family.[23] These were, after all, people she'd known most of her life, loved, and respected. Wartime travel wasn't easy, but Patience made the journey out to Shiplake, walking the last mile or so down the long driveway to the large estate overlooking the Thames. She arrived around teatime, as darkness was falling, and Violet came to the door only to tell Patience she could no longer see her. "You must never darken my doors again," she told Patience, turning her away. "You have shamed your family."[24]

Perhaps Patience naïvely assumed that her present circumstances would not impinge on her relationships with family and friends. But Violet's rejection shattered any notion that she might be able to continue her romance with Thomas Gray and still be accepted by conventional middle-class society. Violet was not the only one to react in such a way. Patience later wrote, "This was only the beginning of almost everyone I knew, outside my contemporaries—including my lovely Aunt [Dodo], my mother, and others—dropping me dead."[25] It was also the beginning of a realization that she was on her own—"a black sheep feeling"—that she would cling to, in some ways even cultivate, for years to come. In hindsight Patience said she was grateful to Violet for helping her "discover in life the true feelings from the false," but at the time the verdict must have come as a shocking blow.[26] In October 1942 Violet's only son, Freeman, was killed in the Second Battle of El Alamein. Several days later Violet was found drowned in the Thames and it is believed that she took her own life.

Whatever the attitudes of others, Patience was confronted with the fact that she was about to become a mother. On January 17, 1941, in an announcement in the *London Gazette*, Patience Stanham officially changed her name to Patience Gray.[27]

A new identity card and ration book were issued shortly thereafter.

❦

Ten days later, on January 27, 1941, Nicolas Gray was born at St. Mary Abbot's Hospital in Kensington. The city was still under heavy fire, and the hospital itself was bombed on three occasions, killing more than twenty staff and patients during the Blitz.

Thomas was now working with the Home Guard in West Bromwich, where Patience and Nicolas later joined him, but it's unclear how much time they spent together during the next year. Thomas was never much of a breadwinner, and sometime after Nicolas was born, Thomas tried to compel Patience to liquidate the shares she had inherited from her great-grandfather's estate. Olive undoubtedly helped financially, as she would throughout Patience's life, but Patience was for the most part left to her own devices. When Thomas joined the Navy in December 1941, their meetings became less and less frequent, and he seems to have done little to support her. Indeed while she was several months pregnant with Miranda, Patience took a job as assistant to the editor of the *Journal of the Free Danes* (*Frit Danmark*), an underground left-wing paper published by the Danish government in exile. By the time Miranda was born on July 7, 1942, Thomas was stationed at HMS Sheldrake, a shore-based training facility near Brighton. (Miranda was born about 25 miles away in Horsham.) Though her name on the birth certificate is Carol Jean, Patience always called her Miranda. On the same document Thomas is identified as an Ordinary Seaman in the Royal Navy and a designer in civilian life. He and Patience no longer claimed the same residential address.

Not long after Miranda's birth, Patience was evacuated to Sandon, a small village in Hertfordshire, where she lodged with another young single mother. (At the time Eardley was in charge of the maternity services of the Ministry of Health and oversaw the evacuation of women from London to Hertfordshire. It is highly likely that he was involved in facilitating Patience's departure and accommodation.) Nicolas had already been dispatched to Fowey, in south Cornwall, where he stayed for a time with one of Patience's childhood nannies. The house in Sandon, Cock's Lodge, was a nineteenth-century cottage purchased by an American émigré and her husband in 1938. (Patience later recounted burying seven pounds of milled oats in a nearby field in anticipation of the German invasion. When she dug it up months later it was covered in mold.[28]) The owners had initially intended it as a refuge for themselves—they were then living in London—but got involved with the evacuation of children during the war and soon used the house for that purpose.

There's a photograph of Patience with Miranda taken sometime in late summer or early autumn of 1942 at Cock's Lodge. Patience, leaning against the brick house with a wide-eyed Miranda in her arms, is smiling and looking directly at the camera. It's one of the few photos in which Patience, who had an aversion to being photographed, looks genuinely happy.

Nevertheless she was beginning to realize that Thomas was hardly capable of ever being a father or husband. He was involved with other women, his drinking had gotten worse (he would die, alone, of cirrhosis of the liver on Christmas day, 1966), and she stood to gain little from staying with him. According to his naval records, Thomas listed Cock's Lodge in Sandon as his address in early 1943. It was presumably the last or one of the last places they spent time together. He was described by one of his superiors as a "rolling stone," with a "good brain," and "a lot of personality," but also "inclined to be non-cooperative" and generally disliked by his fellow officers.[29] Indeed he had a knack for drawing people to him and then just as swiftly being dropped by them. "When those he was with believed in him he was one of the most charming of men," his brother Milner recalled, "but if there were doubts, and there was often plenty to doubt about, that was the end of a happy dream, and others who had no doubts had to be found."[30]

Clearly for Patience, by the time of Miranda's birth, there were doubts, and whatever happiness she had experienced with Thomas had come to an end. She would later describe her brief relationship with him as "pure folly" and compare it to that of Oliver and Anna in A. S. Byatt's first novel, *The Shadow of the Sun*. In the book the seventeen-year-old Anna Severell falls in love with the much older Oliver, an embittered professor and literary critic who is obsessed with Anna's father, a towering novelist, and preys on her vulnerabilities. Pregnant with Oliver's child and on the verge of abandoning him for a fellow student at Oxford, Anna, at the last moment, realizes that she is in some way inextricably tied up with him, and "this really was the feared and expected end."

"Was not Oliver strangely similar to Thomas Gray?" Patience wrote in a letter to her sister Tania many years later. "Myself being the privileged and ignorant girl and he stepping out of some dim background, intelligent, a communist? Determined to punish me?"[31] The difference of course was that Patience left Thomas, who, she later said, was shocked when she did. Not only did she leave him, but she did so knowing she was pregnant with their third child.

If he stepped out of some shadowy background, Patience made sure that he remained an obscure figure, almost entirely unknown to his own children. They would never meet him—or at least have no memory of having done so—though Patience liked to tell the fateful story of rushing them onto a bus in London after spotting him on the street and explaining (or rather not explaining), "That was your father!" Later she instructed her children to tell their classmates that their mother was divorced, which had become increasingly common after the war. Yet even they remained unaware of the true nature of Patience's relationship to their father for years. It wasn't until Miranda was fifteen that Patience told her she'd never married. When they vacationed in Cornwall, not far from where Thomas eventually settled, in Zennor, and stayed with friends who certainly knew him, the possibility of visiting was never raised.

"I think she was absolutely overwhelmed by the mistake she'd made," said Miranda, referring to Patience's misjudging of Thomas's character. "She couldn't forgive herself . . . so it was just a non-subject."[32]

Of course when Patience left for Rogate in late autumn of 1943, to live with Olive, the question of how she would explain Thomas Gray to her children was far from the most pressing of matters. Some of the most difficult years of the war were still ahead of her.

CHAPTER THREE

The Edge of an Abyss

Patience would later liken this period of her life to Thoreau's experience at Walden Pond, which is true in at least one sense. The living conditions at Rogate were spare, even primitive. The cottage, Hill View, belonged to her mother, Olive, who was often away in Shaftesbury, where she volunteered as a librarian at the military hospital. Olive had moved to Hill View in 1939 to be closer to her older sister, Dodo, who had suffered a stroke—Dodo and Sir Eardley had a sprawling 190-acre farm in nearby Wakeham. The country estate, with rose gardens and a swimming pool, had a vast light-filled salon with a grand piano and moon and stars painted on the ceiling. In the hallway there were glass-fronted Regency cabinets filled with Meissen figurines and antique silver snuffboxes. By contrast Olive's house, which had once belonged to a farm laborer, was an unadorned brick cottage (common in West Sussex), with a pebble-dash façade, a porch, and a greenhouse.

There was no electricity, no hot water, and almost no plumbing. Cold water came from a rainwater-filled cistern in the backyard and was pumped by hand to a tank in the attic. Water for bathing was heated in a kettle on a paraffin stove in the kitchen or on a wood-fired range in the dining room. Drinking water came from a nearby 175-foot-deep well, which sometimes dried up.

Patience had no car. Nor would it have mattered, since she never learned to drive. The nearest shop in Rogate, where they went for bread, sugar, and other necessities, was a two-mile walk. Bus service was highly restricted during wartime, a frequently raised issue at Parish Council meetings, so Patience and the children went almost everywhere on foot.

There was no radio and no telephone, and Patience only occasionally saw a newspaper. She described her life in the cottage as being "very much alone, winding buckets from the well, and pumping water from the roof, and picking up firewood and living on £3 a week."[1]

In those first few months, not only was she alone, she was also recovering from the loss of her third child, Bridget, born gravely ill and given up for adoption sometime in September 1943. She was renamed Prudence by her adoptive parents. Although she had given the child up for adoption knowing that she could not possibly care for another infant on her own, Patience was asked to nurse her in the hope that it might save Bridget's life. The uncertainty of the child's fate put her in the unimaginable position of not knowing whether to pray for the baby to live or die. When Bridget did finally succumb just three months after she was born, Patience, who had only just turned twenty-six herself, was asked not to attend the funeral. In a letter to her mother written after the war, Patience said that following Bridget's death she "discovered an endless region of spiritual wastes in which I wandered."[2]

Though Patience was largely cut off from friends and family while living in Rogate, the cottage wasn't completely isolated; they had neighbors, the Woolfords and Crockers, simple laborers who had lived in the area for generations. Colonel and Mrs. Kemmis and their son Patrick lived nearby. And Patience did have occasional visitors from outside the district. One of the few friends who came to see Patience with any kind of regularity was Paul Rosenbaum, a German émigré who would go on to become a legendary dealer in stringed instruments.

Paul, who was born Paul Eric Michael Rosenbaum in 1911 and studied law in Heidelberg, fled Germany in the mid 1930s and settled in London after entering into an arranged marriage (the rest of his family went to America). He was one of tens of thousands of German and Austrian nationals, many of them Jews, who took refuge in Britain in the 1930s. Among them was Norbert Brainin, founding first violinist of the Amadeus Quartet, who would become good friends with Paul and who undoubtedly shaped his interest in music.

Patience almost certainly met Paul through Thomas Gray, with whom he shared a mutual friend, the author and illustrator Mervyn Peake. Indeed it was Peake who introduced Paul to his future wife, Diana Windham, then working for the Ministry of Economic Warfare. Diana had been one of Peake's art students when he was teaching drawing at the Central School of

Art, and she and Peake remained friends until he died in 1968. When Paul and Diana married after the war, he shed his family name and replaced it with "Paul," giving him the somewhat odd-sounding double name Paul Paul.

Like many of the exiles Patience would come to know after the war, Paul was largely self-taught and had been forced to reinvent himself under profoundly difficult circumstances. The past for many of these refugees became a kind of blank screen onto which the present could be projected, and thus family, and what Patience saw as its limitations, were less of a burden. This she found liberating. In their eyes it didn't matter how Patience had arrived at her present station or even where her last name came from. (Incidentally Gray was an extremely common surname.) Perhaps, they might have reasoned, she had gotten divorced, or perhaps her husband had died in the war, or perhaps neither. Well into the 1950s Patience simply referred to herself as "Mrs. Gray," and the assumption was that she'd been married.[3] Among the exiles and refugees with whom she felt most comfortable her situation did not need explaining. Paul's daughter Isabella said that people never speculated—or at least not openly—about the father of Patience's children; she was just a mother.[4] The composer Alvin Curran, who met her many years later, said, "It was as if Patience were born just as she was and no explanations were needed."[5]

But it was more than just this ability to reinvent oneself that attracted Patience to Paul. He embodied a European tradition that Patience, when she was a young student, had greatly admired. He was fluent in several languages, widely read, and at home, it seemed, wherever he went. "He was a bit frightening because he was so bloody clever," said Isabella, adding, "He knew everything about everything."[6] A somewhat restless spirit, he would make trips to France or Italy after the war and return with barrels of wine, which he bottled himself, or cases of olive oil. German sausages arrived regularly by post, and he was fond of buying sides of smoked salmon in Soho, which only he was allowed to carve. He was famous for his zabaglione, an Italian custard made by whipping egg yolks, sugar, and Marsala wine. "It was terribly serious business," Isabella said. "Nobody could talk to him while he was doing it and life wasn't worth living when it didn't work."[7]

In early postwar Sussex, Patience and Paul would hire a taxi (Paul, like Patience, never drove), visiting antique shops and searching for instruments or other items. Paul had a phenomenal eye—he could identify the make and year of an instrument from across a room—and delighted in finding that rare item of beauty that others had overlooked.

They also shared a love of music. In October 1949 Patience and Paul arranged a performance by the Barylli Quartet, founded by Austrian violinist Walter Barylli, at St. George's Church in the small village of Trotton. "There was considerable discussion as to whether applause was to be permitted in the House of God," says Nicolas.[8] Later, through Paul's connections, Patience would have the Amadeus Quartet, opera singer Oda Slobodskaya, or cellist Amaryllis Fleming—Paul's lover—perform in her Hampstead flat. Because of his trade and magnetic personality, Paul knew just about everyone in the classical music scene at the time. When Paul and Diana moved to Iping in the mid 1950s, not far from Hill View, Erich Gruenberg, leader of the Royal Philharmonic Orchestra, would sometimes spend weekends there.

However it was Paul's wit, intelligence, and "sense of wonder" that drew Patience to him. He was, she wrote, "the most 'unaccountable' person I have known, full of feeling often masked by a reckless humor . . . volatility, sadness." They had a relationship "uncluttered by physical adventures," and it was Paul who, more than anyone, helped her through the "long, lonely time" in Rogate. He treated the cottage as a kind of pied-à-terre, which was a great comfort to Patience. "I felt at home with him," she wrote, "at home on the edge of an abyss."[9]

"It was probably her friendship with Paul," says Miranda, "that kept Patience sane in this beautiful but isolated place."[10]

⊱⊰⊱⊰

It was also in this "beautiful but isolated place" that the world of plants and fungi came alive for Patience. Not because of their culinary interest, at least not at first, but because of the landscape itself and their place in it. It was as if she had discovered a hidden world—not unlike the seductive images in Blossfeldt's *Art Forms in Nature*—one that would come to occupy much of the rest of her life.

"It was the sheer beauty of the woods," Patience wrote in an unpublished essay, "that first inspired in me an interest in fungi, the sight of the forest floor littered with the brilliant apparitions, scarlet caps dotted with white, the poisonous Amanita muscaria . . . the brilliant ochre of the chanterelle." She could walk directly from the cottage through the rambling garden and into the pinewood that abutted the property. The patchwork of footpaths and common walkways that traversed the woodlands, hills, and farms of West Sussex was rich with mosses, mushrooms, and ferns. When the children were older, they would walk or bike for miles collecting shells, fossils, and fungi.

Though Patience may not have been aware of it at the time, her mother's cottage was in the heart of some of England's most fertile and extensively studied mushroom territory. The nearby Haslemere Museum, which Patience still consulted when she wrote *Honey from a Weed*, held an annual fungus exhibition in which hundreds of species were displayed. They also held annual displays of wildflowers, mosses, lichens, medicinal herbs, and wayside fruits. Because fungi decay so rapidly, samples were replaced nearly every day, a testament to the region's fecundity. E. W. Swanton, the curator of the museum from 1897 to 1947, wrote in 1934 that the area was "remarkable for the diversity of its Fungus Flora."[11] Indeed it was in these woods, a mix of pine, birch, and Spanish chestnut, that Patience identified more than two hundred varieties of mushrooms for her first book, *Plats du Jour*.

If Patience surprised her neighbors by foraging for mushrooms in the surrounding woods, her interest was in fact part of an unexpected renaissance in mycology—the study of fungi—during the Second World War. There were many reasons for this, including rationing, which compelled ordinary people to find new ways to improve (or replace) otherwise bland food; an influx of immigrants from places where foraging for mushrooms was more common; and a strategic interest in developing penicillin, a mold or fungus to treat wounded soldiers.[12]

In his 1945 presidential address before the British Mycological Society, titled "Mycology and the War," George Smith reflected on how much had changed in the preceding years, explaining, "When war broke out in September 1939 the prospect for this society looked decidedly bleak."[13] Autumn forays had been canceled. Any thought of serious fieldwork had been shelved for fear that it would appear frivolous or indulgent. The expectation had been that mycology, an already embattled and neglected field of study, would retreat further into the shadows.

"But then came a change," he went on, "the primary impulse for which was food rationing. The British public, aided and abetted by a number of more knowledgeable refugees, slowly woke up to the fact that the cultivated mushroom, displayed in the shops at fantastic prices, did not constitute the only means of lending attractiveness to otherwise monotonous dishes, but that there was a wealth of equally attractive food to be had for the picking."

Unexpectedly displays of edible and poisonous fungi at the South Kensington Museum (now the Victoria and Albert Museum) and the Royal Horticultural Society attracted larger and larger audiences throughout the war. Interest in lectures given by John Ramsbottom, one of the country's foremost mycologists, somewhat sparsely attended in 1942, increased thereafter. Forays organized by the British Mycological Society resumed in 1943 and became more ambitious. And Women's Institutes across the country asked for lectures, demonstrations, and instruction in identifying mushrooms. The phrase "fungus conscious" entered the lexicon.[14]

By war's end the annual number of visitors and members of the natural history museum in Haslemere, which, incidentally, suffered bomb damage, were higher than they had ever been. The bombing occurred in August 1940, causing extensive damage and, according to one report, forced E. W. Swanton and his wife to make a narrow escape, "for the windows of the bedroom in which they were sleeping were blown in upon them."[15] Indeed during the war, Swanton, who had written one of the first general guides for nonexperts in 1923, along with his colleague A. A. Pearson, collected and named more than eight hundred species of fungi, samples of which were sent to the mycology lab at Oxford University. They were analyzed for their potential use as bacteriostatic agents, a biological or chemical agent that inhibits growth of harmful bacteria.

Thus it was not a stretch for George Smith to conclude, in his presidential address in 1945, "Not only has mycology been of great service during the war but appreciation of the importance of fungi has become widespread."

Still there were few reliable and easily obtainable field guides, with the exception of John Ramsbottom's 1943 *Edible Fungi*, part of the King Penguin series. In his introduction Ramsbottom wrote, "Since the outbreak of war . . . a good deal of interest has been taken in the possibility of using edible fungi to add variety to wartime diet, an interest which has been stimulated by the presence here of foreigners from many lands where the eating of fungi is customary."[16] Launched in 1939 and initially edited by Nikolaus Pevsner, the King Penguins were the firm's first venture into hardback publishing and sold for one shilling apiece. These slim volumes, elegantly designed and made to easily fit into a pack and be carried in the field, covered a wide range of topics, from flowers and shells to birds and spiders. Remarkably publication was not curtailed by the war, despite the rather esoteric topics and the fact that paper and ink were in short supply.

Ramsbottom, who was president of the British Mycological Society in 1924 and again in 1946 and a public authority on fungi, did more than anyone to help popularize the subject in Britain. Patience's children were introduced to Ramsbottom's book at an early age—"We were brought up on that," says Miranda—and delighted in reading aloud by oil lamp his descriptions of mushroom poisonings throughout antiquity.[17] He was especially fond of recounting a story attributed to Euripides about a woman and her family who gathered fungi and were "strangl'd by eating of them." Several years after *Edible Fungi* appeared, Patience was also given a signed copy of André Maublanc's two-volume study, *Les Champignons Comestibles et Vénéneux*, richly illustrated with color plates, which she swore by as an essential text and used throughout her life.[18]

⋆⋆⋆⋆⋆⋆

As both Smith and Ramsbottom noted, the growing interest in mushrooms was part of a broader wartime push for self-sufficiency, necessitated by a large-scale reduction in food imports and the fallout from rationing. Food imports dropped by roughly half during the war, from 22 million tons to between 11 and 15 million tons a year. To make up for the shortage of foodstuffs, potato and wheat production increased and by 1943 the amount of arable land in the U.K. had doubled. Bread became the staple food and the "National Loaf," introduced in 1942, a symbol of the monotony of the British diet during the war. Through the Dig for Victory campaign, households were encouraged to grow whatever they could to supplement their diet, from potatoes and onions to tomatoes and beans. (Onions, previously imported, were one of the items the British longed for more than any other throughout the war.) In January 1940 butter, bacon, and sugar were rationed, followed by meat two months later. The sale of cream was also prohibited in 1940. Cheese, eggs, onions, oranges, and other fruits and vegetables, the bulk of which had been imported, were difficult if not impossible to obtain. Anchovies and lemons became luxuries. "Variety and palatability were the principal casualties in the diet," one historian has noted.[19]

Although Patience may have been somewhat isolated in Rogate, living in the country had its distinct advantages. The food available in markets would have been pretty much the same throughout England, with some exceptions, but Patience had neighbors who raised chickens and grew a wide variety of vegetables, including onions, leeks, potatoes, root vegetables, shallots, and hazelnuts. Olive herself cultivated fruit trees and berries, including Beauty of Bath apples, black and red currants, raspberries and loganberries, cherries, and gooseberries. Bilberries and blackberries grew wild and were gathered in the woods behind the cottage. The pantry was filled with jams (in fact jam making was championed during the war) and bottled fruit, which contained no sugar (also in short supply), as well as dried mushrooms and dried apple slices threaded on strings. Patience and Olive would exchange plums, the pale-green Reine Claudes, for vegetables and eggs. (The privilege of having access to fresh eggs, at a time when egg powder was the norm, cannot be overstated. Although large-scale egg production declined during the war due to limited supplies of cereal feed, the number of hens kept in backyard gardens more than doubled to 11.5 million.) Pregnant women and children were issued additional or supplementary ration coupons for certain foodstuffs and, if they had the means, could then buy quantities of milk, black currant juice (eventually replaced by orange juice), and the much-despised Icelandic cod liver oil.

Though far less attention was paid to foraging for wild foods, Patience made a point of gathering plants and fungi to supplement their diet. Years later she told the BBC that food gathering during wartime was "absolutely vital" and that invariably "hunger turns you toward what is to hand."[20]

Very little was wasted, and the government even suggested in its propaganda that to do so would be unpatriotic. Patience and Olive pooled together ration books in order to acquire a piece of ham or chicken. "There was the very occasional festive chicken," says Nicolas, "and Patience collected all the bones off our plates to boil up for soup or stock. Olive grew rhubarb, raspberries and gooseberries, and there was a good deal of bottling and jam making. Runner beans were sliced and salted down, and I love them like that to this day."

Patience rarely gave Olive credit for her industriousness or her skills as a homemaker, but she clearly learned a great deal from her time in Rogate. In addition to being an excellent baker—she was fondly remembered for her cottage pies, tarts, and cakes—Olive was an energetic gardener. (Incidentally Patience never took much of an interest in baking or sweets.) After the war, traveling from Hill View to Hampstead, Olive would often break the trip with a stop at the Royal Horticultural Society Garden at Wisley. She was a member of the Royal Horticultural Society, and the Royal National Rose Society, and made a point of visiting private gardens when they were open to the public. Patience's older sister, Tania, was also an avid gardener and after the war became a widely respected plant photographer. In one of the few descriptions of Olive in her memoir, Patience recalls observing her in the garden, where she seemed to spend most of her time, "an appealing and elusive figure in 'gypsy' attire, her jet black hair enveloped in a dark red handkerchief, in long skirts and Hungarian embroidered blouse."[21]

At Hill View the garden was a rambling, semiwild mix of plants, flowers, ferns, and shrubs interwoven with roses and fruit bushes. There was a profusion of bellflowers, foxgloves, and evening primroses, all of which opened out onto a view of the South Downs, that distinguishing feature of gently sloping chalk hills described by one historian as "the symbol of all things Sussex."[22] Here Patience came to see herself as a "pagan worshipping in a lovely landscape," adrift, yes, but also keenly aware of the beauty and richness of her surroundings.[23]

The end of the war brought little in the way of material improvements—rationing remained in place until 1954, the country's infrastructure was badly damaged, and rebuilding would take decades—but it must have been a relief to Patience to know that her years of solitude and isolation would soon come to an end. Rogate was still lacking in basic services:

there was no piped water or drainage system, there were no streetlights in the village, and the bus service was poor at best. Olive eventually inherited a prewar Ford from Dodo, which gave the family a bit more mobility. A telephone was connected not long after, followed by the installation of a Calor gas stove and an indoor flush toilet. The cottage remained without electricity, however, until 1955. Patience stayed in Rogate through 1946, but was set on returning to London and reestablishing her independence as soon as she could. Whenever possible she would leave the children with Olive and take the train to London.

In late November 1946, however, Patience's younger sister, Helen, fell hundreds of feet to her death in the Swiss Alps. She had left in October, at the age of twenty-seven, after completing her wartime service in the Women's Royal Army Corps, to teach English at a private school in Montreux, Switzerland. One Sunday morning she went out for a walk to the Rochers de Naye, a snowcapped peak overlooking Lake Geneva. She lost her footing and plunged 800-feet down the snow-covered slopes and into a ravine. Her body was recovered the next day ("English Woman Dead in Gorge," ran the headline in the *Gloucestershire Echo*), and Olive traveled to Switzerland to identify the body.

The devastating loss of her youngest daughter, who of all her children most closely resembled Olive's late husband, Hermann (Patience described Helen as having the same "blue eyes, noble nose, [and] fair hair" as their father), was followed by the onset of one of the coldest and longest winters of the twentieth century.[24] Some of Nicolas's and Miranda's earliest memories are of that winter "when the birch trees in the glade bent double under the weight of the snow," and they had to haul a sled to Rogate to fetch a hundredweight (about 112 pounds) of coal.[25] Amid blackouts, coal shortages, and rising unemployment, it seemed to many that wartime conditions had only worsened.

Patience, who had lost her own daughter only three years before, was in some ways uniquely positioned to understand her mother's loss, which of course was also her own. But rather than bringing the two closer together, Helen's death seems only to have driven them further apart. Patience would often say that Olive was so shattered by the loss of her youngest daughter that she wished "Tania and I had died instead." She was unable it seems to forgive her mother for indulging "in oceans of self pity." Olive's grief was more than Patience could bear. "I did what I could to comfort my mother," Patience wrote, "but found that this condition of appalling sympathy was killing me."[26]

It's likely that Patience was already preparing to return to London— the children now being old enough to go to school—but Helen's death only hastened her departure.

Before leaving Patience felt she had to come to terms with her sister's death, which she did by taking her own trip to the Swiss Alps and then to Italy in the spring of 1947. "I felt I could only understand it by going into high mountains myself," she wrote.[27] She would later refer to the importance of this journey, of "wandering alone in high mountains," and how it helped her "pinpoint the significant thing and discard the transient."[28]

She did not go to Montreux but instead traveled by train to the Bernina Pass in eastern Switzerland, which connects St. Moritz with the Italian-speaking valley of Poschiavo. Patience walked up the valley making note of the white pasque flowers, *Anemone pulsatilla* 'Alba,' breaking through the snow at the summit, and then made the steep descent down to Poschiavo and eventually, by bus, to Vicenza. From there she continued to Ravenna, "then a village," she wrote, abandoned and primitive, and finally to Urbino, where she wandered among the rooms of the fifteenth-century Ducal Palace, whose landscape paintings by Piero della Francesca "were echoed by the little hills beyond it." After the "horrors of war" it was a rejuvenating experience, and Patience wrote of Urbino that it was the "most harmonious place I had ever been."[29]

In a remarkable letter written to Olive from Hampstead several months later, Patience seems to be reaching out to her in one last attempt to find common ground or a way forward out of the darkness of the last few years. "It is no use turning away from sorrow," she begins. "Each blow of fate starts up an echo of the one before until we seem like dwindling survivors of a universal catastrophe." She recounts the significance of her trip to Switzerland after Helen's death and says, "Tiny was with me in the most wonderful and courage-giving way."

"As I now know where I can find her," Patience continued, "I am not looking back for myself but I cannot help looking back for you. When Bridget died I discovered an endless region of spiritual wastes in which I wandered. I came back in the middle of one night from the dead. Great music seems to me to be an exploration of the spirit leaving life behind, stripping you of all until you are absolutely alone and brings you back. Great voyages and high mountains do the same. Could we only live more in the spirit. Meanwhile the children are chipping away at me like blue tits at the bird bath."[30]

When Patience came back from her trip to Italy, Olive gave her the £4,000 she needed to buy property in Hampstead, where she moved in the spring of 1947. Hill View as home was now consigned to the past, one she was more than ready to leave behind.

CHAPTER FOUR

Hampstead

Although she had severed all ties with Thomas Gray—her own children did not see a photograph of him until they were well into their fifties—Patience continued to rely on his friends, family, and colleagues when she moved to London in the spring of 1947. Indeed this circle of architects, designers, and intellectuals would be instrumental in furthering Patience's professional career as a journalist, culminating in the publication of *Plats du Jour* in 1957 and a staff position at the *Observer* as the paper's first "woman's editor." The deaths of Bridget and her sister still loomed large, but Patience was no longer alone in Rogate and could once again make her own way.

It was likely through her friendships with Misha Black and F. H. K. (Henri) Henrion that Patience found the house at 23 Well Walk in Hampstead. Black, who would become one of England's preeminent postwar designers, lived across the street with his wife and two children. Henrion and his wife, Daphne—a former lover of Arthur Koestler, who had translated his masterpiece *Darkness at Noon*—lived nearby on Pond Street. Other neighbors included the artist and writer Barbara Jones, literary agent Gwenda David, pianist and composer Alfred Nieman, landscape designer Frank Clark, and the writer and painter Olive Cook and her husband, photographer Edwin Smith. Not surprisingly Patience found the vibrant intellectual world of postwar Hampstead a kind of refuge.

Black and Henrion were both exiles. Black had come from Russia with his family in 1912 at the age of two and had set up his own design studio—Studio Z—when he was seventeen; Henrion, who was born in Germany in 1914, arrived in 1936 via Paris, where he had studied graphic arts at the École Paul Colin, a highly distinguished design studio.

They represented the kind of émigré intellectuals Patience was drawn to. Like Paul Paul (Rosenbaum) they had adopted England as their home but without, it seemed, all the baggage Patience had been trying to free herself from. They were also artists, members of the left-leaning Artists International Association (Black was a card-carrying Communist until his death), and had traveled widely.

Both men had worked with the design firm Bassett-Gray Group of Artists and Writers, established in 1921 by Thomas Gray's older brother, Milner. A prominent typographer and graphic designer, later described as "one of the gods" of British design, Milner was at the center of efforts to bridge art and industry in postwar London. Bassett-Gray went through various incarnations and was renamed the Industrial Design Partnership in 1935; Thomas Gray worked with the firm during this period before the war and likely introduced Patience to Henrion and Black sometime in 1939 or 1940. Patience would always say that Henrion considered Thomas Gray a "genius," without, however, offering an explanation why. During the war Milner Gray, Henrion, and Black had all been enlisted to work in the Ministry of Information, where they designed propaganda posters, exhibitions, and public information campaigns.

It was Henrion who gave Patience what she described as her first "9-to-5 job" as one of his assistants during the planning and development of the agricultural and country pavilions for the Festival of Britain, the 1951 celebration of the country's past and future. Black was one of the principal architects on the Festival and had published a futuristic sketch of a South Bank Exhibition Hall as early as 1946. Patience and the other assistants were responsible for all of the plant life—they exhibited live plants and birds in part of the country pavilion called the "Natural Scene"—that had to be brought into the South Bank site. "A lot of the work was on the telephone and had to do with plant measurements, their requirements in the glass building Henri was preparing for them," Patience wrote.[1] Indeed the landscaping of the festival and the furnishing of Henrion's exhibits required the movement of large numbers of plants, flowers, and trees in a very short period of time. Nearly seventy semi-mature trees had to be transported from around the city to the South Bank site. Thousands of tulips, "changed overnight into summer flowers," as Misha Black recalled, were planted, along with a wide array of "architectural" plants such as

Polygonum, Heracleum, Rheum palmatum, Crambe orientalis, Ligularia, and fine-leaved bamboos.[2] At the heart of the Natural Scenes exhibit was an artificial tree made of sculpted plaster—they weren't able to get a live specimen into the space before it was constructed—surrounded by pools of water, woodland plants, and flowers. There were also dioramas that featured the plant and animal life of different regions. In line with the Festival's greater mission, the country pavilion aimed to showcase Britain's native flora and fauna, celebrating the diversity and interdependence of the country's natural landscapes.

Throughout the 1950s Henrion would help Patience find work: at the Royal College of Art; as a freelance writer and editor for *Architectural Review* and *House and Garden*; conducting research for publications like the *Compleat Imbiber* and *Wine and Food.* He also introduced her to Primrose Boyd, with whom she launched an informal research partnership and wrote *Plats du Jour* (Boyd, too, was an assistant to Henrion on the Festival of Britain). "I have often thought what a lot I owe to Henri," Patience wrote to a friend years later. "Not just work but friendship. But it was he who somehow launched me into work."[3] The idea of work, in the French sense of métier, a calling or craft, would become increasingly important to Patience throughout her life.

Henrion also influenced her aesthetic sensibility and approach to the arts more broadly. During the postwar period, there was a concerted effort to better integrate art into everyday life and to bring together a variety of disciplines—engineering, manufacturing, design, and architecture—to solve many of the problems England faced, especially with housing and transport. The Festival of Britain, which brought together professionals from a variety of fields for the first time, embodied this impulse. In their mission statement the Design Research Unit, whose founders included Milner Gray and Misha Black, wrote, "It is necessary to reintegrate the worlds of art and industry, for only on that basis can we progress towards a new and vital civilisation." The Royal College of Art itself, where Patience worked as an assistant to Dick Guyatt, head of the newly created School of Graphic Design, was reorganized in 1948 to help bridge the gap between art and commerce. Robin Darwin, a great-grandson of Charles Darwin, was appointed principal and brought on faculty who were usually also working artists. (Coincidentally, in 1951 Robin's sister Ursula married

Norman Mommens, who would later become Patience's partner.) In his
inaugural address, "Head, Heart and Hand," delivered before the Royal
Society of Arts in 1950, Guyatt, who had worked as a commercial artist,
sought to blur the distinction between fine and applied arts. He elabo-
rated on the importance of commercial art, which had become something
of a pejorative term, and the ways in which it might enrich rather than
debase people's lives. Commercial art, he explained, "has an influence on
our lives which cannot be overlooked."[4]

Thus architects and designers like Henrion and Black—both of whom
would go on to work at the Royal College of Art—were well positioned to
emerge as pioneers of the new design age. The Festival of Britain served as
a laboratory for the kinds of collaborative, multidisciplinary projects they
would embark on in the 1950s. "As for Henrion and my father the Festival
of Britain really made their careers," says Misha Black's daughter, Julia.[5]

In a roundabout way it made Patience's, too. She had of course studied
economics at college but was always more interested in art, literature, and
music. From her year in Germany in 1934 to 1935, when she had attended
lectures on architecture, to the illuminating presentations by Nikolaus
Pevsner in the late 1930s, she had always expressed a profound interest
in the built environment. Indeed she went so far as to say, "The release
from my stultifying childhood expressed itself in architecture, which ever
since has been . . . a fundament of mental experience, or cognition."[6] In
the early 1950s under the direction of Henrion and others, she began to
explore the so-called minor arts—printmaking, jewelry, textiles, and interior decoration—that would become a key, though largely unrecognized,
component of British modernism.[7] As a journalist at the *Observer* later
in the decade, in part because so-called women's subjects like cooking,
fashion, and gardening were already the domain of well-established writers, Patience carved out a niche as someone who focused on the applied
arts, such as textiles, industrial design, and architecture. Moreover in the
late 1950s and early 1960s, in addition to her newspaper work, Patience
began to dabble in various art forms, what she simply called "making
things." She was one of the last designers to work with Alastair Morton,
the director of Edinburgh Weavers, a cutting-edge twentieth-century
textile company, and designed wallpapers for the Wallpaper Manufacturer Limited's innovative Palladio series.

Throughout her life Patience felt that she owed a debt to Henrion both for helping launch her career and for demonstrating that art and commerce could coexist. Writing in a catalogue of an exhibition of Henrion's work at the Institute of Contemporary Art in 1960, Patience celebrated him for having been able to "invade the solid resistances of commercial life" without compromising his artistic principles. As a result, she wrote, the English were finally paying attention to "the look of things" and Henrion had done as much as anyone to bring this about.

"He stands bravely for art in daily life," she concluded.[8]

Hampstead itself had become something of a haven for working artists and writers after the war. Although it had not been as badly damaged as other parts of London—large areas of the borough and "all precious Georgian houses and terraces were unscarred"—it had its share of empty lots, overgrown gardens, and bombed-out houses.[9] (Its population had declined by more than a third, from 90,000 to 58,000 residents, between 1939 and 1942.) A sense of decay and wildness permeated the neighborhood. Nick and Miranda recalled a kind of postwar playground of abandoned tennis courts with tattered nets, untended greenhouses gone to seed, and the occasional empty house. It was still far enough from the city center—sometimes referred to as the "wilds of Hampstead"—to be out of the way and not yet considered fashionable, so rents were cheap.[10] "The outstanding difference from any comparable educated neighborhood group in London today was that we were all so poor—home-made clothes, third-class fares, tramping to and from markets for cheap fruit and vegetables—and nobody minded very much," wrote Maud Murdoch, a neighbor and friend of Patience's at the time.[11] A number of council housing flats were built in the area after the war, and Patience described it as "still a village with its diverse inhabitants." On Flask Walk, there was a pub, always full of writers, and someone outside selling shellfish—cockles, whelks, mussels, and jellied eels. 23 Well Walk was just a stone's throw from Hampstead Heath, a vast and semiwild park with unparalleled views of the city, where Patience would sometimes swim in shaded ponds.

"In the post-war years Hampstead was still a village punctuated with bombed sites," Patience wrote in an afterword to Fred Uhlman's *A Moroccan Diary*. (Uhlman, a German painter and writer best known for his novel *Reunion*, also lived in Hampstead.) "It presented an inexpensive aerial retreat for impoverished artists and writers, attracting many discriminating exiles: once they had accepted the presence of duck-ponds instead of lakes, of little sand and gravel eminences as stand-ins for the sweep of Swabian hills, of horse chestnuts and ash trees in lieu of forests, a glimpse of Thames in place of rushing Rhine and Neckar, with the City of London spread out in the view, momentarily obliterating memories of crags, castles, baroque splendours, sloping vineyards, beer gardens, open air Cafes and lost for ever *gemutlichkeit*."[12]

The rundown Edwardian building Patience purchased with the money Olive gave her had four floors, three of which were converted into flats that she rented out for a modest income. One of her first tenants was the niece of John Maynard Keynes, Polly Hill, who was then working as a civil servant and would go on to have a distinguished career as a social anthropologist. Patience lived on the first floor, which had access to a large rectangular garden that she set out to restore by "sowing rows and rows of potatoes."[13] On the balcony overlooking Well Walk, she grew petunias and magenta geraniums. Well Walk was named after the curative springs that once attracted health seekers from all over the city and was known for the fact that the poet John Keats had lived there in the early nineteenth century. Thus, not long after Patience moved in, the writer Barbara Jones asked her what she had done to merit "living in this sacred spot."[14]

Indeed Patience was not yet writing professionally and seems to have entertained the idea of opening her own antique shop or gallery in Hampstead. In a letter to Diana Paul written in 1948 or 1949, not long after the birth of Diana's daughter, Isabella, Patience said she was exploring the "purlieus of the old Regency Suburbs, pillaging what is beautiful and cheap and creating a clientele in Hampstead of people who welcome the reunion of these two strangers." In Sussex with Paul Paul, she had frequented the antique shops and gotten to know people in the trade. While setting up her house in Well Walk, she exchanged frequent letters with Alec Hill, a partner in an antique shop in Chichester who advised her on purchasing furniture. Mr. Hill put things aside for Patience to look at when she made trips down to Rogate, items he thought she might use to furnish her new flat—a mahogany lampstand, an iron emolument chest, mirrors. "These are waiting for you to see when next you leave the gloom of London and step upon our sacred Sussex soil," he wrote.[15] In exchange Patience told him about the latest gallery openings in London and occasionally tracked down an item he was interested in—a secondhand Chinese typewriter, a chandelier, a tapestry. In one letter Hill asked her when she was going to open "Gray's Galleries," but warned, "Your neighbors will not permit you to turn Well Walk into a business thoroughfare."[16]

As she was not greatly interested in dealing with tenants, however, Patience decided quite soon to sell the house. In 1951 she bought a small part of a Victorian mansion, designed by J. S. Nightingale and known as "The Logs," just around the corner on Cannon Lane. Described by Nikolaus Pevsner as a "formidable atrocity" with its pointed arches and gothic motifs, the building had been abandoned for some time and was acquired by Maud Murdoch's husband, Stanley, who decided to convert it into six separate "maisonettes." The "Billiardroom" with a small garden and a basement flat, which had once been the mansion's kitchens, was Patience's home as long as she lived in London. "One-room living," Patience called it, "an escapist kind of home, which turns its back on materialism."[17]

The architect on the project was Alexander Gibson, a good friend of Misha Black's and also a member of the Design Research Unit, perhaps the most influential design firm in postwar London. For the Festival of Britain, they had together designed the Regatta Restaurant, which accommodated five hundred diners and stood on the South Bank with views of the Thames and gardens designed by Frank Clark. Patience had actually met Gibson a couple of years earlier and "fell in love as if for the first time in my life"—their affair started soon after.[18] Gibson, about ten years older than Patience, was strikingly handsome, affable, and well connected. Patience would later say that he "was the only true friend I felt I ever had in my life."[19] Although Gibson was married and had three children, he and his wife, Molly Gibson, a puppeteer who worked on the BBC program *Watch with Mother*, had an open relationship. Still the long-running affair with Patience, which lasted for most of the decade, was never openly acknowledged. Patience described it as a "strange kind of subterranean life, which no one was supposed to know about, but which the children perhaps sensed."[20]

Indeed the families spent a good deal of time together, Miranda and Julia Gibson were close friends, and Alexander would sometimes tuck Nicolas and Miranda into bed at night before going out with Patience. Every year they exchanged Christmas gifts with Alexander, and for several years, encouraged by Patience, Miranda made Alexander an illustrated book in which he was "always the hero." Despite the Gibsons' purported open relationship—they both had many relationships—Alexander's involvement with Patience and his apparent love for her were difficult for Molly to bear. According to Patience, after a while, Molly "came marching to my door with an ultimatum."[21] Yet Patience and Alexander continued seeing each other in a semi-clandestine way throughout the 1950s.

Unmarried mothers were still a tiny fraction of the population in the early 1950s and the illegitimacy rate extremely low, at or below 5 percent. In addition nearly half of all children born to unmarried mothers were given up for adoption, leaving women who chose to raise their own a distinct minority. Although the war had set in motion certain changes—more women were working outside the home and divorce was somewhat more common—there was still a great stigma attached to having children out of wedlock. As Patrick Kemmis, a young suitor who had known Patience in Rogate wrote, "I was constantly subject to a barrage of propaganda emphasizing how entirely unsuitable a companion you were for me, primarily of course because you were a 'fallen woman.'"[22] This sort of attitude prevailed well into the post-war period, and it was not until the late 1970s that waiting lists for public housing were opened to unmarried mothers. "Marriage itself," as the historian David Kynaston has written of the 1950s, "was the unassailable norm."[23]

Unsurprisingly many of Patience's women friends were also single mothers or unmarried. And it's worth noting that her friendship with such exiles as Paul Paul, Misha Black, and Fred Uhlman rarely extended to their wives. She had a casual friendship with Daphne Henrion, but they were not particularly close. Even her partnership with Primrose Boyd was strictly professional, and they did not know each other well. Indeed Patience was exceedingly jealous of other women, especially if they threatened her in some way. "Patience was really jealous," said Ariane Castaing, who Patience met in the 1950s. "She was terribly jealous. She couldn't help it."[24] However Patience was drawn to some women—typically those who had blazed their own paths or were outsiders like her.

In the early 1950s Patience met the composer Elisabeth Lutyens on the platform at Victoria Station while both were waiting to take their sons to Christ's Hospital, a traditional English boys' "public school" outside Horsham. Strictly speaking, Elisabeth was not a single mother—she'd had three children with her first husband, the singer Ian Glennie, in the 1930s and then left him for Edward Clark, the conductor and BBC music producer, with whom she had a son, Conrad. Elisabeth and Edward married in 1942. But with her flair for the unconventional—she often wore an unkempt fur coat and wide-bottomed trousers—she was, according to her biographers, "not as other mothers."[25] Indeed Patience had first caught a glimpse of this "new woman" in tailored slacks and an Eton crop hairdo in the late 1920s in Sussex at the Barnardos. Even then she carried a 10-inch cigarette holder and had an "air of scorn or aloofness" about her. "It was enough to make you shrink into the ground when these two unconventional ladies came off the train," says Nick, recalling Patience and Elisabeth's visits to Christ's Hospital.[26]

Patience considered Lutyens brilliant and strangely beautiful with her aquiline nose and fantastically long fingers, rarely free of a cigarette. Lutyens embodied a certain devil-may-care attitude and devotion to her craft that Patience clearly admired. By the end of the 1950s, she had carved out a role for herself as a pathbreaking avant-garde composer in a male-dominated field, often resorting to "hack work," such as commissions for radio and film, to earn a living.

In a letter to the critic Peter Heyworth after Elisabeth's death in 1983, Patience recalled, "The brilliance of Elisabeth's talk simply stunned me." She continued, "We had in common the taking of entire responsibility for our own follies and our delightful children. Nothing to do with prematurely 'liberated' women; in those days our situations were simply 'sinful,' having both ignored the bonds of marriage."[27]

Patience identified not only with Elisabeth's strong will and fiercely independent lifestyle but also with her strained relationship with her parents, particularly her mother. Elisabeth's father was the British architect Edwin Lutyens, whose marriage to Emily Lytton in 1897 was unhappy virtually from the start. In the same letter to Heyworth, Patience, clearly with her own experience in mind, says, "Like Marguerite Duras, she [Elisabeth] was born with murder in her heart and no doubt like many of us, unable to admit both love and loathing, would have liked to murder her mother." They remained friends, and one year before Elisabeth's death, Patience sent her a check after learning that she'd suffered a fire in her flat.

Other friends at the time included the architect Rosemary Stjernstedt, an important figure in the postwar design of public-sector housing in Britain and the first female architect to gain a senior appointment at the London County Council; the dancer and teacher Kate Newman, who introduced Patience to the self-sufficiency guru John Seymour; and Ariane Castaing, whom Patience met in the early 1950s and worked with at *House and Garden*. Rosemary and Kate's children, Robert and Sandra, as well as Julia Gibson, would often stay with Nicolas and Miranda at Hill View on weekends or during holidays.

Nicolas, who had been sent to Christ's Hospital in 1950 at the age of nine, considered Hill View his home. This arrangement gave Patience the freedom to work and to travel—she took trips to Italy in 1948 and 1950. "She was mostly away," remembers Nick.[28] Indeed when growing up he and Miranda called Olive "Mummy" and Patience "Patience."

In the autumn of 1951, just before the curtain came down on the Festival of Britain, Patience began part-time work as an assistant to Dick Guyatt at the Royal College of Art. The first year she was there, the faculty of the School of Graphic Design included Edward Bawden, John Brinkley, Abram Games, and John Nash. Nearly all of them, incidentally, were involved in some way with the Festival of Britain. They also had a full-time bookbinder and printer. Henrion joined the faculty in 1953. David Gentleman, who had studied under Guyatt and graduated in 1953, became a junior lecturer in the department during Patience's last year there. Patience would perceptively suggest that Gentleman illustrate her first book, *Plats du Jour*, his first major commission and the only full-length book he would do for Penguin.

When he took over as principal in 1948, Robin Darwin felt that the college had lost touch with the currents of fashion, industry, and art. He wanted to make it a more vibrant, vital place with instructors who continued to work in their fields and who prepared their students to do the same. He appointed Madge Garland, the former editor of *Vogue,* to head the newly created School of Fashion. Guyatt himself had a commercial background—he'd designed ads for Shell Oil—and was a close friend of Robin Darwin. They had served in the same Civil Defense unit as camouflage officers in the war.

Graphic design in particular was a relatively new field. Although Guyatt is sometimes credited with coining the phrase, it had been in circulation since the early 1920s. But he did help to popularize it, and it was the first time it had ever been used in an academic setting. "No one was quite sure what it meant," he later wrote, "but it had a purposeful ring."[29]

Perhaps because it had no single unifying craft that defined it, the graphic design department brought together various disciplines, from illustration and printmaking to typography and poster design. It also gave birth to a small publishing arm called the Lion and Unicorn Press—named after the Festival of Britain's Lion and Unicorn pavilion, which Guyatt helped design—and the trail-blazing student magazine *Ark.* Indeed both of these publishing ventures were launched during Patience's time at the college and showcased the department's commitment to bookmaking as an art form in its own right. Throughout her career Patience would take a strong interest in the design of her own books and in the 1990s worked with a small publishing house in Puglia to produce a series of small books and indeed her own memoir.

The sense of experimentation and presence of "educational amateurs" imbued the department with just the kind of liveliness that Darwin had hoped to foster. Patience became friends with many of the faculty. She used to visit the painter and illustrator Edward Bawden on weekends at Great Bardfield in Suffolk, the locus of a vibrant community of artists and designers. There she met John Aldridge, another painter and avid gardener who influenced her choice of plants in the garden at Cannon Lane. John Brinkley, a designer and typographer, was an admirer and suitor. He once gave her a handwritten poem, "written in an excess of disappointment," that ended, "Fond memory brings the name/of dearest

Patience, distant Patience/chilly remote and unattainable Patience." [30]
Dick Guyatt greatly valued her work and in April 1955 wrote her a note
saying he was "feeling very bleak" about her departure. [31]

Although she had what David Gentleman described as "access to and
friendship with a lot of young and very forward looking people at their
prime," the work itself, for someone of her background and ambition, was
fairly mundane. [32] According to Gentleman, she spent a lot of time writing Guyatt's letters, which she labored at. Moreover women who worked
at the college—with the exception of Madge Garland—were typically in
subordinate roles, and Robin Darwin had little interest in advancing their
careers. [33] The pay was lousy and, though it was a part-time job, the long
commute from Hampstead to South Kensington meant that Patience
routinely arrived home long after Miranda had returned from school.

Thus she continued to freelance, working afternoons and evenings at
home, and to promote her partnership with Primrose Boyd. Around this
time they produced a business card identifying a wide range of subjects they
specialized in, from French and German sources and cartography to indoor
gardening and horticulture. They charged 5 shillings an hour plus expenses.

❦

Among the many areas of expertise listed on the card, the one Patience
perhaps had the greatest interest in was gardening and horticulture. She
had inherited from Olive a love of plants and flowers and had spent considerable time tending to the walled in garden at The Logs. She cultivated
fragrant plants like lavender and a variety of herbs as well as clematis,
hops, and henryana—a climbing plant—which covered the walls. She also
had an abundance of wild roses and let the pink and red London Pride, a
weed that proliferated after the war, take its course. Harpsichordist Trevor
Pinnock, who rented the Billiardroom beginning in 1973 and later bought
it from Patience, described the garden as "a sort of paradise." Her garden
was included in a private collection of photographs of Hampstead gardens
by Susan Jellicoe, the wife of landscape architect Geoffrey Jellicoe. [34] The
photo of Patience's garden captures an aesthetic not unlike the one that
Olive created at Hill View, a carefully tended plot that nonetheless has
the appearance of being semiwild. Writing in the *Observer* Patience

acknowledged the limitations of city gardens—lack of space, poor soil, and "greedy sparrows"—but said these factors should not be seen as deterrents. She advised her readers to use plants that "genuinely mean to live," such as ivies and other climbing plants, hydrangeas—though not the "show-off blue flowered kind," and japonica. She also offered advice on paving materials, iron furniture, and soil. "One needs to aim at a kind of outdoor room," she wrote, "something to be enjoyed on summer evenings, or contemplated from the house, seen from a balcony or through an open window."[35] Susan Jellicoe's 1956 book, *The New Small Garden*, made a very similar argument—she likened the small garden to a kind of "private study"—and focused on making the most of whatever space one had.

Patience's love of gardens and of "all wastes and solitary places" at times compelled her to sneak into some of the well-known private gardens of her day.[36] The thrill of trespassing heightened the pleasure and sense that the garden was somehow a sacred space and also one that perhaps, at least in Patience's view, transcended the limits of private ownership. "Trespassing was definitely more the thing than visiting museums with Patience," Miranda says.[37] When Miranda was about ten, she and Patience climbed along a high wall near the boathouse at Syon Park in search of a suitable place to drop down and explore what Patience described as a "magic garden." As they were making their way down, Miranda recalls, the owner of the house suddenly appeared. "He looked up and asked what on earth we were doing," Miranda says. "Patience was shortsighted but as she drew herself up to her fine height she realized that this person was none other than Robin Darwin, and we turned in our tracks and beat a hasty retreat."[38] Darwin had rented the eighteenth-century Palladian-style house from an old Etonian friend in 1951. On another occasion, while staying at a cottage in Kent owned by her Hampstead friend and neighbor Betty Massingham, a gardening and flower expert who wrote a biography of Gertrude Jekyll, Patience led Miranda on a five-mile walk to a sunken herb garden at Sissinghurst, Vita Sackville-West's celebrated estate. When they heard voices coming from the house, they lay down in a bed of flowering thyme buzzing with bees. A braying donkey probably saved them from being discovered.

Patience's first foray into the formal study of plants, however, began in 1951 or 1952 when she edited and conducted research for a book based on a series of essays that appeared in *Architectural Review*. Written by landscape architect Frank Clark, a Hampstead neighbor, and his sister Margaret E. Jones, a nursery gardener, *Indoor Plants and Gardens* was directed at the nonspecialist and provided an introduction to the cultivation and siting of native species and "exotics which can survive our living conditions."[39] Clark, who oversaw the landscape design of the Festival of Britain, including the interior garden of the Regatta Restaurant, had been influenced by the prewar modernism of Christopher Tunnard, with whom he worked in the 1930s.[40] By war's end though, the emphasis on functionalism and rationality had softened a bit and landscape architects like Clark and Peter Shepheard, who also worked on the Festival of Britain, were more interested in the idea of *genius loci*, or the primacy of place, and its native forms and flora as they set out to define the discipline. (In the immediate postwar period, Clark headed up the Institute of Landscape Architects.) "Native plants are generally, but not always, more likely to fit in than exotic ones," Shepheard observed in his 1953 book, *Modern Gardens*.[41]

Indoor Plants and Gardens was an early example of the growing interest in small gardens and the return to native plants. For Patience it served as a kind of crash course in the taxonomy and nomenclature of a variety of plant species, which would provide a foundation for her later work on the edible weeds, plants, and fungi of the Mediterranean. In a letter to Alan Davidson, who published *Honey from a Weed*, Patience explained that she worked closely with renowned botanist William Stearn while editing *Indoor Plants and Gardens*. "For a time," she wrote, "I seemed to be living at the Royal Horticultural Library!" (now the Lindley Library) where Stearn was head librarian until 1951.[42] A brilliant mind and a keen student of natural history, Stearn was a prolific writer and considered to be one of the great botanists of the twentieth century. His more than 550-page etymological work, *Botanical Latin*, is still a standard reference, and Stearn himself was sometimes referred to as a "modern Linnaeus."[43]

Patience undoubtedly benefited from Stearn's guidance but confessed, in the book's acknowledgements, to "a total ignorance of botany." She was paraphrasing James Mangles, who in 1839 published his whimsical *Floral Calendar*, which *Indoor Plants and Gardens* sought to emulate. "Any strictly botanical shortcomings that may appear in this handbook," she continued, "can be laid without hesitation at her [the editor's] door."[44]

Whatever her misgivings, she found the subject deeply engaging and undertook research for a second book by Clark on the history of nursery gardens that was never published. Nevertheless a great deal of that work—taxonomies of various flowers and plants, descriptions of relevant literature in English and German, and notes on botanical history—made its way into *Honey from a Weed* years later.

Patience was drawn to certain books, mostly Victorian gardening compendiums, like Robert Sweet's *The British Flower Garden* (1838) with lavish color plates by Edwin Dalton Smith, Thomas Rivers's *The Rose Amateur's Guide* (1840), and John Abercombie's *The Gardener's Pocket Dictionary* (1786). She also consulted sixteenth-century herbals, which included woodcuts and copper engravings of plants and flowers, in particular John Gerard's *The Herbal or General History of Plants* (1597). Of the *Dutch Gardener: Or, the Compleat Florist* (1703) by Henrik van Oosten, which covered fruit tree cultivation, tulips, and garden flower culture, Patience noted approvingly that the "'Florist' here is the enlightened amateur and not the commercial gardener." Perhaps more than any other book, though, it was John Claudius Loudon's *An Encyclopedia of Gardening* (1822) that had the greatest impact on her. Loudon, born in Scotland in 1783 and the son of a farmer, would go on to become one of the most influential landscape architects and gardeners of his time. Known for his extraordinary stamina—he often worked 12-hour days without stopping for meals and then wrote late into the night—Loudon was an exemplar of a new generation of naturalists, brimming with passion and versed in an astonishingly wide range of topics, who flourished before the professionalization of many of the natural sciences. He published widely, edited several periodicals on gardening and natural history, and developed a design theory known as the "gardenesque," which emphasized the individual aspect of trees and plants.

For Patience it was his breadth of knowledge and interest in vegetables and their many uses, not only culinary, that set him apart. He also discussed edible fungi and edible wild plants, which he said were deserving of study "to enable the gentleman's gardener to point out resources to the poor in his neighborhood, in seasons of scarcity."[45] Loudon's contemporary Rev. Miles J. Berkeley, incidentally, had identified and described more than 6,000 new species of fungi—a testament to the spirit of inquiry that defined the period. In Loudon's *Encyclopedia of Gardening*, he included a section that he called "Vegetable Kingdom."[46] This he divided into several subsections, including vegetable anatomy, vegetable physiology, and vegetable distribution. The lively and wide-ranging book touches on everything from manures and meteorology to fences and the literature of agriculture.

In addition to the frequent references to Loudon in early versions of *Honey from a Weed*, the first draft of the book also contained a separate appendix called "The Vegetable Tribe," which drew directly from the *Encyclopedia* in its organization and structure. Taking Loudon as her model, Patience initially divided the various vegetables into categories based on "their habits, culture, and uses in domestic economy."[47] She reproduced the same vegetable groupings—the cabbage tribe, esculent roots, and plants used for preserves and pickles, for example—and gave an overview of their origins and uses, at once paying homage to and updating Loudon for the modern reader. Patience considered Loudon not only a "wonderful gardener but a man of voracious curiosity" whose work gave her both a sense of joy and sadness: joy that such an array of culinary plants was included in the nineteenth-century kitchen garden and sorrow that so much knowledge and variety had vanished. "What Mediterranean people still cherish today," she wrote in a 1970 version of *Honey from a Weed*, "a great vegetable variety, was once grown in England and brought to market by nursery gardeners in the vicinity of London, as well as cultivated in walled kitchen gardens of the well-to-do and in cottage plots."

"The Vegetable Tribe" did not make it into the final draft of *Honey from a Weed*, but something of Loudon's approach to gardening as well as his attempt to provide an encyclopedic view of the subject is evident in its pages. In fact the book, in its structure and outlook, probably has more in common with early Victorian books on plants and gardening than it does with the cookbooks of its time. In the end "The Vegetable Tribe" became "Vegetable Heritage," and the published book included chapters on edible weeds, fungi, preserves, conserves, and flowers and fruits.

But in 1951 or 1952, when Patience was first introduced to Loudon's work, she had not yet embarked on a career as a writer, let alone an author of cookbooks. In fact Frank Clark's book on nursery gardens never materialized, but Patience kept her notes in a folder titled "Plant Research."

She was still working mornings at the Royal College of Art and pursuing freelance work on her own and with Primrose Boyd in the afternoons. Sometime in the summer or fall of 1953, they started discussing the possibility of embarking on a cookbook that would include "personal recipes" and "extravagant dishes" from across Europe. In the opening pages of what would become *Plats du Jour*, the authors, in a section on herbs, refer to the "rather confusing" distinction Loudon made between pot-herbs (parsley, tarragon, and dill) and sweet herbs (thyme, sage, mint, and rosemary), one that had unfortunately been perpetuated over the years in gardening catalogues. "As there is no logical basis for these two categories," they wrote, "it is much easier to remember that culinary herbs belong, with a few noteworthy exceptions, to two botanical families, the *Labiatae* and *Umbelliferae*."[48]

Cooking with and even cultivating fresh herbs was hardly revolutionary, but in 1953 rationing was still the order of the day and access to certain vegetables and specialty foods extremely limited. However this was soon to change, and cookbooks like *Plats du Jour* were among the first to reflect the growing desire for a new approach to food and cooking.

CHAPTER FIVE

Plats du Jour

In November 1953 Patience and Primrose Boyd submitted a proposal to Penguin's Allen Lane on "European cookery" that was to be divided by country and subject.[1] The countries were largely confined to those the authors had visited—France, Italy, Hungary, and Spain—and the subjects included soups, fish, pasta, and herbs. It was an ambitious undertaking and something of a departure for two women who had never written a cookbook and had only limited experience as home cooks. Patience would later say that the motivation to publish a book-length work was largely practical—both she and Primrose needed the income—and reflected a desire to produce a book that would be useful to women like themselves with busy working lives and, in Patience's case, two children (Primrose never had children). Thus the book's focus on making a meal of a single dish, or *plat du jour*, accompanied "as a rule" by a simple salad, cheese, fruit, and "wherever possible" a bottle of wine. The book's accessibility—it was the first book of its kind launched as a mass-circulation paperback, at the eminently affordable price of three shillings and sixpence—was mirrored in the authors' rather humble but serious and disciplined approach. These were not cookery experts imparting their knowledge from on high but rather a couple of home cooks inspired by the meals they'd enjoyed abroad and an amateur's zeal for learning as much as they possibly could about the subject. As Patience wrote in a preface to a new edition published more than thirty years later, "I sometimes wonder at the presumption, ours, in embarking in 1954 on a cookery book."[2]

At least one person at the time did not question their credentials or view their lack of experience as an impediment. Eunice Frost, Penguin's reclusive yet powerful editorial director, recognized the proposal's potential and responded with enthusiasm, assuring the authors that she would make certain it received a fair hearing. She advised the authors early on to consider expanding the scope of the book to include other parts of Europe and raised questions about recipes and methods so that they would avoid "errors and ambiguities."[3] Although Frost admitted to not being much of a cook herself, she expressed an interest in the subject that went beyond the ordinary concerns of a publisher, exchanging queries about books and sending Patience copies of Pellegrino Artusi's nineteenth-century classic, *La Scienza in Cucina e l'Arte di Mangiar Bene*, and the popular *Talisman Italian Cookbook*. Indeed, around the same time that she began working with Patience and Primrose, Eunice Frost made a push to acquire the paperback rights to Elizabeth David's first cookbook, *A Book of Mediterranean Food*, published by John Lehman in 1950. "I read it as an artist," she told David's biographer, Artemis Cooper. "And I felt ravished."[4] Frost was something of a painter and writer herself, leaving behind several disconnected refrigerators full of her pictures in the house where she died, and pages of an unfinished autobiography. David later wrote that it was mainly due to Frost's insistence, with the support of Allen Lane, that the firm decided to republish *A Book of Mediterranean Food*.

Frost, who had joined Penguin in 1937 as a secretary and quickly worked her way up the ranks—she was the firm's first female director—would in fact come to rely on David to review manuscripts, including Patience and Primrose's, as an anonymous "cookery expert."[5] Frost's tastes were wide ranging, and she is credited with bringing into the fold some of Penguin's most successful authors, including Graham Greene, Evelyn Waugh, and Dorothy L. Sayers. Such was her impact within the company that the penguin mascot and logo, familiar to legions of readers, is named "Frostie" after her.[6] But in early 1954 Frost was still working diligently to persuade Penguin's editorial board to endorse this new book on continental cuisine by a couple of unknown authors. Elizabeth David had already gained some notoriety as a food writer, but cookbook publishing was still fairly specialized.

Apparently it took several months for Frost to find the right moment—"any earlier attempt," she wrote, "might have been inappropriate"—to pitch the book to her colleagues, but by April 1954 it had been approved.[7] Patience and Primrose were already searching for a title, and in late March Patience sent Frost a postcard mailed from South Kensington, where she was still working at the Royal College of Art, that read simply, "What about *Plats du Jour* for the title?"[8] Primrose had suggested the more prosaic *Foreign Fare: A Choice of Dishes*. An advance of £200, with half being paid up front, was settled on and the authors set to work.

1954 was the year that rationing finally came to an end in England. After years of subsisting on the much-maligned National Loaf—a fortified whole-wheat bread, dense and somewhat grey in color—the availability of white flour was a kind of revelation. (The National Loaf, however, could still be found on shelves as late as 1956.) Restrictions on sugar were lifted in February 1953; butter was taken off the ration in May 1954, and meat two months later. It marked a thaw of sorts and a turning point in the availability of basic foods and cooking habits of the average housewife. There was also a gradual increase in real wages, which fueled an intense, almost feverish desire to eat well. This did not necessarily imply elaborate preparation or even luxury ingredients but perhaps the opportunity to buy certain previously unavailable cuts of meat, a whole chicken, butter, or cream.

Meanwhile the reliance on domestic servants among the middle and upper middle classes had already been undermined by the Great Depression of the 1930s and the war effort—many servants were sent to work in factories, thus compelling an entire generation of British women to rediscover the pleasures of cooking. And they were seeking out the books that would show them how. Elizabeth David's *Italian Food*, published in November 1954, was singled out by Evelyn Waugh as one of the year's best books, unheard of for the genre, and a sign of the prominence cookbooks would attain in the coming decade. The following year, in the preface to the Penguin edition of *A Book of Mediterranean Food*, David marveled at the fact that, compared to just two years previously, "there is scarcely a single ingredient, however exotic, mentioned in this book which cannot be obtained somewhere in the country."[9] Indeed the pleasures of Soho stores and street markets, Patience and Primrose wrote in *Plats du Jour*, "can provoke almost as much interest as an early morning saunter through the market beyond the Rialto Bridge in Venice."[10]

Of course things did not change overnight. It wasn't as if foods that had been rationed for more than a decade were all suddenly abundant or that so-called luxury items such as lemons, anchovies, and olive oil could be found on every street corner. Or even that the sensibilities and tastes of an entire nation had suddenly shifted to the southern shores of the Mediterranean. In fact for the majority of the population, eating habits remained fairly constant in the 1950s, a decade that also witnessed the emergence of frozen and dehydrated foods and supermarkets. But for the adventurous home cook, the possibility of preparing a *daube* or *cassoulet* was within reach.

Still, an "atmosphere of economy" pervades *Plats du Jour*, and the authors go out of their way to appeal to the time-conscious and cash-strapped housewife. In the introduction they acknowledge that "lack of means is just as much a familiar feature of our daily life here in England" as it was in postwar Italy or France, and that "the kitchen is no longer the scene of continuous activity, but a place for sporadic effort."[11] Women, especially those who worked, had far less time to prepare food. With this in mind Patience and Primrose offer a sensible early chapter on refashioning the storage cupboard—instead of being lined with tins, it should contain spices, herbs, and olive oil as well as a few pounds of staple commodities such as rice, pasta, and beans—so that a decent meal can still be prepared when there's little time to shop. They also give advice on what to look for when buying meat, and a guide to affordable table wines.

The recipes and lifestyle embodied in the text reflect the way that Patience lived and cooked at that time. She was fond of shopping in Soho, where she could find such items as black (rye) bread, liver pâté, olive oil, and charcuterie. *Plats du Jour* includes a list of suppliers and specialty stores that she frequented: Harrods of Knightsbridge for its *boucherie francaise*; Parmigiani's for its cheeses, dried herbs, and wine; and above all Madame Cadec's legendary Greek Street shop for kitchenware, utensils, and pots and pans. Indeed Madame Cadec's was, for Patience, an almost sacred space. She described it as a "cook's wonderland" and was particularly fond of the shop's simple copper cookware and glazed terrines with imprints of hares or woodcocks on the lid.[12] Opened around the end of the First World War by Madame Cadec and her husband, the shop originally operated as a supplier for the catering trade. Madame Cadec did most of the purchasing herself, traveling around villages in France and bringing materials back to London. Thus the store was full of otherwise unattainable items. Popularized by writers like Elizabeth David and Patience, it became a fashionable Soho destination and undoubtedly served as an inspiration for David's own cookware shop, which she opened in 1965. Indeed for Patience it represented far more than just a place to buy kitchen supplies, though it was most certainly that, too. When revising *Honey from a Weed*, Patience chastised a copy editor for quibbling with her about Madame Cadec's significance (by then the shop had long been closed). Patience said that she owed her "initiation into the poetic" to Madame Cadec and, though the shop was no longer there, Madame Cadec herself was immortal. "Are you not aware that things that really matter to you are not relegated to the past?" Patience continued, delivering one of her many object lessons. "They belong to the present."[13]

Patience did most of her cooking and recipe testing for *Plats du Jour* in her small Hampstead kitchen, which by today's standards was absolutely tiny. "It was the tiniest kitchen you could imagine," Trevor Pinnock recalled.[14] Nicolas described it as being "more a galley than a kitchen," with just a few appliances, including a small prewar cast-iron gas stove and a fridge decorated with red and black harlequin diamonds, which Patience hardly used and eventually disconnected. "I don't clutter the place up with trick machinery," Patience wrote in an unpublished essay, "because though I love cooking, gadgets bore me." The open kitchen looked out onto the living room, something of a novelty at the time. It may have been true, as Patience and Primrose wrote, that kitchens were increasingly becoming "a part of the living space"; but Patience's arrangement was not yet the norm. Most kitchens were still walled off from the dining room, or at least separated by an open sideboard or shelf unit, and out of view of guests. Patience's Hampstead flat was open-plan living with clerestory windows and a lofted space for sleeping, giving it an almost cathedral-like feel. As she did most of her writing and other activities at the large table overlooking the garden downstairs, "her life and work went on in one room."[15] In a series of articles on modern living for the *Observer*, Patience described the Billiardroom as being roughly equivalent in size to a "normal council house," but that the open plan made it feel substantially bigger.[16] She compared it to a "barn, boathouse, or vacant husk," in a way pointing to the kind of habitations she and Norman Mommens would later live in.

It was at the "Lion Bar" that she both prepared food and entertained. The bar was a simple counter, supported by one of the upstairs gallery's wooden supports, and presided over by an eighteenth-century carved lion's head mounted on the wall. Alec Hill, who found this heraldic relic for Patience, claimed it had washed up on a beach near Chichester. The bar divided the kitchen from the rest of the living room, and guests gathered around it could lend a hand or just observe. Wine flowed freely, recalls David Gentleman, who was a frequent guest—as were Henrion and others from the Royal College of Art. For larger dinner parties Patience would clear the table in the bay window, effectively her desk, and serve the meal under the tall arched windows overlooking the terraced garden. "She cooked like crazy," said her friend Ariane Castaing. "She would have lovely little soirées."[17] And she paid close attention to every detail, from the food and wine to the music and dishware. Food was often served in salad bowls from Italy and on Wedgwood plates in the shape of vine leaves, and the wine in Georgian wine glasses. On Sundays they would often eat outside in the garden where Patience had fashioned a table from bricks and a square piece of slate.

But the food was usually simple, a single dish, followed by salad and cheese, the very principle that underlies *Plats du Jour*. "It was very much how we used to eat," says Miranda, who remembers helping to make the marinade for *boeuf en daube*. "All the attention was paid to this single dish. The book was written for people in her sort of predicament."[18] Indeed Patience was still commuting to the Royal College of Art every morning. Afternoons and weekends were spent in the "damp basement" of the public library at Camden Town poring over "a splendidly illustrated" 1848 edition of Brillat-Savarin's *Physiologie du Goût* or searching the stacks of the London Library for the likes of Maître Carême and Urbain Dubois, nineteenth-century French chefs.[19] When she returned home in the evening, there wasn't a great deal of time left to put together a meal.

Which isn't to say that the book is without its extravagances or appeal to a certain kind of longing for the faraway. Part of the success of Elizabeth David's early books, especially *A Book of Mediterranean Food* and *French Country Cooking*, is attributed to the fact that they tapped into a deep desire to escape the grim conditions of postwar life in England. And of course they drew directly on David's own experience traveling in

Greece, the south of France, and Cairo, where she lived during the war. In a similar way Patience and Primrose made it clear that *Plats du Jour* was in part inspired by their travels abroad, and some of the most delightful passages refer to meals they'd eaten in France or Italy. "What culinary achievements we can claim are the result of enjoyment and the wish to reproduce tastes which have been first experienced in foreign places," they wrote.[20] In the preface to the much later Prospect Books edition, Patience explained "Travel, the hard way, was closely connected with our aim to broaden the post-war approach to island cooking at a time when rationing and 'austerity' were petering to an end."[21] She was referring to the trips she'd taken to Hungary in 1937 and Romania in 1938. Indeed one of the book's most evocative descriptions must have come from Patience's trip to Hungary with Betty Barnardo in 1937: "For anyone who has eaten a well-prepared *gulyás* in one of the little restaurants on the Buda side of the Danube, overlooking the lantern-threaded bridges and the electric glitter of Pest on a warm summer night before the war, this is a dish worth making."[22] But she'd also traveled after the war. In June 1948 she visited Rome, Naples, and Florence with Katharine Watson, a family friend from Sussex. They hiked along the rocky coast south of Naples and ate simple meals, spaghetti, fruit, and wine, which "suited our pockets and our palates," Katharine observed.[23] In 1953 Patience and the children traveled to the seaside town of Locmariaquer in Brittany with Kate Newman and her daughter, Sandra. The tiny fishing village, "outside the track of time," as Patience put it, was still remote, with just a single road connecting it to the mainland.[24] They stayed at the Hotel Lautram, named after the chef-owner, who had served his apprenticeship at Chez Prunier in Paris, famous for its seafood. They ate meals at a large oval table in view of the kitchen, where Patience was able to keep an eye on Monsieur Lautram, "enveloped in an apron down to his boots, a beret on his head."[25] The food was abundant and fresh. The bread was excellent and served with good Breton butter or cheese. There were mounds of local oysters, fresh peas, and red mullet straight from the sea. To try to recreate dishes based on these ingredients, so rooted in a particular place, was not their aim, and in the introduction to *Plats du Jour*, the authors seem to acknowledge as much when they describe the Breton fish soup, *cotriade à la bretonne*, a variety of fish poached with onions, potatoes, and herbs. Thus they noted

"The natural qualities which give this dish its flavor"—the fresh fish, the waxy yellow potatoes, and Breton onions—"are with us partially absent."[26]

In a recipe for *rougets au vin blanc* that she pried out of Monsieur Lautram, Patience's powers of observation and interest in technique are evident (this recipe was not included in *Plats du Jour* but later published in her memoir and in *The Centaur's Kitchen*). The recipe calls for making a sauce from the pan juices—the fish is cooked in nothing more than wine and butter—by thickening with "good butter and a little flour." What Lautram omitted to say, and Patience only learned by watching, was that in order to produce a perfectly amalgamated sauce, the butter is first combined with the flour and then divided into small pieces before being whisked into the pan juices. "This is a perfect example of a 'simple' recipe conveying no idea of procedure, or an instance of a true Breton's reluctance to share his secrets," Patience wrote. "I simply had to beard him in his outhouse kitchen at the crucial moment to watch him make this sauce."[27] Indeed as Nicolas recalled, Patience spent a great deal of time in Lautram's kitchen peppering him with questions.

By all accounts Primrose was also a talented cook, had an interest in fungi, and was an avid gardener. She and her husband, the BBC producer Donald Boyd, lived in Hampstead and moved in the same circles as Patience. "Primrose was a superb cook," says Julia Black, whose mother, Helen, was a close friend of Primrose. Daphne Henrion also remembered her being a good cook whose food was always "highly edible."[28] Patience recalled her hearty pea soups, casseroles, terrines, pâtés, quiches, pickled tongues, salads, and French cheeses in perfect condition because they were "freshly imported and never refrigerated." Born in 1910 Primrose had traveled to Russia at the age of twenty-two and then studied painting in Amsterdam. According to a biographical note that she provided to Penguin Books but which was never used, she received her first lessons in cooking from a Parisian chef. She married Boyd, a journalist and the author of the First World War memoir *Salute of Guns*, in 1943, but it was not a particularly happy marriage. Seven years older than Patience, she was the "living image of the 'professional woman' before her time" who, according to Patience, "sometimes lectured me on 'women's rights' and 'executive dress.'"[29] In a letter to Primrose's niece many years later, Patience described her as having a "stalwart character" and "fierce combative nature" but not being an easy person to get on with, words that might have been used to describe Patience herself.[30]

Although they had launched their very informal business partnership after the Festival of Britain in 1951, Patience and Primrose rarely worked on projects together. For *Plats du Jour* they had agreed in principle to divide the recipes up, but when Patience realized that Primrose's versions were unworkable, she set out to rewrite most of the text. "What shocked Patience is that Primrose hadn't tried the recipes that she wrote," says Miranda.[31] Patience insisted on and prevailed in having her name appear first on the book's cover, out of alphabetical order, bucking a standard publishing convention. When they were accidentally reversed in an announcement in a trade catalogue, Patience wrote a terse note to "Sir Allen," claiming that she had written "seven-eighths of the book" and was therefore "entitled to an un-alphabetical arrangement of authorship."[32] This was the source of much friction and would eventually result in the dissolution of their friendship and the scuttling of a new edition of the book, which was still in high demand, in the early 1960s. They were both formidable personalities, and it appears not particularly close friends. David Gentleman, for example, who illustrated the book and saw Patience frequently during this time, never once met Primrose.

It just so happened that in the summer of 1954, Gentleman received a travel scholarship from the Royal College of Art to spend three months in Italy. Patience had gotten to know him well during her time at the college and suggested to Eunice Frost that he illustrate the book. As she would with all of her books, Patience took an interest in every aspect of production and felt strongly that this cookbook should not only provide readers with a sense of the dishes' place of origin but also be a usable guide to things like fish, cuts of meat, and varieties of pasta. Patience understood well the power of conveying information graphically and wrote to Frost that she wanted the book, for example, "to have recognizable drawings of different fish, as accurate as those to be found in Victorian Treasuries of Natural History."[33] Keenly aware of the "evocative cookery illustrations" that graced the pages of Elizabeth David's first couple of cookbooks—namely those by John Minton in *A Book of Mediterranean Food* and *French Country Cooking*—Patience felt that it would be "a good thing to turn to a more practical approach, which could in its own way be extremely decorative."[34] Minton's drawings, as lovely as they were, tended to be more impressionistic than instructive. Indeed this was a concern to David, who insisted that her second book include drawings of a more practical nature such as pots, pans, and kitchen implements. Frost agreed with Patience and said it would be "essential to have practical and accurate, but elegant, drawings."[35]

Minton was a well-known painter who taught at the Royal College of Art during Gentleman's time there as a student. Gentleman knew him only slightly—he described him once as "haggard yet inspiring"—but was familiar with the layout and approach to the books he had illustrated for Elizabeth David.[36] These books generally followed a formula of a scene-setting sketch at the start of a chapter followed by a few related drawings throughout to illustrate the subject at hand.

Gentleman, who had studied with Edward Bawden and John Nash at the college, was not unknown to Penguin's editors. He'd met the firm's head of design, Hans Schmoller, over lunch at the college and did his first cover—an engraving of a mountain hut for a collection of Guy de Maupassant stories—in 1955. Schmoller, who had taken over from the legendary Swiss designer Jans Tschichold in 1949, was known for his fastidiousness and attention to detail. "Schmoller was a great stickler for perfection," said Gentleman.[37] Though he would go on to do countless covers for Penguin, *Plats du Jour* was Gentleman's first and only full-length commission for the firm.

From the start Patience and Gentleman agreed that *Plats du Jour* would include more detailed illustrations, sufficiently accurate that they mightn't be out of place in a work of reference, of fish, beef, lamb, pork, and veal, and indeed fungi. Patience had given him lists of the items she wanted him to illustrate and also secured him an introduction to the food hall at Harrods, where he spent days watching the butchers at work in the basement. At the end of the day, they would send him home with a bag of fresh sausages as a token of goodwill. He also spent time with a village butcher in Essex, where for part of the year he rented a room from John Lewis, a typographer and book designer and one of his tutors at the

Royal College of Art . It was here that he got lessons in the dismember-ing of whole pigs and sheep. A testament to the book's usefulness in these matters is the fact that Patience herself relied on them years later when she raised and butchered pigs in Puglia. Drawings of fungi were based on illustrations in other books, principally John Ramsbottom's *Edible Fungi*.

But it is *Plats du Jour's* striking pastel pink cover that is best remem-bered. The front depicts a multigenerational French family sitting down to dinner, and the back shows the aftermath of the meal, with the empty table littered with fruit and wine bottles and a couple of well-fed cats occupying the chairs. This was not however the original idea for the cover. Initially Gentleman had suggested an image of a man studying a menu in front of a restaurant somewhere in France or Italy. Schmoller and the authors, who recognized the importance of the cover in setting the tone, felt that it might give readers the wrong impression of what the book was about and suggested that the emphasis be on eating at home to capture the book's personal and informal approach. "The home cooking aspect must be stressed on the cover," he wrote to Gentleman.[38] Thus they settled on the idea of the large family at table, and Gentleman executed the image for which the book is known. However he likely did not inform Schmoller that one of the figures on the cover, the patriarch at the head of the table with a bushy mustache, was based on Gaston Dominici, a French peasant accused of murdering a British family in 1952. The long trial made international headlines right up until Dominici's conviction and sentence to death by guillotine in 1957, the same year *Plats du Jour* was published. (He was, however, later exonerated.)

Gentleman had only limited experience traveling in Europe—he'd been to France—and relied almost entirely on Patience for advice on where to go in Italy. Before he left they looked at maps of the country and Patience insisted that he cross at the Bernina Pass in Switzerland, the same route she had hiked in 1947 after her sister's death, so that his first impressions of Italy would be informed by this dramatic descent through the Val Poschiavo. "Patience mapped out the whole journey," Gentleman said. "I certainly remember the experience of seeing these tiny villages in the fields, what looked like miles below, and gradually walking down and the feeling that it was warm and Mediterranean."[39] In addition to instructing him to visit such prominent cities as Milan, Venice, Florence,

Rome, and Naples, she also suggested he spend some time in places like Verona and Corvino. Toward the end of the trip, he went to Siena and stayed in a small hotel whose chef-owner allowed Gentleman to draw him at home working in his kitchen. *Plats du Jour* is full of domestic scenes—a simple table set for three, stock pots bubbling away on an iron stove, knives and serving utensils hanging from wall-mounted hooks—the occasional French or Italian storefront, and the detailed and delightful illustrations of fish, meat, and fungi.

Gentleman's sketchbooks from his trip to Italy in 1954 served as the basis for the illustrations. "I didn't take any photographs in those days," he said. "The sketchbooks were my most important guides."[40] And they were deeply evocative of the time and place.

As Patience wrote, Gentleman's drawings "reflect the spirit of adventure which informed the undertaking."[41]

During the writing of *Plats du Jour* and throughout the 1950s, Patience continued to make frequent trips to Rogate to visit Olive and to leave the children there on weekends and throughout school holidays. David Gentleman joined on at least one occasion and later made a wood engraving of the cottage, which he gave to Olive as a gift. It was here that Patience did most of the fieldwork for the chapter on edible wild fungi, a highly unusual subject to include in a cookbook at that time. With the assistance of a biologist from the Ministry of Agriculture and others, including John Ramsbottom, Patience identified more than two hundred species in and around Rogate. The Ministry of Agriculture, beginning in 1910, had published a bulletin on edible and poisonous fungi. From these she sorted out the edible species and then those that were "not only edible but also delicious," roughly thirty varieties.[42]

In letters to Eunice Frost, Patience expressed her interest in the subject, difficult though the information was to find, and what she felt was a real need for a fungus identification chart in the U.K. "All I really want to do in *Plats du Jour* is to open up the subject a little," Patience wrote.[43] In 1957, the same year *Plats du Jour* was published, the American researcher and ethnobotanist R. G. Wasson and his Russian wife, Valentina, published their treatise on fungi, *Mushrooms, Russia and History*, in which they divided various cultures and geographic regions into mycophiles, those who love mushrooms, and mycophobes, those who fear them. Britain was firmly in the latter camp. Patience even suggested that Penguin publish a "series of identification charts which could be used as instruction plus decoration in schools, at home, in town halls etc."[44] Relying on Ramsbottom's books, on a new handbook published by E. M. Wakefield in 1954 (*The Observer's Book of Common Fungi*), and on Maublanc's *Les Champignons Comestibles et Vénéneux*, Patience became something of an expert on edible fungi. Fungi, unlike plants and flowers, which can usually be delineated by their leaves or fruit, are extremely difficult to identify with absolute certainty; this is why handbooks and cookbooks always come with a warning and disclaimer. The only completely accurate method, especially for those species that are not commonly eaten, is to make spore prints, which can take up to 24 hours, and examine them under a microscope. Moreover at the time Patience was doing her research, there were still very few up-to-date books available for the general public at an affordable price. "There is therefore considerable demand for books on fungi," Wakefield wrote in the introduction to her field guide.[45]

It wasn't only mushrooms that were of interest to Patience. She had an expansive view of the natural environment and collected everything from starfish and glass fishing floats washed up on the beach to flowers, leaves, and ferns. On walks with the children, they would gather shells, fossils, and the occasional flint tool or arrowhead. They walked and sometimes biked for miles exploring the countryside around Rogate. Nicolas and Miranda, with Patience's strong encouragement, devoted considerable time to writing and illustrating a homemade magazine that they called *The Oil Lamp*, which took its name from the fact that there was no electricity at Hill View until 1955. "We are spending a long time over this edition," they wrote in April of that year, "as it may be the last written under the light of an oil lamp." In their journal they recorded their weekly adventures, featured the writings of such friends as Julia Gibson and Robert Stjernstedt (Rosemary's son), and catalogued the flora and fauna of the region. They often included detailed drawings or sketches of British seabirds, mushrooms—especially the iconic *Amanita muscaria*—and various fossils.

Indeed for Patience drawing was always an important way of engaging with the natural world, and she would remain partial to pen-and-ink drawings or wood engravings of plants and fungi over color photography throughout her life. She admired Maublanc in part for the "botanical truth" of his watercolor plates. Years later she critiqued a new book on Mediterranean plants and flowers because its color photos, so easily forgotten, were no match for drawings or wood engravings. "One broods over a drawing," she wrote. "It is a kind of way into inspiring one not only to dream but to do."[46] She once recalled looking through the watercolors and drawings of her great-aunt Gertrude Jolly, who, like Patience, was nearsighted. "I think her myopic state gave her the key to landscape drawing," Patience wrote to Olive, "which is attack first the shadows, and shape follows."[47] Not surprisingly visitors to Rogate would often spend part of the day drawing. Miranda remembers Barbara Jones and Tom Ingram, painters and illustrators who had both studied at the Royal College of Art, visiting once or twice and walking down the hill into Harting Combe with their sketchbooks.

One of the occasional visitors to Hill View in the early 1950s was Peter Shepheard, a friend of Rosemary Stjernstedt's and one of the principal landscape architects who had worked on the Festival of Britain. Shepheard was an enormously gifted artist—he was never without a sketchbook— and had a particular interest in botany and ornithology. He illustrated two books in the King Penguin series on ducks and woodland birds, and his sketchbooks, archived at the Museum of English Rural Life, are full of masterful drawings of butterflies, birds, owls, moths, plants, trees, flowers, and the female figure. He believed that immersion in nature as a child was an important part of a landscape architect's education and in *Modern Gardens* implored his colleagues to acquire a general knowledge of plants used in horticulture and a "detailed knowledge of those he intends to use himself."[48] His son Paul says, "He was an amateur naturalist in the old school fashion. He was a polymath—plants especially but also fish, insects, and birds."[49] On at least one occasion, Patience and Shepheard's families holidayed in Wales together. Rosemary Stjernstedt, whose mother lived in Aberdovey, spent time there as well, and throughout the 1950s Patience and the children viewed Wales as a kind of retreat. Fred Uhlman also had a place in North Wales on the slopes of the Cnicht, and, as Patience wrote, seemed more at home there, "resembling in spirit the romantic youth of his self portrait in *Reunion*" than he did in Hampstead.[50] Of one of their trips to Wales, Miranda recalled rising early to pick parasol mushrooms for breakfast and Patience gathering maidenhair ferns, which she then pressed to make beautiful pictures and prints. Miranda and Nick later recounted the expedition in an issue of *The Oil Lamp* and even provided the Latin name for the parasol mushroom—*Lepiota procera*—which they described as "sweeter than field mushrooms" and "very edible and good to eat." Patience learned a great deal from Shepheard, sometimes went to shows at the Royal Horticultural Society or to concerts with him, and often consulted him on questions about various plants she was trying to identify. "Patience's botanical sense was developed by Peter Shepheard," says Miranda.[51]

In 1952 Patience received a postcard from Shepheard that shows how scrupulous and exhaustive their efforts were, in regard to not only fungi but also ferns and mosses: "The pincushions are the White Feather Moss, *Leucobryum glaucum*," Shepheard wrote. "Found in Beechwoods on chalk and pine heaths in the south. Grows in some places in tussocks 3ft. in diameter like green sheep. Grows into curious cushions when scratched up by pheasants or rabbits. Common near Fawley, Hants, where known as Fawley Buns. In places like Burnham Beeches & the Northern moors it grows into much larger patches and looks more like what one expects of moss."[52]

For Shepheard, who said his first childhood memory was the vivid yellow corona of a daffodil, drawing was a way of understanding the natural world, as it was for Patience. He was said to draw "with an ease which seemed like part of a universal language."[53] After one visit to Hill View, he sent Olive a thank-you note in the form of a pen-and-ink drawing full of foxgloves, ferns, and other plants that seemed to embody his view that "in any tract of wild ground . . . one finds a miraculously appropriate assortment of plants, each one holding its own fit place and growing as best it may to add its own contribution, whether mean or magnificent, to the living pattern."[54]

Patience took a similarly exuberant approach to the study of mushrooms, and later to edible plants and weeds, that was as much a celebration of the natural world, or the "living pattern" as Shepheard phrased it, as it was an attempt to catalogue and ultimately cook and eat what she had gathered. What Patience said of Loudon—that he was not only a "wonderful gardener but a man of voracious curiosity"—could have also applied to Shepheard.[55]

In late March 1955 Patience and Primrose submitted the manuscript for *Plats du Jour* to Eunice Frost. "We enclose the mss. of *Plats du Jour*, which has received our close attention for more than a year," they wrote, "and we hope this is evident from the text."[56]

Several months later Frost wrote to say that she'd had time to review the manuscript with her "cookery expert" and that, while she was "entirely happy" with what they'd produced, she had several considerations she wanted to bring to their attention.[57] What she didn't say and never revealed was that the unnamed expert was none other than Elizabeth David. In fact David had drafted a 10-page report on the book sometime in June. Although she found the book "perfectly sound" and the recipes "genuine, practical, and clearly and accurately described," she felt that the book as a whole was overwritten and at times pretentious, its worst fault being "long windedness."[58] "If some of the phraseology is a bit terse," Frost warned in a letter to Patience and Primrose, "please do appreciate that reports are usually direct and rather frank."[59]

It is of course a delicious twist of fate that Elizabeth David was the first person to critique *Plats du Jour*. Born in 1913 David was a contemporary of Patience's, and the two have often been compared. Their writing styles and approaches to food were in fact very different but their personae—fiercely independent, intellectually rigorous, and highly opinionated—have perhaps made them seem more similar than they were. Their lives also share a number of parallels: somewhat similar upper-middle-class child-hoods, travel abroad at an early age, and the decisive influence of older male mentors who shaped their outlook, especially with regard to food—Norman Douglas in the case of Elizabeth David, and Irving Davis, an antiquarian bookseller and gastronome, in the case of Patience.

These elements have tempted others, mostly food writers, to speculate on what the two women thought of each other. It is believed that they met on one occasion in 1961 at the home of their mutual friend Irving Davis, who also happened to be an old friend of Norman Douglas's. In a letter to Elizabeth David in March 1961, Irving, who had shared with her some of his catalogues of rare books, wrote, "I wonder whether by any chance you would care to have dinner with me here on Friday next and to meet a great friend of mine, Patience Gray, who would very much like to make your acquaintance? The dinner, if you can come, will be most simple." In his typically unassuming way, he added, "I should not attempt any recipe from your cookery books."[60] If indeed they did meet, neither ever mentioned it. Many years later, in a letter to the American food writer and essayist John Thorne, Patience made an oblique reference to the alleged event: "I set out to tell you about an Irving supper at New End for Elizabeth David to which I was invited," she wrote, "but it is just too hot."[61]

Whatever the case, the general consensus is that the two women would have loathed one another, and there is some evidence to support that conclusion. Over lunch and large quantities of wine at the River Café in 1989, Elizabeth David told the writer Jonathan Meades that she thought Patience "ghastly" and "pretentious."[62] Patience, in some of her letters, criticized David's bookishness and tendency to "look at the published word, not at life," and therefore perpetuate certain errors.[63] She was also sharply critical of the fish drawings in *Italian Food*. But it is also clear that they respected each other—Elizabeth David, who was also very good friends with Patience's publisher, Alan Davidson, sent her a card after *Honey from a Weed* was published saying how much she had enjoyed the book.[64] Patience later dismissed the notion that they were somehow rivals and said that Elizabeth was "a true pioneer" who had "produced an unrivalled body of work."[65]

In 1955, though, when Elizabeth David read the draft of *Plats du Jour*, the two women most certainly had not met. David had already published four books and was becoming well known both as an author and journalist. Thus her opinion on all matters related to food and wine was highly valued. In fact she had already done similar work for the publisher André Deutsch, for whom she also read and sometimes even edited cookery manuscripts.

In the spirit of constructive criticism, David began by commending Patience and Primrose for the "amount of care and practical experience" they had put into the book. She also acknowledged to Eunice Frost that she had herself "fallen into a good many of the traps mentioned in my report" and that it was her wish to "warn others about such pitfalls."[66]

She criticized the authors for the tendency to overwrite, making too frequent use of quotations from novels (something David herself was known for), and what she felt was a certain kind of pretentiousness. She suggested that they go through the text, especially the early chapters, and cut ruthlessly. On their affection for Brillat-Savarin, the French epicure and author of *Physiologie du Goût*, beloved by many food writers, she was particularly scathing: "I deplore the tendency of these authors (although they are not alone) to regard Brillat-Savarin as some kind of deity midway between Shakespeare and Jesus Christ," she wrote. Notably David had been commended by a reviewer for not referencing Savarin in her first book on Mediterranean food. David found the chapter on wine inadequate and raised questions about several recipes: "Can the authors really cook a genuine ratatouille in the oven?" "Is a pint of chicken stock really enough to cook one pound of rice?" And on their recipe for pot-au-feu, she disagreed with their inclusion of cabbage, which she felt the authors should not be encouraging the English to "use more than necessary."[67] In fact a number of errors that Elizabeth David failed to pick up on did creep into *Plats du Jour*, and these Patience duly addressed in the preface to the much later Prospect Books edition.

Perhaps most revealing of the difference in their approaches to food, however, is David's complete dismissal of the chapter on fungi. Ambitious and wideranging, the chapter includes a general introduction to mushroom identification, discussion of several different species (Patience identified at least eleven kinds of *Boletus* in Rogate), and a variety of methods of preparation. David felt that it was beyond the scope of the book, weighed it down, and suggested that the authors cut all but the recipes and, crucially, indicate whether cultivated mushrooms could be used instead. "After all, however instructive the chapter," she wrote, "most of us have to make do with cultivated mushrooms, and as these are now available nearly everywhere and at reasonable prices it would be useful to know how to get the best out of them." She shows a surprising lack of interest in the diversity of edible wild mushrooms to be found in England and seems to see little value in learning about them.

Although David devoted her life to cooking and food, she never kept a garden, only occasionally grew potted herbs, and according to her close friend Doreen Thornton, "hated walking more than an inch."[68] She had bad feet, swollen ankles, and suffered a cerebral hemorrhage at the age of fifty. She preferred to spend most of her time in bed or at the kitchen table, where she often wrote. Thus it is not surprising that she found the chapter on fungi tiresome and perhaps beyond the purview of a cookbook. Patience on the other hand would come to be known for her knowledge of edible wild foods (already evident in the chapter on fungi in *Plats du Jour*), which required a lifetime of foraging, cataloguing, and tasting. As she notes in *Plats du Jour*, "This chapter has been written for people who combine an experimental approach to cooking with an interest in natural history."[69]

Indeed for Patience wild foods were unmatched in their flavor and beauty, and she considered fungi "the most delicate feast the wild has to offer."[70]

Plats du Jour was finally published in April 1957, and one month later Elizabeth David sent Eunice Frost a postcard wishing it every success. "I hope you & Sir Allen are going to revolutionise the cooking of this country," she wrote.[71]

Short of a revolution, the book did reach a wide audience. It sold remarkably well, nearly fifty thousand copies in the first ten months. For the average home cook, *Plats du Jour* became a kind of standard reference. "I make the point that *Plats du Jour* is a necessary possession among all my friends who are interested in the same way in cooking for themselves," one admirer wrote.[72] Muriel Downes and Rosemary Hume of Le Cordon Bleu culinary school said it was their favorite Penguin cookbook and especially liked the chapters on pasta and fungi.[73] Jane Grigson used to search for copies at used book sales to give to friends. The novelist Angela Carter, for whom *Plats du Jour* was her first cookbook, described it as "a book to browse in as much as to cook from, its prose as elegant as its plentiful line-drawings."[74] But the book's impact was not confined to England. Elisabeth Sifton, an editor at Farrar, Straus and Giroux in New York, had been given a copy by a friend and loved it. "Goodness knows I carry on rapturously about it whenever possible and to whomever possible," she wrote.[75] Another friend of Patience's told her she frequently saw it on shelves in Greenwich Village apartments in the 1960s despite the *New York Times*' admonition that it was "entertaining but not explicit enough for any but expert American cooks."[76]

To celebrate the book's publication, Eunice Frost took the authors and Hans Schmoller (David Gentleman was traveling in Spain) out to lunch at Le Bon Viveur, a fashionable club and restaurant in Shepherd Market. It had been two years since the manuscript was submitted—there were numerous delays due to revising the text, copy-editing issues, and the incorporation and layout of the illustrations—and Patience and Primrose were clearly relieved to see it in print with such lovely drawings. "I must say that it is rather exciting that the book really does exist after what seems like years of waiting," Patience wrote.[77] Its rather unexpected success certainly paved the way for Penguin to expand its list of cookbooks, and by 1970 the firm had published more than forty cookery titles.

Plats du Jour remained in print from 1957 to 1961 (an effort to issue a new, revised edition in 1963 fell apart when Patience and Primrose clashed over questions of authorship) and was awarded a silver medal from the German Gastronomical Academy in 1960.

"I am of course delighted that *Plats du Jour* won a silver medal," Patience wrote, adding wryly: "I only wish it was the French Gastronomical Academy that awarded it!"[78]

<hr />

By the time the book was published, Patience had moved on to other ventures. She had left the Royal College of Art in 1955 and continued to freelance and work as a part-time editor, mostly at *House and Garden*, where she had a fruitful working partnership with the photographer Michael Wickham. A latter-day Renaissance man, Wickham was self-taught in a variety of trades, from furniture making and painting to gardening and cooking, and was well known for his carefully choreographed interiors for Condé Nast. "He dreamed things up and then made them," Patience recalled years later.[79] Not surprisingly Wickham, described by the designer Terence Conran as "an 18th-century polymath who ended up in the 20th century," was just the kind of eccentric, willful, and radically independent-minded person Patience was drawn to.[80] Throughout the decade she also continued to collaborate with Henrion, who was still a tutor in the graphic design department at the Royal College of Art. (Misha Black was appointed professor of industrial design there in 1959.) In 1958 Patience and Henrion worked on an issue of Cyril Ray's *Compleat Imbiber*, a literary journal devoted as its name suggests to booze in all its forms, which included essays by Kingsley Amis, Iris Murdoch, Peter Fleming, and others. Henrion did montage illustrations based on old prints that Patience had sourced from the Victoria and Albert Museum, André Simon's private collection, and the National Film Archives. (Henrion served as consultant art editor of the *Imbiber* from 1953 to 1958.) Beginning in 1958 Patience also wrote a handful of articles for *Harper's Bazaar* on everything from buffet parties and ices to innovations in kitchen design and picnicking.[81]

Sometime in late 1957 or early 1958, Patience's brother-in-law John Midgley, a foreign editor at *The Economist*, encouraged her to apply for a new position as "woman's editor" of the *Observer*, one of London's leading papers, then owned and edited by David Astor. The job would largely focus on "home" subjects, including cooking and consumer research, as well as "general topics of interest to women readers."[82] Although Patience had written a cookbook, she did not see herself as an expert on food and was still seeking work in the fields of art and design. Indeed she wrote a letter around this time to Alison Settle, the paper's fashion editor, in which she said she was "keenly interested" in the subject.[83] In March 1958 she reached out to Brian Batsford, the painter and publisher of Batsford Books, to see if he "might have some use for my services as a freelance research worker and/or editorial assistant."[84] She had a meeting with him and pitched an idea for a coffee-table book featuring the homes of forty British celebrities in the fields of design, decoration, architecture, fashion journalism, and food writing. She suggested, among others, Robin Darwin, Henrion, Milner Gray, John Aldridge, Madge Garland, and Elizabeth David, "our leading cookery writer."

But to her surprise Patience learned soon after that she had been shortlisted for the *Observer* position. Her answer to the question "Can a career woman be a good mother?" which was particularly loaded in Patience's case, must have satisfied the paper's editors, including Astor, who had somewhat ambivalent ideas about working women, not to mention unmarried mothers. In early spring, as she was preparing for a trip to Naples and the south of Italy with her friend Irving Davis, she received an "urgent call" notifying her that she'd gotten the job.

CHAPTER SIX

The European Scene

I t was only after the publication of *Plats du Jour* that Patience met Irving Davis, a prominent antiquarian bookseller and bibliophile, who would arguably have the greatest influence on her approach to food and cooking. She always maintained that Irving was shocked to learn that she'd had the temerity to write a cookbook before meeting him. As the story goes he was so impressed by her knowledge of fungi, however, that he invited her to dinner at his flat in Brunswick Square. Patience would later say that it was watching Irving in his austere kitchen, adorned only with engravings and eighteenth-century hand-colored prints of lone men eating at oyster bars, that she came to understand "the master-key to the art of cooking."[1]

Born in 1889 Irving had spent much of his life traveling to France, Italy, and Spain in search of rare books. Even as a young boy, he dreamed of living in Italy and in his memoir wrote, "I would have wished to exile myself to that country ... but I suppose I had not sufficient artistic talent and, as the Italians say, *mancavano i quattrini*, I had no money."[2] Still he would become one of the foremost authorities on early Italian printed books, and in 1953 he organized an exhibition on the subject for the National Book League in London. He was also a celebrated cook in his own right. "His meals were extraordinary," said the poet Oliver Bernard, who met Davis in the 1950s. "They were always marvelous occasions."[3] In *Honey from a Weed*, Patience recalled some of the dinners she had at Brunswick Square in the late 1950s and early 1960s: sorrel soup, marinated anchovies, fresh asparagus, and leeks *à la grecque*; a salad of fennel followed by a matelote of eels, turbot *à la crème*, and lobster; a feast of game birds, including grouse, braised partridges, quail, and pheasant; boiled *zamponi* (stuffed pig's trotter) and *cotechini* served with *pommes à l'huile.* Irving was also a highly regarded expert on French and Italian wine and, in 1934, published a "beginner's guide" to wines and spirits with line-drawn maps and illustrations.[4] Not surprisingly he was a good friend of André Simon, the well-known French wine merchant and founder of the Wine and Food Society, whose journal of the same name Patience contributed to in the 1950s.[5]

Irving not only revealed to Patience what she described as the "full poetic meaning" of classical cooking but also introduced her, in the summer of 1958, to the south of Italy.[6] Just before Patience started her job at the *Observer*, they traveled in a rented car from Naples down to Calabria and then across the coastal plains of Basilicata to Puglia. For Irving it was a journey into the past. "Being with Irving in the South was seeing it essentially through the eyes of Ovid, the younger Pliny, Lenormant, George Gissing, Orioli, and Norman Douglas," Patience wrote in her memoir.[7] In fact they carefully retraced the route that Norman Douglas and his lover, Giuseppe Orioli, had taken when they traveled across the south of Italy in the early 1930s in search of *Magna Graecia* (the part of southern Italy colonized by the Greeks in the eighth and seventh centuries BCE and referred to as "Greater Greece"). In a letter to an editor at the *New York Times* in 1990, Patience explained, "He [Irving] always told me that Douglas had never set foot in the Salento. When Irving and I in 1958 made a journey into Calabria, Basilicata and Apulia, in the steps of Douglas and Pino Orioli, nothing would induce him to explore the Salento south of Lecce.... As far as Irving was concerned, he only wished to go where Douglas had also been."[8]

Indeed Orioli had been Irving's first partner in the book business—they opened a bookshop in Florence in 1911. They were also likely lovers before Orioli ran off with Norman Douglas. "I was not born a homosexual," Irving writes in his memoir. "I can't remember ever feeling in love with a boy until my Cambridge days and later, my Florence days, when homosexuality was almost compulsory."[9] Orioli had moved to London around 1907 and earned a living teaching Italian to young men at Cambridge, where he presumably met Irving. After opening their shop in Florence in 1911, Irving and Orioli returned to London, where they opened a second shop at 24 Museum Street. Irving became sole proprietor in 1931 and after the war transferred to premises in Orme

Square on Maddox Street and finally to his home at New End, Hampstead, where he had a magnificent personal library. Orioli also continued in the book trade and was best known as the first to publish *Lady Chatterley's Lover* (1928).

Though they had separated sometime after Orioli took up with Douglas in 1922, they evidently remained friends and continued to see each other whenever Irving was in Italy. In 1936, for example, at the height of the Second Italo-Abyssinian War, Irving managed to sell a rare manuscript by the poet Torquato Tasso to the Italian National Library in Rome. The writer Richard Aldington suggests that perhaps Orioli was also involved in the acquisition of the Tasso book. "His [Orioli's] two great finds were a folio Shakespeare and a Tasso or Ariosto—I forget which—with notes in the author's handwriting. The former was sold in London for several hundred pounds, and the latter was bought by the Italian Government."[10] The Tasso fetched a handsome sum but, because of wartime disruptions, Irving was unable to bring the money back to England and instead spent half of it on a lavish cross-country tour of Italy and the other half on books. "Irving and Orioli and Douglas spent a lot of the day drinking and eating," Irving's stepdaughter, Ianthe Carswell, wrote in a letter to Patience describing the trip and their stay in Florence.[11] (Irving had married Ianthe's mother, Ivy Elstob, in 1941, and it was through Ianthe and John Carswell, who lived in Hampstead, that Patience first met Irving.) Indeed it was Orioli, a native of Romagna and the son of a sausage maker—the "world's greatest," he liked to boast—who introduced Irving to the pleasures of the table. At that time, Irving writes, "Food became an interest for me and cooking, I gradually realized, the sixth art."[12]

A similar spirit of adventure animated Patience and Irving's trip in 1958. They traveled on remote and rough roads in a tiny Fiat with copies of George Gissing's *By the Ionian Sea* and François Lenormant's *La Grande-Grèce* and *À Travers l'Apulie et la Lucanie* as their guidebooks. Patience kept a fragmentary account of the trip in which she admired the austerity of the landscape, the crumbling architecture, and the wild beauty of the sea.[13] They passed through Bisignano, where Orioli said Greek pots were made; Taranto, because Douglas claimed it was where the cat was first introduced to Europe from Egypt (Irving was a great admirer of cats); and Frederick II's castle in Trani, a seaport on the Adriatic. Meals were simple, often no more than bread, cheese, and wine. Like the hotels, "depressing" and "tomblike" as Patience described them, the meals were also sometimes disappointing. Provisions were scarce.

But there were treasures, too: a truck stop in Trebisacce on the Ionian coast where they ate olives, artichokes, prosciutto, and *maccheroni al forno*; along the quay in Taranto where they had *cozze al forno*, mussels opened over a very hot fire and filled with a mixture of their own aromatic juices, breadcrumbs, garlic, parsley, and parmesan, sprinkled with olive oil and browned in a hot oven—which Patience described as "perhaps the most perfect dish we ate" and for which she eventually included the recipe in *Honey from a Weed*; the strong, lightly sparkling wines of Sava; and the decorative pastries of Lecce. The approach to that baroque city, and the "miraculous lucidity of the Apulian sky," left a deep impression on Patience:

> One could see a long way. The brilliant little white cubes, peasant huts, leading the eye into the farthest distance. Beautiful white castellated farms appeared, enclosed in bastion walls, with square towers, crenellated. Then the delight of the town-villages, long long streets of dazzling white terraced houses (occasionally pale blue, pale chrome, or washed with pink), vistas of rectilinear whiteness punctuated with black garbed peasants at their doorways, sitting on the street.[14]

Though Irving kept to his word and they didn't venture south of Lecce, it was Patience's first taste of the Salento, of that strange and foreign landscape that she would eventually come to view as home. While she and Irving were to make several trips to Agropoli and Paestum, and to the fishing village of Positano, it was the far south that seems to have made an even greater impression on her. In a letter to her mother in 1968, just before she and her partner, Norman Mommens, made their first trip together to Puglia in search of a place to live and work, Patience wrote, "Funny I should have explored that region with Irving. And one or two places have indelibly fixed themselves in my memory."[15]

For Irving the rare book trade and gastronomy were inseparable. He was known for planning his book-buying trips to Florence to coincide with the season's first asparagus and new peas; the acquisition of rare manuscripts was often supplemented with the purchase of casks of wine, cases of extra-virgin olive oil, or aged wine vinegar; and meetings with other collectors almost always involved an elaborate meal. In a 1959 letter to Patience, Irving described a lavish meal with the Neapolitan bookseller Gaspare Casella, which featured an abundance of seafood and pasta all washed down with "real Ischian wine, the sort [Norman] Douglas must have drunk 40 years ago."[16]

Patience seemed to follow Irving's lead and quickly took advantage of the *Observer's* famously relaxed atmosphere to get away from England and her "little cell" in the office whenever she could. The paper's editor, David Astor, the son of wealthy American-born parents who had lived in England for most of their lives, was known to hire non-experts, often his friends or someone in his extensive social circle, who were then left to their own devices. According to Patience, Astor told her that his "ideal candidate" for the job, whom she always assumed to be fashion journalist and former *Harper's Bazaar* editor Anne Scott-James, had been unavailable. A number of young writers who joined the paper after the war—widely considered to be England's leading literary and intellectual forum—were surprised to discover just how informal things were. As Michael Davie, one of Astor's early recruits put it, "The governing principle was that the *Observer* should be written by amateurs."

Patience took it in her stride. Indeed one of her early articles for the paper, "Christmas Joie de Vivre" published under the banner of "A Woman's Perspective," was based on a trip to Paris with Irving in November 1958.[17] He introduced her to some of his favorite places—Le Restaurant des Artistes with its incomparable wine cellar, the famous seafood brasserie Rech, and Au Moulin à Vent—as well as department stores like Hédiard and Fauchon, where "every gastronomic wish is foreseen." He gave her a glimpse of the secretive world of antiquarian booksellers, figures like Tammaro De Marinis, Lucien Scheler (publisher of the poet Paul Éluard), and Blasio Galanti. "I have seen cascades of marvelous books in a famous bookseller's apartment in Auteuil," Patience wrote.

During those few days in November, with temperatures below zero and the streets covered in snow—"It was snowing, staggeringly cold," Patience wrote—Irving showed her a side of Paris she likely would never have seen otherwise.[18] He took her to an out-of-the-way shop that specialized in *andouillettes*, a rustic French tripe sausage. It was a "bookseller's secret resort," and they sat inside at small makeshift tables as the snow swirled outside. They had *soufflé de turbot* and *lièvre à la royale* at Le Restaurant des Artistes.[19] They visited the reclusive Galanti, "a wonderful emaciated figure," who showed them exceedingly rare books, which were stacked floor to ceiling in his small apartment.[20] "His books and papers were scattered all over the floor," one fellow collector wrote, "stacked one upon another reaching dizzying heights."[21] Afterward they dined on *croustade de fruits de mer*, roasted veal liver, and a selection of goat cheeses. It was also during that trip in November 1958 that Irving introduced Patience to the Catalan sculptor Apel-les Fenosa, whose work would have a profound influence on Patience. Fenosa's expressive bronze sculptures, Patience wrote in the *Observer*, "reaffirm an exquisite joy in life against the artistic hammer-blows and cries of the mid-century moment."[22]

To outsiders Patience and Irving's relationship could seem baffling. He was nearly thirty years older and, though charming, had a "fey and eerie" quality to him.[23] He was diminutive, somewhat ancient looking, with wisps of snow-white hair sprouting from his head, and never without his pipe or a cheap cigar, usually an Italian Toscanello. In his memoir *Getting Over It* (1990), Oliver Bernard described him as "looking gnome-like, hook nosed and cheerfully gloomy."[24] Indeed David Gentleman, who said he could never quite figure Irving out, always assumed they had been lovers and couldn't understand why Patience would have been interested in him. Harriet Wilson, Irving's step-granddaughter, remembers her mother, Ianthe, disapproving of Patience wearing a bikini while on holiday with Irving in Agropoli.[25] In fact it seems unlikely that they were lovers—Patience was still involved with Alexander Gibson at the time—and Irving largely preferred men. But it was precisely his somewhat otherworldly nature as well as his intelligence—he spoke five languages, including Latin—and access to unusual people and places that appealed to Patience. Patience saw herself in a similar light—eccentric, refined, and above the fray. "All of Patience's friends were really outsiders," says Ariane

Castaing.[26] She stood out as much as Irving did. Paul Shepheard, Peter's son, who remembers meeting Patience when he was a boy, said she was "fabulously exotic."[27] Elisabeth Lutyens's son, Conrad Clark, recalled her seeming "impossibly exotic and vivacious."[28] Even Patience would later say that she dressed all in black before it was considered chic and that "people were appalled by my appearance."[29]

Irving's interests and frequent travel overlapped nicely with Patience's own mission to give her readers a taste of Europe, in a sense building on what she had set out to do in *Plats du Jour*. "It was the European scene I wanted to bring home to English people," Patience wrote in an essay on her time at the *Observer*.[30] Thus she turned her column into opportunities to travel throughout Europe, covering everything from the Brussels World's Fair and Sweden's glass, ceramic, and furniture factories, to the Italia '61 exposition in Turin and the inauguration of the first direct flight from Heathrow to Sardinia in 1960, which she used as an opportunity for a weeklong tour of the island. This she did in the company of Enzo Apicella, a cartoonist and illustrator who Patience, with her eye for talent, brought onto the *Observer*. In her article on Sardinia, "Crafts from Obscurity," she mused on the "mysterious and beautiful patterns of a native culture not yet destroyed by contact with the mechanical 'civilisation' of today," and delighted in the early morning market at Cagliari with its capers, marbled beans, and zucchini blossoms. She was also struck by the handwoven baskets and rugs made by local people, which incorporated asphodel and other plants from the surrounding hillsides and displayed a high degree of skill and knowledge. "Can you be touched by the delicate pinks, mauves, magentas, poppy tones in the woven hangings without first having seen rock roses, wild mallows, oleander, or cornfields ablaze with poppy, in a landscape of scrub and stone?" Her own role, and that of the globe-trotting tourist, in potentially opening up a place like Sardinia and its subsequent impact on the peasant culture that she celebrated was not lost on Patience. In closing, sounding a theme that she would return to throughout her career as a writer, she noted, "Once the outside world has broken in with its promise of Lambrettas and refrigerators and hire-purchase, the self-sufficiency of a village culture is finished."[31]

Apicella, who went on to become a prominent interior designer and restaurateur in his own right, remembers Patience's boundless curiosity and said that she once spent the better part of a day talking to old men in a small fishing village, many of whom had lost hands or fingers from blast fishing with dynamite. "She was mesmerized by their ability to light a cigarette without help," says Apicella.[32]

Not surprisingly their conversations often turned to cooking. Apicella, who was born in Naples, would tell her about the foods of his childhood and said she was most intrigued by a simple pasta dish his mother used to make during the war, a classic example of *cucina povera*: pasta *con le cipolle,* a dish made from caramelized onions to which pasta, olive oil, Parmesan, and black pepper are added. "We talked endlessly about food," says Apicella.[33]

⟪⟪⟪⟪⟫⟫⟫⟫

Though Patience was a salaried employee at the *Observer*, she continued to freelance, one of her biggest projects being the translation of part of *Larousse Gastronomique*. In March 1958 she received her portion of the text—there were more than thirteen thousand pages altogether, which would take three years to translate. Her colleagues in this enterprise were Nina Froud, Barbara Macrae Taylor (formerly Kuczynski)—her old friend from the London School of Economics—and Patience's neighbor Maud Murdoch, who was also a cookery writer. (In *Plats du Jour* Patience and Primrose had thanked Murdoch "for reading and criticizing the text.") The completed work included an additional reading list compiled by Elizabeth David.

First published in France in 1938 by the celebrated chef Prosper Montagné and with an introduction by Auguste Escoffier, *Larousse Gastronomique* had gone through at least ten printings before appearing in English. This delay may have been in part because of its size—it contained well over a million words, thus presenting a formidable challenge to any translator—but also because there wasn't an English-language readership to justify such an undertaking. By the end of the 1950s, though, the marketplace for cookbooks had changed considerably. They were beginning to sell, as evidenced by the success of *Plats du Jour*. In the two decades that followed, the "flood of new cookbooks . . . became a tidal wave."[34] There was a growing interest in adapting the famously complicated methods and techniques of French cuisine for the English-speaking home cook. Elizabeth David's *French Provincial Cooking* had been published in 1960 and was well received. Other books on the food of France, such as *The Classic French Cuisine* by Joseph Donon and *The Art of Simple French Cooking* by Alexander Watt, were published the same year. The translation of *Larousse* finally appeared in 1961, the same year Julia Child published *Mastering the Art of French Cooking* in America.

Indeed one of the editors of the English-language edition of *Larousse*, Charlotte Turgeon, had been a classmate of Child's at Smith College in the early 1930s. A Francophile, she attended Le Cordon Bleu culinary school in 1937 while her husband, a college professor, was on sabbatical and living in Paris. Her hope, not unlike Child's, was to demystify French cooking for the American housewife. Years later Child wrote that Turgeon had "done a tremendous amount for food in this country" by spearheading the translation of *Larousse*.[35]

In his preface to the original edition, Escoffier, who died long before it was published, noted that the book's mission was nothing less than to chart the "progress of French cuisine" and to "paint a picture of the many stages through which a nation has evolved since distant times."[36] As its name implies, the book is an encyclopedia of French cuisine and includes thousands of entries on everything from apples and Armagnac to woodcock soufflé and zabaglione. The editors were well aware of the many pitfalls that awaited the translation of a sacred text known for its authenticity—the book is often referred to as the bible of French cooking. In the introduction they wrote, "To attempt to 'modernize' or rewrite a classic encyclopedia of this kind would have been, we feel, a great mistake."[37]

It is not known which sections of the book Patience translated, but the painstaking process of transcribing recipes, methods, and techniques undoubtedly left an impression. The project also happened to overlap with her early friendship with Irving Davis, whose knowledge of French cooking and wine was superlative. The translation did pose one problem that would also surface when Patience was revising *Honey from a Weed*: the conversion of weights and measures for both English and American readers, for *Larousse* was published simultaneously in the U.K. by Hamlyn and the United States by Crown Publishing. "Years ago when I translated a quarter of *Larousse Gastronomique*, the 'editing' into American measures was at first insisted on," Patience wrote to Alan Davidson. "The

four translators resisted this energetically & finally won. The transformation of measures leads to inevitable & often deleterious adjustments."[38]
In fact it appears Patience was mistaken about the translators having
prevailed: both the English and American editions included a conversion chart, and the American edition also included cups and spoon-size
measures in the recipes.

Nevertheless some still criticized the translation for not being faith-
ful to the original. Writing in the *Observer* Patience's colleague "Syllabub"
said that it was perhaps "a pity to modernise the book," the earliest
editions of which "contained some touchingly archaic passages."[39]

⸙⸙⸙

While translating *Larousse* Patience was still finding her footing at
the *Observer*. She had been given the somewhat difficult task of writing on women's subjects for a paper where most of the conventional
choices—fashion, plants and gardens, the arts, literature, wine and
food—were already covered by well-known journalists. This problem was
compounded by the paper's laissez-faire approach, which meant that it
was largely up to Patience to determine what appeared on the woman's
page. David Astor, who had taken over as editor in 1948, had cultivated
an open and intellectually freewheeling environment that attracted a
circle of brilliant writers, including George Orwell, Arthur Koestler, Isaac
Deutscher, and later, while Patience was on the staff, Philip Toynbee, Vita
Sackville-West, and Neal Ascherson. Thus Patience would have to carve
out her own niche among this rather formidable roster of writers. When
she had lunch with Alison Settle, who had edited *Vogue* in the 1930s and
served as one of the country's first female war correspondents, "a quite
indomitable professional," she realized just how much she had to learn.

"Inevitably what interested me overlapped with the provinces of
experts, firmly ensconced on other pages," Patience wrote.[40] Settle
covered fashion; Sackville-West, plants and gardening, and Syllabub—
the paper's pseudonymous cookery writer—and Cyril Ray, food and wine.
Architecture, design, and the various crafts—such as jewelry, textiles, and
printmaking—were, however, underrepresented. Given her background
and experience at the Royal College of Art, Patience was well qualified to

explore them. "These themes, rather oddly, began to furnish the Woman's Page," she wrote.[41] She didn't entirely escape what were considered subjects of interest to women and did a handful of articles on the latest kitchenware and home furnishings—refrigerators, domestic appliances, and new design in pots and pans—as well as stories on the latest fashions in eyewear and cosmetics.

Not surprisingly she drew on her connections with Henrion, Misha Black, Milner Gray, and others, who sometimes were featured in her stories. She reviewed student work at both the Royal College of Art ("the print department is very much alive") and the Central School of Arts. She covered new Finnish textile design and an exhibition of Japanese home furnishings at Woolland's, and wrote about Henrion's 1960 exhibition at the Institute of Contemporary Art. "We are slowly coming round to the idea of design as a necessary element in daily life," she wrote, echoing her statement in Henrion's 1960 exhibition catalogue.[42] Other articles covered the British Furniture Exhibition, and the centenary of William Morris's Red House at Bexleyheath. (Patience would later become a member of the William Morris Society.) In all of these articles, she focused on the relationship between art and industry and whether the craftsmen or artists could survive in an age of mass production. Reviewing a new book on crafts, which covered everything from hand weaving and wood engraving to textile printing and toy making, she noted, "Even if our mechanical society seems bent on eliminating the craftsman, there are signs that people are resorting to making things by hand for private pleasure."[43]

She was equally interested in new ways of living and how art and life could be better integrated. This was not an idle concern in a city whose housing stock had been catastrophically depleted and where space was at a premium. Design for living was a theme that cropped up regularly in Patience's articles, and she wrote about everything from student accommodation and housing for the elderly to one-room living and the "working bathroom." She also touched on the interior design of ocean-going liners, the ubiquity and ugliness of mobile homes (here she quoted Peggy Angus, "who has studied the caravan from the artist's point of view"), and attic apartments in Paris.[44] For one story she profiled the brilliant and iconoclastic designer Norman Potter, who had created what he called a platform kitchen in his Canonbury flat. Patience described it as "a new kind of kitchen landscape," a sort of room within a room that concealed nothing, in a sense foreshadowing today's open-plan or island kitchen.[45] About Potter, an anarchist, poet, and design guru, Patience later wrote in a letter, "He was very reluctant about being written up! He knew no one could possibly envisage 'cooking' in this free standing anti bourgeois cucina."[46]

Potter was just one of many designers and artisans Patience was drawn to and with whom she shared a certain artistic, antiauthoritarian sensibility. She also profiled Hertha Hillfon, a Swedish ceramic sculptor and mother of two, whose work moved seamlessly between abstract experimentation and everyday objects, which, Patience wrote, she "infused with life."[47] Patience described the work of Lucie Rie, an Austrian-born potter whose work is now in collections at the Museum of Modern Art and the York Art Gallery, as "art in the absolute sense, even though her pots are capable of holding flowers."[48] She wrote about jeweler Gerda Flöckinger, another Austrian émigré, long before modern jewelry—"ignored since the war"—had been recognized as a respectable art form. Indeed Flöckinger, who took part in the groundbreaking Goldsmiths' international exhibition of modern jewelry in 1961, established one of the first classes in experimental jewelry at Hornsey College of Arts and Crafts the following year. According to Flöckinger, "A few of the more serious journalists had begun to realize that something very different was happening with jewelry design, among whom Patience was one of the earliest."[49]

Although Patience questioned the very notion of "women's subjects" and rarely said anything in her articles about the changing role of women in society, she expressed her point of view through her coverage of female artists like Rie and Flöckinger, who were given their due by others only many years later. In only one of her weekly columns did Patience address head-on the issue of how women were represented in contemporary art and what that said about their role in society. Beginning with the premise that perceptions of women are often mirrored in the ways in which they are depicted by painters, Patience attacked the work of Bernard Buffet and John Bratby, realist painters, for their grim portrayal of the female form. She reserved particular scorn for Buffet, whose women, she wrote, "are like hatchets. Hard as brass bedsteads, plucked hens drooping like desiccated rubber plants. This is hatred etched." Bratby, who often depicted his wife, Jean, in his paintings, wasn't much better. "Haggard, grey and melancholy" is how Patience described the way he represented her. Patience longed for Georges Rouault's mysteriously beautiful Italian women, Modigliani's girls, and Picasso's glorious creatures. "Oh! To be free of the Buffets and the Bratbys," she wrote, "to discard their vision."[50]

Patience never identified herself as a feminist—a word she found distasteful—although this is hardly surprising given that she spurned any kind of group affiliation. She believed more in the overarching autonomy of the individual and described herself as an anarchist with little or no interest in being part of a group. Her feminist heroines, to the extent that she had any, were people such as Harriet Weaver Shaw, champion and patron of James Joyce; Marguerite Duras, whom Patience once described as "an uncompromising friend to women"; and her friend Elisabeth Lutyens.[51] Though an inspiration to many women, Patience "had never developed that feeling that women can have for one another which is strengthening," said Eugenia Parry, a writer who met her years later.[52] In many ways Patience lived a feminist life but rejected the label.

The *Observer*, along with the whole of Fleet Street, was still a predominantly male institution. Although Patience remembered her time there fondly, she was also keenly aware that "a woman was not exactly *persona grata* in Tudor Street."[53] Indeed Astor himself was somewhat uneasy about working women and felt that "only a wife and mother could write about women faithfully."[54] Yet if you were a journalist who also happened to be a wife and mother, Astor reasoned, you should be at home looking after your family and not in the office. The particular challenges facing a single mother were never seriously considered. "In the late fifties," Patience wrote in her memoir, "it was not possible to discuss in print the question of how one might bring up two fatherless children and earn a living while contriving to get home at the precise moment they got back from school."[55] Anyway Patience preferred discussing such matters with Elisabeth Lutyens, in the privacy of a third-class carriage, as they traveled to Christ's Hospital to visit their sons.

Patience though was hardly a marginal figure at the *Observer*. Even among the paper's many strong personalities, she stood out. "She used to wear things like purple stockings," recalls Jean Southon, who was secretary to both Patience and Alison Settle. "She was unusual even at the *Observer*."[56] Jane Bown, who started at the paper in 1950 with little experience and became one of the great portrait photographers of her generation, remembered Patience asking her to do all kinds of impromptu assignments, photographing shop windows, or some out-of-the-way exhibition. "She got me to do unusual things," said Bown.[57] Patience often had her take photos of Madame Cadec's displays. Carol Hall, who was a young secretary at the time and later went on to work as an editorial assistant and then a reporter, says Patience used to send her out to gather material for her columns. "She was a real glamorous sort of figure," says Hall. "She was tall and good-looking. She had impeccable taste and she was always trying to get people to buy very posh things."[58]

In a way Patience fitted in perfectly with the *Observer's* lively and indeed somewhat unruly mix of writers, critics, and intellectuals. "A brilliant dysfunctional family," is how Neal Ascherson described his colleagues.[59] Although she sometimes feared an encounter with Philip Toynbee, "inhospitably ejected from some Soho haunt hours after closing time," whose bearlike embrace she could not evade, she admired his writing. Long after she left England, Olive would send her back issues of the paper, which Patience read cover to cover. In a 1989 letter to Peter Heyworth, the paper's music critic, she noted that he was the only remaining "member of the 'Old Guard' of that other *Observer*, when reading was a pleasure."[60] In her memoir Patience suggested that the arrival of George Seddon, who overhauled the women's pages in the early 1960s, precipitated her departure from the paper, but the truth is she was also beginning to question the life of a journalist always writing about other artists, or as she liked to put it, "about making things," but never making anything herself. "She had good friends and colleagues who admired her," says David Gentleman, who also did illustrations for the *Observer*. "They were a very bright lot. But I think Patience wouldn't have liked that kind of commercially oriented world for very long."[61] If the paper and indeed the country were "heading for Consumerland," as Patience put it, she wanted no part of it.[62]

By that time, though, she'd met Norman Mommens, a sculptor, poet, and willing accomplice, who was not only making things but also becoming increasingly disillusioned with the commercial orientation of the art world. In fact she first met Norman in the summer of 1958, at Peggy Angus's cottage in Sussex, just before joining the *Observer*.

Peggy, who had studied design at the Royal College of Art in the 1920s with Eric Ravilious and Edward Bawden, was a leading postwar designer and educator known for her left-wing politics and decidedly noncommercial approach to art. A member of the Artists International Association along with Misha Black—they both showed work in the group's first major exhibition in 1934—and married for a time to J. M. Richards, a critic and longtime editor of *Architectural Review*, it is not surprising that she came to know Patience in 1950s Hampstead. Peggy was also a close friend of Alexander Gibson, whose son Richard would eventually marry Peggy's daughter Victoria. Patience and Peggy shared a certain kind of fortitude (both raised young children during the war), an independent spirit, and a love of wild places. Like Patience, Peggy was drawn to the simplicity of life in such places as rural Sussex and eventually bought a primitive stone house on the remote Hebridean island of Barra. Patience later described her as "a pillar of the not-then-named alternative society."[63]

Peggy's flint-walled cottage in Sussex, called Furlongs, was very basic and somewhat reminiscent of the house outside Rogate where Patience lived during the war. There was an outdoor toilet, no electricity, paraffin lamps, and no running water. Visitors found it more like camping than country living. Nonetheless Peggy seemed to draw equally creative and eccentric people into her orbit, and the rustic setting of Furlongs became famous for its gatherings of artists and its workshop-like atmosphere. Indeed she had discovered the cottage in 1933, which was the same year Ravilious and Bawden settled in Great Bardfield, attracting an equally talented circle of painters and designers, many of whom Patience had known at the Royal College of Art. Among the architects and artists who spent time at Furlongs during the 1930s were Serge Chermayeff, László Moholy-Nagy, and Alexander Calder. After the war Furlongs continued to buzz with creative life; making art was Peggy's raison d'être.

Full-moon parties with dancing, music, and a bonfire were often held at one of the empty dewponds (a watering hole for livestock) at the summit of nearby Beddingham Hill. "Her invitation lists read like exhibition catalogues of the artists and architects of the day," writes her biographer Carolyn Trant, "the most unlikely people queuing up to sleep on mouse-infested straw mattresses and to overflow into the barn."[64] At each midsummer party a giant ceremonial figure made from recycled materials—perhaps the luggage racks of old railway carriages covered in blue silk from wartime parachutes—would appear over the lip of the hill. One of the creators of the Blue Goddess was Norman Mommens, a frequent visitor at Furlongs, who lived on the other side of the hill in South Heighton with his wife, Ursula Darwin.

One particular evening sometime in summer of 1958, Patience and Miranda took the train to Firle and walked across the fields overlooking the South Downs to Peggy's cottage. John Ravilious, Eric's son, was there, as well as Patience's friends Olive Cook and Edwin Smith.

Norman came with his much younger sister, Ruscha, who coincidentally shares Miranda's birthday. They had both just turned sixteen. In fact Norman and Ursula, very good friends of Peggy's, had come to Newhaven, just a few miles away, when they bought a house and established their pottery there in 1951. Ursula had previously been married to the painter Julian Trevelyan with whom she had a son, Philip, who grew up with Norman as stepfather from the age of eight. In the spirit of inventiveness that animated Furlongs, John Ravilious rigged up a "telephone" between the two homes, stretching miles of found cable by hand across the downs, with coffee tins at each end that made a clanging sound when a handle was turned. Norman, Ursula, and Peggy saw each other frequently and shared a love of festival art, Celtic mythology, and pagan ritual. On that night in 1958, though, Ursula stayed behind to look after her eighty-two-year-old father, Bernard Darwin.

Peggy and Norman shared a fundamental belief in the importance of art to everyday life. One of her favorite slogans, "Art for Life," which she often used as a kind of signature or logo on invitations, could just as easily have come from Norman. (*Art for Life* is also the title of Carolyn Trant's 2005 biography of Peggy.) They were playful in their approach to art, often drawing on ancient myths and legends, as the Blue Goddess demonstrates, yet were also industrious and highly skilled craftsmen. In recent years Peggy has been recognized for her pioneering work in modernist design, especially for her wallpapers and tiles. At an exhibition of her work at the Towner Gallery in 2014, there was a poster titled "The Pop History of Art" that Miranda mistook briefly for a work of Norman's. "There was a definite affinity that Norman and Peggy shared in their work," she says.[65] Thus it must have been especially difficult for Peggy, who had gone through her own wrenching divorce in 1945, to know that she had been the one who unintentionally brought Patience and Norman together. Patience clearly admired Peggy's vivacious and anarchic spirit and was well aware of the ambivalence she felt about her and Norman's affair. "Having been abandoned," Patience wrote in a letter years later, "she [Peggy] can't help feeling bound to the person left. Old history ever getting re-thrashed."[66]

Patience, though, was not a frequent visitor to Furlongs, and after meeting Norman seems to have kept her distance. "How perilous to look at you," she wrote of their encounter in a letter to Norman some time later.[67] Indeed it was not uncommon for relationships and affairs to blossom at Peggy's gatherings. "Furlongs certainly encouraged people to fall in love," Tirzah Ravilious wrote in her autobiography. "The air, fields and downs radiated an open, happy feeling of free-dom."[68] Plus Norman was handsome, vivacious, and full of creative energy. Tyl Kennedy, a furniture designer and Royal College of Art graduate, who knew him in the 1950s, remembered him being "very charming and very offbeat. He wasn't conventional in any sense of the word."[69] Norman's sister Ruscha, twenty years younger and for whom he was something of a father figure, described him as "wonderfully imaginative, playful and joyful."[70]

On the occasions when Patience and Norman were both at Peggy's, they went out of their way to avoid each other. In an undated letter to Patience probably written in 1960 or 1961, Norman wrote of a gathering at Furlongs, "As we shall both be available to others tomorrow night and I daresay quite inaccessible to each other, this letter is as necessary to me as it would be if we were not going to meet at all." Miranda, who between 1959 and 1961 spent a lot of time, along with Julia Gibson, as one of "Peggy's minions" (and later went on to print wallpaper for her in her

Camden studio) says that during that period Patience "did not make a habit of going to Peggy's."

However Patience and Norman continued to see each other. Not long after their fateful meeting in 1958, Norman began working in Peggy's London studio on Adelaide Road, and from there would visit Patience in Hampstead. But nearly four years would pass before they embarked on their first trip to the marble quarries above Carrara.

CHAPTER SEVEN

Departures

B y 1960 Patience and Norman were already contemplating a future beyond England. They were uneasy leading double lives and felt that sooner or later they would have to set out on their own, leaving their families behind, and Patience her career. Norman described this as "doing the horrible thing freedom needs."[1] Their deepening love affair, evident in the many passionate letters they wrote during this time, had led to inevitable complications. Norman was still nominally living with Ursula in South Heighton, though spending more and more time alone in far-off quarries—Bodmin Moor, Hopton Wood, and De Lank—teaching himself to work in stone and camping in his truck. Patience was still involved with Alexander Gibson, who was under the impression their relationship was more secure than it was. Meanwhile she was growing more and more disenchanted with her column in the *Observer* and writing about other people's creative work. Writing about art was a poor substitute for making it.

In a letter to his mother, Muriel, in late 1961, Norman referred to the "tangle" he was in because of his affair with Patience. He was seeking clarity both in his work as a sculptor and in his personal life—this he came closest to finding in the secluded and rugged conditions of the quarries. A year earlier he'd written, "The time has come for me to stake my claim. Where? The answer comes very near sometimes."[2] He may not have settled on a destination, but he was nearly certain that "where" would not be South Heighton. Patience too was feeling restless, and ambivalent about her role at the *Observer*, and in the summer of 1960, according to Miranda, declared that she needed to be "free of her children."[3] Nick had in fact long since left the Billiardroom; sent to Christ's Hospital in 1950, he'd spent most subsequent school holidays in Rogate. "Hill View was my only real home for many years," he says.[4] As for Miranda, she was only sixteen in 1958 when Patience first met Norman, but she too moved out of The Logs in September 1960 to avoid the embarrassment of being under-foot in the open-plan Billiardroom, a lovenest singularly lacking in privacy.

In many ways Norman's was the more difficult predicament. He was still married—he and Ursula had been together for more than ten years—and had been a much-loved father figure to Philip, her son from her previous marriage, who was just six when Norman entered the picture. (Ursula's first husband, artist Julian Trevelyan, left her for the painter Mary Fedden.) Norman and Ursula led a simple but relatively comfortable life and often worked together. Amongst the projects of their artistic collaboration was the series of Staffordshire lion and unicorn figures for the 1951 Festival of Britain. But by the time Norman met Patience he was seriously questioning what the role of the artist in society should be, the coziness of his life with Ursula, and the oppressive atmosphere of South Heighton, where Ursula's father, Bernard Darwin, had moved in 1958, by then needing constant care. Ursula was so taken up with looking after her father that she had little time for Norman. In a letter to Patience in November 1961, he wrote, "It would be more comfortable not to [leave], but comfort kills me."

Patience was struggling with her own entanglements—she referred to her relationship with Alexander Gibson as a "very peculiar kind of marriage."[5] In spring 1961, to tug at her heartstrings, Alexander began returning by post various keepsakes she had given him over the years— one was a glass paperweight found in a junkshop in Belgium, Patience's son, Nick, remembers. When the postman delivered the package, Patience asked him to open it. "He was cut up," says Nick, "and sending her souvenirs back, one at a time, daily."[6] Says Richard Gibson: "My father was losing Patience for good and wanted to try to protect the relationship."[7]

Meanwhile, approaching the age of forty-five, Patience felt that she'd spent most of her adult life working for others—research, translation, writing—and that this was ultimately unfulfilling. "For years I used to do other people's work and it was out of a sort of weird 'humility,'" Patience wrote in 1976. "I loved work."[8] But she was also seeking her own creative outlet and in the early 1960s began designing textiles for Edinburgh Weavers, wallpapers for Wallpaper Manufacturers Limited, a silkscreen mural for a P & O cruise ship, and an exhibition of Mexican crafts at Woolland Brothers department store in Knightsbridge.

(The store's managing director, Martin Moss, was the husband of Jane Bown, Patience's colleague at the *Observer*.) Norman encouraged her to experiment with different art forms—as he had done throughout his own career. "All that is precious in you must be given full play," he wrote.[9]

This was perhaps easier said than done. Though Patience had misgivings about her column in the *Observer*—always writing about other artists but never creating anything herself—she was a successful author and journalist. *Plats du Jour* had been one of the best-selling and most influential cookbooks of the 1950s; she was working on the first translation of *Larousse Gastronomique* and writing for one of London's top newspapers. Plus she had a lively circle of friends and colleagues and had benefited professionally from Hampstead's literary and artistic scene. "Ever since the Festival of Britain she was amongst this very enterprising and cosmopolitan group of people," says Miranda. "Life in London was very rich."[10]

Somewhat surprisingly Patience still felt bound by her past and, as a result, full of what she described as "difficulties and apprehensions." Over the years she had told very few people about her affair with Thomas Gray. Indeed after the war she'd made a confession to the vicar of Rogate, Ken Matthews, who agreed to baptize Nicolas and Miranda at his church in Terwick in 1947. The confession was done in writing, and thus Matthews was the only person she ever fully confided in. Many years later in an account to a friend, Patience wrote, "It has ever been, since, as if my lips are sealed."[11] When she met Norman it had been more than ten years since she'd told her story to Matthews. In the intervening period, though she had hardly ever let the name Thomas Gray pass her lips and had done everything in her power to suppress memories of him, he still cast a long shadow. She was in love with Norman but knew that leaving Alexander would not be easy. Perhaps even more difficult, she felt that she needed to "sweep away" her past in order to make room for a future with Norman.

"I should like to be able to explain my attachments and my peculiar life," she wrote in a letter to Norman, but added, without explanation, that it was not really in her power to do so.[12] But if it was not in her power, then whose? She alluded to the fact that she had "spent a lifetime hurting other people" and wondered if Norman, knowing this, could ever really love her. "Perhaps you and I have no use for a future," she continued, "we can only use the present, what happens then if we have no present?"[13]

In letters to each other at this time, they often invoked the metaphor of a snake shedding its skin, a sign of resurrection, to describe how they might embark on the next phase of their lives together. Patience, who years later shared her studio in Puglia with a large black snake, liked to point out that the ancient Egyptian zodiac symbol of the serpent overlapped with Scorpio—the astrological sign of her birth.

"I wanted to tell you about the snake skins," she wrote to Norman in 1962. "They slough off so slowly the snakes hardly move, it is very hard to do, to slip out leaving the papery skin completely whole."[14]

In 1962 Norman turned forty—about the same age at which French artist Aristide Maillol had completed his first major sculpture, *A Seated Woman*. Maillol, an accomplished painter and printmaker who took up carving late in life, was one of many important influences on Norman. In 1959 Norman had written a letter to his mother reflecting on Maillol's career saying, "It would be poetic genealogy if I was to be reborn a sculptor at Banyuls [Maillol's birthplace]." He added, "It may be so. I have three more years to shake off my chrysalis."

Long before he turned to sculpture, Norman had wide-ranging professional experience in a variety of artistic disciplines: scene painting in the theater, department store window dressing, mural painting, and working in a design studio. At art school in the early years of the war, he had focused primarily on illustration and typography, despite his father's wish that he pursue a career as an architect.

Norman was born in Antwerp in 1922. His father, J. B. H. ("Hugh") Mommens, was one of five children, two boys and three girls, and was apprenticed to a lace maker at age twelve. He had other ambitions and took night classes in engineering, eventually becoming a senior designer for Minerva Motors, one of the premier luxury automobile manufacturers of its day. Norman said his father "created the Minerva car," which for a while rivaled Rolls-Royce.[15] Hugh Mommens came from a family of theosophists, and Norman's sister Ruscha recalled the "terrifying" portrait of Madame Blavatsky that hung on her grandmother's bedroom wall. Hugh practiced yoga regularly, and attended the lectures of Krishnamurti. It was from his father that Norman inherited an interest in astrology and mysticism, which would later shape his ideas about life and art.

Norman's mother, Muriel Lottie Litten, was one of four children born in the village of South Marston, just outside the "railway town" of Swindon. Her father, Thomas Litten, was a master carpenter, and her mother, Kate Elizabeth Cripps, seems to have been remotely, though apparently illegitimately, related to local aristocracy. The story of their meeting may be apocryphal but suggests that the exotic young Belgian engineer, frequently on business in Swindon, spotted Muriel, who was then working at the telephone switchboard. "She was always dreaming of a romantic knight on horseback coming from a distant land," says Miranda.[16] Eventually Hugh whisked Muriel off to the continent, and they settled in Antwerp.

Norman liked to say he was "Flemish by birth and English by adoption."[17] He was fluent in five European languages and was as much at home in one country as another. In 1935 his father was offered a position as chief designer for the automobile manufacturer Kromhout, and the family moved to Amsterdam. Norman spent some time in England attending high school and living with cousins in Swindon, and then in 1939 he enrolled in Elckerlyc, a college for the arts and architecture in Bilthoven, the Netherlands. The school's founder, Hendrikus Theodorus Wijdeveld—a theorist, designer, and architect—was a radical visionary whose teachings attracted attention in the early part of the twentieth century. He was one of the founders of the influential Dutch design journal *Wendingen* and remained an outspoken utopian idealist until his death in 1987 at the age of 101.

Wijdeveld arguably had the greatest early influence on Norman as an artist; the two remained friends and for years to come would discuss their shared vision of creating an artistic community. He would even visit Norman and Patience in 1970 in Puglia at the age of 85, accompanied by his wife, the well-known actress Charlotte Kohler, with the rather fantastic notion of helping Norman establish what he called his "Wonderhouse," a dream that was never realized. Dating back at least to the early 1930s, Wijdeveld had laid out his proposals for an international working community based on a kind of guild model.

"Wijdeveld had a liberating effect," Norman wrote. "The sweep of his imagination was inspiring, but also a challenge to one's own vision." Describing one of Wijdeveld's visits to Carrara, Italy, in the mid 1960s,

Patience captured well his theatrical, wide-ranging, and experimental approach to art and architecture: "We have been the captive audience of a non-stop performance entitled The Daring Life and Works of Prof. H. T. Wijdeveld acted in three dimensions with the aid of gestures, maps, *son et lumière*, the poetry of Keats, graphics, epistles, press cuttings, but, and nevertheless, the old boy has a Heart of Gold. And one cannot help being exhaustedly fond of him."[18] Wijdeveld later asked Patience to write his biography, a proposition she politely declined.

Norman's studies at Elckerlyc were, however, interrupted by the war, and he was sent to live with his uncle Achilles Moortgat in the city of Kleve, Germany, on the lower Rhine, near the Dutch border. The Germans had occupied Belgium and Holland and large numbers of men and women of military age were being conscripted to work in factories. Moortgat was a successful Belgian sculptor who had married Norman's father's sister, Louise. (Kleve, it so happens, was also Joseph Beuys's hometown, and biographies mention that the young artist regularly visited Moortgat's studio. It is, however, unlikely that he and Norman ever met.[19]) It was through the good offices of his uncle that Norman managed, at least initially, to avoid forced labor, Moortgat instead finding him employment as an apprentice projectionist at a local cinema. But when the theater was bombed—the Allied bombardment reduced much of the city of Kleve to rubble—Norman was enlisted to work in a munitions factory. After one of the air raids, Norman returned from his hiding place down by the canal to find survivors desperately trying to lift an enormous concrete slab, attempting to save the lives of a mother and child trapped underneath. This haunting image of men with upheld arms became the leitmotif of Norman's work, a scene of unspeakable horror and desperation later coming to symbolize hope and indeed renewal. Norman and the Moortgats survived the bombardments and were evacuated to a transit camp at Bedburg-Hau, Germany, before eventually returning to Belgium. Moortgat, who lost everything, including his home and studio, lived out his remaining years alongside the Schelde, painting river scenes.

The postwar period, Norman wrote, was marked by "a sense of unreality" as he found himself drafted into the Belgian army's medical corps and then, once demobilized, embarking on a variety of jobs, from stage set design to mural painting for international trade fairs in Belgium and Holland.[20] In 1948 he went to live with old family friends, Jan and Leonore

Hubrecht, in Doorn, the Netherlands. In fact their daughter Lucia had also studied at Elckerlyc, and their son Arend, about the same age as Norman, was a close friend. A former ambassador and astrophysicist, Jan, who Patience described as looking "like an Italian duke of the renaissance," would become a lifelong patron of Norman's work.[21] Leonore was herself an accomplished painter, and Jan, who had traveled widely as a diplomat, was well connected and interested in the arts. "You were both the first people to make me feel 'at home in the world,'" Norman later wrote.[22] They were also responsible for him meeting Ursula, who, along with her husband, Julian Trevelyan, was also a friend. Indeed the connections among the Hubrechts, Darwins, and Trevelyans were longstanding. Jan's father, the noted zoologist Ambrosius Hubrecht, had corresponded with Charles Darwin in the 1880s. Julian Trevelyan's grandmother was a Hubrecht. Thus it was in Doorn that Norman first met Ursula soon after the war and, in 1949, he joined her in England, where they both worked in a handcrafted pottery studio recently founded to provide employment for ex-service personnel. Norman and Ursula married in 1950 and the following year bought Grange Farm, the house near Newhaven, just over the hill from Furlongs, which Peggy Angus had indeed found for them.

According to her son, Philip, it was Ursula's mother, Elinor Darwin (née Monsell), who first encouraged Norman to take up sculpture. Norman's mother-in-law was a talented illustrator and portrait painter: She started her career working with W. B. Yeats, who appreciated and used her woodcuts in a variety of publications; she was a close friend of Virginia Woolf in pre-Bloomsbury days; she encouraged her cousin (by marriage) Gwen Raverat to take up wood engraving. Norman began stone carving in 1952, teaching himself the skills during periodic visits to the granite quarries of Cornwall. Some years later he wrote, "Sculpture and Carrara are part of my daily life because I once did a 'dreadful thing:' I bought a piece of Portland stone from the Newhaven stonemason, then I went to work in a Cornish quarry."[23]

Norman also formed a travelling mime troupe, the Shuttlecock Mime Company, which played in Sussex village halls. He was a great storyteller and poet, and several of the imaginative tales he told Philip, who described him as the "most sensitive stepfather a child could have," were later turned into children's books and published by Faber and Faber.[24] In 1959 the Royal College of Art's Lion and Unicorn Press published his cartoon book *Zoz: A*

Story of Glory, a satirical tale of the temptations encountered by a champion motorcyclist. But the wild and elemental qualities of the Cornish quarries made too great a contrast with the bourgeois comforts of life at Grange Farm. And this was thrown into further relief when Bernard Darwin came to live with Ursula in 1958—the year of Norman and Patience's fateful meeting.

Bernard and Norman had little in common, but Norman got on fine with his father-in-law, as he did with almost everyone; it was rather the stuffy world of bourgeois propriety, which Gwen Raverat memorably referred to in her memoir as "a great fortress of unreality and pretence," that seemed to unnerve him.[25] He complained about the "tyrannical nicety of his [Bernard's] family," their "middleclass pomp and bluster," and described Grange Farm as a "house of sensitive skins, delicate toes, stranded mines and sleeping dogs."[26] Norman preferred to escape over the hill to Peggy's, where he was revived by her "darling plans and ideas plus rum," or to visit Leonard Woolf, who lived not far away.[27] Norman would borrow books from Woolf, mostly in French, and over drinks they would discuss literature, art, and politics. Woolf commissioned Norman to carve a sculpture, which can still be seen in the garden at Monk's House. In a letter to Woolf in June 1957, just after the carving had been completed, Norman wrote to say that he was "happy to hear . . . that you are so pleased with *Goliath*."[28]

There were other important and lasting connections that Norman made through his relationship with Ursula. Leopold Kohr, the Austrian economist and self-declared "philosophical anarchist," was a close friend of Ursula's and visited Sussex often. Philip remembers him talking endlessly on the beach at Newhaven about his economic theories and political philosophy. He must have been gestating his perhaps best-known book, *The Breakdown of Nations*, which was published in 1957. Norman later described him as a "great friend" and a "smiling deaf pataphysician," which coming from Norman was the highest compliment. In fact Kohr at one point asked Norman to illustrate a book he was then working on, *The Overdeveloped Nations*, an indictment of capitalism and the slavish pursuit of economic growth, which was eventually published in German and Spanish in 1962—but not in English until 1977. The collaboration with "Poldi" never happened, but Norman kept a draft copy of the manuscript among his papers.

The artist Cecil Collins was another old friend of the Trevelyans—he and Julian both showed work in London's 1936 International Surrealist

Exhibition. Collins, who taught drawing, as did Mervyn Peake, at the Central School of Art and Design, is perhaps best known for his ruminations on the wise fool—both in his paintings and in a 1947 essay entitled "The Vision of the Fool." He would become an important figure in Norman's life. Indeed the idea of the fool as an artist and poet who resists the deadening effects of industrial society was one that Norman shared with Collins and that he went on to explore in his own work and writing. "Norman and Cecil were peas out of the same pod," says Philip.[29] However, unlike Collins, Norman was still completely unknown; it wasn't until 1961, when the Towner Gallery, Lewes, put on a major exhibition of his work, that his sculptures were seen in public.

That same year, in late October, Bernard Darwin died. The service was held in the rain and the family gathered at Charles Darwin's old home, "a museum suddenly made alive with log fires and drinks."[30] Norman was already distancing himself, spending more and more time in the quarries, free, happy, and alone. "As a sculptor, this is where he found himself," Philip says.[31] At De Lank he struck up a close friendship with the quarry owner, Mr. Coggin. Befriending quarry owners was something he continued to do wherever he worked; he related to these "men of stone." He was finding his voice as an artist and at the same time fleeing the entanglements of life at home. He even began searching for a cottage and workshop somewhere in Cornwall—one that he envisioned sharing with Patience.

As his fortieth birthday approached, he hadn't yet shaken off his chrysalis. Over the winter of 1961–62, back from Cornwall and just before leaving for Carrara, he was spending half the week with Ursula in Newhaven and the other half with Patience in London.

"One must not have ideas about one's relationships," he wrote to his parents in February 1962. "They must be only what they are—they are then all possible and can flourish."[32]

⋘⋘⋘

Patience's last weekly column for the *Observer* was published on October 22, 1961. Titled "Art and Craft in Jewellery," it was a brief review of the 1961 international exhibition of modern jewelry, a display that was later credited with breathing new life into a "dying industry." Patience highlighted the works of French designer René Lalique and of C. R. Ashbee—writing of pieces that had a "worth far beyond the value of their stones." But she criticized the mainstream preoccupation with precious stones, epitomized by an Edwardian choker "which seems to have struck the diamond setting maximum." Patience rarely resisted the urge to take a swing at all things Edwardian. In another essay on jewelry she referred to Edwardian silver work that looks solid but is "cunningly made of thinnest foil, another lie."[33]

Another artist featured in the Goldsmiths' show was Gerda Flöckinger, who Patience had written about earlier and from whom she later requested advice on the tools needed to start making jewelry. According to Flöckinger, Patience told her that the set of tools was to be a gift for a young couple setting sail for the United States—probably Norman's younger sister, Ruscha, and her husband, Stephan Schorr-Kon—and not for her own personal use. Patience and Gerda went to Herring, Morgan and Southon on Berwick Street, where Patience acquired some basic equipment, including a jeweler's saw, mallet, and pliers. Unbeknownst to Flöckinger, Patience would also buy her own set of tools, but it was some time before she used them in earnest.

Patience and Flöckinger had friends in common—Patience's neighbors the Niemans, in whose house they often met. On occasion Patience would refer clients to Flöckinger; one such was *Observer* editor David Astor, who was always on the lookout for unusual gifts for his wife. Their friendship wasn't perhaps particularly close, but frequent conversations were intimate enough for Patience to tell Flöckinger about Thomas Gray and the child she'd lost in 1943. Flöckinger had also left her husband and said that, even though she'd lived with him for six years, she'd never really known him. "We kind of compared notes as to the mystery of the men we thought we loved," Flöckinger says.[34]

In the early 1960s Patience had not yet "thrown paperwork out the window."[35] She was not referring to her work at the *Observer*—though she was on the verge of leaving that behind—but to textile designs commissioned by Alastair Morton of Edinburgh Weavers. Morton, who had taken over the family business and turned it into a pioneering company whose mission was to fuse textiles and modern art, enlisted such artists as Ben Nicholson, Barbara Hepworth, and Paul Nash. By the early 1960s the firm was widely regarded as one of the twentieth century's most important textile companies.

Patience was one of the last designers to work for Morton, who died tragically in 1963. Only one of her designs, *Acanthus*, was produced during his lifetime, and was featured in the firm's autumn 1963 collection. About four feet square, screen-printed on vivid green and orange cotton satin, it is a striking piece.[36] Two others, *The Spurge* and *Wolfe's Tongue*, "both featuring ghostly drawings of plants printed on cotton percale," were completed after his death.[37] According to Morton's biographer, he responded enthusiastically to Patience's work, which he found chimed perfectly with the company's forward-looking mission to show that tradition and modernism were not mutually exclusive but rather "part of the fabric of British life."[38]

Patience's success depended to a large extent on her personal relationship with her employers; it was less her qualifications and experience that recommended her than her force of personality. "I had this wonderful feeling with Alastair that I could do what I liked, as I liked," Patience wrote after his death. "As we had a terrific rapport, with anyone else it will be just selling things or not selling things."[39] Similar to Henrion his approach to work and art was one that appealed to Patience, as it somehow transcended the limitations of the commercial art world without rejecting it altogether. He combined technical mastery and a high level of craft with a sense of artistry and innovation. Although her design work for Morton and for Wallpaper Manufacturers Limited was short-lived, this and other projects such as the Woolland's exhibits, which sold out in one morning, gave her a "new kind of confidence."[40]

Meanwhile the "lower slushy depths of Fleet Street," in Patience's mind no longer held much promise.[41] She was hardly surprised when she received a note in late 1961 from David Astor saying that they'd be "letting her go"—she was replaced by Katharine Whitehorn—and in a letter to Norman admitted to feeling "free and alive." Later she wrote that this marked the beginning of "a different and more creative life."[42]

❦❦❦❦

On the eve of his departure for Carrara in early spring 1962, Norman and Patience had no real long-term plan. In fact it was Norman's intention to set out on his own and have Patience visit him sometime in May. "I shall write an article about you knee deep in Carrara," she wrote.[43] They would take it from there.

For Norman "waving goodbye to Ursula and Philip on Newhaven's west-pier" was agonizing.[44] He found it desperately difficult to reconcile his desire to leave with his remorse for the pain he knew it would cause them. And he even suggested to Ursula that he would return. "I have never known what to say about my leaving her," he wrote to his mother ten years later. "I just did." For Philip, who was nineteen, it was heartbreaking. "After watching him, with my mother beside me, sail off from Newhaven [in the] ferry I felt left to pick up the pieces," he wrote.[45]

Norman crossed the Channel with his Bedford army lorry in driving rain and wind and stopped over with Patience's friend Wolfe Aylward in Paris. Patience had known Wolfe since 1956 or 1957; they met through Diana Paul. Diana was a very close friend of Wolfe's mother, Hester, and was indeed Wolfe's sister's godmother. Born in 1938 in Hampshire, Wolfe was the son of a relatively well-off farmer, Leslie Aylward, who had high hopes of Wolfe following in his footsteps. Wolfe, however, had little interest in farming, instead developing a passion for opera. As soon as he learned to drive, he bought himself a sporty MG, and then, as his sister said, "Nothing could stop him from driving to London and to the Glyndebourne Opera House in East Sussex."[46] On one of those occasions, he had tickets for Glyndebourne and planned to take Diana, but she had to cancel at the last minute. Diana suggested he invite her friend Patience Gray. Patience, too, was an opera fan. She even wrote a feature for *Harper's Bazaar* on "picnicking at Glyndebourne." She suggested the meal should be a "little masterpiece of simplicity and perfection," including Parma ham with fresh green figs, salmon, *courgettes à la provençale*, cheese, and ripe peaches, all washed down with a Pouilly-Fumé carefully set to chill in the lake during Act I. The smart operagoer also kept a thermos of strong black coffee in the car for the long ride home.[47]

Wolfe and Patience became lifelong friends and great devotees of Maria Callas, and Patience dedicated *Honey from a Weed* to him, one of the few people she enjoyed talking about food and cooking with. Tall, handsome, and thin—one acquaintance described him as looking like Rupert Everett—Wolfe had hopes of becoming an opera singer and was taking lessons in Paris, where he lived a somewhat dissolute life.[48] He introduced

Patience and Norman to Madame Coquin's, a small but crowded *bistrot* with flophouse upstairs, just off the Rue de Buci, run by an elderly Breton lady and her daughter, Jo. If she had not had too much to drink, Madame Coquin would cook—simple dishes such as *choucroute garnie, tripe à la mode,* and mussels. Booze and wine flowed freely and evenings often ended with Madame Coquin and Jo dancing on the tables. According to his sister Joanna, "Wolfe had a nose for finding these extraordinary places."[49] "We all stopped at Madame Coquin's when we went through Paris to visit Wolfe," said Nicolas, who was also a close friend.[50]

It was here that Wolfe met Jean Delpech and his wife, Ginette, who'd had a somewhat checkered past and was a regular at Madame Coquin's. Jean was working as assistant to gallery owner and art collector Daniel Cordier. Cordier had served as secretary to Resistance hero Jean Moulin during the war and was indeed writing Moulin's biography, for which Jean Delpech did much of the research. By the time Jean married Ginette, she was working as a gallery attendant at the Petit Palais museum of art and had become the very model of bourgeois respectability. Jean and Ginette were bon viveurs, *gastronomes par excellence*, and would become lifelong friends of Patience and Norman, visiting them often in the south of Italy.

In Paris Norman also visited the Fenosas, the sculptor Apel-les and his wife, Nicole, who, Norman wrote to Patience, were delighted with the pairing. "J'approve," Fenosa said. "Il va marier la seule femme que j'aime," he added to his wife.[51] "He's going to marry the only woman I love." The Fenosas extracted a promise from Norman that he and Patience would visit them in Spain later that summer. For the time being, though, the plan was to drive with Wolfe as far as Vezelay. From there Norman would continue to Carrara, and Wolfe would make his way back to Paris. "Wolfe still thinks we complicated life unnecessarily by not leaving for Carrara together," Norman wrote to Patience from Paris.[52] In the riverside town of Verdun-sur-le-Doubs in Burgundy over *pôchouse*—a soup of river fish, onions, and potatoes—and large quantities of white wine, Norman decided it was indeed foolish to go without Patience. Heeding Wolfe's advice he turned back, dropped Wolfe off in Paris, and showed up on Patience's doorstep. They left together for Carrara the next day.

Fenosa had often talked about Carrara, which had long been a mecca for marble carvers—Michelangelo first travelled there in 1497 to find the stone for one of his earliest major and best-known works, the *Pietà*. Norman, like so many others, hoped to make his mark there. The center of Italy's marble industry, the city has a rough edge—"Italy's Wild West," according to one account—and hardly conforms to the image of Tuscany popularized in so much travel literature and food writing today.[53] In fact Carrara has long been one of northern Italy's poorest and most neglected provinces, with high rates of cancer—a product of industrial pollution— and a feeling of irreversible decay. In 1728 Montesquieu described its inhabitants as "the most brutal and worst governed of all peoples." Charles Dickens, a century later, was somewhat less disparaging and discerned a certain beauty in that which springs from such "miserable ground."[54] Patience preferred to quote Lady Blessington, a nineteenth-century Irish writer known for her *Conversations of Lord Byron*, who described the city, looking down at it from a high mountain pass, as "an earthly paradise."[55]

Perhaps that was because Patience and Norman lived well outside town in the mountain village of Castelpoggio, from which there is a magnificent view over the marble quarries across the valley. At Castelpoggio they lodged with a widow who Patience always referred to in her writings as La Dirce. Dirce was an expert forager—she gathered food not only for herself and her son but also for her menagerie of animals—and she gave Patience her first lesson in the edible plants and weeds of the Mediterranean. Dirce took pleasure in wandering among the high mountain meadows and chest-nut forests, which descended steeply more than a thousand feet from the village to the sea. She gathered everything from bundles of chestnut wood for heating and cooking to wildflowers, most of which she did not identify by name because, in essence, they were "hay to a mountain peasant."[56] She knew the smell of every tree and even had a fondness for snakes, which she said inhabited the forests in great numbers. Patience and Norman arrived in April, and the hillsides were just beginning to fill with narcissus, asphodel, spurges, cyclamen, anemones, orchids, cowslips, and primroses—"a succes-sion of springtime apparitions." As Patience wrote in a letter to her mother from Castelpoggio, "Everything that grows has its peculiar grace."[57]

"Everything that grows" also comprised edible weeds and plants. Dirce covered great distances on her foraging trips, moving animal-like through the fields and forests, and gathered an astonishing variety of mountain plants, which she called *radici*, literally meaning roots. These included several kinds of sorrel, lady's smock, primrose, foxglove, mountain cowslip, mountain orache, plantain, and dock, as well as new shoots of wild clematis, wild hop, wild grapevine, and wild asparagus. Her technique, Patience wrote, was not unlike that of a goat in the hedge "who nibbles at a plant here and a plant there."[58]

At home the weeds and plants were washed under a constantly running tap—piped water being a novelty—boiled, drained, and then dressed with olive oil, a few drops of wine vinegar and served with hard-boiled eggs. Dirce also taught Patience how to make a variety of Castelpoggian dishes, including her version of a frittata, with breadcrumbs and Parmesan cooked in a *padella* (in this case an earthenware casserole with a handle); angel bread, a yeast cake made with anise, lemon zest, and pine nuts ("one got the *anice* by the glass from the bar across the street, and baked the cake in the baker's oven up a little alley"); and *castagnaccio*, a flat, dense cake made from the ubiquitous chestnut flour, water, and olive oil.[59] Much of the cooking was rooted in both peasant tradition and a wartime diet that relied on the staple ingredients of chestnuts, fungi, and weeds. Dirce told Patience that during the war residents of Castelpoggio also ate the tuberous roots of mountain asphodel and the bulbs of the sea squill, *Urginea maritima*, a member of the same family as the hyacinth, *Asparagaceae*. Those daring enough would make the four-day trek on foot across the mountains to Parma, where they would barter chestnut flour and salt for cheese and oil. Of the castagnaccio, Patience wrote, "Some people went on making this cake, baking it in the village bread oven, others preferred to forget it."[60]

When Patience and Norman lived there, the village bread oven was still a regular gathering place. Patience would bake her angel bread in the gradually cooling oven and "by doing so became the focus of intense speculation—passersby curious to know if, by merely lifting the cloth that covered it, they could judge it a success."[61]

They lived a simple life in Castelpoggio, "solid with work and love" as Norman put it, but also ran up against the limitations of having little commissioned work or money, a problem that would plague them throughout the 1960s. Norman did his first marble carvings while living in Castelpoggio, two of which were featured in the third Carrara Biennale, and Patience was still designing textiles for Edinburgh Weavers (it was in Castelpoggio that she did *The Spurge*) and freelancing occasionally for the *Observer* and other publications. But neither was drawing a regular income, and Patience had not yet rented out the Billiardroom, which would later serve as a crucial source of revenue. They lived frugally, eating almost no meat, allowing themselves a bitter Campari only on Sundays, rationing petrol, and drinking the "worst ordinary wines." Still, they somehow managed to spend more on rent and food than they did in London, and Norman described Carrara as "impossibly expensive." In a letter to Olive, Patience wrote, "It seems far too expensive, considering the humble manner in which we live."[62] If they were to stay on, Norman would have to find a studio to work in and to house his carvings—and, ideally, an assistant. Nevertheless it was a season of "unimagined joy," as Norman wrote to the Hubrechts, adding, "I did not know the world had such happiness in it."[63] But by summer they were running out of money and decided to take up the Fenosas' offer of a place to stay in Catalonia. "Very vague at present about the future," Patience wrote to Olive in June. "We are off to Vendrell end of July for I should think a month then we think of coming back here."[64]

With Miranda, who was visiting Patience and Norman at Castelpoggio, they set off in the lorry for El Vendrell, driving through the south of France during the day and "sleeping in lavender fields" at night. One morning they woke to the sound of hundreds of tiny hummingbirds buzzing among the flowers.

Staying with the Fenosas in their sixteenth-century palace, Portal del Pardo, was a far cry from the rugged mountains of Castelpoggio. Patience had been to El Vendrell once before, in the summer of 1960 with Irving Davis and her friend Ariane Castaing, and was captivated by its old-world beauty. "I used to lie on the hay mattress and listen to the carts tinkling and rattling under the wide arch below, rumbling like chariots, at four o'clock in the morning," she wrote, "as the men of Vendrell rode out to the dustblown fields."[65] The Fenosas had bought the house in 1958 with the help of friends and the sale of sculptures and some other works of art, including a painting by Picasso. It quickly became a gathering place for artists, poets, and friends.

During the summer months Portal del Pardo, in the coastal province of Tarragona, was always filled with visitors. Norman had hoped to work—the Fenosas had secured him a rundown barn outside town—but found it impossible to get much done. He described the atmosphere, which tended to revolve around meals and social engagements, as "completely anti-work."[66]

Apel-les Fenosa had come from humble beginnings. Born in 1899 outside Barcelona, he was the youngest of three sons. His father, a restaurant owner, expected Apel-les to follow in his footsteps but Apel-les refused, instead declaring he wanted to be a sculptor. So at the age of fourteen, his father disowned him, and he spent several years studying art in Barcelona and working a variety of odd jobs, barely managing to get by. He later said, "If someone put all the days on which I hadn't eaten together, they would add up to three years."[67] He eventually put himself through art school and then traveled to Toulouse and finally Paris, where he began to work in clay. Despite a trembling left hand, the result of a bout of encephalitis as a young child, Fenosa was determined to work with his hands.

In 1923 he met Picasso, an event that transformed his life. Picasso not only encouraged him as an artist but also became a patron, buying his first sculptures. The story goes that Fenosa, arriving in Paris, went to see his fellow Catalan and told him he was a sculptor; whereupon Picasso asked to see his work, but, having nothing to show, he had to hurry home to make some—five pieces—which Picasso promptly bought. Picasso then commissioned a portrait of his wife, Olga Kokhlova, and eventually acquired more than a hundred of Fenosa's works. "If it hadn't been for Picasso, I would never have done anything," Fenosa said. Picasso called him "my son of an unknown mother." Cocteau, whose likeness Fenosa first sculpted in 1926, considered him "not the best sculptor, but the only sculptor."[68] His work has a lyrical quality to it, a sense of movement barely contained. This he often achieved with very little material, suggesting a certain fullness of form and emotion derived from what he described as a "minimum of means."

"What I remember with Fenosa," Patience wrote, "was that he clasped the clay between both hands and the leaf-like figures would emerge miraculously from unsteady hands." Like a small bird from the hands of a magician. For Patience, who still saw herself as a "bloody intellectual," the spontaneity and anarchic sprit embodied in Fenosa's work was deeply affecting; his ability to work with such a limited palette a revelation. It was Fenosa, she would later write, who inspired in her "the idea of a life dedicated to a chosen work."[69]

One of the first of many works of art that Irving Davis gave Patience was Fenosa's *La Tempête pourchassée par le Beau Temps*, which he had made in 1957. Fenosa had also given Patience a sculpture in Paris in 1958 because she had held it so lovingly, which he then named *Patiença*. Irving had met Fenosa in 1955 through their mutual friend, the poet and publisher Lucien Scheler, and saw him frequently in Paris. He contributed many rare books—including a first edition of Dante's *La Vita Nuova*, a sixteenth-century Petrarch, Luis de Góngora's *Soledades*, and *Las Tres Musas Últimas Castellanas* by Francisco de Quevedo, published in 1772—to Fenosa's library. And Fenosa often gave him bronze or clay figures in return.

But it was in El Vendrell that Irving's interest in rare books and food seemed to converge. He had always loved cookbooks as well as early printed books on the history of science and medicine, and he longed to discover a copy of the fourteenth-century Catalan manuscript *Libre de Sent Soví*, one of the oldest known European recipe collections. Patience speculated that it was partly his desire to locate a copy of the rare manuscript that inspired his interest in Catalan cuisine. Thus during those summers in the early 1960s, he began collecting recipes in a small black notebook, filling it with his nearly illegible script. The recipes were usually relayed to Nicole Fenosa by their cook and housekeeper, Anita Simal Llonch, a native of Tarragona, and then translated into French by Nicole and finally English by Irving.

"You have no idea of how elaborate these dishes are but I think it is a good idea to write them down before they are lost or submerged in the international tide," Irving wrote to Patience in a letter from El Vendrell in 1963. "But," he added, "I hope I shall be able to show the book to you when you come back. It is a huge task & will occupy the rest of my life."[70]

Meals at El Vendrell were usually prepared by Anita and served under the old fig tree in a courtyard overgrown with orange begonias, palm trees, and passion flowers. The food was simple—lunch always began with a salad of fresh green tomatoes, sliced raw onion, and salted anchovies; the first course was followed by paella or fish, salad, cheese, and "pyramids of purple figs." Anita often cooked outdoors on a walled hearth or the nineteenth-century clockwork spit. Fenosa liked to baste lamb himself using a rosemary branch. Wine was drunk from a *porró*, a

Hermann Stanham, ca. 1920. *Courtesy of Miranda Armour-Brown*

Portrait of Olive by painter John Collier, ca. 1906. *Courtesy of Miranda Armour-Brown*

Patience, age two and a half, May 1920. *Courtesy of Nicolas Gray*

Olive and her three daughters: (*left to right*) Patience, Helen ("Tiny"), and Tania. *Courtesy of Miranda Armour-Brown*

The Logs under reconstruction in 1950 or 1951. *Courtesy of Nicolas Gray*

Patience at her desk in the Billiardroom. *Photo by Stefan Buzás / courtesy of Nicolas Gray*

Patience and Peggy Angus in the late 1950s. *Photo by Monica Pidgeon*

Norman carving *Goliath* for Leonard Woolf, 1957. *Courtesy of Nicolas Gray*

A thank-you note from Peter Shepheard, showing the plant life around Hill View.
Courtesy of Nicolas Gray / Archive Masseria Spigolizzi

David Gentleman's front-cover illustration for *Plats du Jour. Courtesy of Penguin Books*

David Gentleman's back-cover illustration for *Plats du Jour. Courtesy of Penguin Books*

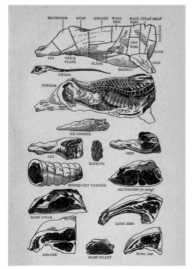

David Gentleman's drawing of cuts and joints for *Plats du Jour. Courtesy of Penguin Books*

Irving Davis with one of his beloved cats at New End. *Photo by Jack Nisberg*

Portrait of Patience taken in 1959 by her colleague at the *Observer*. *Photo by David Sim*

glass pitcher with a very narrow spout that is passed around among the guests in lieu of individual glasses. "The *porró*," Patience wrote, "turns the humblest dish into a cause for celebration."[71]

Shortly before her death in 2013, Nicole Fenosa recalled to me with great fondness the summers spent with Irving and Patience at El Vendrell. "Those summers were radiant," she said, "and the food and meals preoccupied us enormously."[72]

As marvelous as El Vendrell was, Patience and Norman were still eager to find a place of their own for the winter. They discussed many possibilities: the region around Bassano del Grappa, in the Veneto; the San Stefano limestone quarries near Istria; Cornwall's rugged northern coast; and of course Carrara.

1962 marked the beginning of Patience and Norman's long quest for a place to live and work. Before they left for Castelpoggio, Norman had looked at several places in Cornwall, including a cottage and studio that had everything—"even a silent paraffin fridge"—so that they would only have to shop once a week.[73] But even the rudimentarily equipped cottage, they decided, was a bit too comfortable. Throughout the 1960s they looked at numerous properties in France and Italy. Norman's hope was to find an inexpensive retreat that would allow him to complete enough work for a show in Milan or London the following year.

Patience and Norman were not actively seeking the so-called simple life nor indeed communal living, but something else, something that perhaps even they had not yet fully formulated. They were both drawn to alternative modes of living—they'd met at Furlongs after all—and were utopian thinkers who actively resisted the trappings of consumer society. At the *Observer* Patience had written mostly about the role of art and design in modern life. She was open to the revolutionary thinking of iconoclastic design guru Norman Potter, but reserved her greatest admiration for friends and employers such as Henrion and Alastair Morton. She'd also been deeply influenced by Irving Davis and shared his romanticism, European outlook, and love of books. Norman had been deeply affected by the utopian vision of his mentor, Wijdeveld, the playfulness and naïve art of Cecil Collins, and Peggy's radical approach to art and life. He was also increasingly attuned to social and environmental issues essayed by his friend Leopold Kohr. Indeed it was Kohr who is credited with coining the phrase "small is beautiful," which later became the title of the hugely influential classic by E. F. Schumacher, one of his students.

In a way "less is more" became Patience and Norman's guiding philosophy. Norman eventually subscribed to *Resurgence,* the artistic, spiritual voice of the green movement, founded in 1966 and whose contributors included Kohr, Schumacher, Ivan Illich, and E. P. Thompson. When visiting London he scoured Camden Town's alternative bookshops for works on self-sufficiency, eco-building, and alternative technology. He was a longtime member of the Soil Association, which was founded after the war as a pioneer organization promoting organic farming. Ultimately Norman and Patience were seeking their own highly personal form of self-sufficiency and a mode of life that would give free reign to their artistic expression, an endeavor that would take them years to realize.

"During the 1960s Patience and Norman spent a significant amount of time looking for the right place to settle and work," says Nicolas. "They had contacts in the art world and seemed to have followed up a variety of leads. But they soon decided that the ready-made 'artist community' solution wasn't for them and probably neither was the Art World."[74]

By September 1962 they had left El Vendrell and made their way back to Carrara hoping to secure a place to stay. They found a primitive house in a tiny village above Castelpoggio, which Norman described as the "end of the world." But even this proved too expensive, and the idea ultimately came to nothing. Meanwhile Norman was trying to convince officials in Carrara to establish lodging and studio space for visiting sculptors, perhaps along the lines of Wijdeveld's idea for an International Guild, where foreign sculptors could live and work. This proposal, too, went nowhere.

Finally by mid-October they realized that they had no other option but to return to England. In a letter to the Hubrechts, Norman wrote, "Our search for winter quarters failed—we have passed the marble country through a fine sieve and remained roofless."[75] Reluctantly they made their way back to London for what would be one of the snowiest and coldest winters on record. "Both Patience and I seemed to have returned to England to lay our ghosts," Norman wrote.[76]

CHAPTER EIGHT

Beyond and Away

P atience and Norman spent that long brutal winter of 1962–63—the "big freeze," as it was known, the coldest Christmas in London since 1897—visiting family, searching for work, and contemplating their next move. Patience was still designing textiles for Alastair Morton; one, *The Spurge*, was based on the herbaceous plant with vivid yellow flowers that had captivated her in Castelpoggio. She had written to Olive from Italy asking her if she would consult the Royal Horticultural Society library for a monograph on the species. In October 1962, after returning to London, Patience was delighted to see that her *Acanthus* print had been featured in a full-page ad for Edinburgh Weavers in *House and Garden*. Meanwhile she had written what would be her last freelance article for the *Observer*, a review of the third Carrara Biennale, in which she drew attention to "the poetry of a small Fenosa bronze" and to Mommens, "one of the very few sculptors who carve their own marble."[1]

Though Norman had left Ursula the previous spring, they would remain close, exchanging letters regularly, and over the next decade he saw her whenever they returned to England. If he had any misgivings about the decision he'd made—and clearly he did, writing that he could "hardly bear the thought of Ursula's aloneness"—they were eased after visits to Grange Farm, which only affirmed what he already knew: that he did not belong there. "Why shouldn't I have gone on ostensibly being the perfect (and saintly) husband with Patience as a kind of 'auxiliary aid?'" Norman wrote to the Hubrechts. "The artist's training is against this—what I truly feel must be accepted for what it is."[2]

Still, as Patience had written to Norman before he left for Carrara, shedding a snakeskin was far more difficult than it appeared. Perhaps getting as far from England as possible would hasten the process. In *Ring*

Doves and Snakes, Patience's account of the year she and Norman spent on the Greek island of Naxos (1963–64), she intimates that their decision to go was somewhat spontaneous, possibly contemplated over the course of that winter in Hampstead, though more probably made at the last moment. Indeed during their cursory search for a place to live and work in the spring and summer of 1962, Naxos, or anywhere in Greece for that matter, had never been mentioned. They had no contacts on Naxos and knew nothing of what it would really be like to live in such an isolated, out-of-the-way place. "Must people know why we went . . . ?" Patience asked rather pointedly in *Ring Doves and Snakes*.[3] Who these "people" were is never spelled out, but one imagines Patience addressing friends and family, former lovers and colleagues who perhaps wondered why they'd fixed on this remote Cycladic island.

Patience's question was perhaps directed as much to herself as it was to others. Naxos had the requisite quarries of course, and Patience would later write that their Mediterranean odyssey had been dictated by Norman's search for stone. "We went for marble," was her simple answer.[4] But surely Naxos—100 miles from Athens and accessible only by boat—was a long way to go for marble. Moreover neither she nor Norman spoke Greek.

It was Patience's friend and Hampstead neighbor Stavros Papastavrou and his "bewitching Romanian wife," Flora, who told them about the island and the run-down marble quarry above Apollonas known for its half-finished statues left *in situ*, including the famous and colossal 30-foot Kouros. A professor of modern Greek at Cambridge, Stavros not only presented them with old survey maps of Naxos showing its rugged mountains and deep ravines but also furnished them with a letter of introduction, written in the formal diplomatic Greek style, a precious document that Patience described as "a farewell token which could have been written in Byron's time."[5] The letter declared Patience and Norman to be true friends of Greece who, when they returned to England, would be the "very best ambassadors." From the distant perch of Hampstead and based on Stavros's descriptions, Naxos was deeply alluring. "Glittering in the marble light," Patience wrote, "it beckoned, perhaps threatened. Welcoming strangers, it withdrew from them."[6]

Patience and Norman left in mid-May 1963, their lorry packed with carving tools and books—"Robert Graves and other indispensables."[7]

Patience included material she had gathered for a manual of European cooking for Chinese chefs on the Blue Funnel Line shipping company. Many years later this was published as *The Centaur's Kitchen*. It took them a month to reach Naxos after several stops: in Paris to visit Wolfe, the Fenosas, and gallery owner Henriette Gomes, who, Patience wrote, "loves Norman and his work"; in St. Jeannet, where they had the good fortune to find a five-foot-long snakeskin; in Carrara, to retrieve one of Norman's sculptures, *Sibyl*, which they hoped to sell to one of Norman's patrons; then Venice; and finally Athens. In Venice they visited Paul Paul, who was researching a book on Venetian instrument makers—he had in fact recently discovered Vivaldi's birth certificate in baptismal registers of the Church of San Giovanni in Bragora—and they looked into galleries that might exhibit Norman's work the following year.[8] Countess Bianca Coen ran a small private gallery in her palazzo in Calle del Dose and expressed an interest in Norman's proposed series of marble carvings. "Returning was so far from his thoughts that he accepted," Patience wrote. "Yes was easy, sailing away empty-handed. No might have been wise."[9] From Venice they sailed to Athens, where they rented a room looking out at the Acropolis and spent a few days securing the necessary permits for their stay in Greece.

Even with all of their paperwork in order, they still had to find a boat willing to transport the lorry from Athens to Naxos. However, they'd been put in touch with a travel agent, who, when presented with Stavros's letter, said it would be "an honor and my duty to convey both you and the lorry in safety to Naxos."[10] A passage was booked for the very next day. They left Athens in a small *vaporaki* on the evening of Friday, June 14, and 18 hours later, after a brief stop on the tiny island of Paros, arrived at the port of Naxos. A small crane hauled the lorry onto the quay, and they set out over the mountains on what Patience called a "bone-shaking journey."[11] Other than Stavros's letter, the only reference they had was a sort of SOS message written in Greek on the back of a cigarette packet. "Can you tell me the road for Apollonas?" it read, referring to the tiny village on the island's northern shore.[12]

The road, such as it was, took them up a couple of thousand feet before turning into a primitive track strewn with large boulders. The mountain valleys were lined with plane trees and flowering oleanders. When they first caught a glimpse of Apollonas, "a marooned village leaning on the sea," it seemed inaccessible.[13] They had driven only 35 miles from the port but had used 12 gallons of gas and arrived feeling "quite broken and dirty."[14] They were greeted by what seemed like all of the village's 150 inhabitants.

The long journey by boat, the harrowing drive over the mountains, and their inability to speak the language had plunged them into the remoteness of Cycladic life. There was little doubt that they had "shed the snakeskin of fuss, plans, hesitations and other people's claims," but knew not what lay on the other side.[15] Indeed Naxos represented a far more decisive break from England than their trip to Carrara and Catalonia the previous spring. They were nearly unreachable, except by post, which was highly irregular—the postman came by mule two or three days a week and announced his arrival by blowing a horn. Contact with Athens by telephone was unreliable. Only a few people spoke "a kind of English" that Patience and Norman found unintelligible; luckily the quarry owner spoke some Italian. Even Norman, who had a gift for languages and eventually learned serviceable Greek, said in the beginning that he found it unusually difficult to communicate. They had never been so far from home. "This place is the end of the world," Patience wrote to Olive a few weeks after they reached Apollonas. "In itself it is remote, among the Cyclades," she continued, "and the depths into which one is precipitated to finally reach Apollo makes it seem beyond and away. Contact with the world is by sea, but no boat really comes here."[16]

It was on Naxos more than anywhere else that they began, as Patience put it, "to realize who and what we were. . . . And I, whatever I may have been before, achieved a kind of 'invisibility' propitious for creative work, that attaches, so typically Greek, to women."[17] As she'd done in Castelpoggio, Patience immediately began to learn from women and children, whether at the village pump—where wild plants were washed and examined on a daily basis—or at the communal bakery. Indeed edible plants were central to the Apollonian diet, especially during the winter months, when there was little fresh produce available. As Patience and Norman quickly learned, life on Naxos was stripped down to its most basic elements. Norman would later write, "In Greece things are what they are," a notion that seemed to liberate them from what they viewed as the petty entanglements and conventions of life in London.[18] Years later Patience told the BBC that it was a primitive existence, unlike anything they'd ever experienced. Thus Naxos proved to be the perfect antidote to whatever worries or doubts Patience and Norman may have had about their previous lives and their reasons for leaving.

※※※※※

The largest of the Cycladic islands, Naxos in the early 1960s was still relatively unspoiled. Even as late as 1975, there were fewer than ten hotels on the island, nearly all of them concentrated in the capital. The tourist season itself was brief, confined to the summer months of July and August; when Patience and Norman arrived, Apollonas was just beginning to prepare for the influx of summer visitors.

After spending a few days in the Hotel Apollonas, which in the off-season doubled as a storage vault for onions, the island's staple crop, they negotiated the use of a typical Naxian house. The white stone cube (Patience called it a monk's cell) belonged to a couple of peasants who lived in a nearby mountain village. For the house and adjacent onion shed, which Norman used as his studio, they paid £5 a month, far less expensive than anything they had looked at in Italy. The house was a stone's throw from the water's edge and, from the front door, had a view of the bay. It was precisely the kind of living space and work environment they'd dreamed of. "Our wishes have been more than realized," Norman wrote. "They are now out on trial."[19]

It did not take long for villagers to make note of Norman's lorry. Few if any of the villagers had their own vehicles, and bus service was infrequent and highly variable. A few weeks after their arrival, they were woken early one morning and asked to take a sick child to see the doctor. They initially refused because it didn't seem to be an emergency, but when the mother returned later that day with the crying boy, who now seemed feverish, they relented. A few days later another parent with a sick child appeared and Norman took them to Halki, nearly 20 miles away. A week later there was another request for a lift to Komiaki. On their way back they stopped at a café in Koronos, which was presided over by a diminutive elderly woman who served them rustic bread, olives, tomatoes, oil, and wine, the meal finished with walnuts preserved in syrup and thimblefuls of *raki*. This recipe, green walnut preserve, or *Karithó Glikó*, appears in *Honey from a Weed*. During the spring harvest the lorry was also deployed to haul 100-kilo sacks of onions from the fields to the quay, where they were loaded onto *caïques*, traditional fishing boats. The alternative to the lorry was mule transport. Of course these favors did not go unacknowledged. In return Patience and Norman received gifts in the form of food—baskets of potatoes, pomegranates, and beans. "Everyone is drunk with the lorry's possibilities, and we have to be very firm about it, or everyday it would be doing some dreadful feat of endurance," Patience wrote just one month after they arrived.[20]

But the seemingly benevolent act was not without consequences. One day the local bus driver, Andoni, confronted Norman on the quay over these so-called mercy rides and claimed Norman was deliberately undermining his business. Apparently there was a law that buses were not permitted to carry freight, and privately owned vehicles were not permitted to take passengers. Norman wasn't charging for these rides and felt it was one of the few ways he could return the generosity with which they'd been greeted. But there was no question that the use of the lorry had generated a certain amount of resentment among the bus drivers, and as Patience wrote, "war was declared." Nevertheless Norman continued to use the lorry as he saw fit, and the villagers, who undoubtedly benefited from it, generally supported him.

Indeed they were quickly embraced by most of the village's inhabitants, who made offerings in the form of fresh cheeses, wine, and goat's milk. Apostolì, a shepherd who knew how to "draw bread from a stone"—in other words, survive on very little—and Angelos, a father of eleven and the "image of patriarchal plenty in a lean time," became good friends. Angelos, to whom Patience dedicated *Ring Doves and Snakes* and described as the hero of her story, treated them as family. He invited them to the wedding of his firstborn son, for which seven goats were slaughtered. Norman and Wolfe, who had come to visit from Paris in September, took part in the making of Angelos's wine: Crushing the grapes with their feet in a shallow stone pit was a festive, ceremonial right of passage, which Patience described in great detail. "I was hoping to jump into the winepit but it is man's work," she wrote. "'Weak women' are anathema to strong wine: 'strong men, strong wine, potency!' How often I heard this already. One can't help thinking this weakening idea is the ghost of a more ancient notion of female 'pollution.'"[21]

The role of women in Apollonian life was not something Patience dwelt on though she was fully aware of her own unusual vantage point as the "wife" of a non-Greek. Stavros's letter had referred to them as a married couple, and it was generally assumed among the villagers that they were. Patience was happy to learn from the women when it came to identifying plants and flowers or preparing a certain dish, like the preserved walnuts they tasted in Koronos, but she drew the line at certain tasks. Every day, it seemed, was spent washing rugs or linens and "the women, stooping at their work, sometimes called me to work with them," Patience wrote. "But I had my own work to do."[22] Patience even found the Naxian method of cooking beans—by leaving an earthenware pot on the embers of a dying fire—liberating because it allowed her to retreat to her writing desk rather than having to stand over a stove.

With Norman she gained access to the male-dominated province of the café, bar, or quarry—a pattern that would persist throughout their Mediterranean travels and that Patience used to her advantage. She was a keen observer and despite the language barrier managed to record recipes and extract bits of information from the local people—café owners, peasants, and housewives.

They were on the island just eleven months and, during that first summer, they were not the only outsiders in Apollonas. In August the Swiss painter Willi Hartung—"emaciated, bearded, bald"—arrived to work for a month and lived in a "hermit's cell" next to Patience and Norman.[23] As he had no means of cooking, Patience made him a dish of potatoes and beans every day. He would become a lifelong friend and a great supporter and patron of Norman's work, acquiring more than a dozen of his sculptures. There was Kevin Andrews, the American writer, who appeared one day searching for *Acorus calamus*, a tall reedlike plant, which he used for making flutes. Wolfe visited relatively early on, bringing with him his "Parisian's appetite," just as the island's seasonal bounty had begun to dry up. Nicolas and his then-wife, Corinna, came in early autumn, Nicolas having just recovered from a three-month stint in a sanatorium for tuberculosis. They stayed in a little house nearby. "Patience was always a bit difficult about having people to stay with her," says Nick, though Apollonas was one place where they actually had no extra room.[24] Norman Janis, who arrived in Apollonas the following April with his wife, Nia, and spent many evenings with Patience and Norman, described their house as "more of a shelter." At that time, during Lent, there was very little food in the village, and Norman

Janis remembers Patience gathering weeds in the sloping meadows above the village, which she used to make "bitter but interesting salads."[25]

Indeed life on Naxos had a providential aspect to it. As Patience noted in *Honey from a Weed*, each household was more or less self-sufficient, growing most of what they needed in the valleys that rose sharply above the rocky shores. Throughout antiquity Naxos, unlike many of the other Cycladic Islands, was known for its fertile soils and supply of fresh water. However the season of abundant fresh produce was very brief and followed by a long period of scarcity. The three commercial establishments in the village—Manyoli's, a simple *taverna* run by Angelos's younger brother; Kosta's, a small grocery store; and Jánis's *kapheneion*, the café—stocked a few household necessities and basic groceries. During the holiday season they served simple fare such as grilled octopus or marinated anchovies. One of Manyoli's signature dishes was *avgá ke patátes,* which Patience described unflatteringly as "diluted eggs poured over a pan of chips." Kosta's was a place they avoided—"One would have to read Dickens again to discover men as mean as he is." Jánis, the melancholy café owner and father of five, presided over a barren room with an empty meat locker in the corner and "now and then a sack of US famine flour."[26]

They became accustomed to the absence of food and the celebratory feasting it engendered when there was a crop of new beans, a haul of mackerel, or a slaughtered pig. "In every season one confronted an empty prospect redeemed by providential windfalls," Patience wrote. "Here, money can't help you to eat."[27]

❦

They had come, however, at an auspicious time, in early summer, when there was still a good deal of variety in the diet—eggplant, okra, artichokes, zucchini, sweet and hot peppers, sweet potatoes, goat's milk, and "in rare calm weather, fish." Patience became familiar with a number of lesser-known species on Naxos, including dogfish, the fearsome-looking gurnard, red scorpionfish, John Dory, and garfish. When Nicolas and Corinna returned to the island in 1969 just after Patience began work on *Honey from a Weed*, she wrote, "I hope you will be able to draw some of those [fish] with such amazing armorial spikes, etc. and have them named if only in Greek."[28]

Though there was plenty to eat that summer, there were also signs of the scarcity to come. "Have just squeezed what is probably the only lemon on Naxos," Patience wrote in a rare diary entry on June 24, 1963. She made note of the fading spring flowers—"straw colored, brittle, spiny, infinitely fine and delicate"—and before long was training her eye on the local plants. Jánis's daughter Anna, no more than six, served as guide. She was thin-boned, "with eyes like beads of licorice," and named everything in sight. Patience took her cues from the women and children who gathered plants on an almost daily basis and washed them under the village tap. More so than in Castelpoggio, edible wild plants, known broadly as *khórta*, were an essential part of the Naxian diet. In February and March women and children gathered dandelion greens, wild chicory, endive, milk thistles, field marigolds, and chamomile, as well as wild carrot, parsnip, fennel, and chervil. Wild mustard, rocket, thyme, savory, and several varieties of mint were also harvested. Filling her jar at the spring, Patience had a "daily opportunity" to study the rich variety of edible weeds and ask questions. "At the time I was reading the landscape and its flora with as much attention as one gives to an absorbing book," she wrote.[29] She had of course done extensive fieldwork on mushrooms as well as research on plants and gardens throughout the 1950s. And she had spent a few months learning from La Dirce in Castelpoggio, which had similar flora. But she had never lived among people for whom nearly every plant and flower had a common name and function as well as a place in the culinary repertoire. Thus she wrote that it was on Naxos that she first took a serious interest in weeds. She was beginning to learn directly from people, mostly women and children, rather than books, and it was not lost on Patience that nearly everyone in Apollonas was illiterate.

By the beginning of September, though, there was a notable shift both in the availability of basic supplies, even bread, and the general mood of the villagers. Summer was over, the Athenian visitors had fled, and the store shelves were empty. Patience and Norman were getting their first glimpse of what Stavros referred to as the "merciless logic" of island life and the fact that not even the moon, rising up from the sea, manages to give the place a romantic touch.[30] In a letter to Muriel in September, Patience confessed that she was "getting that Island feeling," and explained, "There is practically nothing to eat."[31] They were essentially living on potatoes and beans, the staple winter dish, which they ate twice a day. "Looking for food in Apollonas is sampling the taste of nothing," Patience wrote. "Nothing is a natural condition."[32]

⊰⊰⊰⊰⊰⊱⊱⊱

Naxos also happened to be the backdrop for the writing of her book on European cooking for Chinese chefs on Blue Funnel Line's newly built 480-foot, 8,000-ton luxury vessel, the *Centaur*. Based in Liverpool, the Blue Funnel Line was part of the Holt family's renowned Ocean Steamship Company, founded in 1865, which transported cargo, mostly livestock, and passengers from the U.K. to China. The new ship would be state of the art, with air-conditioned accommodations for its two hundred passengers and, remarkably, would serve fresh milk, cream, and butter obtained from the fifty head of dairy cattle on their way to Singapore. The commission had come through one of the company's managers, a friend of Ariane Castaing's, who was also an admirer of *Plats du Jour*. The £500 Patience was being paid had largely underwritten their trip to Naxos.

Indeed she had done much of the research and recipe testing over the course of the winter before they left, if not previously. In the book's introduction she writes, "There is nothing in this book that I have not cooked at some time in the last few years." Most of the dishes in the book, with a few exceptions, would've been very difficult if not impossible to recreate on Naxos. Very rarely was beef available, for example, and Patience did nearly all of the cooking on an open fire or, in winter, on a one-ring burner. In Apollonas there were no evenings spent lingering over *civet de lièvre* or *boeuf en daube*. However the spirit of the book, with the limitations of the ship's galley in mind, accorded nicely with the kind of life Patience was living on Naxos.

She had nearly completed the manuscript by the end of July—"I am driving my Chinese cookery book to a conclusion," she wrote to Olive. And in fact she was embarking on the much more ambitious *Ring Doves and Snakes*, which would only see publication after the success of *Honey from a Weed* more than twenty years later. Although the cookery manual was written for a very select audience of working chefs, it reveals a subtle yet unmistakable shift in Patience's approach to food and cooking. It is far more opinionated than *Plats du Jour*: "the use of refined salt is to be entirely ignored in cooking," "minestrone without grated parmesan served at table is unthinkable," and "I am as a rule predisposed against tinned goods," are just a few examples. The book incorporates some of the recipes she had learned in Castelpoggio, El Vendrell, and Greece. It includes the recipe for *rougets au vin blanc* that she picked up at the Hotel Lautram in Locmariaquer; a recipe for eggplant "as prepared in the *tavernas* of Athens," as well as the Naxian dish of okra and potatoes; tomato salad *à la catalane* (the dish that preceded most meals in El Vendrell); and "chicken sauté Castelpoggio," a simple dish of chicken braised in red wine that presumably came from Dirce. There were still a fair number of recipes culled from other cookbooks, including a handful from *Plats du Jour*, but Patience was beginning to rely more on her own experience, observing and learning from the cooks and village people she encountered.

Just after Patience and Norman left for Naxos, the idea of reprinting *Plats du Jour* and possibly publishing a new, fully revised edition was raised. Judith Butcher, a young copy editor at Penguin, wrote to Patience on Naxos asking if she had any changes she wanted to make to the text.[33] Given that it took about three weeks for a letter to arrive, Patience said she would leave any revisions to Primrose. But if there were ever to be a new edition, she suggested rewriting the chapter "Pots, Pans and Stoves," replacing or deleting a few recipes, and substantially revising the chapter on wine "because wine has become a real phenomenon in English life!" Incidentally these are some of the same suggestions Elizabeth David had made when she reviewed the original manuscript. Patience also explained that, during the writing of the cookery manual, she had consulted *Plats du Jour* regularly "and have not come across anything of which I was ashamed."[34]

Patience also took the opportunity to pitch an idea for a book she'd been considering for several months. Whereas *Plats du Jour* had focused on a generation that had lived through the war and its aftermath, Patience felt there was another book to be written for a younger generation with a "completely new set of culinary problems." She saw a growing divide between young college students who, after their various expenses, have no money left for food, and an emerging class of yuppies: "posh young things," Patience called them—"drinking whiskey and wine, and having posh little dinners to impress their friends." Patience proposed a cookbook aimed at both camps—the indigent and the affluent—with the title, *Rich Man, Poor Man*. In a real sense she herself was living on the poor man's diet—beans, potatoes, rice, eggs, dried fish, and vegetables. For the well-to-do she suggested a Glyndebourne picnic like the one she'd written about in *Harper's Bazaar*; cold chicken pie; and, once again, Monsieur Lautram's recipe for red mullet. In fact the series of articles Patience wrote for *Harper's Bazaar* in 1958, which included recipes for complicated dishes like *bouchées de volaille* and *civet de lièvre*, were clearly directed at upwardly mobile women interested in entertaining. Nearly every one of the articles included information on hiring caterers or servers to do most of the actual work. "Do you think Penguins [*sic*] would be interested in such a book?" Patience asked. "It would be fun to illustrate these two contrasting aspects, the student crouching over his single gas ring, and the young devotees of Modern Living!"[35] Butcher said she passed the idea along to the handbooks editor, but it was never mentioned again. Patience's idea was, however, rather prescient—Katharine Whitehorn's whimsical and now classic *Cooking in a Bedsitter* and André Launay's *Posh Food* were published by Penguin in 1963 and 1967, respectively. (Whitehorn's book was originally published in 1961 under the title *Kitchen in the Corner*.) Jill Norman, who joined Penguin in 1963 or 1964, says she was never approached about *Rich Man, Poor Man* but almost certainly would have published it if she had been.[36]

Although Patience was "a thousand miles removed from all this," she was still firmly rooted in the social and literary circles of Hampstead. She clearly imagined herself continuing to write books for Penguin and was enthusiastic about the possibility of *Plats du Jour* being published in a new edition, with one condition: that David Gentleman's cover not be replaced. She signed off by asking Butcher to send her regards to Germano Facetti, Penguin's new design director. "I think he is doing wonders with Penguin covers," Patience wrote.[37]

⋆⋆⋆⋆⋆⋆

Winter in Apollonas proved to be exceptionally difficult. In addition to the scarcity of food, Patience and Norman found themselves battling the elements and struggling to work under less than favorable conditions. The house they rented had a northerly exposure and two "windows" overlooking the sea. These windows had shutters but no glass, so keeping out the frigid north wind meant living in darkness. In a letter to Muriel in mid-February, Patience wrote, "Terrible days mean shutters closed, semi dark, heavy cloud, biting wind, don't know the time of day, cold rising off the floor, working with frozen fingers."[38] They seemed to be living at the bottom of the world. Patience observed the old men of the village dressed in "greatcoats to their ankles, looking like the dismissed cast from Gorky's play, *The Lower Depths*. It is as if they are interminably waiting for some alleviation of the human condition."[39]

Norman would split the day's firewood in the morning, and they kept a blaze burning in the kitchen to stay warm. There were fewer distractions in the off-season from stray visitors and villagers alike, and after break-fast—bread, dripping, honey or quince jam, cheese, and coffee—they worked, Patience at her typewriter and Norman in his studio next door. Norman was busy with a series of some thirty carvings, small enough to fit in the palm of your hand, that were evidently inspired by the goddesses found in Bronze Age Cycladic tombs, statuettes that they sometimes viewed at the museum of antiquities in the port city. Patience was drawn to this museum, presided over by an old man who spoke obscure French and passed his days there in solitude. Every time they went to Naxos, they stopped by the museum, whose collection of marble instruments, small arrowheads, and clay pots was displayed without dates or descrip-tive labels. In fact none of the items had been included in publications or written about, Patience noted, and thus one was "left with the things themselves, matchless creatures, island goddesses."[40]

The museum's director told them that the small sculptures were often placed in the hands of the dead or clasped against their breast, their folded arms a representation of the cycle of living and dying. Norman was making his own goddesses, "carvings in wild marble," using pink and white stones found along the beaches as well as the coarse-grained marble from the quarry above Apollonas.[41] It was this set of carvings that he planned to exhibit in Venice in the spring of 1964, coinciding with the city's 32nd Biennale.

"If things go well—if I make money in Venice and publish my book," Norman wrote to his parents in early December, "I'll buy a house here and some fields—I'll grow grapes—dreams? It feels as solid as most things."[42]

Despite the discomfort and the monotony of the winter diet, Norman was content in Apollonas and seriously entertained the thought of settling there.

In early December Patience was obliged to return to London after a cement truck crashed through her garden wall, causing considerable damage. It had happened before they arrived in Naxos and had preoccupied Patience, who was told she'd have to cover the cost of repairing the wall. In addition the tenant who had been renting the basement flat for £100 a month announced that he was returning to America.[43] "The wall makes the £500 I will earn [from the Blue Funnel Line manual] seem a laughable trifle," Patience wrote.[44] Their financial worries were compounded by the fact that Carroll Stuchell, who had agreed to buy one of Norman's Carrara carvings, *Sibyl*, for £600, informed them that she was no longer interested because, as Patience noted, "he wasn't as famous as Epstein."[45]

As she would throughout Patience and Norman's journeys, however, Olive continued to send Patience checks, a crucial source of financial support that often kept them afloat during lean times. "Your amazing cheque arrived and cheerful letter," Patience wrote soon after returning to Apollonas in late January. "What a princely sum to put into the bank."

Her trip to England was stressful and jarring after the solitude and simplicity of life on Naxos—a discordance that was to be repeated on subsequent visits. She described everything being in a state of collapse and complained that the "Beatniks were growing like lichen."[46] In a letter to Muriel, she wrote, "Greece is no preparation for English life."[47] In *Ring Doves and Snakes*, she describes an encounter with an American acquaintance who took umbrage at Patience's claim that US famine flour was of little use to the Greeks. They were too proud to use it. "What they needed," Patience said, "was not charity but a chance to earn money and put shoes on their feet."[48] The American accused Patience and Norman of leading "frivolous" and "trivial" lives that did more harm to the local people than good. Patience replied that Norman had gone in search of marble, that they were neither welfare workers nor parasites, and that they helped however they could, notably by lending a hand with the lorry when asked. "Of course we are not 'solving problems,'" Patience wrote. "But who knows, perhaps the Apollonians feel less abandoned because we chose to see the winter through with them."[49] Indeed after an exhausting seven-day journey from London—the only relief being a stop in Milan, where she saw *Don Carlos* at La Scala with Wolfe—Patience, eager to get back to Apollonas before Christmas, was greeted by a crowd of welcoming village children. Norman, who had been sharing in the monthlong Advent fast, living on beans, potatoes, and weeds cooked without oil, was looking "thin as a pin and rather delicate."[50]

Patience spent the rest of the winter working on what she called her "Apollonic book," which she hoped to sell to the publisher John Murray when they returned to London in the spring. Murray came from a long line of publishers—the family business was inaugurated in 1768 and was famous for publishing Byron—and had managed to breathe new life into the firm by attracting such writers as Patrick Leigh Fermor, Freya Stark, and Dervla Murphy. Murray and his wife, Diana, lived in Cannon Place, just up the road from Patience's house, and they were longtime friends; Diana was also a good friend of Betty Barnardo. Patience was of course familiar with Leigh Fermor's books—he had published *Mani: Travels in the Southern Peloponnese* in 1958 and was widely acknowledged as a leading authority on Greece. Indeed by the time Patience had revised her own manuscript and was ready to present it to Murray, she worried that Leigh Fermor's second Greek volume, *Roumeli: Travels in Northern Greece*, which she had learned of from Leigh Fermor's sister, might "spoil his appetite for mine."[51] Indeed *Roumeli* was published in 1966, whereas Patience's book, *Ring Doves and Snakes*, would not see the light of day for more than twenty years.

The writer who perhaps had the greatest impact on Patience's understanding of Greece, with the possible exception of Robert Graves, was the American scholar Kevin Andrews, although she also admired Henry Miller's *Colossus of Maroussi*. Andrews appeared in Apollonas one day, a Pan-like figure carrying a reed pipe and wearing nothing but a pair of shorts and some of his own handmade jewelry—"barbarous ornaments," Patience called them, admiringly. Andrews was already a well-known Hellenophile, having first explored the country on a traveling fellowship from Harvard in 1947. Those journeys formed the basis of his best-known work, *The Flight of Ikaros*, which Leigh Fermor considered to be "the most brilliant and penetrating book" on Greek village life after the civil war.[52] Leigh Fermor described Andrews as a "blue-eyed scholar gypsy," and indeed he had ranged widely over the Greek islands, often preferring to sleep out under the stars and swimming long distances in wild seas.[53] He had lived in a small village on the island of Karpathos in 1961 and, according to his biographer, considered himself more Greek than the Greeks. When Andrews arrived in Apollonas that summer, "a wild boar disguised as a perfect gentleman," it was a relief for Patience and Norman to encounter someone who knew the country as well as he did and who they could communicate with.[54] "It is very exciting suddenly to be able to talk to someone instead of rubbing along in pigeon Greek," Patience wrote.[55] Not only that, but he shared with Patience a love of literature, Italian opera, and wild places.

Born in China in 1924, Andrews attended private school in England before moving to the United States. He had a complicated childhood. His father, or at least the man he believed to be his father, was an American explorer, Roy Chapman Andrews, who served as director of the American Museum of Natural History from 1934 to 1942. His mother, Yvette Borup, was born in Paris to American parents with an adventurous streak and penchant for risk-taking. After studying Classical Greek at Stowe, Andrews served as a private in the US Army in WWII (seeing action in Italy) and then attended Harvard. However, he felt out of place in the United States, and after marrying Nancy Cummings, the daughter of E. E. Cummings, he moved back to Athens with her in 1954. Even more so than Patience, Andrews was thoroughly dismissive of his "murky past."[56] In the foreword to *The Flight of Ikaros*, he writes unsparingly, "Since personal accounts usually begin with a digression on the author's background, I state first one notable fact about my own: I do not belong to it."[57]

Over the years Patience would maintain "an erratic but lively correspondence" with Andrews, who sometimes stayed with them when they were in London. Patience credited him with inspiring her interest in making jewelry and considered him a trusted authority on Greek life. They sometimes had "violent disagreements," but Patience and Norman were extremely fond of him and admired his intellectual ferocity and adventurous spirit. Thus it must've been all the more painful for Patience when, after the eventual publication of *Ring Doves and Snakes*, Andrews wrote her a devastating letter in which he pointed out the errors in the book and accused her of "an almost colonial disdain" for the Greek people. Its only merit, aside from some "blazing descriptions," Andrews thundered, was the possibility that it might dissuade a few "foreign innocents" from adopting the "simple life."[58]

But in 1964 Andrews was himself impressed by Patience and Norman's fortitude and willingness to spend the winter in Apollonas. In March 1964, in response to a letter they had written asking for advice about shipping agents for Norman's sculptures, he wrote, "I admire your ability to enjoy the place despite discomforts. May spring reward you!"[59]

❦

In early March spring still seemed a distant prospect. On the eve of Lent Patience and Norman were both stricken with flu, which had swept through the village. Patience wrote to Olive, "We have been living for weeks in a kind of nowhere, in which the sun never rose, the damp seeped through the floor and it was impossible to tell the time of day."[60] Spring, she said, was beginning to seem like a myth. She took to wandering the sloping meadows above the village in search of dandelions to keep "alive the little hope I had of spring."[61] On the very day that Lent began, they received a food parcel from John and Carroll Stuchell, Norman's sometimes patrons, containing tinned peaches, tongue, and brisket. Needless to say they needed little persuasion to dispense with the rigors of fasting—Norman was sick of piety, Patience said—and the provisions from abroad gave them a much-needed boost.[62]

When spring finally arrived, it was a euphoric moment, and in her letters Patience made note of the precise day, March 28. The hillsides erupted in flower, water came rushing down from the mountains, and the smell of honey filled the air. There were hummingbirds and giant crickets in the valleys and turtles in the streams. Apollonians were working fifteen-hour days plowing the fields and planting onions, and the village was almost empty, peaceful in its isolation. For Patience it was akin to paradise. "Every day I ran up rocks to fasten on flowers which budded, opened and became seeds in a matter of hours," she wrote. "Bee orchids appeared in several places between the boulders like fantastic Japanese masks crowned with green birds' heads, their brown velvet falls stamped with magic markings. The vetches spread a web of gold along the cliffs, threaded with purple, magenta, indigo, the colors of Byzantium flaring across the headlands. Another kind of asphodel, with tuberous roots and starfish straggling leaves, opened their branched candelabras in high up places where nothing much could grow. . . . The spring corn waved along the hillsides in emerald shoals. The vines sprouted and the silver figs held up new leaves vertically, green hands raised in praise."[63]

The long difficult winter had quickly become a memory, and Patience even alluded in a letter to Tania that they might return to Greece the following year. Norman still held on to the idea of buying a piece of land on Naxos and perhaps growing grapes and making wine—he considered the strength and beauty of the Naxian wine to be incomparable. With few distractions they had both settled into a rhythm structured around their creative work. Patience was spending most of her time writing, drawing, and cataloguing the island's edible plants and weeds. In early April Norman wrote to his cousin that they had finally stopped "thinking about where and how to live," and that this had in a sense set them free.[64] Patience wrote, "In the last months we have lived entirely in the present."[65]

But they still had no long-term plan, and the prospect of Norman's show in Venice and their return to London—for insurance reasons they had to have the lorry back in England by mid-July—began to undermine this settled feeling. They knew that they'd most likely be spending another winter in The Logs, sorting out their finances and searching for work or commissions for the following year. "Shall we be up to modern life?" Patience wrote to Tania. "Or fatally homesick for our rustic companions in this obscure place?"[66]

The dates of Norman's show were finally confirmed and he had just over two months to finish the carvings and get everything off the island. To do so required an inventory of his sculptures, proof that they were not stolen antiquities, and the necessary permits to export them. In the early 1960s there was an active black market in Cycladic sculptures and other antiquities, and therefore Norman's work came under the scrutiny of the Greek authorities.

Around this time Louis Stettner, an American photographer, and his wife, Christine, arrived on the island. Stettner was then working on a novel, and they planned to stay for about eight months. There were no other tourists in Apollonas at the time, and Patience and Norman were largely alone, Stettner recalls. "They had a great love and appreciation of the place," he said.[67]

On April 15, 1964, they were all invited to a party hosted by the quarry master at Manyoli's, the bar/restaurant run by Angelos's younger brother. They drank a good deal of wine and stayed well after dark. But the following day Patience and Norman discovered that two of Norman's carvings, a "splendid Queen" and the largest marble Englishman, both made from large pebbles found on the beach, had been stolen. This was an event that left them stunned and searching for answers. "Apollo where we have been so happy for so long suddenly became another place," Patience wrote in a letter to Muriel.[68] Perhaps against their better judgment, they called the police, who arrived the following day, setting off a wave of suspicion and recriminations that "plunged the village in blackest gloom."[69]

Though Angelos had explained to Patience and Norman that there was a robust trade in stolen Cycladic sculptures and that bus drivers on Naxos had profited from it, they were likely unaware of just how widespread the practice was. In fact the 1960s marked the height of the illegal trade in Cycladic sculptures, which also gave rise to a lucrative market in forgeries. It was a period of intense looting and illegal excavations during which "hundreds of early Cycladic tombs" were plundered.[70] Naxos happened to be at the center of this trade, and Norman's workshop had unwittingly provided an easy target for those involved in the trafficking. Add to this his conflict with Andoni, the bus driver, over the use of his lorry to transport villagers, and Patience and Norman became convinced that he was somehow behind the theft.

It did not take long for Patience and Norman to see how the theft and the involvement of the authorities, who were generally perceived as corrupt, had cast a pall over their relations with the people of Apollonas. Norman wrote an article in Greek for the Naxos paper, as well as a note to the villagers, titled "The Price of a Pebble," in which he absolved the locals of any responsibility and blamed himself for leaving the doors of the studio unlocked.

However his attempts to alleviate the tension seemed to have had little if any impact. They felt they could trust none of the locals and were gripped by paranoia, at one point believing they'd been poisoned. But on the day the theft of the sculptures was discovered, Norman Janis and Nia

Parry arrived in Apollonas. So for two weeks Patience and Norman spent nearly every evening with them. Norman enlisted Nia's help—she had studied art history at Harvard—in cataloguing and pricing his sculptures.

Indeed their main objective at this point was to get off the island. They decided to speed up their departure and to leave before the Feast of the Ascension in early May if they possibly could. Norman later said half jokingly that on Naxos he became a sort of scapegoat but made off before becoming the Easter lamb. When they ran into Norman and Nia in Naxos a couple of weeks later their fear was palpable. "You really couldn't argue with Patience about whether the danger was real," Janis recalled. "I wasn't saying it wasn't, but it wasn't clear to me that it was."[71] Louis Stettner attributed the paranoia to "island fever," a charge Patience refuted at the time. Patience argued that they'd been on the island long enough to know what life was like there, and they were unwilling to attribute "the last nightmare days to a sickness labeled 'island fever.'"[72] They felt so besieged that they asked Norman and Nia, who were returning to Athens, to track down Kevin Andrews's wife, Nancy Cummings, who lived somewhere on Mt. Lycabettus. "We were to go there and give testimony to Nancy that they were in danger, or they might be in danger," Janis said.[73] Patience also wrote to an acquaintance in Athens who ran a news agency and sent a message to a well-known liberal politician, whose name they'd been given before they left.[74]

Their last few days on the island were spent first transporting Norman's sculptures and the rest of their belongings to Naxos and then waiting for the permits to materialize. Patience had been convinced their every move was being watched and that the lorry would be sabotaged as they drove over the mountains. "Leaving Apollonas, and the road, had got inextricably tied up with premonitory dreams and the extraordinary fears which burst into consciousness like terrible flowers in the shadow of night," she wrote.[75]

There is little doubt that Patience and Norman overstayed their welcome in Apollonas—Kevin Andrews said that the outstanding provocation was to settle there in the first place—and that the bad blood between Norman and the bus drivers, the theft of the sculptures, and the involvement of the police had all contributed to the fact that they were no longer welcome. Whether their lives were ever in danger seems doubtful, but they arrived in Athens, after a two-day journey by boat from Naxos, utterly exhausted and relieved. They stayed in a sixth-floor penthouse suite with a balcony and view of the Acropolis. That night, rather than cook, they ordered food—chicken pilaf, salad, wine, and fruit. "We felt like very poor people suddenly become rich," Patience wrote.[76]

❈❈❈❈

They reached Venice in mid-May nearly penniless. Norman's toolbox had gone missing, either stolen or lost, and they were still reeling from their final month in Apollonas. "You could see from the way she was that she was pretty shattered after Naxos," says Miranda.[77] To save money they had planned to make their own monotype posters for the exhibition but needed the tools that had gone missing to do so. "It has just been one blow after another," Norman wrote to his parents.[78]

The show ran from June 15 to 28, 1964, and was not only highly stressful but also in the end a financial burden. Before the opening Norman had been hopeful and wrote to Leonard Woolf to say he wished he could be there. "I think you'd like some of these marble carvings," he wrote. "It's the result of a year's work on Naxos."[79] But sales were not what they had hoped or needed, and they found the gallery owner, Countess Bianca Coen, insufferable. They were unprepared for both the costs of mounting the exhibition and the commission on sales, and subsequently struggled to repay her for months. Coen demanded one of Norman's sculptures, *Ariadne*, "as part of her pound of flesh," Patience wrote.

Indeed Patience was pushing Coen to do more to promote Norman's work and at least try to make the show marginally profitable. When it became clear that she was unwilling to do this, Patience took on the role herself, which only created more tension. By the end of the month Patience could hardly bring herself to set foot in the gallery. According to Norman Janis, who visited them in Venice, it was the only time he ever saw Patience and Norman argue, Norman accusing Patience of being an *entremetteuse*, a meddler.[80] Norman, for his part, was never hugely successful at promoting himself and preferred to give his work away to friends or to exchange pieces with other artists. Even when he completed *Goliath*, which was commissioned by Leonard Woolf, he was uncomfortable asking his patron to pay for it. In his biography for the Venice show, he wrote, "One does not escape

142 — *Fasting and Feasting*

reality. My work is unknown." It isn't clear whether he really wanted to escape that reality. He had deep misgivings about the commercial art world and, though he needed the money, had little interest in haggling with Coen over sums and sales. In the end he vowed that he would never again be pushed into exhibiting his work other than on his own terms. Meanwhile the Biennale was underway. 1964 was the first year that the grand jury prize went to an American, Robert Rauschenberg, signaling the ascendancy of pop art. Nia Parry recalls the brilliant blue hydrangeas outside the pavilion being more beautiful than anything actually in the show.[81]

Patience had always been drawn to Venice, one of Irving's favorite cities and a frequent subject of his letters, and the visit was not entirely overshadowed by the show and financial worries. They saw Paul Paul, who took them to the sixteenth-century Church of San Giorgio Maggiore and to a library where they listened to old recordings of monastic music. Paul, who cut his own witch hazel divining rods and had famously used them in the Venetian church archive where he uncovered the date of Vivaldi's birth, passed the same twig over Patience's manuscript. According to Patience it "twitched and reluctantly responded 'Yes.'"[82] Patience and Norman would later use divining rods or a pendulum to help them make a number of important decisions, which Patience felt perfectly comfortable with despite her interest in and devotion to the natural sciences. "I believe in that really," Patience wrote in a letter to Muriel in 1965, referring to the use of the divining rod.

Miranda and her fiancé, Ashlyn, came through toward the end of the exhibition on their way to Apollonas, following in Patience and Norman's footsteps. (Patience had tried to persuade Miranda to come to the island the previous summer.) Patience and Norman didn't try to discourage this trip, nor did the story of their experiences put Miranda and Ashlyn off. In fact Norman gave Miranda a notebook in which he'd written a list of Greek words, important names and addresses, and detailed hand-drawn maps of the island and Apollonas. "It was as if we were messengers sent to take news that all was well with Patience and Norman," Miranda recalls.[83] When Miranda and Ashlyn arrived in July, they found that the villagers in fact all but revered Patience and Norman, and they went out of their way to welcome their children. Angelos, the great patriarch and hero of Patience's story, showed them a plot of land where he said he was going to build a house for Norman in the hope and perhaps belief that they would someday come back.

CHAPTER NINE

To Work Is to Live

Naxos gave Patience and Norman a taste of the kind of working environment they'd envisioned—one with few distractions and the barest of necessities—but on returning to London in autumn 1964, they faced the same dilemma they'd confronted two winters before: finding a suitable place to work. Naxos had been comparably cheap but too far removed from a larger community of artists. Norman, despite his misgivings about the art world, still felt he needed to be close to his peers in order to exhibit his work, make a name for himself, and eventually fulfill his dream of opening a school or communal workshop along the lines of that dreamed of by his friend and mentor Wijdeveld. They therefore decided to return to Carrara but had yet to come up with a means of financing Norman's work as a sculptor, which required ample studio space, tools and equipment, and an assistant—all with little assurance that the finished works would sell. In an unpublished article on the carvings Norman produced in Greece and Italy, Patience began by stating bluntly, "Stone carving is an impossible business." This hadn't really mattered when Norman was working in England, where the materials—granite, polyphant, purbeck—were relatively inexpensive and he was camping in the quarries. But, as Patience noted, the picture changes if "after working Bath stone or Cornish granite he craves for marble, which, as everybody knows, costs the earth at Putney Bridge."[1]

Meanwhile the commissions from Edinburgh Weavers dried up after Alastair Morton's death in 1963, and Patience was doing less and less freelance writing, though she did publish a couple of articles on design in *The Economist* in 1963 and 1964.[2] The only real income they had was from occasionally letting the Billiardroom, which hardly amounted to much since they still used it themselves on a fairly regular basis. There were also sporadic gifts from patrons and from Olive. Patience had finished the book of recipes for the Blue Funnel Line, and was trying rather desperately to find a publisher for *Ring Doves and Snakes* but had heard nothing positive by the end of the year. Increasingly she was devoting her time and energy to supporting Norman's efforts to launch his career as a sculptor.

Transporting Norman's sculptures first from Greece and then Italy had been expensive, and they still had to pay Bianca Coen for the costs of the exhibition, something they were unable to do until November 1964. In Venice Norman sold few sculptures, mostly to friends, and gave others away. Moreover several pieces were damaged in transit, which reinforced their impression that the whole affair had been misguided. In an attempt to raise funds, they arranged a two-week private exhibition of Norman's carvings in the Billiardroom. Despite their efforts they did not sell as much as they'd hoped and by the end of the show said they were very tired of being "curators." "The object was to discover with the aid of interested persons a place to work," Norman wrote. "This did not materialize."[3] Wolfe came from Paris—"a strong beam of light," in Norman's words—bearing all sorts of delicacies: smoked ham, an assortment of cheeses, *cotechino* sausages, salami, and a king-sized bottle of Saint-Émilion. He took them to Luchino Visconti's production of *Il Trovatore* at Covent Garden, and then just as quickly returned to Paris with blocks of Stilton and other gifts for his "underworld friends."

After the financially disastrous Venice exhibition and the less than successful private show, Norman drafted a proposal that he sent to friends and patrons, seeking to raise enough money—between £4,000 and £5,000—to cover living expenses for the next two years. He sent it to Jan and Leonore Hubrecht, Carroll and John Stuchell, and Leonard Woolf in the hope that they would support his work in exchange for marble sculptures to be completed over the two-year period. "I thought I might now ask some of my patrons and people who know my work to subscribe to my being a sculptor," he wrote to Woolf, "rather in the way 18th-century writers sought support for their books."[4] He was greatly absorbed in his work, and felt that it was only a matter of time before it would pay for itself and allow him and Patience to pursue their larger vision. "Marble sculpture must be a clear affirmation," he wrote to his cousin Lena, just before leaving Naxos. "I feel I could now found a workshop and school on this conviction."[5]

But in late 1964 the most urgent question was how to support themselves in Carrara. "I don't think we really need advice," Patience wrote to
Muriel, "just a series of miracles, a studio popping up like a mushroom,
that sort of thing."[6]

✻✦✦✦✦✦✦✦

This makes Patience's decision not to agree to the publication of a new
edition of *Plats du Jour* all the more baffling. It could have breathed new life
into her career as a food writer and journalist—she clearly had ambitions
to publish other books—as well as providing a much-needed infusion
of cash. Penguin was ready to move forward with a completely revised
edition to appear sometime in summer or fall of 1965. Ever since the
book went out of print in 1961, they'd received letters from readers asking
when the book would be reissued. In a letter from Venice in June 1964
Patience wrote that she was "delighted that Penguin Books are thinking
of a new edition of *Plats du Jour*."[7] Soon after returning to London that
summer Patience, Primrose, and Penguin editor Pat Siddall met to discuss
revisions. In late July Siddall wrote to Patience that she looked forward to
"having a new copy from you round about the end of the year."[8]

However by mid-August Patience and Primrose had severed their
working relationship and plans for a new edition were abandoned. There
were signs of discord even before they'd met to discuss the project. On
July 7 Primrose wrote to Patience that she would only agree to a new
edition under the original terms, which Patience wanted to modify. "We
do the book as we did it before or not at all," Primrose wrote. "We share
the work and we share the profit equally."[9] Patience had long insisted that
she did the lion's share of the work on the first edition and later told Alan
Davidson that she'd written every word of the book herself, testing and
rewriting Primrose's recipes. But the advance and the royalties, as per the
original contract, were always shared equally. In a letter to Siddall, Primrose explained that ever since the idea of a new edition had been raised
Patience had also demanded a greater share of the earnings. Primrose
hoped that they'd be able to smooth things out after Patience returned
to England but said that Patience was relentless and uncompromising.
"I sympathize with anyone who wants more money," Primrose wrote to

Siddall. "It was the manner in which the claim was made and the reasons offered for it which made it painfully obvious that no peaceful collaboration was now possible."[10] There's no firsthand account from Patience of what happened, but Alan Davidson, who republished the book many years later, after Primrose's death, wrote that Patience told him she had asked whether the fifty-fifty split could be adjusted, "whereupon Primrose took offence and declined to have anything to do with the matter."[11] The two women never spoke again. Patience was not even aware that Primrose had died—in 1982—until Alan decided to republish the book in 1990.

There's no doubt that Patience felt she was entitled to a greater share of the book's earnings. Even if she had written most of the book, Patience seemed to be unwilling to acknowledge the work Primrose had done: a good deal of the research and some of the less rewarding tasks such as the indexing—and most of the correspondence with copy editors. It's difficult to understand why she let Primrose's not entirely unreasonable refusal to alter the original terms of the contract stand in the way of republishing the book when she and Norman were desperately in need of money. After all, 50 percent would've been better than nothing. Plus, just a few months before the whole thing fell apart, she'd expressed a real interest in the possibility of a new edition.

But it was more than just her strained relationship with Primrose that had undermined the project. Patience's approach to food and cooking had changed dramatically in the years since *Plats du Jour* was first published. She'd met Irving Davis, whose sensibility—which Patience referred to as his combination of "liberality and frugality"—had a profound influence on her. She'd lived in Carrara, Catalonia, and Naxos, where the preparation of meals perhaps took on a greater urgency because of the limited availability of raw materials. Cooking was not an abstraction, a collection of recipes culled from the books of nineteenth-century French chefs. As she had written to Penguin editor Judith Butcher from Naxos, "Everyone is living here in sun-baked poverty, but the apricots and the mulberries are ripe."[12] *Plats du Jour* had filled an important niche in 1950s London, but Patience had evidently moved on. Around 1980 when the editor Jenny Dereham asked Patience if, yet again, she'd be interested in revising the book, she declined, explaining, "In the intervening years I have completely changed my point of view about cooking."[13]

Plus there was the matter of the book's many inaccuracies. Though Patience was not ashamed of anything in *Plats du Jour*, she also acknowledged that large portions of it required updating, and indeed a handful of recipes needed to be completely rewritten or even replaced. When *Plats du Jour* was eventually republished by Alan Davidson, Patience supplied him with an eight-page list of what she called "vital corrections," and in the preface noted that the detection of errors in the book could become a "parlour game."[14] In the end they decided to make only minor changes to the text and explained that any attempt to bring it up to date would have destroyed its "fabric and integrity." Still, in 1964, after they'd returned from Naxos, revising the book would have been a relatively easy way to earn a bit of money and likely would've paved the way to writing other cookbooks, including *Rich Man, Poor Man*.

As it was Patience would not publish another cookbook for more than twenty years, by which time *Plats du Jour* had been long out of print and was fading into history. Thus the winter of 1964–65 was once again spent scrambling for commissions and freelance work to raise funds to return to Carrara in the spring. In September they retired the old army lorry—"a repository of happy adventures"—and bought a secondhand camouflage-green Land Rover, which Norman attempted to insulate and soundproof by lining the cabin with corks. During the winter they saw a good deal of several old friends: notably John Ravilious, Irving Davis, and Henrion. They invited Russian-born soprano Oda Slobodskaya for Christmas dinner, as they had done in previous years. Patience met Slobodskaya, a highly regarded opera singer who had performed with Chaliapin and Diaghilev, through her Hampstead neighbor, the composer and pianist Alfred Nieman. Something of a gastronome, Oda's favorite dish was roast goose. After a meal she would repose on the couch and sing Russian folk songs and Tatiana's letter scene from *Eugene Onegin*. When Alan Davidson questioned Patience's inclusion of six different kinds of fowl in the chapter on feasting in *Honey from a Weed*, she replied, "Don't forget that I have cooked several geese for Oda Slobodskaya to her perfect satisfaction," as if that settled the matter.[15]

Patience would later claim that she and Wolfe somehow convinced Decca to release a collection of Slobodskaya's unissued early recordings, including the letter scene, which Decca indeed published in 1961. Wolfe frequented a gramophone record shop off of Tottenham Court Road, Mr. Phillips' Collectors Corner, where rare, unreleased, or pirated recordings were sold under the counter to valued customers. It was perhaps here, says Nick, that Wolfe stumbled across the Slobodskaya recordings. "She is like a saga," Patience wrote of Oda. "She has an extraordinary personal resonance." Otherwise Patience had little enthusiasm for London, which she described as a "very heavy lid under which one sits. . . . When we were away it seemed to send out a gleam of eccentricity and idealism, when we are in it, it reeks of custard powder and premium bonds."[16]

❦❦❦❦

In April 1965 they set out again for Carrara in what was becoming an annual pilgrimage. Once again they stopped in Paris to visit the Fenosas and Wolfe, who then accompanied them as far as Beaune—where he insisted on ordering an elaborate Burgundian feast. "After Greece perhaps one simply doesn't want to eat five courses," Patience wrote, "but it is a spectacle to watch the Wolfe."[17]

Patience and Norman arrived in Carrara in early May without a place to stay. They spent nearly two weeks searching for a studio and house before finding a nineteenth-century *casa di campagna* in the hills above the city. "La Barozza" had the charm of a somewhat rundown villa with its ornate iron bedsteads and a spacious hearth containing a large cast-iron polenta pot suspended from the chimney hook. The fireplace served as the only source of heating in what proved to be an extremely difficult winter habitation. Moreover the house was at the top of a steep mule track, a fifteen-minute climb, inaccessible by car. Patience wrote with evident pleasure, "No one has ever rented it because it has no road and no water." The path itself was overgrown and lined with nettles, acacias, sorrel, and snakes basking in the sun. "It is all little hills, steeply terraced, vines, olives and dense woods," Patience wrote.[18] The painter Edith Schloss, who they met in Carrara, described La Barozza as a house "marooned on the saddle of an Etruscan hill." From the terrace they could see the lights of Marina di Carrara, a seaside resort in the distance; and, when drawing water from the cistern, they had a view to one side of the Apuanian Alps—"their summits crowned with plumes of mimosa and dark umbrella pines"—and on the other the Tyrrhenian Sea.[19] Water came from a nearby rain-filled cistern with a hand pump that had long since ceased to function and was closely watched over by the neighboring peasants, "Uncle Nello," as they came to call him, and his wife. Patience and Norman tried to limit themselves to two buckets a day except for Sundays when, presumably, they did the washing. If the cistern was empty, and for long periods it was, they had to haul their water up the hill; during one dry spell in 1969, they did this for two months.

As they did wherever they went, Patience and Norman quickly established a routine structured around their work. Norman was renting space in Carlo Nicoli's studio, a hub for foreign sculptors from all over, and would arrive there at 7 every morning. In a letter to his mother, Norman wrote that, after he left for the day, Patience would slip back into bed to do her "Italian lesson," which consisted of reading Stendhal's *The Charterhouse of Parma* or Pushkin in Italian. Patience had long revered Stendhal, whom she felt captured the excesses and inefficiencies of Italian life better than any other writer. She told Wolfe that she had an epiphany of sorts when she discovered *The Red and the Black* at age seventeen. "The lesson was to be yourself," she wrote, "but it takes years to put it into practice."[20] Stendhal was an Italophile and his first major work, *L'Histoire de la Peinture en Italie*, was written while living in Bologna. He considered Milan, which he first visited in 1800, and in particular La Scala, a sacred space. He had great affection for Italy, and Patience considered his *Italian Chronicles*, a series of historical novellas, essential to understanding the country and its people. She never missed a chance to point out that his staple diet was *les épinards au jus* and years later suggested to Alan Davidson that the dish be included in his *Oxford Companion to Food*.

Patience would meet Norman for lunch at Clara's bar opposite his studio, where they served tripe on Saturdays and salt cod on Mondays, before Patience would spend the afternoon in her "cave," a rented room across town, which is where she started making jewelry. In the evening they'd meet again at Clara's for a glass of wine and then trudge back up the path and sit out on the terrace overlooking the vineyards and fading lights of the seaside. "I would like this life forever," Norman wrote to Muriel in June. "Getting uphill tired at night one cooks the supper and flops into bed," Patience wrote.[21] Edith Schloss's partner at the time, the composer Alvin Curran, recalled being struck by the absence of such basic comforts as electricity and running water at La Barozza. Peter Rockwell, who spent several overlapping summers carving in Carrara and shared studio space with Norman, described it as "fairly rustic living."[22]

The ease with which they settled into life in Carrara was helped by the fact that just after arriving they received a letter from Jan Hubrecht saying he'd put up £1,500 to help finance Norman's work, the only person it seems who responded to his plea for support. Meanwhile rent from Patience's Hampstead flat served to pay for Norman to hire an assistant, Roberto Bernacchi, a stocky twenty-six-year-old sculptor and Carrara native who would become a lifelong friend.

Hard work was central to the lives of the Carrarese and nearly every aspect of life in the city from its food to its politics was shaped in some way by the marble industry. Up until a few years before Patience and Norman settled in Carrara, massive blocks of marble, sometimes weighing more than 20 tons, were still eased down the steep, rubble-strewn slopes on makeshift sleds fitted with oak runners, as they had been for centuries. In a travel piece for *Architectural Review*, Patience admiringly described the men who performed this work, the *lizzatori*, who used thick hemp cables to control the rate of descent, as "a bunch of individualists" and "intrepid freelancers." It was punishing and dangerous work, and throughout the nineteenth century and much of the twentieth, fatalities were commonplace.

In the early 1960s, however, steep roads traversing the seemingly inaccessible mountain quarries were constructed. By the time Patience and Norman arrived in 1965, trucks were beginning to replace the old method of transporting marble on sleds guided by teams of men. Steam shovels and bulldozers were replacing traditional professional skills. High-powered diamond cables and huge chain saws rendered the old method of cutting stone with a rope and abrasive sand obsolete. Patience may have exaggerated when she wrote, "The Carrarese have only in the last fifteen years been precipitated from their medieval past," but it is true that in the mid 1960s the city and the marble industry were experiencing enormous changes.[23] Indeed it was the great era of modernization in the quarries. It did not take long for the *lizzatori* to redeploy as truck drivers, if not abandoning the marble business altogether, which helped to accelerate the booming trade in *carbonato*, the fine dust ground from scrap marble and quarry waste that is used in a variety of industrial materials. Because Norman often transported his own pieces of marble, small enough to be lifted by two men and loaded aboard the Land Rover, they got a close-up view of how the quarries operated. Rockwell remembers Norman exchanging bottles of wine with the quarry foremen for blocks of marble.

The city had also long attracted foreign artists and sculptors—the title of Patience's article for *Architectural Review* was "Sculptors' Eldo-rado." The Carrara Biennale, launched in 1957, quickly became one of the leading venues devoted exclusively to sculpture and drew figures like Henry Moore, who had a summer residence in the area, Picasso, and Louise Bourgeois. In 1965 when Norman rented studio space from Nicoli, some of Italy's leading sculptors—Carlo Signori, Alberto Viani, Pietro Cascella—had their works carved there. Cuban-born sculptor Agustín Cárdenas, Peter Rockwell, and Iranian artist Parviz Tanavoli also worked in the same studio, where, as Patience wrote, "master craftsmen work side by side with brash apprentices."[24] La Barozza, up the hill from the studio and with its terrace overlooking the vineyards and coastline below, became a meeting place for artists and sculptors. Nicoli's was the oldest and best known of Carrara's marble studios, really the last of its kind, and Patience found its drafty, light-filled workshops, littered with plaster casts of fig-leaved Apollos, Sabine women, saints, and goddesses, a sanctuary. "This magnificent place," Patience wrote, "has become, by old tradition and *laisser aller*, and through the commercial inefficiency inseparable from the anarchic resourcefulness of the Carrarese, the marginal land where carving can escape the old bondage which divides conception from execution."[25] For his part, Carlo Nicoli, great-grandson of the studio's founder, remembered Patience and Norman as "strange but wonderful people."[26]

Just a few months after they arrived in Carrara, and clearly influenced by the city's singular devotion to marble, Patience began the difficult task of teaching herself to make jewelry. She had long been interested in jewelry as an art form—she was one of the first journalists to write about modern jewelry—and had been advised by Gerda Flöckinger on buying a basic set of tools. Now, surrounded by the marble workers and sculptors in Carrara, she felt compelled to put these tools to use. "I needed a material as exacting as marble and in its way hard to work, in order to feel at home," she wrote.[27] She had admired Kevin Andrews's clunky bracelets, which she'd first seen when he appeared in Apollonas. Andrews was known for using metal scavenged from scrapyards in his jewelry. A purist, he believed that even soldering, which required mechanical tools, was "decadent," and he made rather imposing pieces—"to be worn like armour," Patience wrote—in any material but gold. When Andrews visited Patience and Norman in Carrara in 1966, she helped him inventory his work—rings, bracelets, and necklaces—which ranged in price from £3 to £18. "Norman and I sat polishing his hardware while he read his newly written work on Athens," Patience wrote.[28] He once gave Norman a "Cretan ring" made out of a solid lump of copper and Patience a spiral ring made from a long iron nail. The copper piece, Patience later wrote, exemplified for her the "will" required to transform metal into art.

In August 1965, with this in mind, Patience began working with small pieces of pure Florentine silver, iron salvaged from wine barrels, or, occasionally, bits of gold obtained from the city's postman, who also happened to make jewelry. Before long she had received her first commission—a pair of silver earrings in the form of two sphinxes suspended from half moons—for the wife of an American sculptor.

Patience never expected to earn a living making jewelry, and like Norman often gave pieces away to friends and family or exchanged them for other works of art. But she took the work seriously—every day after making the rounds of the market, she went directly to her workshop. She kept detailed lists of what she made, who it was for, and the expenses incurred. "What can a person make in nine months?" she wrote on the top of a scrap of paper detailing the pieces she'd made that year. On another she calculated how much she'd spent on silver and other metals between 1966 and 1974. She found herself for the first time completely absorbed in her very own work, doing something other than research and journalism. She later described the sense of losing oneself in time that often attended manual work as "the door into happiness." She wrote, "It is such a small thing, but if you go on doing it long enough it becomes something, a sort of interior song."[29]

For Patience that interior song could only be attained after years and years of work, which she understood in the French sense of métier—a word whose "sacred origins," she once observed, can be traced back to the Latin *ministerium*—meaning "calling" or "craft."

Norman, too, was obsessed with the meaning of work (and finding meaning in work) and with the relationship between the artist and his chosen medium. He was one of the few artists in Carrara committed to direct carving, a practice that eschews the use of mechanical tools and models or preparatory drawings, and he traced what he felt to be the decadence of sculpture all the way back to the Greek use of plaster models and casting to reproduce statues. "The 'pointing process,'" Norman wrote in a catalogue accompanying a direct carving show organized by Rockwell in 1966, "confined the sculptor's creative activity to the preparatory model, and the method, subsequently perfected during each classical revival, reduced the encounter with his material to mechanical reproduction." Alvin Curran remembered Norman using "techniques going back to the time of the ancient Egyptians" and his work having a primitiveness that resembled "early human art."[30] Of course direct carving was far more labor-intensive and therefore less remunerative, but the work itself, in Norman's view, gave rise to a more spontaneous and pure form. "Why do I work so hard?" Norman wrote to Muriel that summer. "Because I passionately want to—it is equal to anything the world has to offer . . . for me, to work is to live." To which Patience added: "There is nothing to say about work. It occupies you intensely if it's what you choose to do."[31] Patience and Norman had made their choice: They would lead the kind of life that allowed them to focus on their art and work, whatever the consequences.

At the same time Patience continued to study the edible plants and weeds of the region as well as the cultivated vegetables available in the marketplace—many of them new to her—supplementing what she had learned in Castelpoggio and Apollonas. Alvin Curran, who sometimes wandered the hillsides with Patience, said that she was always scouring the landscape for plants or fungi. "She had this animal instinct that was absolutely astounding," he said.[32] Although they had returned to Carrara and were just a few miles as the crow flies from Castelpoggio, the plant life of the sparely cultivated vineyards surrounding La Barozza presented an array of new species. As she had done on Naxos, she learned from children, old peasant women, and the occasional cook or innkeeper. She befriended Eugenia, a young girl with "an amazing weed vocabulary," whose father worked one of the local vineyards and who served as her guide.[33] According to Patience, Eugenia divided her plants into two categories: those that were cooked and those used in salad. Inspired by dandelion salads she'd eaten in Paris, Patience wrote to Tania that she was making her own salads using a variety of vineyard weeds. "There are kinds you cook," she wrote, "and kinds for salad," including the flowers of borage, wild rocket, white wall rocket, wild radish, burnet, and fronds of wild fennel.[34] The plants and weeds near La Barozza tended to be more delicate—"small, perfumed, and crisp"—than those she was introduced to in Castelpoggio, where the hillsides were largely shaded by dense chestnut groves.

Unlike Naxos, however, Carrara also had a thriving open-air market that Patience visited nearly every day before heading to her workshop. In *Honey from a Weed*, she offered a eulogy for this market, which sometime after they left, "in the name of progress," was removed to the town's periphery. The market, near a twelfth-century church, was "ruled by very old ladies" and crowded with pork butchers selling blood sausage, hams, and blocks of *lardo*; there were poultry farmers with guineafowl, quail, and game; and fishmongers located in an alley at the bottom of the market, which "resounded with frenzied shouting." Most alluring to Patience were the vegetables displayed in the heart of the market: small winter artichokes, salsify, and the black roots of *Scorzonera*; spinach, cabbage, and wild chicory; white, green, and purple cauliflowers; and orange winter pumpkins. Retired quarrymen sold bunches of wild herbs gathered on nearby hillsides. There was a shepherd who brought fresh ricotta wrapped in beech or bay leaves down from the mountains to the city. "In those days," Patience wrote, quoting Lady Blessington, "it was still possible to feel that the Carraresi were definitely in touch with the 'earthly paradise.'"[35]

Identifying mushrooms remained a constant throughout her travels. If there were fungi, and there always were, Patience was drawn to them. On a visit to the birthplace of Michelangelo—"a pilgrimage inevitably offering a disappointment," Patience wrote—they stayed at an inn where the evening meal was composed of three different fungi dishes: polenta served with a sauce made from the pared stalks of porcini cooked in veal stock; pork chops topped with the porcini caps, lightly floured and deep-fried; and large orange milk caps (*Lactarius deliciosus*) dressed with olive oil and roasted at high heat in the oven.[36] The following day Patience accompanied the cook and innkeeper on a search for fungi, which resulted in a large jar of *porcini sott'olio* (fungi conserved in oil).[37] A careful observer, Patience was also adept at extracting recipes from complete strangers. One afternoon in the mountains above Carrara, considered some of Tuscany's best mushroom country, she came to a seemingly deserted hamlet.

> *Every ramshackle habitation was shuttered, the stone cobbles of the paths were rank with grass, the church roof had caved in; it was invaded by the stillness of the surrounding mountains. Turning a corner I came upon an open doorway and the stooping form of a very old peasant woman carrying a large curved and blackened frying-pan in which were a heap of fungi.*
>
> *I greeted her and asked how she was going to cook them. 'In the usual way,' she replied reprovingly. She invited me into the kitchen, a space so bare it reminded me of Naxian rooms. All it contained was a small table, two broken chairs and a black cast-iron stove with pipe in the centre of the room, a pile of sawn-up chestnut wood beside it. She began to slice up the boletus heads.*

Only then does Patience come to the recipe:

> *She sliced them fine like tripe, simmered them in oil with garlic, mountain savory, thyme, parsley, seasoned them with salt and black pepper, added a spoonful or two of tomato sauce she had bottled and a little stock from boiling the carcase of a scraggy hen. This was simmered and reduced. When fairly dense, some grated* pecorino *was added—her lunch, eaten with some slices of rough bread.*[38]

It's unclear if Patience joined her, invited or not, but one gets the sense that she did.

Patience called the dish *"Funghi Trippati*, boletus cooked like tripe," and the description illuminates how much her approach to cooking and recipe writing had changed in the years since *Plats du Jour*. It was now her larger experience, and not the many books she'd studied and of course still loved, that informed her outlook. The place, the people, and the methods of preparing a dish were all of equal importance.

The outline of a book based on those experiences, one that would be both a collection of recipes and field guide to the edible plants and weeds of the Mediterranean, was beginning to emerge. Indeed it was in Carrara during the latter years of the decade that she began to revise, expand, and prepare for publication *Honey from a Weed*, which was originally titled *Fasting and Feasting*. In a 1968 letter Patience described it as a book "about the approach to cooking experienced in all the wild places we have been living." Even then she imagined it being much more than just a book of recipes. "I feel I have an experience to communicate," she wrote.[39]

Patience still took great pleasure in the diversity of plant life around her and was always identifying new species, edible or not, and making drawings or sketches of them. In a letter to Olive in early spring 1966, she sent a watercolor of *bocca di lupo*, a medicinal plant belonging to the mint family. The arrival of spring, she wrote, had filled the mountain valleys with purple crocuses, flowering heather, and an abundance of salad plants. "Nature's arrangements!" Patience wrote. "How wonderful. Makes gardening seem like knitting."

❦

That first year in Carrara was highly productive and deeply pleasurable, swinging as Norman put it, "between wine and marble." (Uncle Nello, the retired quarryman who lived next door, devoted a good deal of time to making wine and grappa.) Norman felt, as he often did, that he was on the cusp of a breakthrough with his work. "Visions, possibilities, realities, of all kinds occupy my mind and heart," he wrote.[40] In January 1966 Wijdeveld visited, and they continued to discuss their plans for opening a school or workshop. Patience and Norman had found a nearly perfect rhythm, but they still had no reliable source of income, other than from the Billiardroom, and were largely dependent on others. And though they lived simply, they had numerous expenses: the house and two studio rentals, wages for Norman's assistant, tools and equipment, the Land Rover, often in need of repair or parts, and of course the everyday costs of living, which they kept a detailed log of.

By the autumn of 1966, the Hubrechts' £1,500 was nearly gone, and they were once again searching for support. "I have never needed money like I do now," Norman wrote to his mother. Other than the article she'd published in *Architectural Review* in June 1966, Patience had done little freelance work. She was still trying to sell *Ring Doves and Snakes*—she'd sent the manuscript to Penguin—but to no avail. In late October they received £500 from Carroll Stuchell and another £500 from Muriel, enough to see them through the end of the year, perhaps a bit longer, or at least until they were able to find new patrons. "The wolf is not yet at the door," Patience wrote.[41]

On October 18 Paul Paul died of a massive heart attack. Though he had been unwell for some time and had suffered a heart attack years earlier, his death came as a complete shock to Patience. He was one of the few friends who had shared her wartime experience and knew her past. Indeed he was one of the last links in Patience's life to Thomas Gray—who would die later that same year. "I haven't been able to think of anything but Paul," she wrote to Olive two weeks after his death.[42]

For the last several years of his life, Paul had been mostly living with his lover, cellist Amaryllis Fleming, in Venice. "He lived knowing he was going to die," Patience wrote. "Everything was precious to him."[43] But he'd also kept Diana and Isabella at arm's length. The circumstances of his death were wrenching—he'd been in a coma for two weeks, but Fleming never bothered to notify his family. One night they received a phone call from Venice; it was Paul's doctor calling to give Diana the bad news. Patience, however, refused to see the pain that Diana and Isabella had endured and instead felt Paul and even Amaryllis, for whom she had no great affection, should be forgiven. "Paul is a perfect example of the futility of moral judgments," Patience wrote. "There is just loving and not loving."[44]

Diana, consumed by grief, was completely shattered. Yet Patience showed little sympathy for her. "She was brutal with my mother," says Isabella. "Mom was really hurt by it. Patience didn't think anything of it."[45] Her love for Paul and fierce loyalty to him had perhaps blinded her to the pain he had caused. Her unwillingness to acknowledge Diana's suffering, let alone Isabella's, who was only eighteen at the time, was in some ways reminiscent of her attitude to Olive after Helen's death. At the same time, in her assertion that "there is just loving and not loving," there were echoes of the way Patience viewed reactions to her own predicament of having children out of wedlock in the early 1940s: There were those who stood by her and those who turned her away. Needless to say Paul was one of the few who had embraced her unconditionally.

Thus the announcement that Miranda and Ashlyn were to marry in mid-December was overshadowed by financial worries and Paul's death. Olive had offered Patience £200 to travel to London to help organize the wedding, but Patience said that "unless something extraordinary happens" she wouldn't be going. In a letter to Wolfe, she wrote, "All my maternal-wedding-instincts seem suddenly to have dried up."[46] Instead the money, "a godsend," would be used, as Patience put it, "to properly oil the wheels of this *fait-accompli*." It would not be the first time Patience had missed an important event in Miranda's life—she had not gone to her graduation from the Royal College of Art. Olive went instead. In the end Patience made the gold wedding bands for the bride and groom and a silver collier in the shape of a winged eye of Horus, the ancient Egyptian symbol of protection, for Miranda.

※

On the eve of the wedding, however, Patience turned up in London, to everyone's great surprise. Ashlyn's mother, Eilidh, and stepfather, Peter, along with Miranda, had decided to invite only a small circle of close friends and family. This was partly a matter of necessity as the wedding party was to be held at Patience's small Hampstead flat and Tania, with the help of a friend, was doing all of the cooking—and for this very reason Tania had capped the number of guests at thirty. Several of Ashlyn's uncles and aunts, including Patience's childhood friend Betty, had not been invited. Eilidh was of course Betty's younger sister, but she and Patience were never particularly close. According to Patience, Eilidh was "highly critical of her brilliant sister," and Betty and Eilidh tended to move in different circles.[47] It was clear where Patience's loyalties lay.

Patience and Eilidh had shared a similar fate in having to raise their children alone. Eilidh married John Armour Brown, heir to Brown and Polson flour mills, in 1934 at the age of twenty-one. They had a daughter, Fiona, in 1935; Ashlyn was born three years later in Skelmorlie, a village in North Ayrshire overlooking the Isle of Arran. Tragically, just eight days after Ashlyn's birth, John died of a bacterial infection. Tania had recently completed her term at finishing school in Switzerland and was in fact sent off to look after grieving Eilidh, keep house, do the cooking, and help with the children. Patience, Helen, and Olive visited on at least one occasion, and Patience recalled Eilidh being "wrapped in tragedy." As war broke out Eilidh and the children were sent for safety to California to stay with John's American aunt, returning by ship at some risk about a year before the Armistice.

In 1946 Eilidh married John's younger cousin, Peter Brown, who had once been an admirer of Patience. The following year Eilidh and Peter attended Nick and Miranda's christening at Terwick Chapel, Rogate, and were much-loved godparents. (Patience had wanted Diana and Paul Paul to serve as godparents, but because Paul was Jewish that was out of the question.) In 1951, soon after Patience moved into The Logs, Eilidh lent her a grand piano, and Peter used to stop by occasionally to play and sing. "Eilidh felt a strong sympathy for Patience because for eight years she had also brought up her two children alone," says Miranda.[48]

The night before the wedding, Patience explained why she had at the last minute decided to come. She told Miranda for the first time the painful story of Miranda's sister, Bridget, born ill and given up for adoption only to die a few months later. (Miranda knew she'd had a younger sister but had never heard the full story.) The adoptive parents had asked Patience not to attend the funeral. It was this painful recollection, Patience told Miranda, that had compelled her to come to London; she simply could not face the thought of not being at her daughter's wedding.

But she also took it upon herself to invite a number of her Hampstead friends—Irving Davis, Henri and Daphne Henrion, David and Rosalind Gentleman—as well as Betty and Christoph, among others. This could only have been seen as a rebuke to Eilidh, who indeed had a strained relationship with Betty and had not invited any of her other sisters or Peter's siblings. It must've been an especially bitter pill to swallow as Patience had not been involved in the planning and had done little of the work to prepare for the event. Ashlyn recalled that with the addition of Patience's friends there were probably more like seventy or eighty people at the party instead of thirty.

The wedding took place on December 17 at the Rosslyn Hill Unitarian Chapel in Hampstead. Candles on painted broomsticks lit up the aisles of the church. Friends supplied the music, and Nick "gave away" his sister. Irving, who was now in his late seventies and rather frail, offered Miranda a sixteenth-century angel from the Neapolitan *presepio* (nativity scene). Darkness had fallen, and it was gently snowing as they made their way back from the church to the Billiardroom, overflowing with guests.

According to Patience "the wedding was a triumph of affection over organisation."[49]

❦❦❦❦

Days after she returned to Carrara, Patience received a scathing letter from Peter—Patience called it "a Scots letter"—in which he described her behavior as "willful, arrogant, and selfish." He explained that they had been asked not to invite anyone beyond a very small circle of family and friends and pointed out that Patience herself had not been expected. Thus the fact that she had invited so many of her Hampstead friends was interpreted as a slap in the face. He also accused Patience of showing almost no interest in Miranda's new family and could hardly forgive her for introducing him to one of her friends as the person who "paid for the drinks." "You have gone as far as I will allow in discourtesy" and "never again will I allow myself and my family to be subjected to such slights," he wrote.[50] He implored her to write letters of apology to various family members who had not been invited and felt spurned, which Patience eventually did.

But that did not settle the matter. A few weeks later another letter arrived from Eilidh, who said that she'd hoped the wedding would "draw our two families together." Not only had Patience invited half of Hampstead, Eilidh said, but she had also failed to introduce her to anyone. "I couldn't have felt more alone on a desert island," she wrote. She went further and even suggested that all of Patience's friends had heard the story of Violet's rejection of Patience, in late 1940, when she was pregnant with Nick. "Well Patience now you have had your revenge on my mother," she wrote, "a hundredfold and publicly."[51] In a subsequent letter, she included Patience's reply, torn into a dozen or so pieces.

In that letter, Patience had apologized for making them unhappy but quickly defended herself by pointing out that Miranda and Ashlyn married each other, not the entire Barnardo-Brown clan. "We are individuals," she wrote, "and you are the members of a clan. This is the root of our misunderstandings." She also accused them of being preoccupied with convention and unable to live in the present. She dismissed Eilidh's notion that it was out of some deep-seated desire to avenge what Violet had done all those years before that she had behaved as she did. "In fact, I was grateful to her," Patience wrote, referring to Violet, "because cutting me off like that helped me to discover in life the true feelings from the false."[52]

There was something almost operatic about the whole affair—Patience's seemingly inexplicable decision at first not to go to her daughter's wedding; showing up two days before the event; and then inviting so many of her own friends to the party. She had done none of the work but had seemingly stolen the show and must have known that inviting Betty could only be interpreted as a snub to Eilidh. "She could be like a tidal wave, the seventh wave, breaking on the shore," says Miranda.[53] Still the reaction clearly rattled Patience. She wrote letters of apology to each of Ashlyn's aunts who had not been invited to the wedding. Years later she acknowledged that she had suddenly wanted to do things her way and "behaved shockingly." The whole episode overlapped with news that Thomas Gray had died on Christmas Day 1966 just eight days after the wedding. Patience received a letter from Milner, written in his "beautifully calligraphic" script, to inform her.[54]

Meanwhile Norman was in Paris trying to arrange a show with Henriette Gomes, which never came to pass, and Patience was leading what she described as a "dissolute life," hardly working or even getting out of bed. Eventually she sent all of the wedding correspondence to Nick—she needed one solitary witness, she said—but told him to burn it all if he liked.

The fracas over the wedding had hardly subsided when news came that Irving Davis had died. Patience had seen him recently in London and sensed that he was nearing the end. "He has already in life assumed the posture of the Cycladean dead," Patience wrote just a few weeks before his death on May 1, 1967. Still she could not bring herself to tell Norman for several days. Though she had known Irving for less than ten years, he'd assumed an outsize role in her life. She often described him as a mythical figure, a key to that lost world of writers and artists—D. H. Lawrence, Norman Douglas, Max Beerbohm, and others—and for whom Italy had been a loving obsession. They wrote frequent letters—Patience, a prolific letter writer, said he was the only person she'd had a real correspondence with—and they shared innumerable meals. "It is very peculiar these attachments to such an extraordinary person, a very particular anchor, vanished," Patience wrote to Ariane.[55]

Always generous, Irving over the years had given Patience a sixteenth-century engraving by Diana Mantovana, a signed first-edition copy of *Les Secrets de la Cuisine Comtoise* by Pierre Dupin (a 1927 classic of French cookery writing), and an old kilim rug. But perhaps most significant was the tiny black notebook containing the recipes he'd recorded at El Vendrell and a copy of his unfinished memoir. It did not take long for Patience to float the idea of publishing a cookbook based on the recipes Irving had collected, which she hoped would be a "memorial for all the surviving bibliophiles."[56] It would prove to be a formidable undertaking. The script was nearly illegible, and Irving had left much unexplained. Cooking techniques were often glossed over. The particular kind of pan or dish used to make something was sometimes omitted. Mushrooms went unidentified. As Patience noted not long after his death, the book was "unpublishable in its present state."[57]

Beyond the many difficulties of elucidating Irving's notes, the recipes were not easy to execute and some of the ingredients would have been hard to obtain at the time. Hence the title: *A Catalan Cookery Book: A Collection of Impossible Recipes*. Irving thought the preservation of the recipes more important than the practicality of actually preparing them. "This little book," Patience wrote in the introduction, "is not so much a collection of culinary admonitions as the distilled essence of a fast vanishing way of life," a sentiment she echoed in *Honey from a Weed*.

The project took much longer than Patience hoped—the book wasn't published until 1969, at which point she had already started to work on *Honey from a Weed*. Aside from including several of Irving's recipes in her book, they shared a number of overlapping themes: foremost among them was the idea that they were recording recipes rooted in a way of life that was on the verge of disappearing. In *Honey from a Weed*, Patience likened the endeavor to that of a musicologist who records old songs. It was an apt analogy: Just a few years before she and Irving took their trip to Lecce in 1958, American ethnomusicologist Alan Lomax and the Italian anthropologist Diego Carpitella had traveled through the south of Italy, including Puglia, recording folk songs. They started out in Martano, not far from Santa Maria di Leuca, and traveled north, documenting the songs of agricultural workers, shepherds, and peasants. In the text accompanying the recordings Lomax wrote, "It was a mythic time. None of us suspected that that world—made of music, songs, poverty, joy, desperation, custom, violence, injustice, love, dialect, and poetry, formed over the course of millennia—would be swept away in a couple of years . . . by the voodoo of 'progress.'"[58]

By the time Patience started writing *Honey from a Weed* and the Catalan book was published, the "mythic" world Lomax referred to had been indelibly altered by the effects of tourism, industrial development, and the flight of the rural population from the countryside to the city. In many ways, as Patience and Norman saw it, Carrara had already succumbed to the "voodoo of progress." Mechanization was rapidly displacing the quarry workers' centuries-old way of life. The international art market had taken center stage and cultural tourism was being touted as the city's salvation. Before long the old marketplace in the center of town would be moved to the margins and housed in a nondescript modern building.

Patience and Irving's critique, their lament, was by no means a new one. Indeed it was almost synonymous with British travel writing on Italy, and had perhaps reached its high-water mark with D. H. Lawrence's *Twilight in Italy*, which was published in 1916. Based on nearly seven months spent in Gargnano on Lake Garda in 1912, the book, whose title alludes to the coming end of a peasant-based economy and everything that flowed from that, offers a scathing indictment of "the new order," which, Lawrence wrote, "means sorrow for the Italian more ever than it has meant for us."[59] Even if it wasn't a particularly novel observation, Patience and Norman had witnessed their own version of this familiar story as it played out in the 1960s. Moreover they were beginning to feel that Carrara was too close to London—a city they found themselves returning to more often than they would have liked. It is perhaps not surprising then that they were beginning to entertain the possibility of settling in a far more remote place, where they could live a kind of "Greek life" as they had on Naxos. What did they have in mind? As Patience put it in 1968, "We now feel like acquiring a cave and living in it."[60]

CHAPTER TEN

Fin du Monde

In June 1967, just a couple of weeks before the opening of the Biennale, which featured five of Norman's sculptures—"a haven in an otherwise pornographic show," as Patience acidly noted—they set out for the south of France looking for somewhere they could consider settling.[1] They decided to leave La Barozza at least temporarily for a few months that winter—lack of heating and its out of the way location made it virtually uninhabitable—which in part prompted the decision to begin looking beyond Carrara. Through friends, they'd been put in touch with the artists Sven Blomberg and his wife, Romaine Lorquet, who lived outside Lacoste in the Vaucluse. Patience was immediately drawn to Romaine's discreet limestone carvings scattered about the landscape, and to her approach to art in general. She had worked for years in near total obscurity and had little interest in what Patience called the "exhibition racket." Indeed she and Sven had fled Paris sometime in the mid 1950s to live quietly in their farmhouse in Provence. In an essay on Romaine's carvings, John Berger, with whom Sven collaborated on his seminal book *Ways of Seeing*, wrote that Romaine had refused to "place her work in any kind of contemporary artistic or cultural context.... She has simply chosen to remain outside."[2]

It was a choice that Norman and Patience were now grappling with—whether to remain within the more conventional art world circuit, forever pursuing gallery shows and exhibitions, or to strike out on their own in pursuit of a different kind of life. The experience of applying to exhibit in the Biennale had been dispiriting, and in letters Patience referred to the "art snobs of Carrara," who she declared were intent on keeping Norman out. According to her it was only by popular demand and the intervention of a leading communist that Norman's work had finally been admitted.

Thus Sven and Romaine's lifestyle, far removed from the petty backbiting of the art world, was appealing. Patience and Norman spent their days scouring the countryside looking at abandoned farms, old mills, and ruined villas, most of which were far too expensive. Leaving Lacoste they made their way to the limestone region above Montpellier in the Aveyron, to visit Hervé Vernhes, a "shepherd sculptor," and a colony of his disciples, but neither the artist nor his followers seem to have made much of an impression. However, to get back for the Biennale, they cut their trip short, "leaving everything one great question mark."[3] Indeed the questions were many, and after five years living in various parts of the Mediterranean, they were no closer to finding that ideal place to live and work. Sven and Romaine's way of life was in line with what they wanted, but what Provence had to offer seemed too tame to them and beyond what they could afford.

A chance meeting with another artist couple proved to be of far greater consequence. Sometime in the autumn of 1966, the sculptor Helen Ashbee and her partner, painter Arno Mandello, appeared in Carrara. They lived most of the year in Paris but had a house in Ronchi, the seaside resort of Massa. Helen, daughter of architect and designer C. R. Ashbee, had inherited the house in Ronchi from her late husband, the Italian painter Francesco Christofanetti.

Helen and Arno had lived in Paris for many years, but by the late 1960s they were intent on leaving and buying a house and land in southern Italy. As early as 1966 Helen and Arno had discussed their hope of establishing a workshop for artists in Puglia, an idea that naturally appealed to Norman. Helen had long envisioned recreating something similar to her father's Guild of Handicraft, one of several late-nineteenth-century experiments in communal living that combined traditional craftwork— jewelry, furniture making, and bookbinding—with a utopian worldview. Influenced by Ruskin, William Morris, and Edward Carpenter, C. R. Ashbee's Guild grew out of a series of lectures he gave, beginning in 1888, to students in Whitechapel, where the project was based for several years. But by the turn of the century, the back-to-the-land movement was gaining strength, and Ashbee, one of its better-known adherents, relocated the Guild from Whitechapel—a poor, overcrowded neighborhood in East London—to Chipping Campden. The Guild would become most closely associated with this small market town where Helen, one of Ashbee's four daughters, was born in 1915.

By then the Guild had folded, and Helen spent most of her childhood on a large country estate in Kent that belonged to her mother, Janet Forbes. There was a brief interlude, from 1919 to 1922, when the family lived in Jerusalem, where Ashbee had been appointed civic adviser to the Mandate Government of Palestine. Ashbee was a formidable figure, well known in Europe and America, where he often lectured, and one of the chief proponents of the Arts and Crafts movement. As a father he was somewhat remote—it was no secret that he'd always wanted a son—and by the time the family returned to Kent in 1923, he had largely withdrawn from the vibrant intellectual world he'd once been at the center of. He entered into "an early and uncharacteristic retirement," according to his biographer, and enjoyed reading to his daughters aloud from Morris's *Earthly Paradise*.[4]

In Kent Helen attended an English girls school, after which she studied abroad in Germany, and then enrolled at the Royal College of Music in London, where she studied viola and piano. But she found her form as a visual artist and with Christofanetti divided her time between Paris and Carrara. (They also lived briefly in New York City.) After Christofanetti's untimely death in 1951, she took up sculpture and jewelry making. Her meeting with sculptor Alberto Giacometti, who lived not far from her Paris studio, was decisive. Indeed Helen's sinewy, abstract sculptures bear traces of Giacometti's signature style. In the mid 1950s she met Arno, a German Jew—his given name was Grünebaum—who had fled first to France and then Uruguay during the war with his then-wife, the photographer Jeannette Mandello. (When Arno and Jeannette separated in 1954, they both returned to Paris.)

Helen was only four when the family left for Jerusalem, but the Guild and its legacy featured prominently in the children's lives. According to her sister Felicity, Helen had long hoped to recreate the Guild's spirited artistic and intellectual atmosphere: to bring together a group of artists, writers, artisans, and agriculturalists with the aim of building a "small interdependent 'community.'"[5] She and Arno decided on the southern tip of Puglia, a remote and arid predominately olive-growing region where property and land were remarkably cheap. On the surface, at least, Helen and Arno's vision was not unlike Norman's. Over the years he had many conversations with Wijdeveld about setting up a workshop or communal studio that in some ways resembled a nineteenth-century guild. In fact Wijdeveld owned a small plot of land in southern France near Cavalière that Patience and Norman had visited the previous summer (along with the quarries of Beziers), but they concluded, "Only millionaires could make something of it."[6] They did, however, stay in Mèze, a small fishing village and center of oyster cultivation on the Étang de Thau, "full of idle busyness," which reminded Patience of Locmariaquer, the Breton port she'd visited with the children in the early 1950s. "I know that places have been abolished," she wrote, "but this is a place."[7]

Nearing eighty-five, Wijdeveld still imagined leaving Holland, where he felt his work was no longer honored, escaping the "chaos of our time," and fulfilling the "hermit dream" that he and Norman shared.[8] However Norman and Patience were ambivalent about attaching themselves to any kind of community or group of artists—Patience even more so than Norman. Patience later said in an interview that she "could never bear belonging to any group or society."[9] They shared the impulse to flee urban life—as did many in the years following the upheavals of May 1968 in France, including Helen and Arno—to be closer to the land, to grow their own food, and to focus on their art, but they had no fixed idea of what form such a life might take. What Norman had in mind was more akin to monastic life punctuated by periodic visits from other artists and crafts-people: a "hermit dream" rather than an "interdependent community." Patience thought she might start her own herb business, selling wild plants gathered from the countryside, and write books. But they were beginning to realize that if they wanted such a life, they would have to lead by example. "Suddenly we see that we have to do this ourselves first," Patience wrote to Olive. "Then other people may turn up and share it. It is not a community of artists, it is an attempt to establish a more realistic way of life."[10]

❦❦❦❦

In early November 1967, after the *vendemmia*, the grape harvest, they left Carrara for London, stopping on the way to look at properties once again in the Vaucluse, then near Nîmes, and finally in the Ardèche. They kept their studios, where they stored most of their things, but were not certain when they'd return. They now viewed Carrara as more of a summer workshop, a kind of way station as they continued their search for a place to live. Their plan was to spend yet another winter in The Logs, which Norman declared would be a "hive of activity." Patience was working on the Catalan cookbook, which presented numerous challenges, from the decoding of the text itself and the complexity of recipes to the financing and publication. Patience was in discussion with Lucien Scheler, Irving's friend, who had agreed to publish the volume. Scheler, a book collector and authority on the surrealist poet Paul Éluard, had worked at the publishing house Gallimard in the 1950s and 1960s but also printed his own limited-edition books. Nicole Fenosa had offered to do a series of etchings that would accompany the recipes, but reproducing these was proving to be very expensive. Patience also had to consult Ianthe Carswell, Irving's stepdaughter, who had agreed to help finance the project. "It was really Patience who put it together in the end," said Harriet Wilson, Ianthe's daughter.[11] Ianthe would also give Patience permission to use many of Irving's recipes in *Honey from a Weed* since the Catalan book was designed to be more of a collector's item than a working cookbook. "It will be the kind of book you couldn't possibly take into the kitchen as it would immediately get an oil mark on its swanlike pages," Patience wrote.[12]

Patience took an obsessive interest in every aspect of the book's production, from the kind of paper it was printed on ("French printers really are better than English ones," she wrote, adding, "French paper has always been rougher and more suitable") to the functionality and soundness of the recipes.[13] Of course Patience had spent time in El Vendrell and was familiar with many of the dishes that Irving described. Moreover she understood what made a recipe work—why using a tin or aluminum baking dish instead of a copper or earthenware one to make *bacallà a la llauna* (baked salt cod), for example, would be disastrous. She had seen Anita, the Fenosas' housekeeper and cook, make this dish every week using an earthenware *llauna*, which Patience described as a shallow, slightly curved pan "glazed inside and not out." The confusion arose from the fact that in Catalan *llauna* can refer to both tin and the kind of pan described above. That winter she proceeded to test most of the recipes— there were more than forty in the final version—that she culled from

Irving's notebooks. Section headings ranged from soups and omelets to snails and seafood, with forays into paella and game. There were recipes for rabbit with snails and chocolate sauce, calf's head, tripe, partridge, and many variations of salt cod. "It seems we are all being tormented by Irving's innate frivolity," Patience wrote to Ariane. "I mean one would have to cook every recipe to find out what really happens in the oven."[14] Some of the recipes were unintelligible, ingredients that were listed early on sometimes vanished without explanation; and fungi went unidentified. Irving had of course done the important and often painstaking work of recording the recipes, but he had not turned them into usable instructions. This fell to Patience, who observed that nearly everything they ate that winter had almonds or pine nuts in it, one of the staples of Catalan cuisine being the *picada*, a fine paste made from pine nuts or blanched almonds, garlic, parsley, and olive oil. This mixture, a Catalan roux, which sometimes incorporates whole peppercorns, bread soaked in milk or vinegar, roasted chili peppers, or bitter chocolate, is often added to dishes at the very end of cooking to thicken the sauce and elevate the flavors.

The book's final recipe, and one that Patience reprinted verbatim in *Honey from a Weed*, is the feast of the three fishermen of Calafell, which Irving called the "meal to end all meals." It was a three-course affair, and one that took the better part of a day to prepare, featuring several varieties of local fish, including scorpionfish, corb, stargazer, annular seabream, and weever, as well as rice, octopus, and plenty of *allioli*—a Catalan version made without using egg yolks, only garlic, olive oil, and a touch of vinegar. The first course, fishermen's *romesco*, is a kind of Catalan fish stew made with generous amounts of garlic and chili peppers; the second course, *arrossejat*, is rice cooked in the remaining fish broth to which a spoonful of *allioli* is added; the meal concludes with white octopus cooked in a *sofregit* of onions and tomatoes. Needless to say everything is washed down with "*porró* after *porró*" of local wine. After listing the ingredients for the feast, Irving, rather than adapting the recipe for his home audience, if he even had one in mind, provides the following instructions: "First of all take a plane to Barcelona, then drive to Calafell, then find your fishermen and go with them about four o'clock to Villanova and get them to choose the fish as it is landed. . . ."[15] Patience had the good fortune to experience the feast, which took the fishermen hours of "inspired labour," on two occasions.

A measure of how much the culinary landscape had changed in London by the late 1960s was the fact that many of the ingredients called for in Irving's book could be bought at specialty shops. In the introduction to the first Penguin edition of *Italian Food*, published in 1963, Elizabeth David referred to the emergence of "enterprising delicatessens" and "enlightened greengrocers" where all kinds of previously unobtainable ingredients could now be found.[16] Even mainstream supermarkets were beginning to carry some specialty goods. The austerity of the postwar period—after all *Plats du Jour* with its emphasis on economy and willingness to use substitutions when necessary had been published just ten years earlier—had given way to a proliferation of shops and markets carrying all manner of imported produce. Claudia Roden's *A Book of Middle Eastern Food* was published in 1968 and Madhur Jaffrey's first cookbook, *An Invitation to Indian Cooking*, five years later, suggesting that ingredients once difficult to obtain were more and more common. At the same time the audience and market for cookbooks had grown.

Although Patience knew the Catalan book would likely be read by a very small number of people, mostly friends and bibliophiles, she was intent on the recipes being absolutely beyond reproach. Plus Irving, ever the perfectionist, would have settled for nothing less. "I so wish I could have cooked the things for Irving and he could have come along and criticized," Patience wrote.[17]

In Irving's absence she cooked for Wolfe, who drifted in and out of their lives with some regularity and in fact stayed with them for part of the time they were in London that winter. Wolfe had a seemingly insatiable appetite and was much more of an indulgent eater than Patience. He once sent her a copy of A. J. Liebling's *Between Meals*, the *New Yorker* correspondent's classic account of eating in Paris in the 1930s. "Naturally it reminded me very much of you," Patience wrote.[18] But Wolfe was also an exacting cook and critic in his own right. Living in Paris he frequently visited early-morning markets in search of fish or game and consulted neighbors or habitués of the local bar on how to prepare these delicacies. He was one of the very few people Patience trusted to read her work and whose criticism she took to heart. Indeed though it was never entirely clear what Wolfe was doing with his life—his career as a musician seems to have fizzled out by this point—he had always wanted to write a cookbook. Only thirty years old in 1968, he was apparently already writing his autobiography "which consists of recipes interspersed with philosophical remarks."[19] Other than opera, food was his great passion, and his visits, which were often marked by gastronomic and bibulous excess, were memorably exhausting. "Where Wolfe is, it suddenly becomes a restaurant," Patience wrote sometime in 1968 after listing the meals they'd eaten (and that she'd inevitably prepared)—asparagus with aïoli, rabbit with aïoli, pigeon mullet with aïoli, wild strawberries, *tagliatelli alla panna*. "It is almost like Irving, food is the great event in his life. And the great emotional problem is, 'Is there going to be enough wine?'"[20]

The Catalan book was finally published in 1969, edited and with an introduction by Patience. (A paperback edition including Irving's unfinished memoir, which he had given to Patience, was eventually published by Prospect Books in 1999.) In the introduction Patience took aim at the "emphasis placed on gargantuan repasts" featured in so many new cookbooks and the trend in publishing that favored "enormous tomes stuffed with spectacular color photographs." As a result, she argued, the more traditional approach to cooking, embodied in Irving Davis's book, had all but vanished. Indeed, since the appearance of *Plats du Jour*, cookbook publishing had become a far more lucrative business. New books reflected not only changing tastes—greater access to convenience and luxury foods—but also the ascendance of the personality and image of the chef or writer as the main draw. At the same time, by the end of the 1950s, photography had become reasonably affordable and would start to replace entirely the kind of illustrations that had furnished the pages of *Plats du Jour* and Elizabeth David's early books. Robert Carrier, an American journalist with no background in food or cooking, who moved to England in the early 1950s, became famous for his lavish full-color spreads in the *Sunday Times*, which were turned into a book, *Great Dishes of the World*, published in 1963. (His first book had been a box of cooking cards.) In 1960 Paul Hamlyn published *Cookery in Color*, edited by Marguerite Patten, a "picture encyclopedia" with sections on pressure-cooking and television snacks and sandwiches. The recipes were accompanied by double-page spreads of full-color photographs. It sold two million copies. By the mid 1960s Carrier was the highest-paid food writer in England.[21]

It wasn't long before recipes came to be presented as secondary, largely functional blocks of text or a list of instructional steps. Patience always privileged drawings over photographs, whether in field guides or cookbooks, but she wasn't the only one to decry the end of what proved to be a rather brief golden age of cookbook publishing and illustration. When Penguin reissued *Mediterranean Food* in 1963 as part of a new series of handbooks, Elizabeth David wrote a scathing three-page letter to Eunice Frost after learning that John Minton's original cover had been replaced by what she called a "truly terrible, vulgar and inept color photograph."[22]

There is, however, a certain paradox in a book like Irving's, devoted to such humble fare, being printed in a limited edition of 165 copies on sumptuous paper with a series of eleven engravings enclosed in their own soft paper wrappers. The whole thing was presented in a folder-box made of pale green linen with crimson lettering on the spine. "It had transformed from a useful little notebook into this thing which was an artistic enterprise," recalled Harriet Wilson.[23] Patience was well aware of the fact that it was not the kind of book you'd take into the kitchen. It was truly a testament to its author, who had devoted most of his life to the pursuit of rare books. It was also a reflection of Patience's varied background—her interest in design, making books, and food—as well as her strong aesthetic sense. There were no color photographs, to be sure, but the book was more of an *objet d'art* than a cooking manual, in some ways the exact opposite of what *Plats du Jour* had been.

Still it was a serious cookbook at a time when Catalan cuisine had received scant attention from British or American food writers. In fact Irving's book was the first English-language Catalan cookbook of its kind.[24] Elizabeth David's books on Mediterranean food had barely touched on the region, though there were a few recipes from French Catalonia. As late as 1988 one of the few authoritative books on the subject, Colman Andrews's *Catalan Cuisine*, still referred to the region's food as "Europe's last great culinary secret." Despite its rather formidable appearance, Irving's book, largely due to Patience's efforts, did not go unnoticed. A young Jeremiah Tower, one of the early chefs at Alice Waters's Chez Panisse, was drawn to its treatment of traditional Catalan foods, especially snails.[25] "In the early seventies," Tower writes in his memoir, "people thought I was mad for pushing this food and this book."[26]

The winter months in London had been tempered by Wolfe's presence and Patience's singular devotion to Irving's Catalan cookbook. Although Patience had now been on the margins of the food-writing world for some time, she still took an interest in what was being published. She urged her friend Ariane Castaing to push ahead with her idea of translating and bringing up to date J. B. Reboul's 1897 classic *La Cuisinière Provençale*, a compilation of more than one thousand recipes and hundreds of menus from his days as a chef at the Hotel du Luxembourg in Marseille. Patience knew the book well. In *Plats du Jour* she and Primrose cited Reboul and Austin de Croze's *What to Eat and Drink in France* as sources of inspiration. They wrote that *La Cuisinière Provençale* was "an object lesson in the art of setting down meticulous directions." Thus Patience saw the value in translating the book but warned that it would have to be updated for the modern cook and household. "I think all these great 19th century cooks were pioneers of new ways—scrapping the *mode ancienne*—and you have to do this again," she wrote.[27]

She also wondered, half jokingly, if Elizabeth David wasn't already doing something similar. "I mean she must be running out of things to do," Patience wrote.[28] Evidently Patience had been studying David's books closely. In her letter to Ariane, she criticized David for being less than precise with certain species of crustaceans and felt she was too steeped in culinary literature rather than the "raw materials" of cooking. "She thinks *datteri* are tiny little datelike shellfish, in fact they are often very large," Patience wrote. "Mistakes are always perpetuated through the centuries by one work referring to another. They look at the published word, not at life."[29] David had included a recipe for "*Datteri di Mare*" in *Italian Food* and referred to them as "curious little shellfish, shaped like a date stone." In fact they are somewhat elongated, and in *Honey from a Weed*, Patience described them as having "a cursory resemblance to very large dates." More importantly, though, Patience was highlighting a distinction between her own approach to cooking, increasingly based on her travels and direct experience, and David's more scholarly approach. This critique was not entirely fair. Nearly all of David's early work was based on her time in Italy and France. But it is true that her later work, especially after 1970, took a more scholarly turn.

When they returned to Carrara in spring 1968, Patience was considering the possibility of turning her experience into a book of her own. Not long after they had settled back into La Barozza, however, Patience discovered she was pregnant. Norman had always wanted children and often wondered what had kept him from having a large family like so many of his Dutch friends and acquaintances. He and Ursula, who was fourteen years older than he was, had been unable to have children. And by the time Norman met Patience in 1958, Nicolas and Miranda were grown up and Patience had little interest in starting a new family. But after nearly a decade together, they were clearly open to the possibility of having a child. On the verge of a new chapter in their lives, though, the prospect raised a whole host of questions. Would they raise the child in England or somewhere in Italy or France? Would they be able to live and work as they had done? And would they be able to fulfill their dream of establishing a "more realistic life" with a child in tow? At the age of fifty and having had three children, Patience was not unaware of the potential difficulties. In a letter to Ariane, she wrote, "I am living in hope, but it sometimes seems too much in the nature of the miraculous. I shall be the child's grandmother as well as its mother."[30] In a letter to his mother, Norman wrote that the news had "simplified things" and that they were "considering all possibilities and openings," though he did not elaborate on what those were.[31] They wanted the child very much and seemed to be willing to make whatever adjustments would be necessary in bringing it up.

La Barozza, however, with its steep hill and primitive conditions was no longer a suitable place to stay. They needed to be somewhere that was easier to get to and closer to a doctor. Helen and Arno offered to put them up—Patience said she'd been "outlawed"—at their villa in the "flatlands" of Ronchi, a few hundred meters from the sea and about a seven-mile drive from Carrara. Norman commuted every day to his studio and returned in the evening. It was in a letter from Ronchi that Patience first mentioned what would become *Honey from a Weed*. "I am embarked on the cookery book because I think this is probably the one way I can earn some money," she wrote to Olive on July 21, 1968. "I should be able to get it published," she added, confidently. But they were at Ronchi just a couple of weeks when Patience suffered a miscarriage. Even if it did not come as a great surprise—Patience understood fully the risks and complications of carrying a pregnancy at her age—it was a profound disappointment. "Norman had been so happy," Patience wrote. "It was a cruel blow."[32]

Even before the miscarriage they had discussed taking a trip to Puglia with Helen and Arno later that year, suggesting that they did not intend to alter their way of life in any significant way if they had a child. Of course there's no way of knowing how the pregnancy would have colored their impressions of Puglia, comparable only with Naxos in its remoteness. Perhaps it would have seemed a bit too far off the beaten track, too far from family and friends. Or perhaps they would have seen it as precisely the kind of place where they could both raise a child and establish a "way of living that is possible for a working artist."[33]

Indeed they continued to work, the one constant in their lives. In mid-August both Patience and Helen exhibited several pieces in what was billed as Carrara's "first international Biennale of artistic jewelry." An article in the local paper described Patience as a well-known journalist who works "directly" in silver to create earrings, rings, and bracelets that are "original and elegant."[34] The exhibition was held in the lobby of the Michelangelo, Carrara's upscale four-star hotel. Meanwhile Norman was hoping to negotiate a show in New York for the following spring or summer with the help of their friend Jean Delpech, who worked as assistant to Daniel Cordier, co-owner of the Cordier and Ekstrom galleries in Paris and Manhattan. Before their departure, though, signs of strain with Helen and Arno were already beginning to surface. Helen and Arno assumed that they would all travel together in their small car, which Norman wrote "shows up a difference of attitude which I'm afraid may easily become too important to ignore as we proceed."[35] Indeed Helen and Arno were much more committed to settling in Puglia to establish a commune or guild and by the end of the summer would sell their Paris studio and home in Ronchi. They imagined other artists and friends, many of them associated with sculptor Jacques Lipchitz's studio in Pietrasanta or with their life in Paris, coming to join them.

For Patience and Norman, Helen and Arno had already made too many firm decisions. "Their idea of what is going to happen," Norman wrote, "the land we are going to acquire, the buildings we will need to erect, the way we are going to provide for water and electricity, what we are going to grow and possibly live on, the company we are going to attract, the interest we are going to awaken in the cities at the other end of the Autostrada del Sole . . . their idea, I say, has already been formed before we have even set eyes on anything or even know what we feel about the place at all."[36] Indeed on the eve of their departure Patience and Norman were far from certain that they would settle in Puglia; it was just one of many places they were considering.

Nonetheless on September 25 they set out for the far reaches of Puglia, more than 650 miles from Carrara, Patience and Norman in the Land Rover and Helen and Arno in their tiny red Simca. "Dreams or not," Patience wrote to Olive, "we are going to look."[37]

⥷⥷⥷⥷

They spent two weeks in the Salento, the jagged peninsula that forms the heel of Italy's boot, camping along the beaches and touring the "Neolithic" countryside. Indeed the landscape, relentlessly flat and dominated by ancient olive groves and pale blue seas in every direction, was spellbinding. Patience had trouble putting into words the feelings it evoked in her. (She had traveled to part of Puglia before with Irving but had not ventured south of Lecce, the province's largest city.) It was both bracing and somewhat terrifying. In her eyes it seemed to strip away everything incidental and lay bare what really mattered. Helen said that the "olive-studded, rocky landscape and blue skies" reminded her of her childhood in Palestine.[38] In an unpublished essay Patience described Puglia as "an image of wilderness," not only in the sense that it was relatively untouched but that it was somehow impenetrable and unknowable. In a letter to Ariane, she said it was like seeing the world "before there was a single human being on it." She added, "Of course I can't explain. Anyway it is a bare and desolate place where nothing earthly really matters."[39]

Of course they had gone to look at property and were dealing with the very earthly task of buying a house or farm. On the Ionian coast they found what Patience described as a "ruined farm"—"it was just like Greece," she wrote, "a fortress built on rock, and covered with aspho-del"—which they nearly rented for a year before discovering that they would have had to share it with "beasts and people."[40] Many of the old farmhouses, the *masserie*, though somewhat abandoned were still used by farmers, peasants, and shepherds who sometimes smoked their cheeses in the vaulted rooms or simply used them for shelter. Other buildings, which looked promising from afar, turned out to be nothing more than "palatial cow stalls." "We longed to acquire a few stone huts and an almond orchard," Patience wrote. "But everyone offered us hectares of olives and agricultural responsibilities!"[41]

The dazzling landscape was complemented by the glorious autumn weather. Temperatures were in the mid 60s and the air bone-dry. The sea was still warm enough for swimming. Norman, who succumbed easily to colds and the flu, found the climate favorable compared to the frequent cold and damp of Carrara. They camped on the beaches, sleeping in the back of the lorry. Patience gathered what she called "small narcissus bulbs," in fact a sea daffodil growing on the dunes, that she later sent to Olive. She made note of a "delicious salad weed called *rugola*" (rocket), which she described as "a sort of wild mustardy dwarf cabbage." She collected herbs everywhere and had her first real taste of the macchia, the dense scrubland that defines so much of the coastal Mediterranean. It was a completely foreign landscape in many ways—fantastically diverse—with a profusion of wild herbs, edible plants, and dwarf trees. Her only point of reference was Greece, and of course Puglia was part of that swathe of southern Italy colonized by the Greeks in the eighth and seventh centuries BCE, which Ovid referred to as *Magna Graecia*, Greater Greece.

Puglia had a far greater impact on Patience and Norman than any other place they'd seen since leaving Naxos. Moreover there was a good deal of inexpensive property and land available on offer. However they were no closer to making a decision when they made their way back to Carrara in mid-October. They returned via Agropoli, where Patience had stayed with Irving all those years ago, and Rome, where Norman had to retrieve a couple of carvings. One week later, back in Carrara, bronzed and rejuvenated, Patience wrote, "Puglia is a very intoxicating place but probably altogether too remote to settle in. It really is the *fin du monde*."[42]

⋘⋖⋇⁕

Though Patience said very little about what she simply referred to as her "cookery book," it was beginning to take shape. It was going to be different from everything she'd previously worked on, with the exception of Irving's Catalan cookbook. In the manual for the Blue Funnel Line, she'd included a few recipes from her Mediterranean travels, but this new book would be drawn entirely from her own experience, which, in the realm of cookery, she was gradually beginning to privilege over knowledge gleaned from culinary literature. For her birthday Olive had sent her a book by Sir Peter Quennell, the poet and historian who had written several volumes on Byron as well as a book on Edward Lear in southern Italy. Patience described Quennell as "an old literary spinster" who "lived very much at second hand." By contrast her book, far more passionate than anything Quennell ever wrote (he had published dozens of books), would be based on "first hand experience."

At the same time she was becoming increasingly interested in the ecology of wild plants and flowers, far more so than in garden varieties. This was not just a culinary preference. Patience found certain patterns in nature—the ochre-colored spiral of a snail's shell or the delicate leaves of a maidenhair fern—both illuminating and somehow instructive, an idea she'd first explored with Peter Shepheard and in her textile designs for Alastair Morton. Many of her jewelry designs were also based on patterns found in nature or natural forms employed in ancient Egyptian and Greek art. For Patience the contrast between nature and horticultural art was heightened by the fact that they were now staying with friends, sculptor Michael Noble and his wife, Ida Borletti, who kept what Patience felt was an overly manicured villa, Idania, with its garden on Lake Garda. Designed by a botanist from Kew, the extensive park combined English and Italian styles with sweeping lawns, elaborate rock gardens, and a floral staircase. Patience said it was regularly visited by English horticultural societies, and described it as "a perfect example of *Il Troppo Bello*." In a letter to Olive, she wrote, "Idania had lawns like billiard tables, emerald green, gardeners to water them, and shrubs and rock plants. Ugh!"[43] She said she was interested in gardening only if it involved "growing things to eat," even though at this point she and Norman were not doing any of their own vegetable gardening.

Norman had met Michael Noble in Carrara, and in need of temporary quarters for another winter, they were offered the use of a small house, studio, and workshop on Lake Garda for a few months. Muriel, Norman's mother, would join them for part of the time, staying in a nearby house that belonged to Noble's mother. Noble was Scottish and had studied under Frank Dobson (who was known for his pioneering work as a direct carver) at the Royal College of Art in the late 1940s. During the war he had been stationed in Italy and returned there in 1951, first living in Venice and then on Lake Garda with Ida, who came from a wealthy Italian family; her father had been the business manager of the opera house La Scala. In the late 1950s Noble established and directed a painting and ceramic school at a psychiatric hospital in Verona where he'd received treatment for alcoholism. The school, at the San Giacomo hospital, was known for championing the work of outsider artists, like Carlo Zinelli.

Patience found the atmosphere at Garda somewhat oppressive and lifeless, especially compared to La Barozza, but good for making headway on her book. She had a small studio (she called it a "cupboard") that looked out onto lemon trees with views of the lake and mountains beyond. It was here that much of the first draft of *Honey from a Weed* was written. "The absolute absence of life here forces me to conjure up the things which make life worth living, and I feel that that is probably the point of being here," she wrote.[44]

She was aided by frequent visits from Wolfe, whose "gigantic appetite" spurred her on, as did their proximity to Verona, which offered a wide variety of foods unavailable in Carrara. It did not take long for Wolfe to acquire a Veronese pheasant, a guinea hen, and a Garda chicken, which Patience described as "a revelation." In the Piazza Erbe market, there were mounds of black and white truffles, lake fish—salmon, trout, and whitefish (*lavarelli*)—and all manner of wild game. Patience compared the displays of game in the shops to the plenty pictured in Victorian lithographs and nineteenth-century illustrated books such as Oliver Goldsmith's *Animated Nature*. "Its [Verona's] food shops are arranged with an order inspired by artistry," she wrote.[45] Sometime in December Jean and Ginette picked them up in a luxury Citroen and took them to a château in southern France owned by Cordier. They stayed there for the night and had a regal feast in a "desolate mansion stuffed with art works."[46]

By the end of February, Patience had completed a rough typescript of the book and sent it to John Wolfers, a literary agent known for his high standards and radical politics, who had worked with the publisher John

Murray before setting up his own agency in the mid 1960s. (Patience also sent a draft to Penguin.) The book, titled *Fasting and Feasting*, consisted of about thirty chapters, alternating essays and reflections on the places she and Norman had lived with recipes organized under section headings such as "Pig," "Weeds," and "*La Polenta*." "The Vegetable Tribe," which drew heavily on Loudon, was included along with a glossary of "fruits, nuts, fungi and insects." Many of the vegetables were those Patience had encountered at the market in Carrara. In a cover letter she said the book would provide a picture of what life was really like in these relatively primitive places. A couple of years later she described it as a "study of culinary practices and their origins."[47] Its appearance, she imagined, would have something in common with *Plats du Jour*, and she had already asked Miranda and her then-daughter-in-law, Corinna, to do the illustrations. In a letter to Nicolas and Corinna in 1969, Patience said she was thinking of end piece illustrations of various insects and animals like the praying mantis, stag beetle, cicada, salamander, and swallowtail butterfly. Like *Plats Du Jour* she hoped the book would include drawings of less common vegetables, Mediterranean fish, and a wide variety of herbs and plants, a guide for the uninitiated. Most of all, though, she said the book was meant to be "an inspiration not a manual."

Like Irving she hoped to bring a taste of what she believed was a fast-disappearing way of life into the "*gran vuoto*," the great void of the present. Though she had "violently enjoyed" writing the book, she worried that the enthusiasm and immediacy she felt for the subject would be lost on the publishing world. Completing the manuscript coincided with their departure from Lake Garda, and Patience was greatly relieved to once again breathe the "anarchic air" of Carrara.

⊰⊰⊰⊱⊱⊱

After their trip to Puglia, Patience seemed drawn to wild plants and flowers in a new way. She had reacted strongly against the neatly ordered gardens of Lake Garda and relished the opportunity to wander the hillsides of Carrara in search of plants and flowers. "I have this peculiar passion for flowers growing wild," Patience wrote in May.[48] She had been making drawings of cyclamen, hellebores, and anemones, as well as gathering "huge flowered" primroses and what she called wild hyacinths. In a letter to Olive, she discussed her fondness for "wild plants, old old roses, and passion flowers."[49] There were purple crocuses in the mountains and wild cherry and white plum blossoms that reminded her of images of Mt. Fuji. "Do you ever borrow that marvellous book of Tania's of old herbal plates and engravings?" she wrote to Olive. "I have one too, and it has been a very great pleasure."[50] (The book in question was most likely Richard G. Hatton's *Handbook of Plant and Floral Ornament from Early Herbals,* originally published in 1909.) Edible plants were at their best in early spring, and Patience gathered a variety of wild plants—carrot, parsnip, radish, sorrel, and many others—to use in the "most delicious little vineyard salads."[51] She made marmalade from bitter oranges growing at hand and watched as their old neighbor Uncle Nello tended the vines.

There was news that the Catalan book was finally going to be published, and Patience received proofs from Nicole, which she was pleasantly surprised with. In June Norman learned that two of his works, *Sibyl* and *Athena Promachos,* had been accepted in the upcoming Biennale, which would also feature work by Louise Bourgeois, Michael Noble, and Peter Rockwell. Helen and Arno, who had finally acquired a house in Puglia, passed through on their way to Paris. Wolfe, who had spent much of the winter with Patience and Norman, making Patience "cook the most marvellous things," had gone to South Africa to visit his sister Joanna. "He plans to cross over to Casablanca, eat a couscous and find some way of visiting Joanna in Natal, an idea which started with the vision of a camel carrying him into the heart of Africa," Patience wrote.[52]

It was another one of his adventures, which Wolfe built up in his typically theatrical fashion with talk of Casablanca and journeying into the heart of Africa. In reality he flew from Paris to South Africa. The next day, April 12, 1969, he was driving with Joanna's then-husband, Ireneu da Cruz, a Portuguese surgeon, along the Drakensberg Escarpment. Da Cruz somehow lost control of the car, which skidded on the dusty road and flipped over, leaving Wolfe seriously injured. Da Cruz was unharmed.

It soon became apparent that Wolfe was unlikely to regain much movement or sensation from the neck down. Patience and Norman received a telegram from Joanna two days later telling them that Wolfe's fate was uncertain. He'd stopped breathing several times and then contracted pneumonia. Yet somehow he survived. On April 16 they got a letter Wolfe had written from Paris before he left for Africa. "He seemed to be in two places," Norman wrote. "The Wolfe we know, thinking of us in Paris, and the impossible one lying prostrate in a South African hospital."[53]

Patience clung to that image of Wolfe in Paris, studying music and French, sipping a Pernod at Madame Coquin's, and preparing meals in his tiny apartment; the other one was simply unimaginable. Wolfe, only thirty-one at the time, had always described himself as Oblomovian, having "an inexhaustible ability to dream." He was an urban creature. He loved the theater, opera, and art. Patience and Wolfe had a passion for Stendhal and an almost obsessive love for Maria Callas, subjects they could talk about forever. And of course there was food, which Wolfe said he'd always had a "profound interest in." Patience would later say that he was one of the few people she actually enjoyed cooking for. "He inhabited the world of pleasure," Patience wrote, "and suddenly is precipitated into a pit of sorrow."[54]

By July his condition had stabilized, and he was transferred to Stoke Mandeville Hospital in Buckinghamshire, established during the Second World War and famous for its spinal injury clinic. Patience, with Norman's help, forced herself to see him as a "free spirit" and not someone who'd simply be confined to a wheelchair for the rest of his life.

"One must have faith in him," Patience wrote later that month just before the opening of the Biennale. "The conception of life as a success story has to be replaced by love of the person as he is. This is a very important year for realizing things."[55]

⚜⚜⚜

The Biennale proved to be a great success. Norman received invitations to teach and lecture in North Carolina and New York. Young sculptors from the United States, Tunisia, and Lithuania adopted him as their "maestro." Japanese sculptor Isamu Noguchi, who had lived in Rome in the early 1960s and worked in marble from quarries south of Carrara, was deeply impressed with Norman's work. Noguchi visited his studio and promised to show photos of Norman's work to the Cordier and Ekstrom gallery in New York, where Noguchi had held his own exhibitions. "It is so strange after such a prolonged period of obscurity that people now see Norman's work," Patience wrote to Muriel. "Hasn't it been there all this time?"

"Nevertheless," she continued, "I also feel that a certain anonymity is the perfect climate for making things, and I have always rather dreaded Norman being famous."[56]

Indeed there was a certain paradox between Patience's belief in the importance of anonymity and the artist's natural desire for public recognition. It wasn't really just a question of either working away in obscurity or being famous. Rather it was about participating in what Patience referred to dismissively as the "exhibition racket"—finding galleries to show Norman's work, taking part in the Biennale, always chasing commissions and patrons to buy his carvings. Much of this promotional work fell to Patience. Norman was conflicted: He seemed to want both the career of a successful artist and a more ascetic life free of such material concerns. He wanted to be able to convey his ideas through his sculpture and his writings—he was constantly working on books of poems, children's stories, and philosophical tracts, which Patience usually typed—without having to deal with the commercial side of things. Moreover he was a gifted teacher and always attracted students and admirers wherever he went. He still entertained the idea of establishing his Wonderhouse, which would mean finding cheap land far from the centers of the European art world, but was also keen to reach a wider audience. Throughout his career he firmly held on to the idea of the artist as a full "member of society." And after four years in Carrara, he was finally gaining the recognition he had sought since he took up carving in the 1950s. "I'm getting very expensive you know," he wrote in a letter to Muriel. "I sold a 12″ carving for £400 the other day."[57]

In any event the Biennale was a much-needed boost for Norman, and he started work at once on a series of large carvings. With the very real possibility of a show in New York the following year, he felt it could be the "working year of my life."

Meanwhile they were overwhelmed with visitors—friends and foreign sculptors alike—and decided to take another trip to Puglia in mid-September before heading to London for yet another winter. They had become somewhat exhausted with the never-ending search for a place to live and work and were growing resigned to the fact that the semi-nomadic lifestyle they'd established was perhaps no longer temporary.

"The more places we look into the more indecisive I feel," Norman wrote. "Perhaps I don't want to settle down—maybe I just am unsettled and that's why I do the work I do?"[58]

Before Patience and Norman left for Puglia, Norman and his assistant, Roberto, wandered up the Colonnata riverbed, "searching for ruins" they might acquire to convert into studio and living quarters. Instead they came upon Carrara's last functioning brothel, run by a lady with a "spun-sugar hairdo." She actually had a reasonable three-bedroom apartment to let, but one of her call girls apparently lived above it. "Too noisy at night for us," Patience wrote. "Too much of a temptation for Roberto."[59]

Though they did intend to do some "barn hunting" in the Salento, unlike their previous trip this one was less explicitly about finding a place to live. In a letter to Wolfe, Patience said, "We are going off to Puglia to recover, camp, wander, and restore ourselves."[60]

They camped out on deserted beaches but also stayed with Helen and Arno, who had already transformed their house in the countryside near Torre Mozza into a studio and workplace. Named after the livestock once stabled there, it was known as the The Bufalaria. According to Patience they were "making a far from ideal home in their inimitable way."[61]

Puglia, however, was still sublime. They spent nearly two weeks exploring the Ionian side before they happened upon a place that seemed to have everything they'd been searching for. One afternoon they left Helen and Arno's and were heading east on their way towards the village of Presicce when they stopped to picnic at a high point with views of the sea. They found themselves on the grounds of a masseria on 11 acres of land; the house had vaulted rooms and panoramic views overlooking the tip of the peninsula, *finibus terrae*, land's end. Just over a mile and a half from the sea, the house was surrounded by wild scrubland, views to the north and east of olive groves as far as the eye could see, and to the south and west glimpses of the Ionian Sea and largely unspoiled coastline. "In every direction one can see for miles," Patience wrote, "a sea of olives at the easterly side on an enormous plain, and a great stretch of sea to the west, one cannot begin to explain it."[62] On survey maps the spot was marked as "Spigolizzi," a name possibly derived from the nearby *specchia*, one of a chain of ancient crude stone lookout mounds erected by local inhabitants in bygone days to warn of Turkish invaders.

On that afternoon, though, the largely deserted countryside must have seemed like uncharted territory, a kind of *tabula rasa* that would become Patience and Norman's home for more than thirty years. They'd arrived at land's end and a new beginning.

CHAPTER ELEVEN

A New Life

Throughout the 1960s Patience and Norman had maintained a somewhat uneasy relationship with England, returning periodically to spend winters at The Logs. As late as 1968 they had not completely ruled out the possibility of settling there. In the winter of 1967–68, they traveled to the area around Brecon in central Wales, once known for its limestone quarries, to look for a place to live and work. However they found the Brecon Beacons "bleak and off putting," and Patience told Ariane they'd be "happy to leave England forever."[1] If anything trips to London only confirmed why they left in the first place. They had long been disillusioned with the preoccupations of urban life and what Patience called the drift toward "consumerland." In 1966 she described England with its "perpetual leaden sky" as being in "full middle age" and "a monument to triteness."[2] Much later she described modern consumer society as "terrifying" and akin to "being trapped inside a machine."[3] According to David Gentleman, over the years Patience became somewhat contemptuous of those who followed a more conventional career path and made the compromises and sacrifices needed to survive in a city like London. Even Henrion, for whom she had the greatest respect, and Gentleman himself came in for some of that. "I think Patience always thought that she was right all along, but I felt that she was probably silently thinking the same things about my setup here [Gentleman had moved to a spacious townhouse in Camden Town] as she did about her other friends who indeed hadn't necessarily used their lives as single mindedly or creatively as she did."[4]

By the late 1960s, though Patience kept in touch by post with her English friends and family on a regular basis, she saw them less and less often. Patience and Norman complained that Carrara was too close to

London—a rather fanciful notion—but the truth is they visited rarely.
Meanwhile Nicolas and Corinna were living in Bristol, Miranda and
Ashlyn in London. Patience now had four grandchildren, though she
seldom saw them. In fact over the years Tania would become much closer
to Patience's grandchildren and some of her London friends than Patience
ever was. Rosy, Nicolas's daughter, said that for years she assumed Olive
was her grandmother and wasn't sure where Patience fitted in. "She wasn't
the kind of granny who sits you on her lap," said Lisa, Miranda's second
daughter.[5] Marushka Delabre, Miranda's eldest, said, "She had difficulty
feeling and expressing unconditional love. For her grandchildren there
was little recognition and just a bare sliver of interest if we were doing
something that was 'interesting' in her eyes."[6] Patience visited Nick and
his family only once over a twenty-year period after 1962 when they
moved to Bristol. Even when Nick was in Ham Green Hospital with
tuberculosis for twelve weeks in 1963, while Patience and Norman were
on Naxos, she did not make the trip to visit him. Miranda, too, saw her
infrequently—Patience visited the young Armour-Brown family twice
while they were living in Greece in the 1970s—and it was more often the
case that she went to visit Patience and Norman, whether in Catalonia,
Carrara, or eventually Puglia.

Olive, now in her eighties, was still living in Rogate. Tania was in
London and Patience often relied on her for sundry tasks such as circulating her manuscripts or looking up the name of some rare plant or
flower at Kew Gardens. Patience continued to employ the services of
a literary agent in London and held on to her Hampstead flat, which
contained most of her worldly possessions and research materials. Even
living abroad she kept up with the British newspapers—she retained a
certain fondness for Fleet Street as she'd known it in the 1950s—and
Olive regularly sent them the *Observer* and other periodicals. Despite
what Patience referred to as their "essential vulgarity," she read them
avidly and cherished the work of a "few friends" like Peter Heyworth and
Philip Toynbee, "who gets more human as he gets older."[7]

But settling in the south of Puglia would put them about as far from
London as they could possibly be without actually leaving Europe. And
in those days getting down to the heel was not at all easy. Nick described
the journey from Bristol, with stops in London, Paris, Venice, and finally

Lecce, where Norman picked them up, as "agonizing," though always an adventure. Later on, when even Lecce was too far for Norman to drive, they would take the slow local train to Presicce and had to be sure to arrive on a Tuesday or Saturday, the days Patience and Norman came to market.

Even their friends in Carrara only half jokingly considered the move a "descent into Africa."[8] Puglia, and the *Mezzogiorno* more broadly, had long been considered not only backward but also somehow separate, another world. As early as the sixteenth century, Jesuit missionaries referred to the south as "Italian India."[9] In his letter to Muriel from Puglia describing the masseria, Norman reassured her there was an airport near Taranto, about a two-hour drive, and that Rome, thanks to the newly built *autostrada* (highway), was only a day's drive away. "Don't be alarmed at the distance," he wrote, somewhat unconvincingly. Patience had once written to Olive, from La Barozza, that she imagined one day having a place that was "more guest worthy." (Neither Olive nor Muriel visited them in Carrara.) Had electricity been installed, and hot water—and the luxury of a bath—Spigolizzi would still have been so far for friends and family to travel that whether it was guest-worthy or not was hardly relevant. Of course there was a post office in the nearby village of Presicce, and it would become the vital link connecting Patience and Norman to the outside world.

Not long after they moved to Puglia in spring 1970, at Patience's request Olive began sending them the weekly papers. "The *Observer* is very welcome," Patience wrote. "Quite apart from its content it is the only source of paper, and very useful for lighting the bonfire, on which the recalcitrant *fichi d'India* (prickly pear) eventually expire."[10]

⊰⊰⊰※⊱

When Patience and Norman had left Puglia the previous autumn, negotiations for the purchase of Spigolizzi were well underway, but the terms of a deal were still far from clear. They spent the winter months in London, Patience working on *Honey from a Weed* and visiting Wolfe at Stoke Mandeville whenever she could, bringing him roast chickens, aïoli, and caviar. She was waiting for news from Lelio Martelloni, the agent and banker they'd met through Helen and Arno, who was orchestrating the sale. Patience and Norman finally traveled to Puglia in April, but it took more than a month to sort everything out. The chief obstacle was the fact that ownership of the house and the 11 acres of land were shared by five different peasant families, though the greater part of the property belonged to a single owner who still worked the land and harvested the olives. On top of the complications of bringing the various parties together and getting them to agree on the sale, there were a number of unexpected delays. Patience said the deal nearly fell through half a dozen times. During the negotiations they stayed briefly with Helen and Arno, and then started "camping out" in the masseria's two most habitable rooms. "The five peasants were not easy to round up," Patience wrote, "and it took a month to unite the old masseria into a single piece."[11]

In early May they finally closed the deal. Ashlyn, who had recently come into his share of the Brown and Polson family fortune, put up the money, about £3,000. That night, by the light of an oil lamp, Patience cooked on their newly acquired gas stove, and they drank a bottle of champagne that Jean Delpech had given them especially for the occasion. "As we sat down to our first supper," Norman wrote, "we said grace because we were both suddenly overcome with gratefulness—a feeling of a prayer—a real deep-down prayer—having been granted."[12] Just as they had been beginning to doubt they would ever find a suitable place to settle, they'd stumbled upon Spigolizzi, which, with its seemingly endless vistas and its raw beauty, seemed full of possibility. In her first letter to Olive after finalizing the sale, Patience described the "wild and savage" landscape full of cacti, wild plants, herbs, and peas, "which seem to thrive on nothing."[13] She called it a "flowering wilderness" and told Wolfe that her letters had been reduced to three topics: beetles, erosion, and luxury. "Luxury is washing your feet," she wrote. "A pee out of doors on a rock in the sun, a juicy *nespola* [loquat] after a bout of road mending work."[14] Norman was already imagining Wijdeveld designing small structures to be scattered about the landscape—he called them "cells"—that would be used as studios for his students or visiting artists. Norman and Wijdeveld immediately began a correspondence about the project, and Wijdeveld, intoxicated with the idea of southern Italy and the possibility of collaborating with Norman, sent Patience and Norman a check for £300. Patience and Norman took it as an auspicious sign when a large black snake, "like a rivulet of pitch," appeared soon after they'd moved in.

The house itself, an L-shaped structure with lime-rendered dry-stone walls 3 feet thick and vaulted ceilings made from hand-quarried tufo blocks (the local stone), had been used largely for agricultural purposes. There were still cow byres in what would become the kitchen, and Norman's studio was full of bales of straw and manure. The studio floor was paved in roughly leveled stones that, Norman noted with evident pleasure, had "received a most beautiful dark brown patina by being trampled and peed and shat upon by generations of buffaloes."[15] Like most of the masserie in Puglia, the building and surrounding land had once served several families—as evidenced by the vast bread oven in the garden—producing everything they needed from oil and wine to grain, dairy products, and meat. Just off of the kitchen, there was a tiny room with a large open fireplace; the hearth had provided heat for ricotta making but also smoke for curing cuts of meat hung under the cell's high vaulted ceiling. Since the Second World War, the building had primarily been used for stabling cattle and sheep, and storing hay, grain, and firewood. It was no exaggeration when Patience declared in *Honey from a Weed* that they'd moved into a cowshed.

There was a small vineyard just below the house, and part of the hillside was planted with olives, but much of the land was now largely uncultivated, several acres of once-terraced escarpment having served most recently as rough grazing. As part of the arrangement, a previous owner retained the right to harvest the olives for the first two years of Patience and Norman's tenure. The field was overgrown with waist-high weeds—chicory, couch grass, and thistles—and the encroaching macchia. There were cultivated fruit trees such as pear, fig, pomegranate, and cherry, which had been neglected and run wild. Fichi d'India had spread across the lichen-covered rocks. "They seem to be the avant garde," Patience wrote. They were breaking up the rock and making way for all manner of weeds: wild parsnip, carrot, oats, rye, and peas. Patience likened the land to Prospero's island in *The Tempest*—stark, isolated, and unforgiving. Yet it was also undeniably beautiful. In those days there was just a narrow unpaved road that traversed the countryside. (The road was eventually paved.) Water was hauled from a cistern—"a jar in the ground"—just opposite the house on the other side of the dirt road. Villages, with their clusters of small white buildings, could be seen in the distance. The near total darkness of night was pierced only by the flashing of the lighthouse at Santa Maria di Leuca, the tip of the peninsula. "In Puglia," Patience wrote, "ideas of comfort are replaced by intangible moments of poetry and delight."[16]

They had found their Eldorado, as Peggy Angus would write the following year.[17] But Norman had been somewhat overly optimistic when he wrote, after their first visit to Spigolizzi in September 1969, that the masseria needed only modest repairs. In fact they would spend the next four months making the place habitable, overseeing a motley crew of laborers, and doing little if any of their own work during that time. They made one last trip to Carrara in mid-May and arranged to have a tomato delivery driver, who traveled regularly from Puglia to Bologna, retrieve Norman's sculptures—10 tons' worth, which took six hours to unload with the help of a crane. Patience recalled being lectured by friends in Carrara about the madness of going to the Salento, where there were "wolves in winter" and no people.

Indeed they had to have Spigolizzi weatherproof by winter, an unpredictable season characterized by the damp *scirocco* blowing off the sea, or a cold north wind, the *tramontana*—the house was north facing—and sometimes torrential rain. When they moved in there were no doors or windows on the masseria. The earth floors needed to be leveled. The walls re-plastered. Parts of the roof needed to be repaired. There was no running water. The 20-foot-deep cistern on the other side of the road was filled with rainwater piped from the roof and was capable of holding more than 15,000 liters. Norman and Patience installed a two-stroke Briggs & Stratton motor pump to bring water from the cistern to a tank on the roof, which fed an outdoor tap and sinks in the kitchen, bathroom, and guest room. Domestic plumbing was so new in that part of Puglia that the choice of fittings was limited, and Norman brought brass taps from Carrara, along with three marble sinks. They also carted down some furniture, including a few bentwood chairs and a large marble slab to be used as the kitchen table. "Norman says anyone who comes here has first to spend a week dragging water from the well so as to know how precious, rare, and amazing this tap water is," Patience wrote.[18] Indeed over the years Norman was famous for handing guests carafes of wine upon arrival and telling them, "Drink your fill. We make new wine every year. But go easy on the water. Or it will run out."

Throughout the renovations they were for all intents and purposes living with the builders in what Patience described as a state of siege, everything covered in dust and debris. The summer heat and lack of privacy added to frustrations over how long things were taking. The workers—carpenters, plumbers, and stonemasons—were all "so harassed, penniless, vain, [and] undependable" that they had to be constantly leaned on to finish a job.[19] Every new transaction seemed to be shrouded in layers of intrigue and obfuscation, and Norman found himself exasperated by the endless negotiations. They also had to put up with a near-constant stream of visitors curious to see who these foreign artists settling on the hillside were. Needless to say progress was slow. By the end of July, after nearly three months, Norman said that the masseria was "becoming less of a cave and more of a habitation."[20] In late September they were still waiting for doors and windows to be installed. It wasn't until October that Patience unpacked her tools and began to set up her studio.

Early that month, on the feast day of Saint Teresa, they celebrated with their neighbors, Teresa and Salvatore de Mira, and their young daughter, Laura: large bowls of spaghetti with tomato sauce, boiled weeds, a cock "beautifully cooked and finished with capers," salad, and new walnuts—which, in the Salento, are considered vital winter fare.[21]

⋘⋖⋇⋗

Teresa and Salvatore were among the last *contadini*, peasant farmers, to actively work the marginal land on the Spigolizzi hillside. They were both from the nearby village of Salve but, in the mid 1950s, left home in rebellion against their parents who refused to give their consent for them to marry. Having been disowned by their families, they fled to the countryside and lived in a *pajara*, a windowless stone hut that Salvatore constructed himself. Laura was born soon after, in 1956. In the mid 1960s Salvatore was one of many young men from Salve who went to work in Switzerland. It is estimated that between 1952 and 1968 more than 2.5 million Italians, in what the press at the time called "the hemorrhage of the Mezzogiorno," migrated from the south to the north and abroad. But unlike many who found employment and stayed abroad, Salvatore chose to return to the Salento, whatever the difficulties of earning a living. In a sense they were outliers, having defied convention both in marriage and in occupation, and continued to live on their own terms. "He's made his own life," Norman wrote. "He's a bit odd-man out ... busy and essentially contented."[22] By 1970, when Patience and Norman arrived, Salvatore and Teresa had moved back to the town of Salve but spent at least half of the year living in the country and tending a small plot of land and olive trees just over the road from Spigolizzi. Even this part-time arrangement was considered somewhat unorthodox—the idea of living out of town and the hardships of working the land having been largely rejected by most Pugliese. There were a handful of other contadini in the area, but none would become so intimately involved in Patience and Norman's lives.

They met almost immediately—Salvatore and Teresa were just getting settled in for the summer when Patience and Norman arrived in May—and Salvatore was hired by one of the building contractors to work on the interior of the masseria. He proved to be indispensable both as a laborer and helping hand. He was an expert mason and builder, and Patience wrote, "What has been done would have been inconceivable without him."[23] They helped clear the land around Spigolizzi, overrun with weeds and macchia bushes, and regularly appeared with vegetables and fruit they'd grown—baskets of zucchini, yellow plums, *nespole*, onions, or new potatoes—or things to plant such as, that first season, lettuces and basil. Patience was especially struck by the fresh "emerald green" chickpeas they delivered one evening. "I had never imagined they were fresh or green," she wrote.[24] In those early days Salvatore encouraged Norman to make his own wine with the Negroamaro and Malvasia grapes harvested from Spigolizzi's vines, small, black, and sweet; the vendemmia would become an annual event. The homegrown harvest was usually supplemented with grapes purchased from the nearby village of Gemini or from their neighbor Maria Vittoria, who had a mix of grape varieties planted by the old Duke of Salve, an amateur agronomist. In some years Norman would make more than 160 gallons of wine, requiring 10 *quintali*—one ton—of grapes. Over the course of the next thirty years, Salvatore would be instrumental in helping Patience and Norman establish a life very much rooted in the land. And it was Teresa who introduced Patience to many of the traditional elements of Pugliese cooking. "I taught her," Teresa recalled. "I helped to make the sauce, the olives for the oil, all those things."[25] They were vital links to a way of life that was fast disappearing. Planting cucumbers once with Norman, Salvatore quipped: "Watch well how I do it, because if I die there aren't many others like me; of people like you there are millions!"[26]

In Carrara Patience and Norman had not grown any of their own food, having had neither the time nor land to cultivate. And when they made their first trip to Puglia in 1968, Patience referred somewhat dismissively to being offered "hectares of olives" and "agricultural responsibilities," suggesting that they were not greatly interested in working the land, or at least not devoting the bulk of their time to such activities. Their focus was still primarily on their own work—sculpture, jewelry, and writing—though they had expressed an interest in growing some of their own food, and Patience was of course an experienced gardener. Nor was the land around Spigolizzi particularly favorable for small-scale production. The soil was calcareous and stony. Ashlyn, who visited with Miranda in 1971, remembers little other than fichi d'India growing at that time. No trees had been planted, and the house was rather exposed. According to Miranda, "the light was dazzling and the heat overwhelming. A wild warm wind was blowing sand as if from the Sahara."[27] To make the land viable required an enormous amount of hard labor, traditionally done by hand or perhaps with the aid of an old horse. In those days Nick, who first visited in 1972, recalls most of the farming on the hillside amounted to "old men scraping a bit of soil together between the rocks with a *zappa* (a mattock) to plant a half dozen tomato seedlings."[28] Perhaps the only thing going for it was the relatively mild year-round climate. As novice farmers Patience and Norman leaned heavily on Salvatore, who possessed an unusual mix of the kind of knowledge obtained over a lifetime of working the land and a sort of enlightened curiosity. He was illiterate, yet, according to Patience, had a "Pythagorean clarity of mind," which was apparent in the way he mapped out the use of his own land.[29] Norman was at ease with him and marveled at his ability to "take unexpected flights of the imagination."[30] A sometimes-barber, he also cut Norman's hair.

It was Salvatore who introduced them to a number of the agricultural activities practiced in the Salento: the olive harvest; wine making; and cultivation of a wide variety of vegetables and legumes such as zucchini, cucumbers, beans, and chickpeas. Later on they would purchase potatoes together, half a quintale each (about 110 pounds), cut them—which was "an art," Patience wrote—and plant them by hand. In 1973, the first year they harvested their own olives (with Salvatore and Teresa's help), they produced close to 150 pounds (65 kilos) of oil. By 1975 they were cultivating kilometers of peas, broad beans, garlic, barley, wheat, and tomatoes, and they observed, "Agriculture has taken over."[31] The following year they added fennel, onions, peppers, and runner beans. They had also acquired two pigs, which they butchered themselves. "With *Plats du Jour* drawings of David in one hand and knife in the other Norman operated on the pig," Patience wrote in early 1978.[32] She also relied on Jane Grigson's *Charcuterie and French Pork Cookery*, as well as local input for some of the recipes.

The first five years in Puglia, they rarely planted without Salvatore's assistance, and Patience called him their "sowing planting clock." It wasn't until 1976, when Salvatore took a job at an olive oil mill in order to earn money to buy an "Ape" (Italy's ubiquitous Vespa-based, three-wheeled mini-truck) that they were largely left to fend for themselves. By that time, though, Patience declared that they'd become "gardening pioneers" and were living to a considerable extent off of the fruits of their labor. During the winter of 1974–75, Patience wrote that they were eating their own dried peas, dried haricots, dried broad beans, and harvesting their own chicory, "a pleasantly bitter salad."

At harvest time, whether of tomatoes, olives, or figs, agricultural labor dominated their lives. *La salsa*, bottled tomato sauce, for example, was a several-days-long undertaking that Patience admitted likely would not have happened without Teresa's help and guidance. The sauce requires hundreds of pounds of Leccesi tomatoes, which are cooked in large vats over an open fire, with red onion, thyme, rosemary, sea salt, and very little water, before being put through a *passapomodoro* (mechanical tomato sieve), which separates the skin and seeds from the juice and pulp. Some of the seeds, extracted before cooking, were dried and reserved for next year's planting, sown in February in cold frames or covered with plastic sheets. While making the sauce, several other traditional ways of preserving tomatoes would not be neglected: the thickest pulp exuded by the passapomodoro would be sun-dried on plates on the roof of the masseria and eventually spooned into glass jars for use as concentrated tomato

paste; and plum tomatoes would be quickly blanched and then labori-
ously peeled for preservation. The effort yielded enough sauce for winter
with plenty more to give away. "Like a military operation," Patience
described it, "only peaceable."[33] She took it seriously and was known to
turn away friends or even family members when the floor of the guest
room was covered in ripening tomatoes (the tomatoes were harvested
in early July and left to ripen in a covered space). She once told one of
her granddaughters, who'd shown up unexpectedly on her honeymoon,
that she would have to sleep in her van until the floor was cleared. In
addition to the bounty of vegetables grown, olive oil and wine produced,
Patience gathered wild plants and herbs year-round, and mushrooms in
season from November to February, continuing to rely on Maublanc's
field guide to identify new species. On their land there were also fruit
trees—quince, wild pear, fig, pomegranate, Amarena cherry, Damascus
plum, the strawberry tree (*Arbutus unedo*), nespola, several varieties of
citrus fruit—as well as several large almond trees. Thus the wilderness at
their door provided a secondary harvest.

Years after they'd settled in Puglia, Patience recalled her initial
amazement at seeing Teresa, Salvatore, and Laura picking up thousands
of olives from the damp earth; at the time she thought, "Well, that I
would not even think of doing."[34] In *Honey from a Weed* she compared the
labors of olive picking to the pains of childbirth. Over time of course her
outlook on olives and on other laborious crops changed, and she came to
value the "endless harvesting," the gathering, threshing, and preserving.
Ada Martella, who met Patience and Norman in the 1980s, remembered
Patience spending hours sifting through "millions of black olives" in order
to select the very best specimens for conserving. Their lives were in many
ways structured by these yearly rituals: la salsa in July, the drying of the
figs in late August, the vendemmia in September, the olive harvest in
October or November, and the autumn and spring sowing and planting.
Letters were almost always peppered with the agricultural equivalent of
the shipping news, what was going in the ground and what was coming
out of it. Patience even referred some years later to "doing so many things
a liberated woman should never do" but derived great meaning from the
work itself and the communal spirit that it gave rise to.[35] She had in a
sense found her métier.

A number of these practices not surprisingly made their way into *Fasting and Feasting* (as it was still called), which continued to evolve as the circumstances of their lives changed. Patience had continued to work on the book after she sent the initial draft to John Wolfers, who evidently failed to show much interest in it. The winter before they moved to Puglia, she'd sent what she then considered a finished draft to Deborah Rogers, a well-known literary agent and friend of Henrion's. (Patience and Rogers did not meet in person until 1977.) Rogers, who often championed work that did not necessarily conform to mainstream literary tastes—the avant-garde novelist B. S. Johnson, for example—loved the book and longed to have a bound copy for her shelves. She said this was "long the best incentive for an agent to persevere."[36] In June Patience received a letter from Diana Athill, editor at André Deutsch (Patience had also sent them the manuscript), who said that there was "marvelous material in it" but that it was a "connoisseur's book rather than one for the mass market." Athill, who seemed genuinely interested in the book, said that they'd tried to convince Penguin to co-publish a paperback version, which would have made it financially viable, but that Penguin had declined. "I am afraid this leaves us hopelessly stuck," Athill wrote, "and we have no alternative but to say no."[37] Throughout the 1970s the book seemed to elicit the same kind of reaction. Rogers called it "publishing enthusiasm coupled with economic temerity."[38] An editor at Faber and Faber apparently loved it but knew that the firm would never pursue it. When presented with the manuscript, Louise Gault of Doubleday, who'd published books by James Beard, said they were more interested in basic recipe books that catered to an American audience. She suggested getting in touch with Judith Jones at Knopf, the legendary editor who had published, among other groundbreaking cookbooks of the 1960s and '70s, Julia Child's *Mastering the Art of French Cooking*. Jones did in fact see Patience's manuscript sometime in the early 1980s and confessed to falling in love with it—she said she copied several pages and "tucked them away to read again when I needed that kind of refreshment"—but knew that it wasn't something Knopf would be willing to take a gamble on. "Twenty years ago I wouldn't have hesitated but the sad fact is that it is getting harder and harder for a conglomerate, such as we are when it comes to the sales force, to publish the odd and unusual."[39]

Patience also enlisted the services of Tessa Sayle, another distinguished literary agent and admirer of *Plats du Jour*, who she'd been introduced to through an old friend from college. In a letter to Sayle in 1971, Patience acknowledged that the book "falls into no obvious category" but described it as an "attempt to return to the meaning of cooking."[40] (She also sent portions of the manuscript to the Italian publisher Feltrinelli in 1972.) Though it still largely focused on the 1960s—Naxos, Catalonia, and Carrara—it was gradually being reshaped by her experiences in the Salento. The list of edible weeds was growing, and Patience had begun to identify the up-to-date Latin nomenclature for many of them. (There are roughly 450 species of edible wild plants in the Salento, many of which are used for medicinal purposes and known primarily by their dialect name.) She was also incorporating some of the culinary practices she'd been introduced to in the Salento, including the long, slow cooking of beans and pulses in a glazed earthenware jug-shaped pot, the *pignata*.

Even as the book met with resistance from publishers, Patience felt that the information in its pages and the way of life it embodied were actually becoming more relevant. Although *Fasting and Feasting* had started out as an exploration of traditional cooking methods, Patience was beginning to view it as a handbook for the "times to come."[41] She was keenly aware of the broader social changes underway, of the fact that John Seymour, an early self-sufficiency pioneer, had been translated into several languages, that "twee books about dainty herbs" were being published, and that so-called survivalists were having something of a renaissance.[42]

Indeed there was a growing interest in both self-sufficiency and organic farming, part of the broader cultural transformation of the 1960s. The oil shock of 1973 and the period of inflation that followed spurred a new back-to-the-land movement inspired by a wish felt by many to produce their own food, to be able to "grow your own." This was coupled with a reaction against what Patience called the "triumph of consumerism" and its negative impacts on the environment, food, and water. There was no shortage of books and journals devoted to the subject. *Mother Earth News*, a magazine that covers alternative living and environmental issues, was launched in 1970. Helen and Scott Nearing reissued their

classic text *Living the Good Life*, with an introduction by Paul Good-
man, that same year. Richard Mabey published his popular book on the
edible wild plants of England, *Food for Free*, in 1972 (and since then it has
never been out of print). Seymour's *Farming for Self-Sufficiency* and E. F.
Schumacher's *Small Is Beautiful* were both published the following year.

Many of these books made an explicit connection between the
pursuit of self-sufficiency and environmental stewardship, something that
Patience and Norman were beginning to take more seriously. In the first
chapter of *Small Is Beautiful*, Schumacher, a disciple of Norman's old friend
Leopold Kohr, devotes considerable space to the finite limits of "natural
capital" and the implications of continued growth on the environment
and society. Patience and Norman subscribed to *Le Sauvage*, an influential French environmental journal, and *Resurgence*, its British counterpart,
both still in publication. They also received copies of *The Ecologist*, another
British environmental journal, whose 1972 *Blueprint for Survival* painted
a rather stark picture of the planet's ecological crisis. After reading it
Patience wrote, "I feel we must have fewer and fewer things."[43] The first
issue of *Le Sauvage*, published in 1973, was no less pessimistic and bore
the headline "1973: Utopia or Death" over the image of a heavily polluted
cityscape. *Resurgence*, founded in 1966 by peace activist John Papworth,
regularly ran essays and columns by Schumacher, Kohr, and Seymour.

Patience never imagined *Honey from a Weed* being a polemical tract
along the lines of Frances Moore Lappé's 1971 *Diet for a Small Planet* and
was well aware of the dangers of striking too prescriptive a pose. After all
the book was both an account of the places they'd lived and a celebration
of the people and food they'd encountered, not a manual for living. Yet it
was not lost on Patience that the themes of the book overlapped in many
ways with emerging interest in agriculture, food, and the environment.
"As life gets more difficult I can't help seeing F & F [*Fasting and Feasting*]
as a source of sustenance!" she wrote in the mid 1970s.[44]

Still Patience was becoming increasingly disillusioned with the
publishing world's unwillingness to take a risk on a cookbook that seemed
to defy all of the genre's conventions. As early as 1972 she was beginning
to doubt whether it would ever see the light of day. A few years later, in
a letter to Olive, she described the book as a "monument to a life which
has all but vanished," and said that she would make one final push. If no

one wanted to publish it, she wrote, "It will be a historic something for Nicolas to inherit and publish in 2020."[45]

⟿⟿⟵⟵

Meanwhile Norman was busy developing his plan for an art school, his Wonderhouse. He referred to his project as a "sanatorium of the soul." In more prosaic terms it was to be a summer sculpture school that he hoped might evolve into a more ambitious eco-artistic community. In summer 1970 Norman was putting together a proposal and brochure, based in part on Wijdeveld's earlier vision of a work community, in an attempt to solicit support. Norman kept one of Wijdeveld's poems and a sketch of his "dream house" pinned to the wall of his studio. He and Patience hoped to put four small stone pajara-like buildings on the hillside, overlooking the promontory, which they imagined serving as studios for visiting artists. The main room—Norman's studio—would be the Wonderhouse, a center for study groups, classes, and lectures open to the public. Their hope was to appeal to local artists and intellectuals, at the same time maintaining professional contacts abroad and cultivating a guild-like atmosphere. They also imagined the visiting artists would provide them with a modest income.

The idea in some ways drew on an artists' residency established by Countess Catherine Karolyi in Vence, France, that Patience had visited in 1960. Madame Karolyi had set up the colony, a collective workshop with several studios around it, at Le Vieux Mas to honor her husband, the first president of Hungary, after his death in 1955. (They were forced into exile in 1919 when Béla Kun's regime came to power.) Looking to escape from Paris for a summer, Wolfe had applied for one of the residencies (then in its second year), and Patience wrote his recommendation; he billed himself as a poet. That summer, on assignment for the *Observer* and before a rendezvous in Venice with Irving, Patience decided to visit Wolfe and was invited to stay in one of the little houses on the hillside. There wasn't much of a collective spirit—the place was surprisingly empty— and the residents who were there "tended to drift off to Vence and simply get drunk," as Patience recalled.[46] Wolfe wrote "19th-century poetry" in the mornings and, like the others, got fabulously drunk in the afternoons.

Karolyi herself, whom Patience clearly admired—she called her a super-woman who had an old-fashioned idea of culture—entertained the likes of Jean Dubuffet, Sir Isaiah Berlin, and Gordon Craig.

The Karolyi colony served as a kind of model, or perhaps more accurately a cautionary tale, as Patience and Norman fleshed out their own idea for some kind of summer school. "We have often brooded on this Karolyi thing," Patience wrote in 1970, "because it is in a way something like what we could offer sculptors here."[47] But in Patience's view the Karolyi model was inadequate. Artists were given a place to stay but nothing to live on, so they had to figure out how to cover everyday expenses. (She remembered a German painter who'd brought along a suitcase filled with tinned sardines to live on.) However Patience admitted they, too, would be unable to provide stipends. The biggest issue, though, as Patience saw it was that the Karolyi colony had no unifying idea, nothing to bring people together. Instead, from what Patience observed, everyone did their own work—or nothing at all—and maintained independent lives. The Wonderhouse would be a more cohesive and focused endeavor with visiting artists, primarily sculptors, also offering classes and engaging in some way with the larger community. Patience and Norman believed that something like this would have particular resonance in Puglia, which had long suffered an exodus of young people and artists, not to mention peasant farmers. Judging by what Patience described as "the hundreds of people" who came to observe what they were doing, even in those early days, the Spigolizzi project would fill a void.[48] Plus Patience and Norman would benefit. Norman was wary of becoming isolated and felt that they would need to maintain contact with other international artists. "There is something parochial about just going somewhere to do your own little bit of work," Patience wrote, "and not trying to do with others something for the glory of god."[49]

Remarkably at age eighty-five Wijdeveld still entertained the possibility of moving to Puglia and working with Norman. In April 1971 he made good his promise to visit Patience and Norman and traveled to Puglia with his wife, Charlotte Kohler, now almost eighty herself and not in the best of health. Well aware that Spigolizzi would be too rustic for their more demanding friends—"two pearls dressed in the latest trouser suits," in Patience's words—they put them up in a hotel. The journey from

Amsterdam had been exhausting, and when they arrived in Brindisi, more than 70 miles from Spigolizzi, and discovered that it was midwinter—cold and windy—and not the southern Italy they'd imagined, they nearly turned back. But Wijdeveld was deeply moved by Spigolizzi—the landscape, the architecture, and most of all Norman's work. He felt that Norman's sculptures spoke on a deeper, almost primal level. "When I saw the beauty in simplicity of architecture and the mystery of vaults inside your home and studio, there was no end of thinking and longing," Wijdeveld wrote.[50] With Wijdeveld there really was no end of thinking and longing—his curiosity and idealism were boundless—but his visit to Puglia forced him to "accept the unavoidable"—that he was too old to undertake a venture like this. Though he acknowledged that he was "still glowing fire deep inside," his vision of creating an ideal school or utopian community—in a way a continuation of Elkerlyc, his school of art and design, which did not survive the war—would be left to Norman. "I have to give in," he wrote. "My sun of life passes slowly on below the horizon."[51] (In fact he would live another sixteen years and die, in 1987, at the age of 101.)

Norman would tinker with the idea of a Wonderhouse for much of the 1970s though it never came to fruition, at least not in a formal sense. Sometime in the early 1970s, he and Patience went to hear a lecture by Lanza del Vasto, an Italian philosopher and activist, who had established a spiritual commune—Community of the Ark—in the south of France in 1948. (Del Vasto was born in Puglia.) Spigolizzi was also something of a gathering place for a circle of young activists and Maoists, as Patience referred to them, including Pippi Corsano and Francesco Radino, who were interested in land-use issues and agricultural reform. Corsano's collection of historical documents and other materials related to the local peasants' revolt following the Second World War is archived at the municipal library in Presicce. Of greater consequence, though, was their neighbor's decision to turn part of her estate, Fano, into a summer school for artists. Maria Vittoria Colonna-Winspeare came from an aristocratic Neapolitan family that traced its lineage back to a poet and friend of Michelangelo's. Maria Vittoria's husband, Baron Carlo Winspeare, had inherited Fano from the Duke of Salve, though he spent little time there and ultimately left the estate to his wife to manage. She was a formidable woman and lived there for the better part of the year on her own, presiding over the 50-odd hectares. She spoke French, was interested in the arts, and was well connected to what remained of the landed aristocracy in the Salento. Patience described her as a "true *nobildonna*" and aristocratic in the sense that she possessed "a great refinement, a sort of detachment, and a deeply Christian spirit."[52]

In 1973 Maria Vittoria had read about an international architecture competition in France won by Slobodan Dan Paich, a conceptual artist, designer, and teacher from Yugoslavia. His plan was based on several years of work at the Further Education College, an experimental school outside London, where he had developed a scheme for a series of underground buildings that he called "a playground of experience." Maria Vittoria had some thirty abandoned small stone buildings on her property and felt that Slobodan could put them to use, establishing a kind of educational village based on his earlier vision. Slobodan, who Patience described as a "fiery individual with blue eyes" and someone "who thinks everything is possible," made his first visit in 1975.[53] In 1976 the Fano Foundation Educational Village inaugurated its first summer season and for the next five years brought artists, architects, and musicians to help cultivate the land, repair the buildings, and do their own creative work. Norman, absolutely delighted about the project at the outset, was called upon to teach sculpture. Patience described him giving lectures in the ravine, "talking to famous Milanese architects" and "looking for a new point of departure."[54] But being a seasonal endeavor with different participants every year, the project failed to establish anything more than a passing connection to the land and its people. Patience and Norman felt that the young artists who spent summers there weren't really interested in devoting their time and energy to making it work, so they distanced themselves from the school. Owing to financial complications, the Fano Village was disbanded in 1980.

Helen and Arno, meanwhile, were also busy establishing their own "cultural community" at the Bufalaria a few miles away toward Torre San Giovanni. In just a few years since their first trip to Puglia together in 1968, the two couples had drifted apart. Norman had accurately predicted that their respective visions of the simple life were incompatible. They saw each other infrequently, at most once a month, and maintained largely separate social spheres. Patience was dismissive of Helen and Arno's plans to establish a small theater company, a sculpture Biennale, and a modern painting wing at the Ugento art museum. She feared that their ambitious plan would attract the wrong crowd, individuals who had no real interest in working the land. After a "cultural evening" at the Bufalaria in 1972, Patience wrote, "I sincerely hope Puglia will resist such an invasion which might lead to serious consequences, i.e. the whole of St. Paul de Vence moving down here."[55] It was clear that they had taken very different paths since settling in Puglia: Helen and Arno had indeed worked to create a cultural atmosphere at the Bufalaria not unlike the one they'd left behind in Paris and Carrara; Patience and Norman on the other hand were spending more and more time tending the land and had little interest in the sort of lifestyle Helen and Arno were intent on cultivating. Yet both the Bufalaria and Spigolizzi would over time become regarded as "cultural lighthouses," attracting local youth and foreign artists, many of whom stayed on and eventually bought houses in the area. Helen and Arno were much more systematic in their attempt to establish an artistic community, requiring founding members to pay dues and recruit other artists. They even drew up a manifesto that outlined their desire to create "an international cultural community" centered on agriculture and the creative arts. "The ideal of the Bufalaria is to create an egalitarian, cultural community, which is both creative and self-supporting," they wrote.[56] It seemed promising at first, but most of the artists who came eventually bought their own property, having shied away from communal living. In the end Helen and Arno were unable to meet the requirements of Italian law, which stipulated that such a community must have at least nine permanent members.

Despite their differences Patience and Norman remained grateful to Helen and Arno for introducing them to the Salento and to Lelio, the banker who helped them close the deal on Spigolizzi. "We are indebted to them as instruments in making a new life," Patience wrote.[57]

In the early 1980s Helen loaned Patience a copy of Fiona MacCarthy's biography of her father, C. R. Ashbee, *The Simple Life*, which covered his years running the Guild of Handicraft in the Cotswolds. In a letter to Olive, Patience explained that they hadn't appreciated the extent to which the intellectual origins of the "simple life" could be traced back to late nineteenth-century England or that it had such a "mythical background," one that was rooted in the ideas of such figures as Ruskin, Edward

Carpenter, and William Morris. But establishing a so-called simple life, as MacCarthy pointed out in the introduction to her book, is never as straightforward or as "simple" as the phrase implies. Even Ashbee's experiment, in many ways a success, had been undone by a combination of factors: financial difficulties, internal disagreements, and the inability to market the Guild's products successfully.

Patience and Norman understood the challenges involved in setting up any kind of community and worried that what they'd set out do, on a far smaller scale, might be mistaken as little more than a pastoral or romantic throwback. Patience took their way of life—whatever one wanted to call it—utterly seriously and expected others to do the same. "She took her 'simple life' with Norman so seriously," Philip Trevelyan, Norman's stepson, recalled. "And of course made it a great success."[58] Indeed she was very critical of the artists, mostly young, some of whom came to the Fano Village or stayed at the Bufalaria, who seemed to want an alternative lifestyle but were unwilling to put in the time and labor to make it happen. The undoing of the Fano Village and of Helen and Arno's commune likely contributed to Patience and Norman's decision in the end not to move ahead with their Wonderhouse. However Norman never let go of the idea altogether. In 1979, when the Scottish artist Richard Demarco embarked on a journey from the Hebrides to the Cyclades as part of the Edinburgh International Festival and passed through the Salento, Norman went to great lengths to prepare an exhibition that embodied his "visionary world" and included everything from painting and sculpture to geometry, philosophical writings, and geodetic toys.[59]

Increasingly, though, the idea of the simple life, fairly or not, was becoming associated with growing one's own food and the rejection of industrial agriculture. The handicrafts that underpinned Ashbee's Guild—metalwork, furniture design, and bookbinding—were no longer widely practiced. Of course self-sufficiency, or at least producing some of one's own food, had always been a key part of the back-to-the-land movement—even Ashbee included smallholdings in his original plan. But the back-to-the-land movement of the 1970s was much more a direct response to the overwhelming scale of agricultural production and its related impact on human health and the environment. (It was in 1973 that a young Ed Behr, who describes himself as a "kind of back-to-the-lander," moved from outside of Washington, DC, to Vermont, the heart of the self-sufficiency movement in the United States. Behr, who founded the *Art of Eating* magazine in 1986, was one of the great champions of *Honey from a Weed*.[60]) Even Patience and Norman, who were deeply rooted in the arts and design and had long sympathized with the critique of industrial capitalism that gave rise to the Arts and Crafts movement—Patience had, after all, been an honorary member of the William Morris Society— were devoting more and more of their time to growing their own food. "Here, like so many others—foreshadowing the age to come—inscribed as artisans we also cultivate some acres of stony red earth," Patience wrote in *Honey from a Weed*.[61]

In January 1975, far removed from the so-called food world—what Eda Lord dubbed a "closed circle" of cooks and writers in Europe and America, whose anointed members were perhaps more interested in the "good life" than the "simple life"—Norman and Patience had their first pig slaughtered at Spigolizzi.[62] They would continue to raise pigs, feeding them overripe figs and boiled potatoes, into the early 1980s. Using David Gentleman's drawings in *Plats du Jour*, Norman did the butchering, and Patience spent several days making sausages, *rillettes*, pancetta, lardo, and hams cured and then smoked in the little room with the fireplace next to the kitchen. The rillettes were a revelation, "a sublime kind of potted pork," Patience wrote.[63] And she described the prosciutto, which they sliced away at in the evening, as being "like a poem." Based on these efforts, she later wrote a lengthy article on how to make coppa, which, in its own circuitous way, led to the publication of *Honey from a Weed*.

CHAPTER TWELVE

An Image of Wilderness

Though Patience had completed what she regarded as the final draft of *Fasting and Feasting* in Carrara and over the next few years had drawn a blank with a long list of potential publishers, she was unwilling to abandon the project. If anything, her experience in the far south during those early years at Spigolizzi had, in Patience's view, given the book an even greater urgency. Cultivating her own plot of land had brought into focus what the book was about: the relationship between a way of life, observed in various parts of the Mediterranean, and the culinary practices that sustained it. In part this was due to the fact that she and Norman had finally settled down and were no longer searching for the next place to live and work. They were developing a far deeper relationship to the place and its people than they had in Naxos or Carrara. They had become close with Salvatore and Teresa—Norman said they were like family—and were largely living from what they could grow. For Patience life had been stripped down to its essence. "So much I feel has dropped away," she wrote in 1976, referring to the time that had passed since she finished the first draft of her book.[1] Even her relationship to food had changed. In 1974 Patience wrote that she was "not particularly interested in food anymore" but "in what people do on whatever food they swallow."[2] However in the same letter she recounted the experience of tasting a truffle for the first time, grated over some scrambled eggs. "It does something extraordinary to the palate," she wrote, "even the next day." For years now they'd been living among marble workers and peasants who tended to eat variations on the same simple dishes every day. In the Salento one of Patience's favorite rituals was the *merenda*, which she felt embodied "food in its simplest form." Equivalent to the Greek *mezethes* or Catalan *refrigeris*, the laborers' midmorning snack always accompanied by a glass of wine, it was often little more than bread, tomatoes and garlic, raw quail eggs ("pale blue with tawny freckles"), or marinated anchovies.

It wasn't that Patience had reduced food to a functional role—she would always insist on the poetic and celebratory nature of fasting and feasting—but that she was no longer interested in food for food's sake. She wanted to know what gave rise to certain culinary traditions, their significance and meaning, without at the same time demystifying them. She resisted suggestions from friends and agents that she rewrite the book in a way that would more closely resemble the work of other food writers. "Why does 'my' book have to resemble E. David or Alice B. Toklas?" she wrote to Ariane in 1975. She admired both writers and considered Toklas's popular cookbook, published in 1954, "a masterpiece of dramatic revelation" but felt that if *Fasting and Feasting* became "just another cookbook" much of its meaning would be lost. (Some might take issue with the notion that Toklas's book was, as Patience put it, "just another cookbook," but by the 1970s it was widely regarded as a classic of literary modernism and had become equally famous for its hashish brownie recipe.) One of the primary criticisms of Patience's book, at least from the point of view of publishers, was that it lacked cohesion, in part because it ranged over so many distinct regions and combined personal essays with recipes.[3] To say that it was about Mediterranean cooking would be a wholly inadequate description of the book; it would also ignore the fact that the Mediterranean covers an incredibly diverse set of culinary practices. Patience acknowledged that the book was a somewhat unorthodox compilation of recipes and essays based on the course of their travels but also felt that this comparative aspect gave the work its resonance. If the book was "on the margin of the fashionable world of cookery" so be it, she concluded.[4] She would sooner leave it unpublished, a family heirloom as she liked to call it, than make the kind of concessions necessary to turn it into a more conventional and marketable cookbook.

Still she understood that the book needed to be revised. She had to incorporate new material from their years in Puglia. Many of the sections were too long. Certain subjects, such as vegetables and fungi, had not been treated with the kind of thoroughness she felt they deserved. And the text as a whole had to be more cohesive. Sometime in 1975 she sent the manuscript to her friend Ariane Castaing in the hope that she might come down to help her overhaul it. "If you could come," Patience wrote, "perhaps we could get to grips with the thing."[5] In April 1976 Ariane made the long journey down from her summer home in the Loire Valley, to spend a week working on the book. She had not been to see Patience and Norman in Puglia before and was struck by the harshness and monotony of the landscape. "The first thing that really horrified me was the landscape," she recalled. "I couldn't stand to see the vineyards with these horrible concrete poles. I mean it absolutely shook me rotten because in my part of the world, in the Vouvray, they were all lovely wood."[6]

Patience had known Ariane since the mid 1950s when Ariane first moved to London from Australia. Patience had taken Ariane, who was some twenty years younger, under her wing, finding her a place to live and introducing her to many of her friends, including Irving and Wolfe. (Patience and Ariane vacationed together with Irving in Agropoli in 1959.) Patience introduced her to the American photographer Jack Nisberg, whom Ariane married in 1963. Nisberg was famous for his photographs of Parisian high society—intellectuals, artists, and celebrities—which appeared regularly in the French edition of *Vogue*. They lived in Paris much of the time, but Ariane continued to write for British glossies and was well connected to people in the food-writing world. She was a friend of Jane Grigson, whose books she regularly gave to Patience, and she was one of the few people Patience trusted to read her work. Indeed, after Ariane's trip, Grigson, a great admirer of *Plats du Jour*, wrote to Patience, "We both rejoiced at another Patience Gray book. . . . If you can ever bear to tell me anything about it, I should love to hear from you."[7]

Though Patience had sought out Ariane's advice and said she was "all for sacrifice and slashing," she was actually much less willing to accept her editorial suggestions.[8] Ariane recalled the weeklong visit being dominated by their arguments over what should be cut—Ariane felt that much needed to be left out—and how to restructure the book. "It was terribly difficult because Patience just got screaming mad when I'd cut something," she said. The manuscript, she recalled, was on little bits of paper and lacked any real sense of order. Ariane felt that rather than organize the book around various subject headings and the recipes that went with them—soups, pasta, fish, and so on—that it should be driven by the narrative itself. Indeed the idea of organizing the book around the sculptor's "marble odyssey"—in the introduction to *Honey from a Weed*, Patience wrote that "a vein of marble runs through this book"—was Ariane's. She considered *The Alice B. Toklas Cook Book* to be one of the most important cookbooks of the postwar period and urged Patience to study it. "It's the story of these two old ladies living in France through two world wars, everything that happens to them, and the recipes are incidental," Ariane said.[9] "This is how I wanted Patience's book to be and not to be a conventional cookbook with veg, fruit, and so on." In other words she felt it should be less of a cookbook and more of a memoir, an account of her life with Norman.

However Patience's approach was more anthropological, and she was too serious a student of cooking and food to turn her book into a memoir. She was committed to organizing the book around the variations on different foods and edible plants and fungi she'd encountered in Greece, Catalonia, and Italy—with personal reflections folded in. Plus she felt that readers simply wouldn't put up with the same kinds of dishes cropping up again and again in different chapters. "I don't think the public would stand for this," she wrote. "They would start yelling: why aren't all the bean soups lined up together for easy reference?"[10] Moreover for Patience the recipes were anything but incidental—they were the heart of the book.

Despite their differences and frequent arguments, they battled on. According to Miranda, Ariane put her friendship with Patience on the line during that visit. "She said something none of us had the courage to say," Miranda recalled, "that there was sort of a peevish tone to Patience's writing in reference to England."[11] Patience later thanked Ariane—"like thanking one's surgeon"—for tearing the manuscript apart, which she said had helped her see the book's true meaning. "I'm so grateful for what you have done on the book," she wrote, "and certainly would never have been able to revise *Fasting and Feasting* without you."[12] What Patience didn't tell her was that after her departure she spent the next two months "resuscitating the corpse," putting back material that Ariane suggested cutting and rewriting it in the way Patience originally envisioned. She devoted new chapters to edible weeds and fungi, and scrapped most of the "vegetable tribe," which had drawn so heavily on Loudon and her research in the 1950s. By the end of August, she had sent the revised version to Tessa Sayle and would later send a copy of the same version to Deborah Rogers. "Apart from a great reduction of the text," Patience wrote to Sayle, "it has I think gained in impact and found its form."[13]

Aside from her agents and a few editors, Wolfe was the only other person Patience had asked to review the text. He had been around much of the winter of 1968–69 at Lake Garda when she was working on *Fasting and Feasting*, and Patience kept him up to date on its progress. He visited Spigolizzi regularly, the first time as early as 1970—only a year after his accident. By then he'd bought a decommissioned British ambulance, which he refitted and used during summers to travel in. That he made the journey at all was remarkable. Spigolizzi of course had no hot water or other modern conveniences that someone in Wolfe's condition would normally depend on. In fact he treated his annual sojourn to Puglia as a tonic, one that would somehow sustain him, along with Norman's wine, for the remainder of the year. "The highlight of his summers was to go down to Spig," said his friend Julia Farrington.[14]

Given that eating and drinking were the only carnal pleasures Wolfe could still indulge in, his visits revolved around Patience's cooking. "Wolfe used to say the nearest thing he gets to sex is having a grape," Farrington said. "He used to make it last forever. And would describe it in great detail."[15] Patience's devotion to him was unconditional. Of course this meant accommodating not only Wolfe but also his caregivers, whose interest in simple, rustic living, let alone food, was never a given. Several, particularly Dave Maddams and Doreen and Terry Wingate, were absolutely heroic and not only shared Wolfe's vivacity and appetites but learned to cook at his behest. Doreen once recalled Wolfe instructing her to make Irving's version of Christmas pudding and having to crush almonds by hand until her arms nearly dropped off (the recipe calls for 1 ½ pounds of almonds, skinned, dried, and reduced to a fine powder in a mortar). In an essay by Wolfe, published in *Harpers & Queen* in the late 1970s and titled "Cooking by Proxy," Wolfe is described as "shouting recipes to his helpers through the kitchen doors of his homes in Hampshire and Frosini." The recipes included in the article—baked turbot with tarragon butter, brains in batter, and guinea fowl with cream and dried mushrooms—suggest that he had very high standards. Thus visits to Spigolizzi, sometimes for several weeks, always required an extraordinary effort. "At every meal," Patience wrote in 1972, "Wolfe expects a culinary miracle."[16] They feasted on everything from dorade (sea bream) and lobster to wild turtledoves and sea urchins. After one visit Norman described the garden, littered with pigeon feathers, fish gills, chicken carcasses, and oyster shells, as looking like "the mouth of a prehistoric cave." For Patience it meant suspending her own work and setting aside the measured way of life they'd established. By the end of a visit, she was inevitably exhausted and longing for little more than bread and tomatoes. "I have lost my appetite," she wrote after Wolfe departed in 1973. "This always happens when too much devotion is paid to food."[17] Of course his visits were also filled with love, joy, and endless conversation. Wolfe's enthusiasm for art, theater, film, and literature, as well as whatever Patience and Norman were working on, never wavered.

Wolfe generally stayed in high summer and sometimes he and his entourage overlapped with other guests. In 1972 Christine Bullin, then a rare-book librarian at Harvard and a friend of Norman Janis's, paid a visit to Spigolizzi on his recommendation. In her early twenties, she was in Italy on a book-buying trip and was curious to meet these artists who Janis had been so enamored of. "Patience was sort of a Byronic figure," she said.[18] When Norman Janis and his then-wife, Nia, met Patience in Apollonas, they were also in their early twenties. Janis had a traveling fellowship from Harvard, where he studied philosophy—one of his professors had also taught Kevin Andrews—and they were making their way on foot across the island. At a crowded cafe in Apollonas one evening, Patience, dressed in a large colorful shawl, and Norman entered. "Patience was very glamorous," Janis recalled. "She was a presence."[19]

For Bullin and other young visitors who met Patience and Norman, there was a Bloomsbury-esque quality to the whole affair. The starkness of the setting and distance traveled to get there only added to the mystique. "They were singular," Bullin recalled. "Who else do you know who leaves society and commits to that kind of life forever?"[20] With Norman's sculptures dotting the landscape and his playful mural painted on the kitchen ceiling—the figures bore a distinct resemblance to Cecil Collins's images of the fool—it was as if you'd walked into an art gallery. Patience herself was strikingly beautiful, with a deeply lined face and complexion burnished by an outdoor life under the Mediterranean sun. Even in the wilds of Puglia, according to Philip Trevelyan, who visited for the first time in 1971, "she had a way of occasionally striking, cigarette in hand, the flirtatious, sophisticated pose of a starlet or member of a younger generation."[21] They were on the margins but still fashionable, engaged, and interested in the world around them. "Her wit and intellect weren't hidden," says Bullin. "She had opinions about politicians and knew what was going on in the art world. It was not as if she'd cut herself off from current affairs."[22] Bullin also recalled the rich cast of characters—friends and guests as well as strangers—who seemed to drop in with startling regularity. There was always plenty of wine, Patience and Norman's latest vintage, and conversation. Food seemed to appear with little effort. As there were no lights in the masseria other than the oil lamps, Patience often cooked in near darkness. "They [the meals] just seemed to come from nothing," recalled Leila McAlister, who visited in the early 1990s.[23]

The truth is that Spigolizzi was not as isolated as Patience and Norman might have wished. It did not take long for them to feel that the peninsula had been discovered. Soon after they arrived in 1970, other foreign artists began to buy up summer homes in the vicinity. Some, such as Klaus and Ulrike Voswinckel, came because of Helen and Arno, and others were simply seeking the same kind of solitude that had attracted Patience and Norman. Then there was the Fano Village, which from 1976 to 1980 brought at least thirty visiting artists to the neighborhood annually. Beginning in the late 1980s, several teams of archaeologists undertook projects near Spigolizzi, exploring the confluence of the early Greek and Roman civilizations. Several of them—Emmanuel Anati, Bruce Golan, Ted Robinson, and Duane Roller—became good friends and sometimes stayed with Patience and Norman. (In 1973 Patience and Norman had an extension built onto the masseria, the "tower," which provided an additional guestroom.) By the end of the 1970s, Patience said that during the summer months it was not unusual for them to host upward of twenty usually unannounced visitors of an evening. She referred to August as the "season of the herd, the flock, the *invasione.*"[24] Indeed there was an annual pattern to the wave of visitors, and Patience and Norman were all the more careful to reserve the long winter months strictly for their own work.

There was a paradox, though, in the fact that Patience and Norman had ventured so far to escape the downside of mass tourism only to find that they now served as a draw for all kinds of travelers. Of course they weren't the only draw nor even the primary one. The Salento's unspoiled beaches had already been discovered by northern Italian and German tourists, and the coast would soon be built up to accommodate the summer visitors. In 1978 Patience said that the Salento had become a destination for disaffected urban dwellers, architects, journalists, and professors of sociology. "I think it is so peculiar living in a kind of desert and so many people popping up," she wrote.[25] At the same time more and more roads were being built, beachfront property was developed, and electricity pylons erected over the hillside to power new seaside holiday villages. In 1980 the Italian government selected the as-yet-undeveloped coastline between Torre Mozza and Lido Marini, just down the road from Patience and Norman, as a possible site for a nuclear power station; Norman, who had long studied the potential risks of the nuclear industry, was aghast.

Julia Farrington, who first visited in the late 1970s, remembered Norman discussing his fear that Spigolizzi would become just another "thoroughfare," a route to somewhere else and no longer a place in its own right. It was a notion he'd expressed, in a very different context, as early as 1962, before he and Patience left England—and it would become inextricably tied to his artistic vision. "I make stone sculptures because I believe the earth will cease to be a spiritual battleground and become a place to live in," Norman wrote. "Sculptures need places. Places are holy. Thoroughfares are useful—look what usefulness has done—it has disemboweled the earth."[26]

⸙⸙⸙⸙

Patience may have been content to work away in obscurity, but Norman still felt the need to show his work and engage with other artists. From the moment they arrived, he'd expressed his fear that they might become isolated, and the Wonderhouse scheme, designed to bring artists to them, was a way of guarding against this. Early on a few artists indeed came to stay and work at Spigolizzi, notably Daphne Henrion and Willi Hartung. In January 1973 Patience and Norman had a joint show in Zurich with

Willi. (The show Norman had been hoping to arrange at the Cordier and Ekstrom gallery in New York soon after they moved to Puglia never materialized.) Patience exhibited some of her jewelry and Norman a selection of sculptures. "Zurich will remind me that I am an artist!" Norman wrote, "which is after all a sort of 'member of society.'"[27] It was their first extended period away from Spigolizzi, and the contrast was striking. Upon returning in February Patience wrote, "After all that central heating in Switzerland, I was amazed, do we really live here?"[28]

A more ambitious show was Norman's solo exhibition at the Whitechapel Gallery in March 1975 titled *Figures in Stone and Drawings from Spigolizzi*. The twenty-five sculptures, most of which had been completed in Puglia, had to be transported to Carrara and then dispatched from there to London. There were all of the usual headaches in dealing with a gallery—the show was delayed several times, and the director who had initially commissioned the exhibition was gone by the time it opened. But for Norman it was a happy reunion with old friends, and he was able to reconnect with Cecil Collins, Peggy Angus, and others.

Norman was never entirely at ease with his decision to live on the margins of the art world and had yet to strike that balance between the asceticism he felt he needed for his work and his desire to engage with a larger audience. The Wonderhouse had not moved beyond the drawing-board stage, and Norman still felt he had a universe of ideas to communicate. In late 1975 he acknowledged that Wijdeveld, now ninety, would have likely been disappointed in his "torch bearer."[29] Thus when he was offered a job to teach sculpture part time at the Central School of Art and Design in London, the prospect was hugely appealing. In December 1976 Norman received a letter from Patrick Reyntiens, head of the fine art department and a well-known stained glass artist, informing him that the principal lecturer in sculpture had died and that Norman's name had been raised as a replacement. Reyntiens worked with Cecil Collins, who taught painting and life drawing at the college and likely recommended Norman for the position. Norman was also a friend of Paul Bird, the school's vice principal, who had taught at the Royal College of Art under Robin Darwin. It would be a part-time post running through the spring and summer terms with a working field trip to quarries in Cornwall or to other venues of Norman's choosing. It would pay reasonably well and, aware of Norman's commitments in Italy, the school was willing to tailor the position to his needs. A week later Norman wrote saying he would accept the position and enthusiastically described possible visits to quarries in Dorset, Shepton Mallet, and Bodmin Moor, his old stomping grounds.[30]

Intellectually and professionally it was the kind of opportunity he'd always hoped for. He'd be teaching, which he loved and by all accounts had a gift for. And he'd be plugged back in to the art world, surrounded by colleagues and friends. He'd even convinced Patience that it would somehow be an extension of what they were doing at Spigolizzi. "Everything seemed beautifully tied up," he wrote.[31]

Yet leaving Spigolizzi and Patience for such long periods would have serious implications. Norman would be leaving at the height of the agricultural season, when his labor was most needed. Patience would have to look after the masseria on her own for at least four months at a time, a formidable task. And, worse, there'd been a rash of thefts in the area, and Patience and Norman never felt entirely secure. (Over the years the house would be broken into all too frequently, as would Helen and Arno's Bufalaria.) Norman Janis recalled Patience disapproving of the idea altogether—she'd become sharply critical of life in England—and discouraging Norman from going.

Though he had accepted the position, Norman was not entirely comfortable with the prospect of leaving Spigolizzi every year. Around that time their friend and Norman's former assistant, Roberto Bernacchi, came down from Carrara to visit. He was captivated by what they'd done with the masseria and the possibilities it afforded. This made an impression on Norman, who was gradually coming to the conclusion that he could be more effective working and teaching in Puglia, even if he reached far fewer people, than in London. Spigolizzi was an example of living art, he said, whereas London would have little to offer beyond museums and galleries. He became convinced that if he left he'd be abandoning his larger vision rather than building on it.

In early February he wrote a second letter to Reyntiens declining the job.[32] Reyntiens was not surprised and replied, "I'm not sure you wouldn't have been stifled by all the red-tape and the student indifference." In a separate letter to Collins, whom he felt he'd let down, Norman wrote, "I was hooked intellectually but the whole of me had other things to attend to."[33] "He felt that becoming this character in Southampton Row was a sort of putting off of actually making his own Wonderhouse and making a . . . final statement," Patience wrote in a letter to Ariane. "He suddenly sees he can illuminate something for a few people, why not the few people who come to his door?"[34]

They were both relieved. For Norman, now in his midfifties and fully aware that such an opportunity would never come again, it was a turning point. His life's work, or as Patience put it his "final statement," would be firmly rooted in their labors at Spigolizzi. They opened a bottle of champagne from Maria Vittoria and celebrated what felt like yet another new beginning.

⚜

Norman had been planning to visit his mother in London later that year, but now that he'd decided not to take the position at the Central School, she agreed to come to Puglia instead. She'd been once before in early 1971 for what was a particularly stormy visit. Indeed at that time she'd even entertained the idea of finding a house nearby and living out her final years there. Patience warned her that it was nothing like the view from Lake Garda or the "Italy you dream of."[35] The fact is she and Patience had never gotten on well, and Muriel, who'd always been close to Ursula, had difficultly, at least initially, accepting the kind of life Patience and Norman had embraced. During that first visit in 1971, she and Patience had clashed, and there was a kind of falling out. "Every cup of tea she offers me is a poison cup," Patience wrote to Wolfe.[36] In a letter to Norman after her visit, Muriel concluded, "You will live and work at Spigolizzi, darling, but I shall never come again, my dreams are finished." Olive had visited once as well in 1971, but that had been much more successful. According to Patience, Olive shelled a million peas, and Norman had to wrest the gardening tools from her hand. "That is all that is required of visitors to Spigolizzi," Patience noted.[37] Needless to say the notion that Muriel might move to Puglia was dashed.

They were hoping for a rapprochement of sorts in May 1977—Muriel was now seventy-eight—but on May 10, three days after her arrival, she died of a stroke. Norman found her in the bathroom at 3 a.m. and in darkness rushed to Presicce in search of a doctor. They held a mass for her at the local church and she was interred amongst the peasants of Salve.

For Patience, Muriel's death opened a number of old wounds. (Muriel's death was followed over the next several years by the passing of many old friends, former lovers, and colleagues, including Alexander Gibson, Jack Nisberg, Philip Toynbee, and Elisabeth Lutyens.) On a recent trip to London, she'd sorted out her affairs and updated her will—in fact Patience had gone to London just before Muriel's departure from England, and they had traveled down to Puglia together. She'd also seen Olive and, as they so often did, parted on less than favorable terms. Patience felt that Olive had never been able to get over the death of her youngest daughter, Helen, and that she somehow blamed her and Tania. She was also convinced that Olive had never been able to forgive her for her relationship with Thomas Gray and the circumstances of her life in the 1940s and '50s. "Have I done you a wrong?" Patience wrote to Olive a few days after Muriel's death. "Perhaps in my life simply by not being what you hoped and expected me to be."[38] On subsequent visits before Olive's death in February 1984, Patience often referred to the "black sheep feeling" and the continuing power struggle provoked by the rare family gathering. "It felt a bit like stepping into a Harold Pinter play," Miranda recalled, "where everyone is talking at cross purposes, getting the wrong end of the stick."[39] Patience described a visit to Olive in 1981 as "horrific" and summed up their relationship by drawing on one of her favorite metaphors: "You live in a garden, and I live in a wilderness," she wrote. "You are a pillar of society and I am a person in the wild. We can wave at each other."[40]

Though they may have been, so to speak, on opposite shores, Patience and Olive kept up a regular correspondence. Patience often found it easier to maintain relationships over great distances than in person, and though she rarely saw her grandchildren she made her presence felt in her letters and the drawings she sent. "There was always a letter on the table or sideboard," Lisa recalled. "I loved reading them."[41] In those last years of Olive's life, Patience asked her to recall everything she knew about the family's past, especially her father's. "It helps one to understand oneself," Patience wrote.[42] Around this time Patience became increasingly interested in the fact that her great-grandfather had been a rabbi and her grandfather a

Hebrew scholar who converted to Christianity. In later life she placed more and more significance on this aspect of her heritage, even attributing her "disrespectability or inability to come to terms with society" to the suppression of her Jewish roots.[43] For this she blamed her parents, who "put a lid on it and buttered the outside with Edwardian gentility: So I now see why I spent a great part of my youth blowing the lid."[44] Though her interest in Judaism was never more than intellectual, she and Norman did take it upon themselves to summon a rabbi to serve as confessor when Arno was dying in 1989. They hatched the plan with their friend Aldo Magagnino, who contacted the Chief Rabbi of Rome, Elio Toaff. To Aldo's surprise Toaff was keen to help out and said he would send one of his subordinates. Several days later Aldo picked the rabbi up at the airport and drove him to the Bufalaria. Patience and Norman never let on that they'd engineered the improbable visit, and Helen and Arno—self-avowed atheists—were undoubtedly shocked when the rabbi appeared at their door. Apparently, though, Arno and the rabbi hit it off, and Arno was pleased to be reminded of his spiritual roots. They conversed in Yiddish for about an hour, and then the rabbi departed. Arno died the following day. The rabbi did not have time to stop by Spigolizzi, but Patience had prepared a kosher meal in anticipation of his visit. According to Aldo she was "thrilled at the idea of receiving a rabbi at Spigolizzi."[45]

Patience admired Olive's vigor and independence—she was still splitting her own firewood at the age of ninety—and was deeply grateful for how much she'd helped them over the years. She called Olive, along with Willi Hartung and the Hubrechts, one of their few "benefactors." After Muriel's death she suggested that they both bury the hatchet before it was too late. The obstacle between them, she said, was the inability or unwillingness to forgive: "Not just those who have to be forgiven, but she who forgives," Patience wrote pointedly. Several years later, in 1982, Patience struck up a correspondence with Ken Matthews, the vicar of Rogate, who'd played such an important role in her life just after the war. Questions of faith were clearly on Patience's mind. She'd recently written to Olive that she thought she leaned "too much towards the dark side" and confided to Matthews that she felt Olive had "resolutely refused to accept Christ's message." "Has she?" Matthews replied. "I never thought that when she used to come steady to Church at Terwick."[46]

Patience last saw her mother in 1983 on a dispiriting winter visit to London. Olive had the flu and managed to pass it on to Patience. By then Olive had moved from a flat overlooking the churchyard in Rogate to a nursing home in Midhurst, not far from Fyning. (Olive had sold Hill View in the mid 1960s.) When she died the following February, Patience did not return to England for the funeral.

The wilderness was no longer a metaphor—since moving to Spigolizzi, Patience had been living in it. In her letters she referred to the restorative power of wild places and lamented the fact that there was so little wilderness left. *Fasting and Feasting* was, she now said, essentially about wilderness, "the limestone one."[47] Nowhere was she more at ease than in the macchia, which she described as the "cradle of every valuable herb."[48]

Indeed after nearly a decade of living with the macchia at her door, Patience had come to know its plant life with a degree of intimacy she'd been unable to attain in Greece or Carrara. Visitors often recalled her as a kind of spectral figure drifting through the landscape. Unlike Norman, though, she had little interest in teaching. She rarely took anyone other than her dog on her foraging trips. She was just as unlikely to invite anyone into the kitchen. And though she continued to learn from the local people—even for those who had moved out of the countryside, gathering weeds was still common—she preferred to wander alone. In autumn she picked mushrooms almost every day, particularly varieties of the species *Lactarius*. These included the *mucchiareddi*, which were often found growing beneath cistus and in local dialect was known as *mucchia*. She had even come across the excellent but rare *Hygrophorus poetarum*, fungus of the poets, which Alan Davidson always maintained did not exist in Puglia and was a "fantasy of [her] imagination."[49] Patience continued to identify varieties that were new to her well into the 1990s. At times she said the autumn harvest was bountiful enough to provide a three-course dinner consisting entirely of fungi. "If it's a bad day," Patience wrote one November, "I fall back on weeds."[50]

Weeds had long been a staple of the Salentine diet as well as a reminder of the region's enduring poverty. Abundant and easily accessible, they were gathered more out of necessity than by choice. During the Second World War, when bread was severely rationed and there was little else to eat (dried figs were the other staple), weeds were one of the few dependable foods. But after the war as the economy gradually improved and many workers left for northern Italy or Europe to find employment, the reliance on edible weeds declined. At the same time produce from supermarkets, including cultivated chicory, began to supplement and in some cases replace the traditional diet. Inevitably perhaps, much of the knowledge passed down from one generation to the next, traditionally from mothers to daughters, began to fade. By the 1970s when Patience and Norman had settled in the area, the knowledge seemed in danger of disappearing. For many this was hardly viewed as a loss: Weeds had come to symbolize privation and hunger.

Patience of course viewed them differently. Over the years she had come to believe that weeds were a source of energy—she said an afternoon's work could be performed on a dish of weeds alone—and she and Norman ate them regularly. A typical lunch was an assortment of edible weeds boiled, drained, and then sautéed in olive oil and hot peppers and served with bread and cheese. "I think one has to eat them daily," she told Alan Davidson.[51] These were often supplemented with other edible wild plants, depending on the season, including wild asparagus, beets, or fennel. The herbs of the macchia, which Patience pointed out have higher concentrations of essential oils than their cultivated counterparts due to the harshness of the environment they grow in, were a ubiquitous presence in all of Patience's cooking. At certain times of year, particularly early spring and autumn, the richness of what the macchia had to offer was staggering.

Ada Ricchiuto, a friend who met Patience and Norman in the 1970s, recalled first catching sight of Patience walking in the macchia with her basket. Ada had grown up in the nearby village of Acquarica and knew well that a certain stigma was attached to those who gathered weeds. Her husband, Mario, came from a better-off family whose father grew his own fennel, cauliflower, and chicory and looked down on those who had to scavenge for food. Thus it wasn't that Patience taught her how to identify or cook edible weeds, she said; she taught her to value them. "Patience could have bought her vegetables but chose not to," she said. "That was significant."[52]

As she ranged over the macchia, Patience also began to collect shards of Bronze Age pottery, fragments of ancient tools, pieces of bone, and the occasional arrowhead. She and Norman had always maintained a peripheral interest in archaeology and ancient history. They had a library of books on everything from Celtic runes and the cave paintings of Lascaux to Stonehenge and the pyramids of Giza. Being a stone carver, Norman knew his "porphyry from his soapstone." As Nicolas wrote in an unpublished essay describing their collection of artifacts amassed over a thirty-year period, "A chip of flint turned up by the plow in a calcareous landscape would not have escaped his notice."

On Naxos Norman had discovered a handful of obsidian arrowheads and other prehistoric tools, and Patience made a point of visiting the museum of antiquities in the port city whenever possible. "Islands do funny things to time," she wrote from Naxos. "You don't know the day of the week, you can't remember the recent past, but the Stone Age 4,000 years ago seems quite near."[53] In Puglia the past came into even sharper focus. From the moment they set foot on the hilltop near Spigolizzi, they recognized what must have been its strategic and historic importance. Patience wrote an unpublished essay, "Speculations on Spigolizzi," in which she explored the meaning of the masseria's name and the likely function of the specchie, the stone mounds that dotted the landscape.

As early as 1975 Patience was writing with great excitement about the fragments of Bronze Age pottery she and Norman discovered near Spigolizzi. Whereas before they'd only encountered rather crude Neolithic objects on the hillside, these pieces were delicate, even refined. At that time there were no professional archaeologists working in the immediate area—studies had been made in the past, however, and throughout the 1970s several keen local amateur archaeologists were active around Spigolizzi—and Patience and Norman simply put the objects away, occasionally displaying them for friends or visitors.

In 1978 Patience wrote to Professor Emmanuel Anati, the authority on rock art who had done extensive fieldwork at Val Camonica in Lombardy in the 1950s. Her letter described the rock incisions she'd observed on an excursion to the Pangaion Hills near Kavalla while visiting Miranda in 1974. Ashlyn, who was doing geological work in the region, had in fact discovered these drawings of various animals and sticklike figures with outstretched hands several years earlier. The correspondence marked the beginning of a long friendship. Anati, who taught paleo-ethnology at the University of Lecce beginning in 1979, would sometimes visit Patience and Norman and examine their collection, which was growing in size and scope. He informed them that the flints they'd discovered were not quite as old as they had thought—roughly 13,000 not 30,000 years old—which placed them in the Mesolithic period, just after the retreat of the last ice age, when rising sea levels submerged the coastal plain. The land around Spigolizzi, a couple of kilometers from the coast but on a hillside, would have been strategic, which accounts for the presence of so many Mesolithic artifacts.

According to Anati Patience and Norman were more interested in archaeology from a cultural and aesthetic point of view rather than as a science. What did the objects signify? How were they used? What did they say about the people who'd made them? Indeed their approach was thoroughly unscientific in that they did not record the dates or precise locations of the finds, nor describe the objects in any kind of detail. It was the "aesthetics and the meaning of the forms of the artifacts" that mattered.[54] In December 1983 they discovered a trove of artifacts in one of the unplowed fields beyond the masseria, which included flint blades and tools and their first arrowhead. A year later the superintendent of antiquities in Lecce inspected the collection and declared Patience and Norman to be its "curators." "We are custodians of a museum," Patience wrote with evident pride.[55] Their collection would eventually number some three thousand items, and they were required to keep it under lock and key.

For Patience the objects opened a window onto the food-gathering habits of the Mesolithic people who had first settled the hillside millennia ago. She felt strongly that there was a link between the tools she and Norman had discovered and the region's food-gathering culture up to the present. She speculated that after the gradual disappearance of large fauna, whose habitat had been severely diminished by rising seas, the diet of Mesolithic people slowly began to change. Over time hunter–gatherers turned their attention to mollusks, small birds, frogs, and snails, thus necessitating the development of such refined tools. She liked to point out that in her dictionary of Salentine dialects the largest entries were for snails, frogs, and wild chicory, respectively. "I think one can say that the mesolithic people . . . were pioneers in gastronomy," she wrote in *Honey from a Weed*. "Their artefacts are not only small, often minute, but also made with incredible skill—fish hooks, *mezzalune*, tiny blades to prise open the reluctant bivalves, refined points to tease out the land and sea snails."[56]

Still, as with fungi so many years before, it was the beauty of the objects—"jewel-like fragments," as she called them—that initially drew her. For Patience their significance and meaning went far beyond whatever material application they might have had. "I have often thought that it is in the *Musée de l'Homme* that one realizes that the exquisite beauty of the earliest artefacts in ivory and flint and bone prove that civilisation began long before cities, commerce, etc.," she wrote to Anati.[57] She viewed the interest in and knowledge of wild foods as a connection to that remote past.

It was Patience and Norman's hope as official "curators" of the collection that it might serve as a kind of cultural bulwark against the ongoing development of the hillside. They were encouraged in this by several archaeological digs that were undertaken nearby throughout the late 1980s and '90s.[58] Duane Roller, an archaeologist who taught Greek and Latin at Ohio State University and conducted work in the Salento throughout much of 1990s, said it was a blessing to be introduced to Patience and Norman and that his own project was greatly enhanced by the work they'd already done. He described them as "gifted amateurs," which the discipline has long relied on, albeit grudgingly, and dedicated his final report to them.[59] Though Patience felt that she and Norman were, in a way, guardians of a sacred landscape, she was not blind to the many threats it faced from the dumping of toxic waste in abandoned quarries, the widespread use of pesticides, the construction of holiday bungalows, and the specter of a nuclear power plant. In 1984 she acknowledged that "practically the whole of the Salento is 'desecrated'" and had little conviction that what was left would be protected.[60] If anything a retreat into the ancient past, its tools, customs, and practices, was a way of effacing the horrors of the present.

CHAPTER THIRTEEN

Honey from a Weed

By the early 1980s Patience had been unpublished for more than a decade. It had been even longer since she'd brought out anything written specifically about food. She said she was happy to work away in obscurity and sometimes invoked Stendhal's "Happy Few" to justify writing and making jewelry only for a select circle of friends. Meanwhile she had drifted ever farther from the food-writing world and the Hampstead literary scene and saw her way of life as being entirely at odds with the values of the publishing industry. The hope of publishing *Fasting and Feasting* had largely faded, but Patience continued to revise and circulate the manuscript. In 1980 she sent it to her Hampstead friend and former neighbor Gwenda David, a well-known editorial representative for Viking Press in New York; David said it was the "most enchanting book" that she'd read in a very long time.[1] Deborah Rogers continued to work on Patience's behalf as well. In 1982 there was a flicker of hope that John Murray would publish the book—in the end nothing came of it. Patience even made another attempt to pitch the book to André Deutsch's Diana Athill, who she visited in London during her trip to England in February 1983. Patience's pendulum suggested a favorable outcome, but this meeting, too, went nowhere. By spring 1984 Rogers seemed to have exhausted all options and wrote to Patience, "The sad thing is I am no nearer to finding a publisher for the book at the moment. I love it myself, as you know, but just haven't managed to overcome the tedious—but I suppose realistic—reservations that are voiced by all the hardnosed publishers I have tried so far."[2]

In late 1982 Patience sent an article and selection of recipes titled "Just in Case You Want to Make Coppa," based on her experience raising pigs, to Ann Barr at *Harpers & Queen*. (In 1970 the magazine, previously known as *Harper's Bazaar* merged with *Queen* magazine and changed its name; in 2006 it reverted to its original name.) *Harper's Bazaar* had long been one of the leading lights of food journalism—Elizabeth David started writing for them in 1949—and was one of the magazines Patience contributed to in the late 1950s. The article was a detailed account of how to make not only coppa but also a variety of cured meats and other delicacies. The piece was based on a letter Patience had written to Philip Trevelyan and his wife, Nelly, which began, "You asked how to make a salami," and was followed by three pages of densely typed instructions on how to make *prosciutto crudo*, coppa, pancetta, and rillettes. The article ended up in the hands of Paul Levy, food and wine editor of the *Observer*, who also freelanced for *Harpers & Queen* and worked closely with Barr (they published *The Official Foodie Handbook* together in 1984). They declined to publish Patience's lengthy article, but Levy passed it along to his friend Alan Davidson.

Davidson held an esteemed, if somewhat peripheral, position in the food-writing world. A former diplomat, he had published a highly regarded cookbook and reference work, *Mediterranean Seafood*, in 1972. The book was a product of the years Alan spent in Tunisia in the early 1960s, where he and his wife, Jane, had been overwhelmed by the variety of fresh fish and seafood available, most of which they'd never seen before. Alan, a classical scholar and bibliophile, was unable to find a decent reference work to help with the task of identifying what was on offer in restaurants and local markets. So he decided to write one himself, essentially for the benefit of his wife and perhaps other travelers who were similarly flummoxed. The problem was that Alan had no scientific training and could find little published documentation to help him untangle the vast and complex subject. To his good fortune it was at this very moment that the Italian government dispatched the world's foremost authority on Mediterranean fish, Professor Giorgio Bini, to Tunisia as part of a delegation to investigate a maritime dispute in the Gulf of Tunis. Alan, the scholar-diplomat, and Bini, the gastronome-naturalist, made a deal.

"I discovered that Bini, who weighed a ton and broke three of our dining room chairs, loved birdwatching," Alan later recounted. "My Ambassador had a big car with a chauffeur. I told Bini, 'I will fix you up with some really good birdwatching times if you teach me the scientific names for all these fish.'"[3]

With Bini's help Alan produced what he described as a "primitive little booklet" titled *Sea Fish of Tunisia and the Central Mediterranean*. It was nonetheless an ambitious undertaking and included the names of 144 species of fish in several languages, as well as lists of mollusks, crustaceans, and other sea creatures. Recognizing its value, one of Alan's colleagues, Roger Eland, who had known Elizabeth David in Cairo, passed the booklet along to her, and she praised it in her weekly column for the *Spectator*. David was impressed with the thoroughness of the work and Alan's "gift for conveying memorable information in a way so effortless that his book makes lively reading for its own sake."[4] David's popular column was undoubtedly responsible for the booklet's runaway success, and in June 1963 she wrote to Alan to report, "A lot of maddened *Spectator* readers and friends are still shrieking for copies of your book."[5] Not surprisingly they struck up a correspondence, and she eventually encouraged him to publish an expanded version of his work in the U.K., putting him in touch with her friend and editor Jill Norman.

Their relationship did not end there. After Alan retired from the Foreign Office and returned to London, he set up a small publishing house, Prospect Books, and a journal, *Petits Propos Culinaires*, whose first issue appeared in 1979. Something of a lark, *Petits Propos Culinaires* was the brainchild of Alan, Elizabeth David, and American food writer Richard Olney, who was then editing the Time-Life Books Good Cook series but was hamstrung by the fact that he was permitted to use only recipes that had been previously published. He and Alan conspired to publish the desired recipes not yet committed to print in *Petits Propos Culinaires* under a handful of pseudonyms. Elizabeth David was one of the early contributors.

It was of course *Petits Propos Culinaires* that Levy had in mind when he sent Patience's article on coppa to Alan. Alan sat on it for about a month and finally wrote to Patience to say that he wasn't going to use it, but that she might try the newly formed American Institute of Wine and Food, which had plans to launch its own quarterly journal. They eventually published Patience's essay in two parts in spring 1983, but failed to pay her.[6] Alan, feeling in some way responsible—he had told Patience that the Institute planned to pay "generously"—came to her defense. And Patience, who eventually—following Alan's intervention—

received $150 for the article, called him the "St. George of the culinary world."[7] The misunderstanding marked the beginning of a long and extraordinary friendship.

In one of her very first letters to Alan, Patience told him she was an admirer of *Mediterranean Seafood*. She also said she'd asked Deborah Rogers to send him a copy of the draft of *Fasting and Feasting* some years before but that Deborah had said she didn't "know" him. Patience had come across *Mediterranean Seafood* on a rare visit to England in 1981 and was impressed by its exhaustive treatment of the subject and the quality of its illustrations. As someone who had spent a great deal of time sorting out the Latin names of edible weeds, she could sympathize with Alan's efforts to provide taxonomies of unfamiliar fish and crustaceans. While living in Carrara Patience had also made use of Bini's catalogue of fishes prepared for the Food and Agricultural Organization in 1965 in her own attempt to identify Mediterranean fish.

Alan, ever curious, expressed an interest in reading Patience's book but explained that he was not in a position to publish anything other than "trouble free" facsimile reprints. This was in part due to Prospect Books' precarious finances but also because Alan was principally occupied with *The Oxford Companion to Food*, which he'd begun work on in 1976 and wouldn't finish for more than twenty years. One writer, who profiled Alan midway through his work on the project, said the tome, which eventually numbered more than one million words, "assumed in his life the status of a jealous and insatiable kept woman."[8] (Indeed his wife, Jane, eventually bought a small flat whose sole purpose was to house reference material related to the encyclopedia.) Yet Alan was tempted by *Fasting and Feasting* and agreed to help Patience find a willing publisher even if Prospect Books couldn't take it on alone. He proposed pitching it to John Harris of Aris Books or to the University Press of Virginia, which sometimes distributed Prospect Books' titles in the United States. From the beginning he sensed that the book had great potential.

He was also uninhibited in his critique of the manuscript, suggesting early on that Patience bring it up to date, greatly expand the bibliography, reorganize some of the sections, include common names alongside the Latin for edible weeds (Patience initially resisted this, believing it would be too confusing given the number of languages and dialects involved), and come up with a new title. Alan had some concerns that *Fasting and Feasting* was too close to Bridget Ann Henisch's 1976 book *Fast and Feast: Food in Medieval Society*. However he also made it clear that the book should not be edited in a way that made it more like a conventional cookbook, which he thought would "destroy its special virtue."[9]

That Patience, famously hostile to editorial intervention, was not put off by Alan's comments was the result of several factors. Alan had already endeared himself to her through his efforts to secure payment for the American Institute of Wine and Food article; she respected his scholarship and evenhandedness; and she finally saw the possibility of publishing a book she'd been working on for close to fifteen years. Plus he wrote lovely whimsical letters.

Thus, by the end of 1984, though the book had no firm backing from anyone, not even Prospect Books, Patience agreed to move ahead with the revisions Alan recommended. This was not undertaken without a certain degree of doubt as to whether it would bear fruit; Patience had gone through a similar process with Ariane in 1976 to no avail. In June 1985 she and Norman traveled to London to deal with Patience's Hampstead flat, which she'd been trying to sell since 1983. They had dinner with Alan and Jane at their home in World's End and discussed the possibility of financing a pilot edition of the book, perhaps along the lines of Irving's Catalan cookbook—in other words a limited print run primarily for friends and family. One idea was to see if Norman's brother-in-law, Stephan Schorr-Kon, would provide an interest-free loan. Plan B was for Patience herself to supply the loan if the sale of the Billiardroom went through. The meeting, according to Alan, was a "landmark occasion," and he was especially delighted to receive as a gift from Patience the complete 13-volume set of Curnonsky and Rouff's classic guide to French restaurants and inns, *La France Gastronomique*.[10]

Later that summer the sale of the Billiardroom was finalized (she sold to her longstanding tenant, Trevor Pinnock). In August Patience sent Alan a check for £5,000—an interest-free loan to be paid back within two years of publication—to cover the costs of publishing a pilot edition. "As I have never written a check of this kind in my life," Patience wrote, "it gives me an especial pleasure to send it in your direction."[11] According to Alan's sister, Rosemary, "He called me up and said we seem to be publishing this book."[12]

Editing the manuscript began almost immediately. Over the course of the next year, Patience and Alan exchanged at least seventy working letters. Patience insisted that they be sent express—ordinary letters sometimes took three weeks to arrive in Puglia—which amounted to an additional cost of more than £100 for Prospect Books. For Alan it was well worth it.

He later wrote that his correspondence with Patience "proved to be by far the most voluminous and in many ways the most fascinating of any I have ever conducted."[13]

Patience and Alan's friendship was in many ways an unlikely one. Alan was a career diplomat who had devoted thirty years of his life to the Foreign Office, culminating in a post as ambassador in Laos from 1973 to 1975. He'd studied classics at Oxford, abstained from alcohol, and was something of a technophile, reading avidly about the latest gadgets and taking an early interest in computers (he kept Patience abreast of periodic developments in the field). He loved to talk and write about food more than he liked to actually prepare it, a preference exemplified by his founding of the Oxford Symposium on Food and Cookery, an annual academic conference known for its unapologetic devotion to esoteric topics. By all accounts, even his own, he was a lousy cook. Moreover some of the things he most liked to eat, the foods he had grown up with, would have shocked Patience: corned-beef salad, white sliced bread and butter, steak and kidney pie, and such sweets as spotted dick, jam roly-poly, and suet pudding. "Many of Alan's 'food' friends were horrified by the sort of food we sometimes ate for lunch," wrote Helen Saberi, who worked for Alan for fourteen years (they published a book on trifle together in 2001).[14] According to his daughter Caroline, "Everybody dreaded Alan's meals."[15] Patience on the other hand was a self-described anarchist who extolled the virtues of wine and had turned her back on modern life. She was also very much an intuitive cook who thought nothing of butchering half an animal in her kitchen or scouring the macchia for mushrooms or edible plants most people would never touch. One can only wonder at what she would've thought, if she'd had a television, of Alan preparing kippers and toad-in-the-hole to the delight of an American audience on *The Martha Stewart Show* as part of a tour to coincide with the US publication of *The Oxford Companion to Food*.

Yet in other ways they were kindred spirits. Patience was familiar with *Mediterranean Seafood* but did not have a copy of her own; she promptly ordered one from Alan and called it a "triumph of wit and logic."[16] While much narrower in focus than her own book, *Mediterranean Seafood* had managed to present more than two hundred species of fish with various names in several languages in a clear and concise manner, with levity and a sense of history. "It also makes me laugh," Patience wrote. "I have this vision of you surrounded by fantastic ladies polishing their already shining copper pans in the hope that you may arrive for dinner."[17] The book also relied entirely on drawings, some of which were culled from nineteenth-century texts, instead of photographs.

Patience was deeply touched to see that Alan had included Irving's Catalan cookbook in his bibliography, and she noted that he and Irving were both classical scholars. In fact there was a certain resemblance between Alan and Irving: They were both diminutive, slightly disheveled, and elfin in appearance. Moreover she admired his independence, willingness to publish books he believed in, and unpretentious approach to food. She also came to appreciate Alan's nonculinary interests: He'd written a novel, *Something Quite Big*, a romantic thriller set in Brussels, that was partly based on his diplomatic career; he was obsessed with film stars of the 1930s and '40s (he planned to write a book of essays on the subject but only got as far as Carole Lombard); and he drove a 1953 Bentley. When he and Jane lived not far from Elizabeth David in Chelsea, he used to give her rides to the London Library at 14 St. James Square, where she often worked.

It was not only film divas who piqued his interest but also the group of fashionable food writers who came to prominence after the war— Elizabeth David, M. F. K. Fisher, and Patience. Alan was friends with M. F. K. Fisher, as well, and visited her on trips to America. He introduced

Patience to her work and felt their writing shared certain stylistic simi-
larities, a point he made when he was promoting *Honey from a Weed*.
Though Patience enjoyed reading her books—she described her prose as
"witty" and "voluptuary"—she considered Fisher a "culinary Medea" and
"hardly a cook."[18] "Patience was definitely among the top three hero-
worshipped women, and Alan considered her a wonderful stylist," said
his daughter Caroline.[19] "He was of course completely overcome by the
strength of her personality," his sister, Rosemary, recalled.[20] He was also
fascinated by her way of life, bits and pieces of which were described in
her captivating letters, and by Norman's works of art.

The uncertainty over financing the book left them with just about
a year to complete the revisions and the illustrations. As early as 1969
Patience had asked Miranda and her then-daughter-in-law, Corinna
Sargood, to illustrate the book. Corinna had already done some drawings
on Naxos when she and Nick visited in 1963 and on a return trip in 1969,
but the majority of the artwork was completed after Prospect Books took
the project on. Corinna spent a week in Puglia with Patience in early
October, and in the end the book contained more than one hundred of her
drawings. Beginning in September 1985 Patience and Alan went through
the book chapter by chapter, Alan sending Patience comments and questions and Patience returning detailed lists of corrections and amendments,
in red and black ink, all performed on her Olivetti typewriter. Notwith-
standing the occasional postal strike or the fact that her typewriter ribbon
sometimes dried up in the Salentine heat, Alan was quite impressed with
how fast Patience was able to turn things around. "Patience is being very
quick with her responses to our copy-editing suggestions," he wrote in
November. "Indeed her celerity puts us to shame!"[21]

Patience made it clear early on that she was only interested in dealing directly with Alan and not his copy editor and assistant, Candida
Brazil, though Brazil's insights often made their way into Alan's letters.
In one of the few letters Patience addressed directly to Brazil, she wrote,
"You mustn't think I don't appreciate your labours, I do, and thank you—I
also stick to my guns."[22] "She preferred to get letters from Alan," Brazil
recalled. "We learned that quite quickly."[23] Not only did she enjoy reading Alan's letters but she also responded favorably to his suggestions. He
was a tactful editor, perhaps drawing on his experience as a diplomat, and

had a way of getting his writers to come round to his point of view. "Alan of course was very clever in that he knew how to work with people in the nicest possible way," said Helen Saberi, whose *Afghan Food and Cookery* was published by Prospect Books the same year as *Honey from a Weed*. "He knew how to get the most out of me or any of his authors."[24]

Alan and Patience quickly entered into a lively and intellectually charged editorial exchange. They were both well versed in the history of cookbooks, especially ancient Greek and Roman texts, and in natural history, and indeed linguistics. "He understood her," said Brazil. "She was very ready to be angered and misunderstood, and he didn't fall into any of the traps. He knew how to handle her completely. And she immediately respected him for that."[25] Perhaps Alan's greatest asset as an editor was the same quality that set his own writing apart: an ability to convey scientific and scholarly information in a highly readable and indeed entertaining fashion. And as a publisher who specialized in cookbooks, he knew how to present recipes concisely, especially when dealing with several different languages and complex, little-known subjects. Alan may have steered the ship when it came to editing *Honey from a Weed*, but there was plenty of input from others, including his wife, Jane, and his children. He kept a small blue notebook on the cover of which he'd written "Patience Gray: Fasting and Feasting," to which Candida, and later her replacement, Idonea Muggeridge, and others, contributed questions, comments, and queries. In it they addressed everything from grammar and word usage to the merits of various recipes and questions of style. On one page someone wrote, "Ask AD if he finds this chapter confusing."

From the outset Alan made it clear that the book should be user-friendly and accessible, with some of the attributes of a reference work. The layout was especially important since many of the recipes were part of larger narratives and needed to be delineated without completely disrupting the flow. The recipes of course also had to make sense, and Alan and others tested many of them, including the Naxian fish soup, about which Alan and Patience exchanged several letters. There also needed to be a standard way of organizing the various entries in chapters on vegetables, fungi, fish, and flowers. "We want to have readers become familiar with the layout," Alan wrote, "so that they 'know their way around' the material in the book and have a feel for the construction of the recipes, etc."[26] Yet he also made it clear that this emphasis on clarity and organization would not interfere with Patience's style, which is what had drawn him to the book in the first place. Patience at times had a tendency to write overly long sentences, by the end of which the reader had lost his way. Angela Carter would later compare the cadence of her prose to the seventeenth-century writer Sir Thomas Browne. "The verve and poetic qualities of your style are entirely compatible with total lucidity," is how Alan put it. "The latter is desirable, especially in imparting recipes."[27]

Which isn't to say that she took everything Alan said as gospel. On the contrary she challenged him at every turn and at times complained about his unrelenting scrutiny of her text. But in the end she almost always came to accept his point of view. She even came round on the question of including American cups and measures in the recipes, a practice she loathed and had vigorously opposed when working on the translation of *Larousse Gastronomique*. "You really put me through it with those fish and fungi!" she wrote in November 1985. "But thank you! How lucky I am to be rapped over the knuckles by you."[28]

Yet there were numerous points of contention that went unresolved and issues that they returned to over the course of their correspondence long after the book was published. There was one recipe Alan simply couldn't fathom. Ironically it had to do with a dish that involved no cooking and in its purest form required only three ingredients. *Pa amb tomàquet*, the simplest of Catalan dishes, consists of nothing more than bread, tomatoes, and olive oil. The ripe tomato is squeezed or crushed onto both sides of the bread, which is then doused with olive oil, and sprinkled with salt (occasionally garlic, anchovies, or thin slices of ham are added). Variations on this merenda can be found throughout the Mediterranean, and it was something Patience and Norman ate frequently, especially in summer. Alan thought it impossible to crush the tomato onto both sides of the bread without pieces falling off the underside and making an unpleasant mess. (Perhaps it was difficult to envision with the tomatoes available in London in winter.) In his little blue notebook, he wrote incredulously, "What? How do the tomatoes stick?" Though she disagreed vehemently, Patience, who had actually eaten it this way in Catalonia, eventually relented, describing the dish in the book as a "slab of bread onto which are crushed some ripe tomatoes" and leaving the question of whether both sides are used somewhat ambiguous.[29] (The recipe itself was omitted.)

They also disagreed on the question of whether weeds are a source of energy, Patience relying on her own experience and Alan insisting on some sort of scientific evidence to prove the point. They had a similar dispute over whether the small amounts of potassium bicarbonate present in certain plants—chicory and dandelions in particular—were capable of breaking down beans during cooking. It was common practice in the places Patience had lived to add a handful of blanched chicory or dandelion greens to the pot of beans during the last quarter hour of cooking. "Judging from Mediterranean practice, beans are more digestible when cooked with these plants," Patience wrote. "This I regard as a fact, and do it myself."[30] Alan for his part consulted a chemist in London who told him that while most plants do contain traces of potassium bicarbonate, it wouldn't be enough to soften the skin of even a single bean. Rather, he said, it could be some other enzyme present in the plants, the common salt used in cooking, or simply prolonged boiling. In the end Patience said she "suspected" that the wild chicory or dandelions were alkaline and that using the recent crop of beans—as well as cooking them in earthenware—lessened their indigestibility.

Perhaps most interesting, they had a long-running conversation about whether elephant garlic was properly classified as a variety of giant garlic (*Allium scorodoprasum*) or as a cultivar of the wild leek (*Allium ampeloprasum*). Patience said she'd been interested in the question ever since Jane Grigson told Ariane that the wild leek did not exist, even though Patience had been gathering them since they lived in Carrara. On this matter Alan did not have a strong opinion, but he encouraged Patience in her inquiry; eventually she sent several specimens of wild leeks, including one in Paul Levy's suitcase after he visited Spigolizzi in 1987, for Alan to bring to Kew. Ultimately Patience's view was corroborated and the Kew herbarium now contains two specimens of *Allium ampeloprasum* from southern Italy courtesy of Patience Gray. Throughout all of this back and forth, what became apparent was Alan's scrupulousness and attention to detail on matters large and small. Indeed when he republished *Plats du Jour* in 1990, he asked David Gentleman to redo the drawing of grey mullet because he found a couple of minor inaccuracies. "He was very particular about the fish, and he made me add a bit more flesh on the top of one," Gentleman recalled. "I thought he was crazy myself."[31]

Of course years had passed since Patience had written the first draft of the book, which posed certain challenges. In the food-writing world much had changed. Scores of new books on everything from edible fungi and vegetarian cuisine to the science of cooking and the ethics of eating meat had been published. *Petits Propos Culinaires* and other journals devoted to the subject of food were attracting larger followings. In 1980 John Thorne started publishing his quarterly newsletter, *Simple Cooking*. Ed Behr's *Art of Eating* periodical would be launched in 1986, the same year *Honey from a Weed* was published. The term "foodie" was coined in the early 1980s to describe someone for whom gastronomy was a way of life, or perhaps more accurately, a lifestyle. Not surprisingly Patience found the very notion abhorrent. Nouvelle cuisine, with its emphasis on lighter fare and the aesthetics of eating, had firmly taken hold. Meanwhile the organic food movement, and environmental issues such as the use and abuse of pesticides and GMOs, had begun to impact a whole new generation of cooks, writers, and consumers.

Not that much of it mattered to Patience. As she confessed to Alan early on in their correspondence, she'd stopped reading modern cookbooks and preferred to gather recipes "from the horse's mouth."[32] Since 1970 some botanical names had inevitably changed, and there were a number of new field guides on edible plants and fungi. Thus Patience wrote to Nick asking him to look for a copy of a modern French work— modern being post-1975—on edible weeds, as well as reprints of old herbals. She conferred with Jane Grigson about using her husband Geoffrey's comprehensive work on plants and flowers, *The Englishman's Flora*. Alan, too, began sending her books, facsimile reprints he had published, and articles from back issues of *Petits Propos Culinaires*. Working on the *Oxford Companion*, he had amassed his own extensive library of rare cookbooks, food histories, and other obscure sources. There was rarely a book Patience referred to that Alan hadn't heard of. This led to what Patience called "revolutionizing the bibliography," a task that dominated much of their correspondence.[33] Eventually Nick found and sent her a copy of François Couplan's *Plantes Sauvages Comestibles*, a field guide to fifty edible plants with color illustrations published in 1985. Patience couldn't resist pointing out to Alan that Couplan, an ethnobotanist by training, echoed her conviction "so fiercely denied by you, that weeds are a source of energy."[34]

Patience had long studied plants and fungi and was well versed in how to identify and catalogue them. However there was one region she'd largely neglected to examine closely or to write about: Catalonia. There were several reasons for this. She'd only spent two brief summers there, and during that time the Fenosas' housekeeper had done most of the cooking. There were few opportunities to search for, let alone identify, fungi. And even though she'd edited Irving's book, he hadn't bothered to distinguish the many varieties of fungi used in Catalan cuisine. There was also the challenge of reading Catalan, and the section on Catalan fungi in *Honey from a Weed* is appropriately titled "Assaulting the Language Barrier." In fact the region is known for its rich diversity of fungi, many of which were identified in the early 1930s by the botanist Pius Font i Quer. His comprehensive study, published in 1937, identified well over one thousand species. Thus Patience spent considerable time poring over Catalan cookbooks as well as encyclopedic works on medicinal plants and fungi. She found that she was able to read them without a great deal of difficulty, and the bibliography grew to include more than a dozen Catalan works. She attributed her ability to read Catalan to "the underlying anarchic spirit of the language," to having translated some of the poems of Salvador Espriu, and to her years of studying Salentine dialects.

The book that left the greatest impression on her, however, was Josep Pla's *El Que Hem Menjat* (That which we have eaten), a copy of which she obtained from Nicole Fenosa. First published in 1981, the same year the author died, Patience described it as "a definitive and nostalgic work."[35] (A Dutch translation was published in 2013; it has yet to be translated into English.) Pla is considered one of the great twentieth-century Catalan writers, and his work often drew on his experience among the people of his native Empordà, up the coast toward France, especially its fishermen and farmers. Pla described himself as a gentleman farmer who also happened to be a writer, and his approach to food was very much in line with Patience's. He favored the peasant cooking of his homeland and admitted to not being terribly interested in other cuisines. "Luxury, in food as in everything, depresses me," he wrote, a sentiment Patience would have agreed with.[36] He also felt, as Patience and Irving did, that the cultural traditions that supported this particular way of life were under siege. "It's a world that's bound to be lost," he once wrote of his beloved Mediterranean.[37]

Patience found the re-engagement with the book and the layering on of new sources intellectually satisfying and at times even revelatory. She was thrilled, for example, to learn that Alan had obtained a copy of the seventeenth-century English translation of Dioscorides's work on medicinal plants, *De Materia Medica*, widely considered to be the first botanical compendium of its kind. Alan and his sometime assistant, Marcus Bell, who worked exclusively on the bibliography, were particularly helpful in hunting down and verifying classical sources, confirming dates of publication, and unearthing rare or out-of-print works. However great the pleasure she derived from this exercise, there was a certain tension between Alan's more scholarly approach and Patience's commitment to presenting the simple food of village people, most of whom, as Patience noted, would never read her book. Patience, of course, adored books and was "devoted to the written word" but had spent the past fifteen years reading the landscape and learning from the peasants who owed their livelihood to it. In *Honey from a Weed*, she argued that it was "country people" and "fishermen" who were responsible for creating recipes rather than "chefs of prelates and princes," who, she maintained, merely refined and wrote them down. Thus she did not want her book to be cluttered with references to other texts. Nonetheless Alan continued to send Patience works by scholars, historians, and food writers, and encouraged her to incorporate references to them if she could. For Alan, Patience once remarked, "nothing existed that was not in print."[38]

Ever a perfectionist, he was also determined to avoid errors in translation and, through his diplomatic connections, located someone in the Greek embassy to help with the sections on Naxos. At one point, when it appeared that publication would be delayed for a variety of reasons, Patience shuddered at the thought of spending the winter "studying Greek aspirates."[39]

Despite the challenges of editing the book by post, by late 1985 they'd made considerable progress. However there were still a number of pressing issues, and Alan felt it would be easier to address them in person.

In fact he had long been considering a trip to Puglia in order to hash out remaining edits, discuss book design and production, and go over any last-minute questions. Plus he was deeply fascinated by the place and life he'd been reading about on an almost daily basis and wanted to see it first-hand. He decided to visit in mid-December, during some of the darkest and coldest days of the year.

Alan flew to Rome on a Sunday, took the overnight train to Lecce, where Patience and Norman had arranged for him to be picked up by "a young man in dark glasses," and arrived at their door the following day. Patience had been somewhat wary of his visit from the beginning and warned him (and Jane) of the primitive conditions. She described Spigolizzi as a "gypsy encampment" and said that one had to think of it as "camping indoors."[40]

Of course Alan had lived in far-flung places, including Tunisia and Laos, and loved to travel. But diplomatic posts were a far cry from the accommodations at Spigolizzi, which lacked modern plumbing, adequate heating, and electricity. He may have been drawn to a certain idea of the simple life, perhaps the one that emanated from the pages of Patience's book, though he did not aspire to live that way himself. His sister, Rosemary, with whom he was close, had a rustic farmhouse in Yorkshire, where she "sort of pretended to live a peasant life."[41] But over time she'd increasingly come to rely on modern conveniences. Thus when Rosemary herself went to visit Patience and Norman some years later, it was, according to Caroline, "like an ideal come true."[42] Alan perhaps approached his trip with similar romantic notions.

It's easy to imagine that the south of Italy is warm and sunny most of the time, but the winter months in a stone farmhouse can be exceedingly frigid, colder inside than out. Darkness fell around 4:30, at which point the only source of light was from oil lamps and candles. In anticipation of Alan's visit, Patience and Norman moved a small gas stove from Norman's studio into what Patience called the "ambassadorial suite." However Alan seemed to be largely unconcerned with the hardships of Spigolizzi and was determined to make use of his time. According to Patience, he gradually imposed his working hours on her, starting at 8:30

in the morning and continuing late into the night. Meanwhile Patience understandably felt a certain pressure to cook elaborate meals, which she described in a letter to Nick:

> *Freshly caught tunnyfish, some Sarpe, a chicken neatly braised with peppers, dutch herrings cleaned and soused, anchovies de salted, a zampone cooked to a turn with cabbage made to resemble sauerkraut by dousing it with fresh bitter oranges from the laden tree, dolmades, an excellent frittata, home grown haricot beans cooked in earthenware and made more digestible by last minute addition of the wild beets growing luxuriously at the door, dwarf octopus also cooked scientifically (my science this) in order that they are delicious, pasta in a mushroom, zampone and cream sauce, to mention only a few of the dishes.*[43]

Patience's reference to "my science" exposed a fundamental difference in her and Alan's approach to food and cooking. Alan of course did not consider himself a serious cook and never pretended that he was. His idea of bliss, according to his daughter Caroline, was to watch somebody else cook while he took notes. Moreover he wasn't interested in spending a great deal of time preparing food, hence his affection for the kipper, which requires little more than pouring boiling water over the smoked fish. Caroline says that most people who knew him through his books found this relative lack of interest in food and eating hard to reconcile with his career as a food writer. "He really wasn't that interested in eating," she says.[44] "The sensual side of eating doesn't interest him," Paul Levy once said of Alan Davidson. "When we talk about food, we're more likely to discuss things like species."[45] But that doesn't mean he didn't take the process seriously. His was a scholarly and at times scientific approach, whereas Patience's was largely intuitive. She had a way of humming, almost chanting to herself, while she cooked or washed up, which she almost always did alone and in the dark. She handled ingredients, whether fish or plants, with a kind of reverence, "like a little dance."[46] "She made food seem terribly exciting," her granddaughter Lisa Armour-Brown recalled.[47] In Patience's view Alan, with his scholar's lens, seemed to have the opposite effect. After his visit Patience likened herself to a peasant who'd come up against a "data processing mentality."

Yet they had matters to resolve, one being the recipe for pa amb tomàquet, which they both felt strongly about. Though very much out of season, Patience had managed to procure a tomato of the "Catalan size" and postponed the experiment as long as she could in the hope that her precious acquisition would ripen. But when they set out to try the dish, the tomato was still unripe, and Alan "was triumphantly convinced that his scruples were justified."[48] However apparently even this firsthand experience was not enough to satisfy Alan completely. On a trip to Catalonia in 1987, he sought out the dish, and he and Jane sampled it several times, "always with tomato juice on one side only," he wrote to Patience.[49] He and Jane also visited a small publisher who, it so happened, had printed a small pamphlet on the very subject (it was called *Teoria i pràctica del pa amb tomàquet*) in which the author, Leopold Pomés, "gives the orthodox recipe as very definitely requiring juice (but not pulp) on both sides."[50] Alan concluded that the two-sided technique had, over time, given way to the one-sided because it was easier to eat. Patience replied that she thought Alan was making too much of the matter, but noted, "You must feel at peace on the subject, for which I am glad."[51]

By the end of his visit, there were heavy rains and water had seeped up into the guestroom where Alan was staying. Patience had grown tired of preparing elaborate meals for someone who, she was beginning to realize, was not terribly interested in eating. He likely would've been happy with whatever she put in front of him. She was also beginning to feel that he was more interested in cataloguing food than he was in celebrating it. For Patience and Norman eating even the simplest of meals was meant to be convivial. All of the elements mattered: the food, the company, and especially the wine. Yet despite their differences they'd accomplished a great deal, and Alan marveled at Patience's ability to "combine so much literary work with the production of all those delicious meals."[52]

After returning to London, though, Alan, usually an animated storyteller, was surprisingly mum about his experience. Friends and colleagues remember him mentioning the trip, but only in very broad strokes.

In a letter to Patience after his visit, Jane referred rather obliquely to Alan's adventures in Italy, "which left him highly stimulated."[53] Years later she told the *New York Times* that he "came back shaken."[54] Alan would later describe the week he spent with Patience and Norman as an "experience of remarkable intensity," and Caroline said it had the quality of a "Joycean epiphany" for him.[55]

Shortly after he returned he sent Patience a copy of British gardener and diarist John Evelyn's 1699 *Acetaria: A Discourse of Sallets*, which is believed to be the first English-language book ever written on salads.

"To Patience and Norman," he wrote, "with happy memories of acetaious food and talk at Spigolizzi."

One matter left up in the air after Alan's visit was that of the book's title. A number of alternatives had been raised—*Wolf at the Door*, *Apropos of a Salt Herring*, *A Marble Odyssey*, *The Enchorial*, *Aeneas's Feast*, and *Escaping from My Kitchens*, among others—but *Fasting and Feasting* was still the favorite. (Alan had softened a bit on his concerns about using the title but was still not encouraging it.) For Patience it best captured the spirit of the book and what she had come to see as the foundation of the way of life she'd been writing about. Though fasting had been a part of life on Naxos, observed during Advent and Lent, Patience used the word more expansively to refer to seasonal periods of relative scarcity, which characterized the Mediterranean. The title also captured Irving's approach to food and cooking, striking that perfect balance between liberality and frugality, which Patience felt gave eating so much of its meaning and pleasure. In Patience's view fasting and hunger—sometimes a function of poverty, ritual, or season—were no less important than the particularities of slaughtering a pig or making paella. In fact she felt there was an intimate connection between the two, that the pleasure of feasting was in part derived from the specter and memory of hunger.

Sometime in late February the final words of William Cowper's poem "The Pineapple and the Bee" occurred to Norman as providing a suitable title for the book. Cowper was a popular eighteenth-century English poet whose life had been beset by tragedy. His mother died when he was six, and Cowper was sent away to boarding school. He suffered a nervous breakdown in his early thirties and converted to Evangelicalism before embarking on a career as a poet and hymn writer. His work drew in large part on this spiritual crisis and religious awakening. After spending a year in an asylum, he found solace first in Evangelical Christianity and then in simple everyday activities like gardening, animal husbandry, and drawing. His great work, *The Task*, a poem in blank verse, addressed everyday objects (the first book is titled *The Sofa*), nature, and religious faith. Though "The Pineapple and the Bee" is not considered one of his better poems, the final couplet was widely quoted and well known. (Patience and Norman had a copy of Cowper's complete works.) Observing the bee's efforts to alight on a pineapple plant under glass, "pervious only to the light," Cowper mused on the folly of man's attempt to pursue that which he cannot have. (Cowper did in fact grow his own pineapples, so he knew a thing or two about the bee's predicament.) Longing for the unattainable fruit, he writes:

> *With hopeless wish one looks and lingers;*
> *One breaks the glass, and cuts his fingers;*
> *But they whom Truth and Wisdom lead,*
> *Can gather honey from a weed.*

A nearly identical phrase appears in Shakespeare's *Henry V* in the opening scene of Act 4, where King Henry at Agincourt, on the eve of battle, tells his brother that though they may be in great danger, perhaps they can somehow use this to their advantage, "Thus may we gather honey from the weed / and make a moral of the devil himself." For Shakespeare, and to a lesser extent Cowper, the weed represents a rather pernicious object from which some sort of lesson or truth can be derived. Taken alone, however, the phrase captured Patience's long love affair with and reverence for wild plants and her desire to find in them some sort of deeper meaning.

If Patience had acquired most of her knowledge of edible wild plants from peasant women, she was well aware that most of her readers would have to rely on books and field guides—"a slower and more uncertain method," as she put it.[56] She pointed to Roger Phillips's *Wild Food*, published in 1983, by way of drawing attention to the risks associated with gathering edible plants in the face of widespread pesticide use and the fallout from industrial pollution. It was a question that she and Alan had discussed early on. They differed to some extent on whether a cookbook was an appropriate venue to raise such concerns. In a letter to Alan after reading *Mediterranean Seafood*, Patience noted that he had relegated the subject of pollution to a tiny footnote on scorpion fish and that he had not really addressed the ways in which fish, especially bottom feeders, absorb dangerous toxins. "Can you really say how fortunate are the English in the wide variety of fish," she wrote, "without mentioning the effect of Windscale-Sellafield [a nuclear power plant that caught fire in 1957] on those in the Irish Sea?"[57]

The issue of nuclear waste was of particular concern to Patience and Norman as plans to build a nuclear power station just a few miles from Spigolizzi had recently become a very real threat. Moreover the Salento, despite its remoteness, was hardly pristine. The use of pesticides and chemical fertilizers was widespread. A Mafia-controlled waste disposal industry had marred much of the landscape. Just a few miles from Spigolizzi and visible from the masseria was a disused quarry where household and industrial waste was burned in an open pit day and night. These problems and the Chernobyl nuclear disaster of April 1986, which sent clouds carrying radioactive waste over Europe, compelled them to stop filling the cistern with rainwater from the roof; instead they had to resort to buying 12,000-liter lorry-loads from a well in Presicce. "Culinary preoccupations have been rather put in the shade by a cloud of dust, don't you think?" Patience wrote to Alan a couple of weeks after Chernobyl. Perhaps the most revealing and haunting description of the compromised state of the landscape came from BBC broadcaster Derek Cooper, who visited Patience in 1988:

> *I was anticipating some kind of unpolluted terrain where peasants cherished the land in the old traditional ways. From a distance it does look a bit like that. But as you drive past the gnarled olive trees and the deep-rooted vines you see, by the roadside, what at first sight might be construed as some device to scare birds away. The empty plastic bottles hang like dead men from the branches of trees and are meant to scare people away—these fields have been sprayed with toxic chemicals, they say. Trespass at your peril.[58]*

A postcard of Apollonas in the early 1960s. *Courtesy of Nicolas Gray*

Wolfe Aylward visiting in Carrara, ca. 1967. *Courtesy of Nicolas Gray*

Norman at the foot of a quarry in Carrara. *Courtesy of Nicolas Gray*

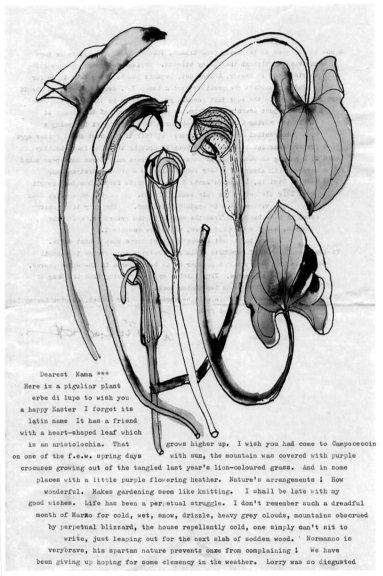

Dearest Mama ***
Here is a piguliar plant
erbe di lupo to wish you
a happy Easter I forget its
latin name It has a friend
with a heart-shaped leaf which
is an aristolochia. That   grows higher up. I wish you had come to Campococcin
on one of the f.e.w. spring days   with sun, the mountain was covered with purple
crocuses growing out of the tangled last year's lion-coloured grass. And in some
places with a little purple flowering heather. Nature's arrangements ! How
wonderful. Makes gardening seem like knitting. I shall be late with my
good wishes. Life has been a perpetual struggle. I don't remember such a dreadful
month of Marzo for cold, wet, snow, drizzle, heavy grey clouds, mountains obscrued
by perpetual blizzard, the house repellently cold, one simply can't sit to
write, just leaping out for the next slab of sodden wood. ' Normanno is
verybrave, his spartan nature prevents once from complaining ! We have
been giving up hoping for some clemency in the weather. Lorry was so disgusted

One of Patience's illustrated letters sent from Carrara in spring 1966. The drawing is of *Arisarum vulgare*, a member of the Araceae family and commonly known as Friar's cowl. In the letter Patience writes, "Nature's arrangements! How wonderful. Makes gardening seem like knitting." *Courtesy of Nicolas Gray*

Patience in her workroom wearing one of her rings, 1971. *Photo by Francesco Radino*

Olive during her visit to Spigolizzi in
1972. *Courtesy of Nicolas Gray*

Norman in the 1980s. *Photo by Tania Midgley*

Patience being interviewed by the BBC's Derek Cooper, July 1988. *Courtesy of Nicolas Gray*

Patience at Spigolizzi in the mid 1990s. *Photo by Doris Schiuma*

Alan Davidson receiving the Erasmus Prize in 2003, shortly before his death, from Prince Bernhard of the Netherlands. *Courtesy of the Praemium Erasmianum Foundation / Wikimedia Commons*

Norman and Patience, February 1992. *Photo by Grace DiNapoli*

Indeed by the mid 1980s, as *Honey from a Weed* was being revised, Patience and Norman had become increasingly preoccupied with environmental issues. Norman kept boxes and boxes full of press cuttings on ecological problems and devoted particular attention to genetically modified foods and nuclear power. His was an apocalyptic view. As Patience put it, "Norman thinks that the end of the world will come, as forecast in the Bible, while everything is going on as usual."[59] What they saw before them was deeply troubling. The wilderness they'd come to in 1970 was rapidly disappearing. Coastal development, just beginning when they'd arrived, had spread unchecked. New holiday villages, seaside villas, and shoddily constructed second homes were the product of a larger building boom fueled by tourism and a growing middle class. The excesses of consumer society, what Patience referred to in *Honey from a Weed* as *stare bene*, which literally translates as "living well," and the waste that it engendered were reshaping the landscape. For Patience this transformation was epitomized in the spectacle of the *cucina Americana*, an expensive gadget-filled kitchen paid for by speeding up "the ripening of a crop" or boosting its "weight by every means known to science."[60] Ironically these shiny new kitchens were usually left entirely unused; cooking was still done on an old stove in some out-of-the-way passage so as not to "impair the brilliance of stainless steel nor dull the lustre of polished granite surfaces."[61] In Patience's view all of these developments were responsible for the demise of the peasant way of life embodied in Salvatore and Teresa.

Patience had little interest in glossing over these dilemmas but nonetheless recognized that a cookbook was perhaps not the best place to dwell on them. To an extent she did raise some of these issues in her concluding chapter entitled "A Parting Salvo," though she did so only indirectly by arguing that her book belonged to an era of "food grown for its own sake, not for profit."[62] Meanwhile Patience and Norman had recently been involved in a local antinuclear campaign—they were initially enlisted by a group of young activists from Presicce. This proved to be a fruitful relationship. Norman encouraged several of the campaigners, notably Marina Pizzolante, Fabio Ponzo, Rolando Civilla, and Vito Pignatelli to start a street theater group called Anteo. This loose-knit group of students and artists eventually became known as the *ragazzi*—Klaus and Ulrike made a film about the theater group for German television in 1989 titled *I*

Ragazzi—and they spent a great deal of time with Patience and Norman at Spigolizzi. Marina, whose father had helped negotiate the purchase of the property in 1970, called Spigolizzi a "second home" and Patience and Norman her "spiritual parents."[63] She later wrote a collection of poetry illustrated by Norman. (Chloé d'Aujac, an artist affiliated with the Fano summer school, who studied with Norman, also described Patience and Norman as "spiritual parents.") Ada Martella, who lived in Chieti but spent summers in the Salento, heard about Patience and Norman from friends in Presicce and felt compelled to seek them out. "It was like finding the mother ship, the mother ship that they [the ragazzi] could dock with," she said.[64] According to Nick, "Such was the importance of these informally 'adopted children' to Patience & Norman that in the late '90s Norman seriously envisaged leaving Spigolizzi to them."[65]

Patience and Norman were also strong supporters and advisers to Rolando Civilla and Luigi Quaranta when they launched their printing press and publishing house, Levante Arti Grafiche, in 1989. Over the years Patience and Norman would publish several small books and Patience her collection of autobiographical essays under Rolando's imprint, Leucasia Editore. In addition Rolando and Luigi published an occasional cultural broadsheet, *A Contrappunto*, which Norman was closely involved with in an advisory and editorial capacity, sometimes contributing essays or drawings. Though far from his original vision of an artists' school or utopian community, this ongoing collaboration was in a way the fulfillment of his Wonderhouse dream.

In *Honey from a Weed*, Patience, perhaps taking a cue from Alan, dispensed with the issue of environmental degradation by saying that she did not "wish to depress the reader by examining the effects of industrialisation."[66] Yet she felt that food writers had an obligation to confront the grim realities of their world and that for the most part they had fallen short. Throughout the 1990s she talked about making war on Monsanto, the alarming color of "falsified tomatoes," and the "un-Godly deformation of nature."[67] "You might almost say that food writers have taken refuge in the history of food," she wrote to Corby Kummer in 1992, "in order to avoid this baneful subject of contamination."[68]

By summer 1986 the editing of the book was in its final stages. Not surprisingly it was longer and far more expensive than Alan had anticipated, and he was forced to raise the price and increase the print run. *Honey from a Weed* had been settled on as the title ("fasting and feasting" remained in the subtitle). Wolfe, to whom the book was dedicated, came to visit in June, and Patience took a brief though welcome respite from revisions in order to "cook for dear life." Meanwhile Alan was busy making last-minute visits to Kew to consult various experts: Dr. Alan Pegler, their top mycologist; an allium specialist; and an expert on fruit trees. (Pegler gave a brief mention of the book in the scholarly journal *Mycologist*.) Alan even had a meeting with "the famous professor" William Stearn, whom Patience had worked with in the 1950s when she was researching *Indoor Plants and Gardens*. "An extraordinary man," Patience wrote to Alan. "I am so glad he is available, indeed sometimes wondered if he was still alive."[69] Right up until the publication date, they continued to have impassioned discussions about the geographic origins of various fruits, nuts, and vegetables, the role of commerce in gastronomy, and the correct spelling of "oregano" (or "origano": Patience insisted on spelling it with an "i," not an "e," which she argued was an American corruption of English).

Printing of the book was completed in mid-October, and a few days later Alan sent proofs of the first few chapters to M. F. K. Fisher, Alice Waters, and Judith Jones, describing it as "a highly unusual cookbook which in my opinion will become a classic."[70] He had also dispatched Harold McGee to show the first sixty-four pages to Jack Shoemaker of North Point Press in California, the publisher of McGee's second book, *The Curious Cook*. "I thought it was amazing," McGee recalled.[71]

In his last letter to Patience before the launch, held at David Mellor's design shop in Sloane Square, Alan updated her on the state of his computer ("still ailing"), on *PPC* issue 24 ("running later and later"), and on the busy program for the week.[72] Patience was picking olives until the day she left, early on the morning of November 4. When she arrived at Heathrow Airport, Alan, dressed in a white linen shirt and V-necked sleeveless jersey, met her at the terminal, whereupon they set out for London in his newly refurbished bottle-green Bentley.

CHAPTER FOURTEEN

Discovering the Salento

While Alan Davidson certainly had high hopes for *Honey from a Weed*, its reception far exceeded his own expectations. Jeremy Round, food critic for the *Independent*, with whom Patience agreed to do an interview at Alan's behest, dubbed her the "high priestess of cooking" and said that *Honey from a Weed* "pushes the form of the cookery book about as far as it goes."[1] Irish food writer Theodora FitzGibbon said, "It is not like any other book written in the past fifty years and its memory will stay forever."[2] Jane Grigson considered it one of the best cookbooks of the year. Food writer and historian Christopher Driver said that Patience's "earthly-visionary-prose" suggested a "George Fox of the open fire, a cook without an oven."[3] Angela Carter, in the *London Review of Books*, deemed it nothing less than "a summing up of the genre of the late modern British cookery book."[4]

However not all reviews were positive. Writing in the *Sunday Times*, Fiona MacCarthy, though acknowledging that the book might someday become a classic, described Patience as a "snob" and the book as having "a quality of lunatic conviction." She said the recipes were mostly useless and came to the conclusion, based on the chapter titled "Chopping and Pounding," devoted to the mortar and pestle, that the book was "all about sex."[5] Patience attributed the review to a "Presbyterian rationalist attitude at war with Dionysus" and told Alan she hoped it would lead to a run on mortars.[6] Incidentally the book's launch party had taken place at David Mellor's shop, which carried a long line of cutlery and cookware, including mortars and pestles. Mellor was MacCarthy's husband, and she attended the event.

If anything MacCarthy's review led to the selling of more books. Despite its high price tag—it sold for £17.50 in 1987, what would be about

£45 today—*Honey from a Weed* quickly became Prospect Books' best-selling title, and by January Alan was having more copies bound. Macmillan Publishing bought the paperback rights almost immediately. Soon after, Harper and Row snapped up the American rights, paying an advance of $15,000, a sum beyond Prospect Books' wildest expectations. "We didn't have a rights department or anything like that," recalled Candida Brazil. "And we didn't usually do deals like that."[7] This was a great relief for Alan, who feared that publishing *Honey from a Weed* risked plunging him into even deeper debt. Even with Patience's loan, which was a not inconsiderable sum for Prospect Books, *Honey from a Weed* needed substantial investment on his part, with total costs approaching £17,000. However he was able to cover the printing and to pay back the loan much sooner than anticipated.

Later that year the book was awarded a special prize by the André Simon Memorial Fund in the U.K. and shortlisted for the prize itself, and was runner-up for the 1987 Glenfiddich Prize in Australia (first prize going that year to Claudia Roden for her book *Middle Eastern Cookery*). "He believed in it," Alan's sister, Rosemary, recalled. "But I think he was taken aback by how it was received."[8] Patience was both amused and astonished by the publicity. "It certainly seems to have flummoxed the food writers," she wrote to Ariane. "Alan is happy because he can now pay the printer! And nothing he has published in 20 years has caused such a stir."[9]

Reactions in the United States were even more enthusiastic. The book was published virtually unedited and in the same format in October 1987 with a print run of ten thousand. Though it ultimately sold poorly in the United States, it received high praise from a wide range of food writers and magazines. *Gourmet* said the book was sure to become a classic and put Patience in the same category as Patrick Leigh Fermor, Freya Stark, and Elizabeth David. Christopher Driver in his review also made the comparison with Elizabeth David and said the two were "rivals." Patience thought this absurd and wrote to Alan that Elizabeth David "has no rival. . . . She is in a class of her own." John Thorne in his newsletter *Simple Cooking* said that not since Richard Olney's *Simple French Food* had a cookbook "revealed more of the sheer possibilities inherent in food writing." Ed Behr in the *Art of Eating* described as it as "a mixture of brilliant essays, careful recipes, and practical information about basic foodstuffs." And Paula Wolfert said that Patience had "placed herself in the forefront of serious food writers." Harold McGee, who in fact had won the André Simon Food and Drink Book Award in 1986 for the British edition of *On Food and Cooking* and who would visit Patience and Norman several years later, said it was one of the first books to treat wild foods, plants, and fungi in a comparative context. But above all it was the writing that drew him. "I remember thinking I'd never read anything quite like it before," he recalled. "It's still a kind of gold standard."[10]

Unsurprisingly interest in the book translated into interest in its author, who'd last written a cookbook nearly thirty years before, when *Plats du Jour* was published. The autobiographical nature of the text, its vivid descriptions of remote places, and the singularity of the writing itself painted a picture of a remarkable but elusive woman. The book had the same sort of appeal that Elizabeth David and M. F. K. Fisher's work had engendered—what Angela Carter described as "upmarket bohemian-ism"—but was laced with a rugged eccentricity. Above all, perhaps, the way of life described in it was deeply compelling.

The first of the food writers to profile Patience was Paul Levy, who traveled to Puglia in the summer of 1987. Over the course of the next half-decade, Derek Cooper, Harold McGee, Ed Behr, Corby Kummer, Nancy Harmon Jenkins, and a handful of other food writers would also visit. Patience, who relished her privacy, did everything she could to discourage Levy from coming. She told Alan, who acted as intermediary, that she and Norman saw no reason for him to make the journey in order to write the piece and that, as anonymity had enabled her to observe and learn from country people, she wished to remain anonymous. "Our life is well beyond the norm," she wrote, "and thus is wide-open to ridicule—to the delight and reassurance of the reader."[11] But Levy was insistent, and Alan, as he always seemed to do, eventually won Patience over. In a some-what terse letter to Levy, Patience implied that since she and Norman "rarely talk about food" and "seldom have time to prepare it," there would be little of interest for the food writer. And since he'd be coming during the height of the holiday season she warned him of "culture shock" and said that it would be too hot to cook. "Perhaps at dawn I may be able to knock something up," she wrote.[12] Levy, who was born in Kentucky and studied philosophy at the University of Chicago and Oxford before turning to journalism, wrote back to say, "The prospect of culture shock is one I greatly look forward to."[13]

Levy had begun writing about food for *Harpers & Queen* in the late 1970s, contributing to the magazine's Private Cook series, in which he discussed the pleasures of tending a vegetable garden and making simple dishes like ratatouille. His annual six-thousand-plus-word roundup of the year's cookbooks was something of a novelty at the time and, according to Levy, "started a near-riot among grateful publishers."[14] He met Alan Davidson in 1978—they had the same literary agent—when he wrote a profile of him for an obscure American magazine. They became friends and in 1980 spent a month together on a gastronomic tour of China. Levy regularly wrote about the Oxford Symposium of Food and later became involved in running it. The publication of his book on "foodie culture" with Ann Barr in 1984, *The Official Foodie Handbook*, marked a turning point of sorts in the world of food writing. Somewhat tongue in cheek it was nonetheless notable for the fact that it had less to do with food and cooking and more to do with being in the know. In a way it mirrored some of the trends of nouvelle cuisine, not to mention the boom years of the 1980s, all of which had turned food into a fashionable commodity (the book's subtitle was *Be Modern—Worship Food*). Elizabeth David, included in the section titled "A Foodie's Who's Who," was outraged—it contained numerous factual errors—and wrote an article attacking it. Patience had read the piece and told Alan she "much enjoyed 'a whiff of grapeshot' from her [David's] pen." "The foodie thing," Patience wrote in a letter to Alan, "is full of false sociology, surely, with such an elitist slant." Elsewhere she added perceptively, "It's not a word really, just very big business."[15] During Levy's visit, Patience later wrote, Elizabeth David's dislike of him "was a topic he returned to frequently."[16]

Levy arrived on July 24 in the midst of a crippling heat wave, which they would later learn caused the death of hundreds in nearby Greece. (Because they had no radio or telephone, nor even a thermometer, they were unaware of just how severe the heat wave was.) Indeed it was so hot—temperatures topped 113°F (45°C)—that Patience did very little cooking and no one had much appetite. That probably worked in Levy's favor, as it gave them plenty of time to take refuge indoors in the masseria and talk. Patience later wrote that she thought Levy surreptitiously "turned on some minute Japanese instrument to record my lifelong recollections."[17]

The article, which appeared in the *Observer* in October 1987—a slightly modified version was published the following month in the *Wall Street Journal*—accompanied by a portrait of Patience taken by her former colleague Jane Bown, presented Patience as a modern witch. Levy suggested that Patience's knowledge of local plants and herbs surpassed even that of the locals. He concluded the article by noting that peasants now came to her seeking herbal remedies. "Do they, I asked her, regard you as a doctor, or as a witch?" Levy wound up with. "Dragging on her cigarette, Patience Gray smiled serenely."[18] He wasn't the only one who saw this quality in Patience. Corby Kummer, who visited in the 1990s, described her as "witch-like" with a "strange perceptive intensity."[19]

Elsewhere Levy described her as an "Italian peasant" who got up at 5:30 every day to work the fields. "Norman's phallic sculptures," he wrote, punctuated an otherwise barren landscape. Levy clearly hadn't bothered to talk to Norman about his work—the sculptures referenced the wartime image of men holding up a concrete slab in order to save the women and children trapped underneath. Despite its somewhat caricatured version of their lives, the article also offered the first sketch of Patience's early years, with a discussion of her trip to Romania in 1938, her brief affair with Thomas Gray, and her fraught partnership with Primrose Boyd. However Patience had been less than forthcoming about certain things, and the article is riddled with factual errors regarding her age and the nature of her experience during the war, which she described as "Walden"-like. Somewhat surprisingly, by today's standards anyhow, Levy provided Patience with a draft copy of the article and said he had no "intention of printing anything you find objectionable."[20] Patience objected to the whole enterprise and, though she professed to be unhappy with the final product, offered no corrections or suggestions.

Patience and Norman may have been uneasy subjects, but it wasn't the first time life at Spigolizzi had been written about. As early as 1973 an Italian art journal described them somewhat awkwardly as "new Neolithics" working away in isolated, primitive conditions.[21] According to the article they had rejected the contemporary art world in favor of an older, archaic way of life, which was reflected in the materials they worked with—stone and metal. Patience approved of the notion that they were "Levy Strauss individuals structuring themselves back into Neolithic life" and told Wolfe, "I don't think any other category would've appealed to me more."[22] In 1982 Klaus and Ulrike Voswinckel made a fifty-five-minute documentary about them for German television; *Sonne, Mond* portrayed Patience and Norman as living in a paradise, in tune with the cycles of the sun and moon.[23] There are scenes of Patience using a divining rod to search for the "energy" of a building they conjectured had been built as a place of worship, and of her climbing a tree to pick figs. Much of the film focuses on Norman's speculations on the significance of Salentine architecture. Patience said that it had taken Norman years to agree to the project, and they were both unhappy with the final result. They actually traveled to Germany by train, a twenty-two-hour journey, to attend the film's opening.

The film confirmed their worst fears—that the romantic view of what they were doing would obscure the day-to-day labor and discipline that made it possible. Klaus and Ulrike "kept veering away from real themes—work, agriculture—into a series of picture postcards," Patience wrote to Alan Davidson.[24] Not only did this perspective gloss over the role of work in everyday life—of utmost importance to Patience and Norman—but it also neglected the unpleasant realities of environmental degradation and the erosion of a centuries-old traditional way of life. In fact Patience believed that what she and Norman were doing was so far removed from modern life that any depictions of it would necessarily fall short. Julia Farrington, who was visiting at the time the film was being shot, remembers Norman referring to the camera as a "dumb idiot" incapable of capturing the larger picture.[25]

When Alan Davidson asked Patience to recommend "picturesque local scenes" that might be included in an upcoming television documentary on Mediterranean cultures hosted by Claudia Roden, Patience replied with a long disquisition on the superficiality of the medium and the disastrous impacts of consumerism on local customs. "There is an interesting film to be made here," she wrote. "The fairytale come to life."[26] In this case the "fairytale" was Patience's old hobbyhorse, *benessere* (literally "well-being", but which Patience understood to be the excesses of consumer society), that she felt had irreversibly corrupted the local culture. Yet for many who read *Honey from a Weed* and later visited Spigolizzi, they expected to see a different kind of "fairytale"—Patience and Norman's life—that seemed to emanate from its pages. Indeed the book jacket showed the inside of the masseria and Norman's frescoes painted on the ceiling. Alan's reference to the picturesque, he said, had come directly from the pages of her book. It was a dilemma Patience had confronted while revising the manuscript: how far to pull back the veil on peasant life and expose what she saw as its dissolution, a process she and Norman had witnessed firsthand. In fact by the time *Honey from a Weed* was published, Patience said she'd stopped using the word "peasant"—preferring the slightly cumbersome "agriculturalist" instead—since peasants had ceased to exist. "This to me is a great sadness," she wrote, "the collapse of Salvatore and Teresa in relation to absolutely meaningless ideals of *benessere*, the triumph of consumerism."[27]

The fate of the peasant and, more broadly, local cultures in the face of an ever-expanding industrial juggernaut was emerging as a central question among food writers. The Slow Food movement, founded by an Italian sociologist and political activist, Carlo Petrini, had its beginnings around the same time that *Honey from a Weed* was published; in fact the organization that preceded it, Arcigola, was launched in 1986. In 1987 French farmer José Bové formed the Confédération Paysanne, an agricultural union committed to organic farming and environmental stewardship. Both groups would galvanize support through their vocal and sometimes militant opposition to the opening of fast-food restaurants in France and Italy, seen by many as an existential threat to European identity. In Bové's case, he drove his tractor into an Aveyron McDonald's and demolished it. About a decade later, after reading a letter sent by Monsanto to American farmers that was published in *Resurgence*, Patience wrote, "As all American farmers have guns, one wonders when the shooting will begin."[28] These various movements, combined with a growing concern over genetically modified crops and the overuse of pesticides, gave rise to a new genre of food writing that was more overtly political than it was culinary. "She [Patience] was one of the canaries in the coal mine," says John Thorne, "warning us of the rapid degradation of agriculture, the loss of the integrity and character of the food we eat, the traditions that sustained it."[29] But it was the book's deeply personal nature and sensuality that captivated and moved so many readers. Ed Behr recalled, "It was the first really earthy cookbook like that that I ever encountered."[30]

Not surprisingly Patience was sought out as an authority on Mediterranean cuisine and culture. In January 1988, just two months after *Honey from a Weed* was published in the United States, Corby Kummer, food writer for the *Atlantic* and a "fervent admirer," invited her to participate on a panel on "preserving regional traditions in Italy" as part of the American Institute of Wine and Food's sixth annual conference on gastronomy in New York.[31] Patience said she was flattered by the invitation but that it was "entirely misdirected." She was not a soothsayer, could not submit to three days of discussing and sampling food, and would inevitably flee to the Museum of Modern Art. Moreover she took issue with the premise itself, arguing that "preservation or conservation normally occurs when their object is already dead."[32] This was the case, she pointed out, for country houses, eighteenth-century kitchen gardens, and the historical center of every ancient village in Puglia, not to mention much, though not all, of the region's traditional dishes. "What are they eating today?" she wrote, referring to the local people. "Enormous quantities of unwholesome 'plastic' food. I am not going to cross the Atlantic to elaborate the distressing news. . . . People should be studying the baneful effects of the new industrialized diet on health; the Salento would be a good place to do it."[33]

One prominent journalist, known for his willingness to engage with the titans of industry—often getting the better of them—was Derek Cooper, presenter of the BBC's *Food Programme* from 1979 to 2001. Something of a muckraking journalist but with a light touch, he had published two books—*The Bad Food Guide* and *The Beverage Report*—excoriating Britain's restaurant culture and beverage industry. He was also a connoisseur of Scotch whiskey, about which he wrote several books. He believed food should be unfussy, straightforward, and prepared with the best ingredients. Like so many others, he was drawn to *Honey from a Weed* for its learned but no-nonsense approach to food, and in the spring of 1988 he wrote to Patience expressing an interest in interviewing her for a radio program on the politics of food. As she had been with Levy, she was reluctant to give interviews, but she felt obliged to welcome Derek Cooper as a favor to Alan for all that he had done. But she wrote in a letter to him, "It is impossible that what I might have to say on the 'politics of food' would be worth the tiring trip to Spigolizzi."[34]

Cooper and his producer, Vanessa Harrison, arrived in late July, almost a year to the day after Levy's visit, in the middle of another lacerating heat wave. Patience had prepared a simple lunch of cold chicory, hard-boiled eggs, and tapenade, and they ate outside in the shade of the fig tree. Cooper, who disliked the heat, was already wilting. Harrison recalls Patience being a thoughtful but hesitant speaker, and there were many very long pauses, which they feared would jeopardize the program. Needless to say it was a somewhat inauspicious start—they had less than two days to do the recordings—and Patience was clearly uncomfortable with the whole thing. Thus when someone suggested that they go for a swim, they all felt it would be a good diversion, even though Derek himself was not a swimmer.

Patience took them to a shallow bay and set Derek up under a large beach umbrella festooned with big blue flowers. As the sand was unbearably hot, he moved into the water up to his chest and Patience swam around finding him little bits of edible seaweed to sample. It turned out to be the perfect icebreaker, and they all began to loosen up. However, when it was time to return to Spigolizzi to start recording the interview, they discovered their rental car had gotten stuck in the sand. They were far from the nearest public beach, and there was no one in sight. Meanwhile it was getting hotter and hotter as the afternoon wore on. Eventually they spotted a snorkeler some ways out in the water.

Derek, known for his deep baritone voice, asked Patience what the Italian word for help was and began to shout "*Aiuto!*" hoping to get the snorkeler's attention.

"His voice really came into its own," Harrison recalled. Still for several minutes the snorkeler did not look up. Finally he turned and began to swim toward them. When he looked up he saw Patience, tall and thin, standing on a rock "with her stream of long grey hair," and next to her a shorter man, "scarlet with heat and exertion," shouting "Aiuto!"[35]

The snorkeler drove up to Spigolizzi and fetched Norman, who came down with the Land Rover to pull the car out of the sand.

Patience and Cooper shared a similar sensibility, and the rest of the visit was a great success. The interview, which aired in August, opened with the sound of herbs being pounded in the stoneware mortar and Patience saying, "I feel that I'm not really a real cook because I don't want to astonish and surprise. I only want to satisfy people." To which

Cooper replied, "That perhaps means you are a real cook."[36] In his piece for the *Listener* recounting his visit, Cooper was one of the few journalists to present an antiromantic view of the Salento, one that most closely echoed Patience's own. The land, he wrote, was saturated with chemicals. Vegetables at the market had been reared with "pesticides, fungicides and artificial fertilizers." The sea was no less polluted. And the way of life that informed *Honey from a Weed* had been "almost entirely lost." Where then did Patience and Norman fit in? Rather than build them up as latter-day peasants, Cooper portrayed them as outsiders, artists, attempting to grow their own food in an inhospitable environment. They were regarded as "eccentric" and their adherence to more traditional methods of farming as an "aberration." "Spigolizzi," he wrote, "is a time-warp of sanity in a world corrupted by the cash advantages of chemical farming."[37]

Alan was always eager to hear about these visits and, after Levy's trip in 1987, was intrigued by the idea of Patience writing her autobiography. Levy was convinced that if she did it would be a bestseller. Jane wanted Alan to commission it. "I must say Paul's wild enthusiasm has rather infected me!" he wrote to Pat Brown of Harper and Row. "Did you know (no, how could you?) that Patience was born on Halloween?"[38] In fact during the course of editing *Honey from a Weed* and in the months after its publication, Patience had sent Alan the occasional autobiographical essay, what she called *fascicoli* (pamphlets), which she'd been circulating to friends and family for years. When it seemed unlikely that *Honey from a Weed* would ever be published, she started to devote more time to these vignettes. Alan filed them away and began to encourage her to turn them into a collection.

Meanwhile he was busy promoting *Honey from a Weed* and acting as Patience's de facto literary agent. In August 1987 she had sent him the manuscript of *Ring Doves and Snakes*, the account of her and Norman's year on Naxos that she had been unable to publish at the time. Alan, surprised to learn of another book, quickly advised her to pitch it to Kyle Cathie of Macmillan Publishing, who was overseeing the paperback version of *Honey from a Weed*. Cathie was keenly interested, and after some initial editing by Alan, Macmillan agreed to publish the forgotten manuscript.

Alan had also revived an interest in republishing *Plats du Jour*, which he told Patience was still in use and considered a prized possession by many. Patience, who'd refused offers to resurrect the book over the years, now saw it in a different light. Negotiations over a reprint would be easier now that Primrose was no longer alive. And Patience felt Angela Carter had put the book back on the map.[39] In her review in the *London Review of Books*, Carter opened by saying that *Plats du Jour* had been the first cookbook she ever bought and that, with *Honey from a Weed*, Patience had "helped to instigate the concept of the cookery book as literary form—part recipes, part travel book, part self-revelation, part art object." Plus she liked Alan's idea of doing *Plats du Jour* in hardback and in slightly larger format, which would showcase David Gentleman's illustrations.

Ring Doves and Snakes was published in January 1989 with a cover illustration and seven monotypes by Norman. In the introduction written in 1987, Patience explained that one of the reasons given for not publishing it in the 1960s was that "it could have only happened to me." She was delighted that a book then thought to be "too far out" should now appear and, looking back, said that their experience on Naxos was "the most significant we have had together."[40] But she was unhappy with the final product, especially the quality of the paper—it was printed in Hong Kong on cheap semitransparent stock—and with her treatment at the hands of Macmillan, so different from what she had become accustomed to working with Alan. "Macmillan are no longer publishers as understood by Anthony Burgess," she wrote, "but computerized business people."[41] Despite the poor quality of the paper—Norman felt it had been "priced for pulping"—the book was expensive. Still Patience traveled to London in February for the launch and was featured on a BBC roundtable, hosted by Melvyn Bragg, with John Kenneth Galbraith, whose book *Capitalism, Communism, and Coexistence* had recently been published.[42] Though Patience and Norman hoped *Ring Doves and Snakes* would have a paperback run, the book was largely ignored.

However a curious review appeared in the *Times Literary Supplement* in July 1989. Written by Elizabeth Herring, it described Patience and Norman as naïve, blundering travelers—"innocents abroad *à la* Daisy Miller"—who had grossly misunderstood the village Greeks. Herring wrote that the unrelenting narrative of hunger, privation, and fear failed to "transcend the bitterness with which it ends" and had none of the redemptive qualities of, say, Lawrence Durrell or Patrick Leigh Fermor. If it had, she continued, "the author and her mate would begin to view Naxos, Greece, the Mediterranean, as a movable feast."[43] Herring did not address the matter of the stolen sculptures directly but suggested that Patience and Norman's paranoia was unfounded, a product of unreasonable expectations and plain ignorance. Nor did she consider the book in relation to Patience's later work, *Honey from a Weed*, which offers a very different picture of life on Naxos. (Indeed the chapter titled "Fasting on Naxos" is as much about the pleasure and ecstasy of feasting as it is about the hardships associated with island life.)

By the time *Honey from a Weed* was published, of course, Patience and Norman's understanding of village life and their place in it had changed considerably. The Salento was not quite as remote as Naxos, but nevertheless their presence, at least initially, aroused a great deal of suspicion. They'd become accustomed to being robbed and yet never again thought of going to the police as they had done in Greece. Moreover Patience's appreciation of the time they spent on Naxos is evident in the introduction to *Ring Doves and Snakes*: "In Apollona we enjoyed a freedom, a reciprocity, which we felt as happiness," she wrote. "What finally happened in no way cancels this experience."

Herring, it turns out, was deputy editor of the *Athenian*, an English-language magazine read mostly by expats. She was an acolyte of Leigh Fermor, and for a very brief period before Kevin Andrews's death had been his lover. She and Andrews had met at a party in Athens for Leigh Fermor in 1988, belatedly celebrating the publication of *Between the Woods and the Water*, now regarded as a classic; at the time Herring was launching a literary journal of her own and hoped Andrews and Leigh Fermor would contribute to it. Indeed it was Leigh Fermor who had recommended her to the *Times Literary Supplement* as a reviewer.

One month before Herring's review appeared, Andrews had written Patience a blistering four-page letter in which he laid out his own unsparing criticisms of the book. (According to Herring she and Andrews never discussed *Ring Doves and Snakes*.[44]) Having lived in Greece for more than forty years, he could relate to Patience and Norman's predicament—he had even spent nine months in the remote village of Ikaria, where he was accused of being a spy—but felt that Patience had presented a one-dimensional and unfairly negative portrait of village life. He seethed at her "deafness to the Greek language," misunderstanding of local customs, and failure to see things from the point of view of the local people. Andrews said it was well known at the time that antiquities from the island of Naxos were being plundered and sold for large sums throughout Europe; there was even a rumor, he said, that they were being loaded from a *caïque* onto a German submarine in the bay of Naxos. How they could have overlooked this mystified him. "The penalty for exporting antiquities can be anything up to a life sentence," he wrote. "Clearly, if only just for good measure, you were better out of the way. Your own misfortunes there leave you no room to inquire into the Apollonians' viewpoint. They could only have felt threatened—by the Greek state via yourselves."[45]

Others, however, felt the book was a bracingly honest portrait of the parochial nature of island life. Nia Parry, whose grandparents were from Sparta, said that at that time "Greece was really very raw and mean in a lot of ways."[46] Nancy Cummings, Andrews's estranged wife, with whom Patience struck up a correspondence after his death, told her she found the book "very startling because it was so accurate." She added, "The writing is a lot like Kevin's, with a certain Greekness of impact."[47]

Andrews was not one to mince words—he seemed to delight in tearing down other people's work, especially if it had anything to do with Greece—and he assured Patience in that same letter that it would not imperil their friendship. It turned out however to be the last letter she would receive from him. In late August he and Herring took a boat to the island of Kythira, just south of the Peloponnese. On September 1 Andrews, an indefatigable long-distance swimmer who thought nothing of swimming for four or five hours, set out for the tiny uninhabited island of Avgo. Herring was left waiting on the shore. Andrews never returned, and his body, battered on the rocks by pounding surf, was recovered the following day.

❦

Patience could be equally withering in her own treatment of other people's work. She considered a paper on the history and uses of garlic, delivered at the Oxford Symposium on Food and Cookery in 1984, to be subpar.

"If we are to call up on the Ancients, I think we should do so worthily," she wrote to Alan, who had published the article. "Don't be cross but Ms. Hicks garlic document in this respect is a shocker. And so are the recipes. She should read Horace."[48] Even Alan wasn't spared. After announcing that the 1993 Oxford Symposium was to be devoted to the "look and feel" of food, including its shape, size, color, and texture, Patience wrote to say that she found the very premise offensive. "Apparently nothing whatever to do with nourishment or taste," she wrote to the symposium's organizer, Harlan Walker. "Just something to gawp at, something to prod. As if we were suddenly transported back to Earl's Court circa 1958 with the spun-sugar kings and hallucinating chocolate molds."[49] Alan, who'd been sent a copy of the letter, was astonished. Were the shapes of breads and various kinds of pasta of no interest, he asked? What about certain foods such as krill, which, if turned into an "ocean paste," would be "almost perfect little packages of nutrients" and a "dream food in terms of economics and nutritional values," but was unlikely to catch on because of the way it looks and feels? Finally he referred Patience to her own discussion of the "sculptural pleasure" of making gingerbread in *Honey from a Weed* and asked if such things had suddenly gone out of fashion.[50] Patience wrote back to say that it was really a question of word choice—form, taste, and texture would have been more appropriate. (Incidentally the subject of the 1988 Oxford Symposium, "The Cooking Pot," was chosen by Patience.)

Patience was often generous in sharing her knowledge: Her judgments were always intellectually rigorous and sharply critical. In 1989 Alan sent her a copy of a new translation of Giacomo Castelvetro's *The Fruit, Herbs & Vegetables of Italy*; Alan's daughter Caroline, who had uncovered the manuscript in the Natural History Museum, was one of the book's editors. Castelvetro, who came from an aristocratic family, wrote the book in 1614 while living in England in exile, as a gentle reproach to the English, whose diet was so heavily dependent on meat and sugar. What follows is a seasonal account of the fruits and vegetables of his native Emilia-Romagna, with basic instructions on how to prepare them and reflections on daily life. Circulated in manuscript form and known mostly to scholars, the book was not published during Castelvetro's lifetime—he died in 1616, impoverished and homesick—and appeared in Italian only in 1974.

Patience considered it a mediocre work that, she argued, drew primarily on the earlier labors of doctors and naturalists, whom Castelevetro—"a mountebank and a snob," in her words—failed to acknowledge.[51] Indeed it was Patience's conviction that Castelvetro had essentially plagiarized the work of Costanzo Felici, a botanist and doctor whose *Lettera sulle Insalate* (*Letter on Salads*) was written in 1567. A little-known provincial doctor, Felici had a long-running correspondence with Ulisse Aldrovandi, one of the great collectors and naturalists of his time. Because of Felici's breadth of knowledge—he also wrote on birds, fungi, pasta, and bread—and his engaging, straightforward prose, Aldrovandi asked him to prepare the treatise on salads, which covered all wild and cultivated plants of the Marche. Patience had read the "salad letter," which was published in Italian in 1982, and she considered it a masterpiece.

There is little hard evidence to support the plagiarism claim, though Felici and Castelvetro knew many of the same people, and it's entirely possible that Castelvetro was familiar with the letter. Most of all Patience felt Felici more deserving of translation and credit than Castelvetro. She admired his inquisitive mind, systematic approach, and interest in the great diversity of plant and animal life. In a letter to Caroline Davidson, she wrote, "This knowledge belonged to people who cultivated the earth and to doctors and botanists. The translator disregards the tradition (practice) but also the studies of the herbalists, as does Castelvetro."[52] She included a list of more than two dozen corrections, and told Alan that as food historians "it is not our task to disseminate ignorance."[53]

The translator was Gillian Riley, who would go on to edit *The Oxford Companion to Italian Food*, published in 2007. Riley briefly took up the issue of Felici's possible influence in her introduction, noting that there were some overlapping elements in both books, and pointed out that Castelvetro was not a botanist but "an enthusiastic amateur," and that he may very well have read Felici's manuscript. However in *The Oxford Companion to Italian Food* she dismisses the notion that Castelvetro borrowed from Felici's earlier work, calling the claim "plain daft." Though Riley never met Patience, the basic tenor of her comments were relayed to her. "Her reply was quite outspoken," Riley recalled, "so much so that they thought I should not be shown her letter."[54] When John Thorne published an enthusiastic review of the translation for his newsletter *Simple Cooking*,

Patience wrote to say that she was astonished at his "whole-hearted approval of Castelvetro" and asked if he could read sixteenth-century Italian, in which case she'd be happy to provide him with Felici's letter. Patience laid out her defense of the unknown author whose treatise on plants, she argued, had "nothing to do with the tables of the rich, but with the knowledge of wild plants and their uses as food, and as medicine, derived from centuries-old practices of mountain peasants and confirmed by the Ancients—Dioscorides, Theophrastus, etc."[55]

Like John Claudius Loudon, the Scottish botanist and gardener whose work Patience had studied in the 1950s, Felici was a polymath, self-taught in a number of disciplines, and a pioneering naturalist. Whereas Loudon had focused almost exclusively on the cultivated land-scape—his great work was after all an encyclopedia of gardening—the sixteenth-century Italian naturalists, apothecaries, and herbalists were interested in the full range of plant and animal life that surrounded them. Felici even set out to send Aldrovandi specimens of every sort of fish, rare or common, that were found in the nearest port to his hometown of Piobbico. In her own work Patience had adopted a similar approach and, though she continued to grow vegetables, her real interest was in the staggering diversity of the macchia, which she described as "nature unimpaired by human hand." Thus she wrote that she was particularly interested in Felici's letter "because it is the first time I have read about weeds and plants in the way I myself approach them, as living forms, but also because of the spirit of discovery in the Renaissance."[56]

Patience was far more interested in food history and "the Ancients" than she was in contemporary food writing. As she'd told Alan in 1984, she'd pretty much stopped reading modern cookery books when she and Norman left to live in Carrara in the 1960s. By the 1990s she admitted to being "far from the subject [of food writing], of which I am almost entirely ignorant."[57] She also said she was "sick to death of food writers."[58] Thus when Alan solicited recommendations for his anthology of food writing—*On Fasting and Feasting*, published in 1988—she offered passages from Knut Hamsun's *Hunger* (fasting), which was published in 1890; George Gissing's *By the Ionian Sea* (feathered food), published in 1901; D. H. Lawrence's *Sea and Sardinia* (meat), published in 1921; and the Greek historian Xenophon (odd diets), who lived from 431 to 354

BCE.[59] Alan included a passage from *Hunger* in which the narrator, an impoverished writer, procures a raw bone from a butcher—he tells the butcher it's for his dog—and tries to eat it but cannot keep it down and instead vomits and weeps over the wretched object (he calls it a "gorgeous little bone"). Alan also published the piece on pa amb tomàquet by Leopold Pomés and two selections from *Honey from a Weed*: "*La Salsa*" and "The Christmas Fish"—an almond-paste confection made in Lecce to celebrate the birth of Christ. Patience felt that Italo Calvino should be recognized as a "food historian" for his novel *Mr. Palomar*, which includes a section on the eponymous narrator's visit to various specialty food shops in Paris. She thought Fritz Brenner, the cook and butler in Rex Stout's Nero Wolfe stories, who kept busts of Escoffier and Brillat-Savarin as well as hundreds of cookbooks in his living quarters, worthy of closer study.[60] She recommended Will Self, whose weekly column appeared in the *Observer* beginning in 1995, for a Glenfiddich Award because he reached "far beyond the boring topic of food and drink." Plus, she said, he'd be the "best promoter you could wish for the virtues of whiskey."[61] A few years later John Thorne introduced her to the work of Anthony Bourdain, the enfant terrible of American food writing whose *Kitchen Confidential* was published to great acclaim in 2000. Patience enjoyed it, especially its evocation of the drama of cooking, and described Bourdain as a "reckless romantic." Thorne also sent her a copy of Richard Olney's *Lulu's Provençal Table*, which she appreciated, though she took issue with the recipe for tapenade because it strayed from J. B. Reboul's classic version.

For a special issue of *Simple Cooking* on books that writers would like to see reprinted, Patience chose Daniel Spoerri's highly unorthodox *The Mythological Travels of a Modern Sir John Mandeville*, a sort of diary with recipes that recounts the author's year on the tiny Greek island of Symi in 1967. It also includes a lengthy digression on the origins of the meatball and is more a work of conceptual art—Spoerri is best known for his collage-like presentations of found objects, or "snare-pictures"—than it is a cookbook. Though initially repelled by his attitude to women and his treatment of animals, Patience came to admire his honesty and intelligence, and even felt the book shared some affinities with *Honey from a Weed*. It was clearly a book written by someone who had little interest in catering to anyone, least of all to critics or food writers. "Spoerri is probably a Ram (Aries)," Patience wrote to Ulrike Voswinckel, who had given her a copy of the book. "He likes butting the reader!"[62]

⚜

The success of *Honey from a Weed* led not only to publication of Patience's previously written books and the new edition of *Plats du Jour*, which appeared in 1990, but also to the occasional commission from magazines and journals. In the years following its publication, Patience wrote a few short pieces for *Simple Cooking* and *Petits Propos Culinaires*. But her name had reached beyond the often insular world of food writing. In 1989, Nancy Newhouse, the editor of the *New York Times*' biannual travel magazine, *The Sophisticated Traveler*, asked Patience if she'd be interested in doing a feature on the Salento. Newhouse was also an admirer of *Honey from a Weed* and felt Patience would offer a compelling introduction to the region, which was still relatively unknown to American travelers. It was the kind of assignment Patience might have scoffed at, given her lack of interest in America—the United States stood for everything that was wrong with the world and with food in particular—and her disdain for tourism more broadly. But after the reception of *Honey from a Weed* in the United States and her correspondence with several American food writers, Patience's feelings had softened a bit. Alan, whose wife, Jane, was from Washington, DC, was also quite keen on America. He once wrote Patience a letter after visiting friends in Berkeley, California, in which he referred to "the ritual of going to Peet's in the morning for one's three mugs of coffee, the wealth of bookshops, [and] the Berkeley Coop in which half the foods are labeled with warnings not to buy them."[63] When Wolfe took a trip to New York City and reported that he'd found copies of *Honey from a Weed* on sale at the Frick, Patience was delighted.[64]

Still she found it challenging to conjure an image of the well-heeled American traveler, and her interests and predilections. It wasn't until Newhouse told her that readers would probably be completely ignorant of the Salento, and that most of them would never actually bother to go there, that Patience was able to write the piece in the way she wanted, as a kind of travelogue rather than tour guide. "In telling me her readers were 'armchair travellers' she relieved me of a good deal of anxiety," Patience wrote.[65] Originally titled "Discovering the Salento," it is an intimate portrait of the place that Patience had come to consider home.

Published in the spring 1991 issue, the article covers much of the region's ancient past, especially its Greek influences, and muses on why the peninsula "has been a closed book to all but a little stream of dedicated travelers."[66] Even Norman Douglas, as Patience liked to point out, hadn't bothered to set foot there. "The Salento has always been exposed, invaded, settled by people from across the sea," she wrote, echoing Carlo Levi.[67] It was this very vulnerability that had given rise to a culture of self-sufficiency and conservatism that had protected many of the region's traditions, including the time-honored production of wine and olive oil. In this version the Salento is alive and well, its "Neolithic way of life" flourishing in various small villages and old fishing ports. Patience starts off in Lecce, giving an overview of the city's architectural history and its culinary treasures: *cotognata* (quince paste), *fichi mandorlati* (dried figs stuffed with almonds), smoked mozzarella, ricotta, *pucce* (small loaves of bread baked with olives), and *rustici* ("little featherweight pies of *pâte feuilletée* filled with melting mozarrella").[68]

The only inkling we get of the incursion of modern life is an offhand reference to the congestion in Lecce (elsewhere she had referred to the "chaos of apartment blocks and maze of motorways" that surrounded the city).[69] But the city is just a gateway to the dozens of tiny villages that make up the southernmost tip of the peninsula. Mostly traveling back in time, Patience writes that the cultivation of the olive and the vine, the stone structures that dot the landscape, and the traditional crafts displayed in the Museum of Popular Traditions are all emblematic of a "rural civilization both heroic and refined." She takes us to some of her favorite places: villages where Griko, a dialect that can be traced back to Homeric Greek, is still spoken; tiny chapels with Byzantine and Renaissance paintings; and forgotten fishing towns. At one point she even seems to veer into the kind of romantic pabulum she could be so critical of. To the traveler, she writes, "the peninsula proposes personal adventure, a new-found freedom, a gift of timelessness." Along the Ionian coast "you may feel a sudden euphoria borne on an easterly breeze from the mountains of northern Greece."[70] This is decidedly not a picture of a place ruined by pollution or the disintegration of a centuries-old way of life. Needless to say such a critique would never have made its way into the pages of a glossy travel magazine, and Patience was writing from the point of view of someone who had come to love and cherish the Salento, particularly its wild landscapes. Yet the piece also highlights the fact that Patience had not reconciled in her own mind whether the way of life she was writing about was "fast vanishing," as she put it in the introduction to Irving's book as early as 1969, or more durable.

She memorably wrote in the introduction to *Honey from a Weed*, "As with students of music who record old songs which are no longer sung, soon some of the things I record will also have vanished."[71] But, she told Alan, this was not the message she wanted people to come away with after reading the book, and she discouraged him from using that sentence on the jacket copy. There were plenty of traditional methods of cooking that lived on and were not yet in need of being "preserved." It was a point she made repeatedly despite the overwhelming sense that regional traditions were in peril. Just after the book was published, she told Jeremy Round, "Although the world's crumbling, what I describe is still going on."[72] A decade later in a letter to John Thorne, she explained, "We have many young friends who cook with pleasure grandma's dishes, keeping alive *la cucina povera*."[73] And she made the point to Alan that at its heart *Honey from a Weed* was about the intrinsic "excellence of raw materials and their treatment," which she considered eternal.[74]

Her *New York Times* editors were supremely happy with the piece, and Patience could have continued to write for them, and perhaps others, but it was to be the last article she wrote for an American magazine.[75] The inevitable challenges of working on an article over such a great distance—though Patience now had access to a fax machine, which speeded up communications—seemed to outweigh the benefits. Patience was happier writing for friends and family. Increasingly, throughout the final decade of her life, she turned her attention more to local projects, one of which was involvement with the *tipografia* (print shop) and Rolando's publishing activities, and to writing autobiographical essays.

CHAPTER FIFTEEN

Reflections

Patience's interest in design, publishing, and handmade books went back at least to the early 1950s when she worked with Henrion and at the Royal College of Art. It was later informed by the remarkable early Venetian and Florentine woodcut books in Irving Davis's personal library. Throughout her career Patience always paid close attention to the visual presentation of her work and felt that illustrations were not simply decorative but integral to the text itself. "The marriage between text and drawings is essential," she wrote to Alan just before the publication of *Honey from a Weed*. "Everything depends on it."[1] Even her own letters were artfully composed with red and black typewritten text often wrapping around photocopied images from newspapers or photos, portraits of beloved writers like Stendhal or Kafka, or drawings of flowers and plants. The images were carefully chosen, and Patience said that she often used a letter heading that was relevant to the "as yet unwritten text."[2] As with Irving's Catalan cookbook and even *Honey from a Weed*, she was interested in making books on her own terms without much regard for profit or readers' expectations. Thus in 1989 when Rolando Civilla started his *tipografia* it was for Patience "a kind of miracle."[3]

Rolando was among the group of friends and students who'd been attracted to Spigolizzi and Patience and Norman's unconventional lifestyle. He'd been a founder member of the theater group Anteo but never pursued acting as anything other than a hobby. (Anteo disbanded in 1991.) His real passion was books, printing, and typography. The son of contadini, Rolando had in fact met Patience and Norman in the early 1980s on one of his weekly walkabouts with a friend through the countryside. Every Sunday morning for about five years, Rolando and Vito would stop by Spigolizzi to see Patience and Norman. Initially it was curiosity that drove them; then a desire to escape the monotony of village life; finally Spigolizzi became a beacon of hope, a sign that it was possible to make a life in the Salento despite the insistence by many that emigration was the only way forward.

Rolando had long been interested in books, even though his family had very few, and considered every letter of the alphabet a work of art. Throughout his childhood he would visit the small public library in Presicce whenever he could and knew it from top to bottom. After National Service he studied graphic design in Lecce and then typography in Milan, but decided to return to Presicce to pursue his dream of opening a print shop, which he called Levante Arti Grafiche. Along the way he conferred regularly with Patience and Norman, learned from them, and ultimately collaborated with them on numerous projects, culminating in the publication of Patience's collection of autobiographical essays, *Work Adventures Childhood Dreams*.

Every Tuesday, after doing their shopping in Presicce, Patience and Norman would stop by the shop with a merenda of *panini* and beer. In the basement workshop crowded with printing presses, including an antique treadle platen machine and a newer, more sophisticated Heidelberg, they'd discuss their work, local issues, art, and politics. Patience had complete faith in Rolando as a publisher—she liked the fact that he was willing to take on "impossible things"—and they saw eye to eye. "They were like two bees who met in flight," said Ada Martella. "They had a language of their own."[4]

Though by 1989 Patience had finished most of her *fascicoli* (a word she used to refer to her miscellaneous self-published writings) in 1989, it was the work of another author that she initially sought to bring to light. Don Andrea Giovene, the scion of an aristocratic Neapolitan family, had been introduced to Patience and Norman in the early 1970s through their mutual friend Riccardo Winspeare, Maria Vittoria's brother-in-law. Soon after they met, Don Andrea and his wife, Adeline Constance Schuberth, came to Spigolizzi for dinner, and he brought the second volume of his great novel, *The Book of Sansevero*, which Patience considered a neglected masterpiece.

One of the more memorable meals recounted in *Honey from a Weed*, the only feast Patience felt "impelled to describe," was with Don Andrea and Adeline in what had once been a trattoria near Ugento, where the

Giovenes spent their summers. In the bare whitewashed room, they dined on spaghetti in a deep red tomato sauce, scorpion fish, lamb roasted over an open fire and served with red peppers, a dish of grilled red mullets, and fresh goat's cheese from Gemini, followed by green melon and almond cakes.

After another visit Don Andrea sent them an old Bourbon map of the Salento from 1830 that he had washed, cleaned, and ironed by hand. It showed a mostly uninhabited landscape with the occasional watchtower along the coast and a few villages inland. Patience wrote that meeting Don Andrea was like a bolt from the blue that "reminded me of the sudden appearance of the bee orchid among the stones."[5] They saw each other infrequently—Don Andrea lived most of the year in a small flat in London—but maintained a lively correspondence.

Like the Winspeares, Don Andrea gave the impression of belonging to an earlier epoch. He saw himself as an outsider, was "happy to work away in total obscurity," and had a noble heritage that appealed to Patience. By the time of Don Andrea's birth in 1904, the family's wealth had largely dissipated and its status faded—this long, unhappy decline would become the subject of his own fiction. Don Andrea took an interest in books and writing at a young age and founded an avant-garde literary magazine, *Vesuvius*, in the 1920s. He served as a cavalry captain in the Second World War and, after Italy's capitulation, he was taken prisoner and held in camps in Poland and then Germany. Among his friends, some of whom Patience corresponded with and whose letters she said, "[resembled] those of a nineteenth century novel," were fellow cavalry officer Detalmo Pirzio-Biroli and the artist Emilio Ambron.[6] Though nearly blind by the time he met them, Don Andrea sent Patience beautiful handwritten letters decorated with drawings.

Don Andrea was also a bibliophile and had a collection of more than ten thousand books, which he housed in the family's last remaining monument to its storied past, the twelfth-century Palazzo Cerevo in the medieval town of Sant'Agata dei Goti (the library included a signed copy of Proust's *Swann in Love*). The first volume of *The Book of Sansevero*, the work he would become best known for, was published in Italian in 1967. Don Andrea told Patience that he'd pondered the book for twenty years before beginning to write it. It eventually ran to five volumes, but it was only after Don Andrea self-published the second volume in a limited run of one thousand copies that it received the attention of the literary world; it was translated into several languages and Don Andrea was even floated as a possible recipient of the Nobel Prize for Literature. An epic generational novel based largely on Don Andrea's own life, the book tells the story of the second son of a declining Neapolitan family—Giuliano Sansevero—through the early decades of the twentieth century. It is evident from his books that Don Andrea, who was sometimes compared to Giuseppe Lampedusa, author of *The Leopard*, clung to an older vision of Italy, one ruled by romance and chivalry. In the first volume of his "autobiography," he bemoans the "cipher of the modern world which has abolished the distinguishing emblems" of an earlier time.[7] The book is full of evocative descriptions of Naples and its decaying, worldly elegance, a romantic vision that Patience wrote, "calls forth my so long held Italian feelings."[8]

Don Andrea equally admired Patience's writing and told Alan at the launch of the paperback edition of *Honey from a Weed* that it was much more than just a cookbook: It was a book of great spiritual depth. In late 1986 he asked Patience to translate a "sacred drama" he'd recently completed, *The Third Day*, which Patience did the following year. Set between Palm Sunday and Easter, it is a retelling of the Gospels story—the third day being the resurrection of Christ—a text Don Andrea had read over and over while a prisoner in Poland in 1943. Years later, in what he described as a trancelike state, the play was written. In 1996 with Rolando Patience published a limited edition of thirty-five copies for friends; the original Italian edition of five-hundred copies apparently disappeared without trace, making the translation the "only printed testimony to the original poetic work."[9] Patience also brought out a collection of Don Andrea's poems, *Lirica dell'Insonnia*, which he had composed at night to overcome insomnia and then sent to Patience; and a selection of his "poetic letters" titled *Immagini e Chimere*. These were in fact letters written to Patience and Norman over a twenty-year period. Lamenting what she called "the indifference of editors towards the great writer," Patience included a brief account of the publication history of the Sansevero novels as well as her discovery of them. She concluded with a plea for the books, along with a number of Don Andrea's other works, to be republished "for the consolation of the young."[10]

She also admired Fred Uhlman's *A Moroccan Diary*, which she reprinted with Rolando in 1995, feeling it deserving of a wider audience. An account of the author's journey to Morocco after the war, the slim volume with pen-and-wash drawings was originally published by Penguin in 1949. In the early 1990s Miranda spotted a copy of the long-out-of-print book in a Cambridge market stall and sent it to Patience, knowing she'd be interested in this forgotten story of her one-time Hampstead friend and neighbor. Uhlman had not been a particularly close friend, but Patience recalled him giving her a copy of his autobiography, *The Making of an Englishman*, in the early 1960s. Trained as a lawyer, Uhlman had fled Stuttgart in 1933 after receiving a phone call with the coded message, "Il fait beau à Paris aujourd'hui." He spent time in Paris, and then Spain during the civil war, before settling in England. Like so many German Jewish exiles, including Henrion, he was interned on the Isle of Man for several months, which Patience described as a "fatal reversal of expectation." Patience clearly identified with this group of émigrés and said they "acted as an instant leaven . . . on the stodgy pudding of English life." It wasn't long after the war, while on holiday in Wales as Patience recalled, that she told Uhlman the story of her paternal grandfather, another Jewish refugee who'd fled to England.

The last of the small books Patience and Rolando published was a collection of poems by Antonio Lupo, a friend and neighbor from Salve. "Antonio was writing these poems on little scraps of paper," Rolando recalled. "She [Patience] turned them into a book."[11] She had in fact done earlier translations from Italian of a few stories by Ezechiele Leandro, a scrap-metal dealer turned self-taught sculptor, whose writing eschewed punctuation altogether.[12] These she copied and distributed to friends. In a biographical note accompanying one of the stories, Patience, mimicking Leandro's style, described their first encounter in Lecce. She and Norman "saw some pictures hanging inside a sort of garage we went inside & found Leandro alone with his painting they were on bits of board they seemed magic in this empty garage we looked at the paintings & at once we wanted one Leandro spoke like a rushing torrent like a waterfall a cataract in dialect we could not understand what he said he was so fierce the whole world seems to be against him . . ."

Rolando also published Norman's philosophical treatise on the role of art and culture in human history, *Remembering Man*. The book grew out of an invitation to attend a conference on the origins of art to be held at the Val Camonica National Museum of Prehistory where their friend Emmanuel Anati was director; Anati had recently published a book titled *The Origins of Art and Conceptuality*, a systematic study of the history of rock art. Initially Norman asked Rolando to attend the conference with him, and they embarked on a series of conversations on the subject, which Norman had long studied. But they soon realized that they had far more to say than would be possible at the conference or in an academic paper and decided to turn their attention to publishing a book. According to Rolando it was Patience who convinced them it wasn't necessary to make the journey to Val Camonica, thus "initiating another creation."[13] The book summed up, in largely impenetrable prose, Norman's thoughts on everything from the creative act to man's assault on nature. Even Patience, who edited the manuscript and read it more than a dozen times, admitted to being unable to fully understand it. The book itself, however, is a striking work of art illustrated with lithographic reproductions of some of his later acrylic paintings and line drawings.

Meanwhile Patience continued to toy with the idea of publishing the fascicoli, the essays she'd been sending to Alan, the first of which was written as long ago as 1966. She continued to work on them intermittently, but most were completed in 1988 and 1989. In the early 1990s she put them aside, telling friends and family she wasn't interested in undertaking a large-scale project in the midst of so much global conflict and unrest. "I have somehow in these stressing times lost the conviction that they really matter," she told Nick about her collection of essays.[14] Later she told one of her granddaughters, "I stopped writing in 1991 during the gulf war, because then I felt nobody would listen."[15]

The truth is she was never entirely comfortable with the idea of publishing an autobiography. The fascicoli were strikingly personal, photocopied, simply bound, and sent with letters, and were never intended for a larger audience. It wasn't until she began to view the endeavor as less of an account of her life than an imaginative, creative act that she warmed to the idea of publishing the essays, which Alan Davidson had long encouraged. She'd also been reading a number of experimental autobiographies:

Boris Pasternak's *Safe Conduct*; Carl Jung's *Memories, Dreams, Reflections* (to which the title she eventually chose for her own book most certainly alludes); *The Autobiography of Alice B. Toklas*; Saint Thérèse of Lisieux's *Story of a Soul*; and Don Andrea's fictional autobiography. "I now realise that Don Andrea and Gertrude Stein have one thing in common," she wrote. "They both have written somebody else's autobiography."[16]

Patience may have wished to do the same, and in the introduction to *Work Adventures Childhood Dreams*, she makes the somewhat dubious claim that autobiography, because of its selective nature, belongs "in the realm of fiction." This is undoubtedly a stretch, but it absolved her—or perhaps from her perspective liberated her—from any obligation to adhere to the facts of her own life, or, perhaps more importantly, to a conventional linear narrative. Later in the book, when introducing the subject of her own childhood, she quotes writer, biographer, and novelist Jonathan Keates: "Autobiography, what suppressions, what lies!" Patience insisted there was a message in the book but wrote in the postscript, "It is up to the reader to decipher it." Despite the roundabout narrative and her professed contempt for the genre itself, the book is clearly a work of nonfiction, and Patience, while she takes liberties, is still presenting a snapshot of her life. "The result is a kind of patchwork," she wrote, "in which time is not strung out in an orderly way. . . . However far from 'ordinary life' the picture may seem, it certainly reflects my life."[17]

Not surprisingly this approach did not lend itself to the expectations and wishes of mainstream publishers. Even Tom Jaine of Prospect Books, to whom Alan had sold the company in 1993 and turned over the material Patience had sent him, found it too discursive and hard to follow. In a letter to Patience, he explained that it would be too costly for Prospect Books without significant pruning, and indeed cutting several of the essays altogether, while Patience was reluctant to revise the work at all. He felt it lacked cohesion. There were structural issues, in part because the narrative did not proceed chronologically. Ultimately the book demanded too much of the reader, who had to follow the various threads without any guidance from the author. Throughout the collection Patience mentions people and places without providing any context or explanation of who they are. "It is autobiography," Tom wrote, "but the facts and figures are buried deep in the text and need much pre knowledge and forensic ability to tease out."[18] Plus it wasn't a book on food or cooking, which, he speculated, readers had come to expect from the author of *Honey from a Weed*. The book does contain a single recipe, one of Patience's favorites, for *rougets au vin blanc,* which she'd pried out of the cook and innkeeper in Locmariaquer in the early 1950s. Even this, as one reviewer noted, was a recipe that "in its reliance on technique impossible to learn from the page, proves the pointlessness of cookbooks."[19]

Tom Jaine's response hardly deterred Patience. If anything it reinforced her desire to publish the book herself, which gave her complete control over everything from the typeface (Bodoni) and kind of paper used to the images included, many of which were photos she'd taken throughout her travels with Norman. "It must be said that no publisher could have published it as it is," a reviewer in the *Spectator* aptly noted, "but I don't suppose Miss Gray cares very much about what publishers think."[20] For about three years, beginning in 1997, she and Rolando worked on the project together, digitizing the text, correcting proofs, and designing the book. An army of beautiful women, as Rolando referred to them, transferred the typewritten essays to a computer. Images were culled from Patience's archive. Like the director of a film, Patience presided over every aspect of the book's production until it took on the quality of a living, breathing thing.

Indeed the book presents a collage-like portrait of its author, one in which images of the past and present overlap and the "facts and figures," as Tom Jaine referred to them, are mostly submerged. Many of the photos, linocuts, and other images are in fact displayed in collage form, and it has the feel of a lovingly made art book. The first section, titled "Work," broadly follows the contours of Patience and Norman's life after they left England in the 1960s. There are essays on Greece and Norman's 1964 exhibition in Venice, on life in Carrara and the history and archaeology of the Salento—all of which serves as a companion piece to *Honey from a Weed*. The second section, "Adventures," plunges further into the past with pieces on the trip to Romania with Tania in 1938, an account of the family holidays in Locmariaquer, a pivotal journey to St. Jeannet in 1961 while on assignment for the *Observer,* and a long, rambling tour of the Palladian villas of the Veneto with striking photographs of the deserted, crumbling architecture. (Some of the essays, with their mix of autobiography, storytelling, and photographs, bear a resemblance to the work

of W. G. Sebald.) "Childhood," tellingly the briefest section, addresses
Patience's early years but is more revealing for what it leaves out than
what it includes. The final section, "Dreams," the least conventional in
form, covers everything from Don Andrea's fiction to the baroque architecture of the city of Lecce. It closes with a fond remembrance of Irving
Davis and Patience's whimsical rumination that he had returned, on the
occasion of the sale of his collection of books at Sotheby's in 1985, in the
form of a bluebottle fly.[21]

Perhaps not surprisingly the name Thomas Gray does not appear
in *Work Adventures Childhood Dreams*. Patience does, however, devote
considerable space to the question of why she never married—while
never really getting to the heart of the matter. Knowing nothing of her
past, one would surmise from the book that her decision not to marry was
a sort of feminist reaction against the domestic arrangements of Edwardian life, which is not altogether untrue. "Why I never married," begins
the section on childhood. The answer: "The kneeling upset me. I used to
suffer appalling embarrassment when my mother went down on her knees
to implore my father, who was sitting in a low armchair stretched with
well-worn leather and completely absorbed in the *Times* Fourth Leader,
to come to dinner."[22] Acknowledging that she has perhaps skirted the
question, Patience returns to it several pages later. "Isn't it transparently
clear?" she asks. And then answers herself: "Something definitely out of
tune even before emerging from childhood in my response to convention,
something fatally dissonant in the observable models. Wedlock seen by a
schoolgirl was far from inspiring; life must surely mean more than repeti-
tive 'domestic bliss.'"[23] At the end of the same essay, after referring to her
desire to "live my own life irrespective of family patterns," she dispenses
with saying anything at all about Thomas Gray and concludes, "How in
due course I became a black sheep is far too painful to write down."[24]
That there might have been a link between becoming a black sheep and
why she never married is never explored. It is hardly noticeable given the
book's structure, but the years 1940 to about 1947 are almost entirely
absent; the war itself, arguably one of the most significant periods of her
life, is mentioned only in passing. As Patience liked to say, her adult life
could be divided into two distinct periods: raising her children in postwar
London and her travels with Norman.

The specter of Thomas Gray, though, had not been completely vanquished. It was in 1991 that Miranda reached out to Thomas's siblings—his brother, Milner, and sister, Margaret—to find out more about the father she never knew. Milner at that point was in his nineties and in poor health (he died in 1997). However she struck up a correspondence with Margaret, who was fairly candid in her assessment of Thomas's life. "Some of the things he did (or failed to do) were quite outrageous," she wrote in one letter. "And I am sure your mother had valid reason for feeling bitter towards him."[25] She also provided Miranda with several photographs and a few details about Thomas's life after the war. "It is the first photo of our father that I have ever seen as far as I am aware," she wrote to Nick. "It strikes me that he is rather like you."[26] Patience was not particularly sympathetic to Miranda's efforts to learn more about Thomas Gray. However she largely concurred with Margaret's analysis of his character, suggesting only that Margaret might have somewhat understated his flaws. For her own part Patience still considered the matter a closed topic and told Nick that digging around in the past was "a form of 'voyeurism.'"[27]

It was Norman, Patience often wrote, who helped her reinvent her life, and *Work Adventures Childhood Dreams* is as much a tribute to him as it is an autobiography. Patience dedicated the book to him, and his presence is felt throughout. Photos of him appear at the beginning and end of the book; the closing image is one of Norman leaning over a wine barrel listening to the "song" of fermentation. A painting he did of Patience, titled *For My Darling*, graces the cover. The first essay, "Patron Saint and Patron," and much of the first section on work are clearly a homage to Norman. In relation to her own work, she credits Norman with "'giving me the right' to make things because, before I knew him, any creative thing I undertook seemed to be a kind of madness."[28] It was, she writes, "*l'uomo di pietra* who long ago handed me not so much a completely new life but more mysteriously a life that is always new."[29] According to Patience's granddaughter Rosy, "She always said 'life for me started when I met Norman.'"[30] "What Norman did was to give Patience freedom to be her creative self," Miranda recalled. "Because he just assumed that that's why we are alive."[31]

The feeling was reciprocated, and their relationship was a symbiotic one in every respect. Norman had met Patience at a pivotal moment in his own life, and she was both inspired in her own work by his creativity and a great encouragement to him in his. "Norman reveled in her ability to respond to all of his ideas," recalled his sister, Ruscha.[32] Norman once told his mother that "life begins at Spigolizzi," echoing Patience's own sentiment. She became his muse and provided him with the spark he needed to break free from his life at Grange Farm. Every year beginning in 1978, the year after his mother's death, Norman made Patience an elaborate and strikingly beautiful handmade book for her birthday. He devoted the time between the winemaking and the olive harvest to writing and illustrating these objets d'art, which took the form of illustrated poems, plays, or parables. The first book, inspired by the presence of two new moons in the month of October 1978, was an illustrated diary containing fragments of poetry, newspaper clippings, and the day's events superimposed over Norman's geodetic drawings. Norman called it *Come Hallowe'en: Breviary for a Lunar Advent*. It closes with an image of the second new moon, which is clearly an idealized portrait of his muse, and a quote from the book of Solomon: "All good things together came to me with her, and innumerable riches in her hands" (Wisdom of Solomon 7:11).

Patience never displayed these books and showed them only to very few people. When, after Norman's death, she eventually wanted photocopies of three of her favorites, she insisted on being driven to the printers in Presicce—in this case not Rolando—so she could hand them over in person. She considered them to be her secret, and though they were undoubtedly among Norman's finest creations, she refused to have them included in a catalogue raisonné of his written works and illustrated books.[33]

⚜

By the time she published *Work Adventures Childhood Dreams*, Patience and Norman had in fact gotten married, which Patience made note of in the postscript. Apparently they had considered doing so years earlier, and had even made an attempt in Hampstead sometime in the 1970s, but were unable to, for what Patience described as "tax reasons." Norman and Ursula had divorced in 1972, and of course Patience and Thomas had never married. Still it wasn't easy as foreigners to get married in Italy. Even though she had never married Thomas Gray, she was required to prove that he was the father of her children and that he was no longer alive. For this Miranda's research proved useful as she managed to obtain a copy of his death certificate. Norman was required to document his places of residence since birth in case he'd been previously married and had other wives in Europe. They had to obtain what is bizarrely called a Certificate of Competence, which was furnished by Michael Burgoyne, then British vice consul in Naples. Even so, on the day of their marriage, there was a discrepancy discovered in Patience's papers, one of which said she was unmarried (*nubile*) and the other married (*coniugata*). They were obliged to reschedule the event for the following week. "This Balkan or even Byzantine experience makes one realize where we are!" Patience wrote.[34]

However, on February 10, 1994—a rare sunny midwinter day—they were married by the mayor in the town of Salve. Their friends Ada and Mario Ricchiuto served as witnesses. (Norman had witnessed Ada and Mario's wedding in the early 1970s.) That morning Patience had prepared a meal of anchovies, artichokes, *pampasciune* (tassel hyacinth bulbs), "asparagus chicory," hard-boiled eggs, and stuffed sun-dried tomatoes and mushrooms, followed by a dish of braised pork, *pezzetti di maiale*, and potatoes tossed in butter. They'd saved a bottle of 1982 Moët & Chandon d'Epernay from Jean Delpech for the occasion. "In your mind's eye you could see the original Morandi bottle," she wrote to Wolfe, "but can you taste the contents? This was nectar."[35]

This would be almost the last of Patience's letters to Wolfe, who died the following month, just before his fifty-sixth birthday. His last visit to Spigolizzi had been in 1992. Though he had planned to come in 1993, Patience for the first time told him they simply could not face another visit. "At the moment I really do not know if we are going to be up to your visit," she wrote. "Getting old. One has to admit it."[36] He'd been to Spigolizzi more than twenty times since 1970, the year they moved there, and considered the annual trip a great source of sustenance.

Over the years they wrote each other hundreds of letters—Wolfe had perfected a method of typing using a rubber-tipped stick tied to his fingers—and Patience often replied with a recipe for Wolfe's helpers to regale him with. Collected together over the years, they made a remark-able personal cookbook. Always forthright in her correspondence with others, Patience was especially open with Wolfe. "Truth has always been the goal in my writing to you," she once told him.[37] And she was a singular presence in his life, her letters a lifeline. "Patience's care and love for Wolfe absolutely would just pour out of her letters," said Julia Farrington.[38]

Wolfe's health had been precarious ever since the accident but had declined considerably in the early 1990s, and he'd been receiving treatment at Stoke Mandeville nearly all of February. He returned home to Brighton extremely frail and very ill, but determined as ever to continue to go to the theater and opera whenever possible. On March 20, 1994, just over one week before his death, he had managed to go to London to see a play, in spite of his doctor's orders not to make the trip. In his last letter to Patience, dated March 25, he congratulated her and Norman on getting married, described an exhibition of ancient Greek and Egyptian sculptures he'd gone to see, and said he still planned to go to Italy later that year. "A touch of spring is in the air," he wrote, "thank god. I imagine the weeds will be growing rapidly and sometimes think of you at the same time as *Le Grand Meaulnes*."[39]

Three days later, after a frank conversation with his doctor, Wolfe, recognizing the end was near, chose to forgo further treatment and readmission to hospital. He died at home on March 29, surrounded by friends and family.

≈≈≈≈≈

Wolfe had often been the first to hear about the various food writers who, long after the publication of *Honey from a Weed*, continued to make the journey to Puglia to visit Patience. Now in her midseventies, Patience found the interest in her book and her life somewhat bewildering, but she was always welcoming. It was the Americans who most sought her out and this, too, came as something of a surprise. "Among a certain group of cognoscenti she was very, very well known," says Nancy Harmon Jenkins, the author of several books on Pugliese cuisine.[40] In a letter to Wolfe in the early 1990s, Patience admitted to being amused that food writers from Vermont, Boston, and California would travel to the Salento to "eat a merenda at Spigolizzi." But rather than brush them aside, she seemed to enjoy their occasional visits and willingness to come from so far. It was, she said, the "absurd pretensions of the Brits" that she found more troubling.[41] "I think there was a certain humility, like she couldn't believe these people responded to her book with such praise," recalled Ed Behr.[42]

As she did in her letters, Patience took some pleasure in debunking the popular image of Italy as an unspoiled paradise. She was just as quick to point out the environmental catastrophes unfolding at her doorstep as she was the edible plants and herbs of the macchia. And although her admirers knew from her book that she lived frugally, they were often struck by the Spartan conditions at Spigolizzi, the large number of cats and dogs (Patience and Norman refused to have them neutered or spayed), and especially the quantity of cigarettes Patience smoked. She had been a heavy smoker since at least the early 1950s, as were many of her friends and colleagues. Dick Guyatt, whom she worked for at the Royal College of Art, for example, smoked sixty cigarettes a day. By the 1990s, though, attitudes to smoking—particularly among those in the food industry—had changed dramatically. Even among chefs and line cooks, who often considered smoking something of an occupational hazard, the habit was beginning to go out of favor. When Nancy Harmon Jenkins made the trip with R. W. Apple Jr., an associate editor of the *New York Times* known for his writing on food and travel, he was rather amazed by the fact that Patience smoked as much as she did.[43] Ed Behr wrote that he was surprised to learn that "she was devoted to cigarettes, with a smoker's deep wrinkles and gravelly voice."[44]

Behr and his then-wife, Grace DiNapoli, first visited Patience in March 1992. They drove from Naples, where he was researching an article on pizza, and brought with him several traditional cheeses—*mozzarella di bufala*, *provola affumicata*, and *bocconcini alla panna*—"setting a standard of offerings impossible to emulate."[45] The following month Corby Kummer, who was in Italy for a conference sponsored by the International Olive Council on the virtues of the Mediterranean diet, made the diversion to Puglia; he came with Carol Field, the author of several books on Italian food, who was researching a book on the merende of Italy. Having gotten lost on the way, as most everyone did, they arrived nearly an hour late. As a gift they'd brought with them a wreath of cherry tomatoes to hang to dry for winter, and a loaf of bread. "Patience gave them both right back to us and said, 'Wouldn't you both like these?'" Kummer recalled. She invited them in and served them a variety of small dishes, including some incredibly dry but flavorful chickpeas cooked with onions. After about an hour she said, "Well, we must go plant again. You'll be leaving." As they were getting into their car, Patience told Corby that an article he'd written for the *Atlantic* on pasta in the 1980s "didn't exactly send one rushing to the pots and pans," Patience's measure of what made a piece of food writing successful.[46] Despite the rather chilly reception, Corby—captivated by Patience, her manner of speaking and way of life—continued to visit throughout the 1990s, cherishing his friendship with her. In 2002 she endorsed his book, *The Pleasures of Slow Food*.

Patience regarded the notion of exporting the Mediterranean diet elsewhere as pure folly because to do so would inevitably separate the local cuisine, the dishes themselves, from the way of life—precisely the agricultural labor—that was the diet's foundation. Simply put, the food she served and wrote about wasn't the kind of thing that could be transposed readily to another place and time. The label "Mediterranean diet" also failed to take account of what Patience considered central to the local cuisine, namely scarcity and "doing without." Plus the kind of food she'd come across in Carrara and Puglia was far from the sort of light fare of fish and olive oil that had come to represent the Mediterranean diet in the United States and elsewhere. Rather it was heavy, rich in starches and greens, caloric, and designed to satisfy a huge peasant appetite. She found the obsession with food and nutrition itself unhealthy and a sign of decadence. "Modern fear of cholesterol seems to have replaced the concept of sin," she wrote, and concluded that a conference at Harvard on the American diet, a report on the proceedings of which Corby had sent her, proved "that Americans are invalids, they do nothing but count their cholesterol, and are terrified of fat."[47] After Corby's visit Patience wrote to him, "Those writing about food should be less concerned with the subject of reckless variety, and more concerned with the quality of basic ingredients."[48]

Honey from a Weed had itself inspired a similar critique from Harold McGee, who in a letter to Patience wrote that the increasingly widespread availability of exotic foods from all over the world, while undoubtedly interesting, had a tendency to obscure "what in essence they are and should be." "We Californians like to make much of our climatic, agricultural, and gastronomical ties to the Mediterranean," he wrote, "but what do we really know about the olive or the grape, or the thyme and rosemary that we coddle in patio pots or sprinkle from supermarket cans?"[49]

He told her that her book had in part inspired his next long-term project, a book about the natural history of some common foodstuffs, and that he would be in Italy in August 1992 for a conference on molecular gastronomy and was interested in visiting. He hoped roaming the macchia with Patience might give him a better sense of the native habitats in which some of the herbs and plants of the Mediterranean flourished. Patience was of course familiar with McGee's book *On Food and Cooking*, as she and Alan had referred to it in their discussion of various matters during the editing of *Honey from a Weed*. In a letter to John Thorne one week before McGee's visit, Patience wrote, "I am piling up tomes for his instruction! I'm terrified."[50]

McGee spent a couple of days at Spigolizzi touring the countryside by bike, or on foot with Patience, identifying herbs and plants. Being August it was extremely hot, and they would occasionally stop in the shade of a fig tree to cool off. The dining table itself happened to be under a fig tree, and McGee, like many other visitors, recalled figs falling directly onto the table at breakfast. "Those were the best figs I'd ever had," he said. To McGee, Norman's tomato crop recalled Californian dry farming, and he remembers the "saddest looking tomato plants" he'd ever seen, yet they produced some of the most delicious tomatoes he'd ever tasted. McGee did a lot of exploring on his own, and in the evenings they'd gather again for dinner. One night a physician and his wife came from Lecce to join them. The conversation seemed to turn inevitably to Norman's great theme: how science and technology had "ruined much of what was good in the world."[51] Though he sympathized and even agreed with many of Norman's concerns, McGee, an authority on the chemistry of cooking, felt that for Norman he and the doctor somehow represented the dark side of science and technology. Sitting around a fire after dinner Norman, who had a flowing Old Testament white beard and halo of hair, looked like a Greek god. "He was a very intimidating character," McGee recalled.[52] Behr also recalled being intimidated by Norman and said that he didn't think he and Patience were "great admirers of the importance of science in cooking."

Patience could be equally intimidating in a different way. Her letters were often full of references to classical scholars, works of literature, especially Russian and French, and early cookbooks.[53] She was more likely to cite an ancient herbal or a pioneering nineteenth-century bota-nist than anything published in recent memory. Nick remembered her in her eighties telling him that she'd been rereading Hesiod. "I found it diffi-cult to keep up with her erudition," he said.[54] Corby Kummer said he was overwhelmed by the depth and richness of her letters and told her that they "provide endless, incalculable pleasure. Not to mention intimidation, since of course I feel I should have read every citation you mention."[55] Ed Behr said she was "an incredible letter writer" and that he had trouble matching the frequency and range of her dispatches. Receiving a letter from Patience in its signature yellow envelope was always an event. For John Thorne his correspondence with Patience "was one of the high points of my life."[56] Bruce Gollan, an Australian archaeologist who stayed at Spigolizzi in the 1990s, once wrote that her letters were "harbingers of hope and deliverance" and that he "could not have survived without them."[57] They were like shafts of light that punctured his otherwise dreary academic life. Despite her occasionally arch tone, Patience was always generous with her knowledge and keen to hear from other writers, friends, and family. She wrote with warmth and a sense of urgency—letter writing was the lifeblood of her relationships. "One begins to think letter writing is a sin," Patience wrote to Ulrike, adding: "I cling to letter writing."[58]

Patience maintained an ongoing correspondence with John Thorne, who was something of an iconoclast among the world of established food writers. In fact Thorne was the first of the American food writers to contact Alan Davidson in 1987 after the publication of *Honey from a Weed* to express his enthusiasm for the book.[59] He and Patience shared an outsider's sensibility, a willingness to forgo the conventions of the publishing world—Thorne had published his own newsletter, *Simple Cooking*, since 1980, as well as a number of limited-edition books on a variety of topics—and had a disdain for the elitism, snobbery, and assumptions that so often prevailed in food-writing circles. In a blurb for his book *Outlaw Cook*, Patience celebrated him—an "intelligent" and "dangerous" man—for undermining "the culinary pretensions of our time." Though they approached the subject of food from radically differ-ent points of view—Thorne was not terribly keen on weeds, for example, and once wrote that "a mouthful of tiny dandelion leaves is as tender as you could want, but they still make me all but gag"—Patience admired his writing and considered his essay "Learning to Eat" a masterpiece. Norman called him a poet and the only food writer who made him laugh. He was not afraid to criticize the giants of the food-writing world and, after publishing a several thousand–word essay titled "My Paula Wolfert Problem"—in which he attacked the popular author for the tone of condescension and exclusivity in her cookbooks—he was not exactly considered a member of the tribe.

Needless to say he was not among the nearly one hundred journalists, writers, and nutritionists who descended on the city of Lecce in May 1995 for a conference sponsored by the Oldways Preservation Trust, a nonprofit body devoted to healthy eating and one of the chief proponents of the Mediterranean diet. The full title of the conference was "Celebrating Puglia's Healthy, Traditional Mediterranean Cuisines," and its mission was to "introduce the Mediterranean Diet to Americans." It was precisely the kind of event Patience found so loathsome, with its quasi-scientific approach and obsessive focus on nutrition. What could possibly be gained from a bunch of well-to-do American writers touring the Salento "seeking 'enlightenment' while gorging on banquets?" she wrote to Nick.[60] Patience was courted by the conference organizers but declined to participate. Yet she knew or had corresponded with a handful of the participants and agreed to a lunch organized by Nancy Harmon Jenkins with a small group of about ten attendees, including Corby Kummer, Ed Behr, Mary Taylor Simeti, and Carol Field. Benedetto and Claudia Cavalieri, friends of Patience's, were also invited; Cavaliere, a well-known local pasta-maker, had recently landed a deal with Williams-Sonoma to distribute his products in North America. (Patience had been consulted over some of the recipes included on the packaging.) According to Jenkins there was some jockeying over who was to be invited and a minor controversy ensued. Paula Wolfert was particularly distressed not to be included.

The almost four-hour lunch was held at Mimì's, one of the only restaurants Patience and Norman patronized. They not only liked the food but Patience also knew and was fiercely loyal to Mimì, the owner, whom she'd first met on one of her trips to the Amalfi coast with Irving Davis in the late 1950s. He had been the young waiter who served them at a restaurant in Positano and, in a remarkable coincidence, moved to Puglia the same year that Patience and Norman did. He opened his restaurant overlooking the cliffs at San Gregorio a few years later. Despite her misgivings about the conference, Patience seemed to enjoy being fêted by the food writers. She found the president of Oldways, Dun Gifford, a former aide to Robert Kennedy and successful restaurant owner himself, engaging and down to earth. She and Norman didn't hesitate to supply him with information about the widespread use of pesticides in the Salento. The air of competitiveness among the journalists, especially the women, reminded Patience of a Women's Institute jamboree in Rogate long ago, and in letters from then on she took to calling them "the Divas." Even Paula Wolfert managed an appearance and introduced herself to Patience.[61]

Some weeks later in a letter to Corby, Patience wrote that she was no longer concerned with the "the thought of so many well-to-do Americans prying into the secrets of *la cucina povera* in order to save themselves and others from heart attack." She had come to see the interest in Pugliese cuisine and traditional foods as a kind of ongoing conversation, "an occasion for protracted conviviality," that was perhaps missing from American life.[62]

For Oldways it was the first of many conferences in Puglia: They held subsequent events there in 1999, 2006, 2007, and 2013. The brochure for a weeklong culinary tour in 2013 opened with a passage from *Honey from a Weed* in which Patience described the search for a workplace in Puglia and the "feeling of being marooned in an older kind of time." Indeed the 1995 conference took place on the cusp of a long-running love affair with the region spearheaded by British and American food and travel magazines eager to showcase a relatively unknown part of Italy and its culinary heritage. Since then nearly every major American food magazine has devoted a feature story to Puglia, which *Food and Wine*, in 2004, dubbed "Italy's next great escape."[63] The Salento had indeed been discovered.

CHAPTER SIXTEEN

Things Are Sacred

Patience's last trip to London was in 1990 for the launch of the new edition of *Plats du Jour*. She was happy to see Alan, and by all accounts the event at his home in Chelsea was a success. David Gentleman was there, and Patience said he was delighted to see the illustrations presented in such a favorable way. "It is as if his drawings appear for the first time," Patience wrote.[1] She had a chance to see old friends such as Christoph von Fürer-Haimendorf, whose wife, Betty, Patience's childhood friend, had died a few years earlier.[2] (Henrion had died just a few months before Patience's trip.) Vanessa Harrison, the BBC producer who'd accompanied Derek Cooper to Puglia in 1988, recalled meeting her for lunch at a pub not far from Patience's old school, Queen's College, in Harley Street. "The pub was full," she remembered. "As Patience came through the door, the place more or less came to a halt. Her appearance was so striking. She had a huge blue shawl flung around her shoulders and she had enormous presence. She was unforgettable."[3]

Patience's perceptions of England had changed very little since she and Norman had moved to Puglia in 1970. Her understanding of the political and economic changes taking place there, especially during the Thatcher years, was largely shaped by reading back issues of the *Guardian*—they sometimes arrived two months late—and by corresponding with friends and family. Maud Murdoch, who had been a friend and neighbor in the 1950s, wrote to Patience thanking her for *Plats du Jour* (her original copy had been borrowed and never returned). She congratulated Patience on "achieving such a fine renaissance" and said the book brought back a flood of memories from "those days when we were all young and full of *joie de vivre* and bright ideas—the children, the gardens, and everyone knowing everybody else." But she had since moved to Scotland, she explained, in no small part because of the way money and wealth had "obliterated the Hampstead we knew."[4]

Indeed Patience was sweepingly dismissive of life in London and could be severe in her judgments. When asked by the BBC in 1989 about her impressions of the city, Patience described it as "a mass of people living in a forest of material objects and mechanical devices."[5] When she visited David Gentleman and his second wife, Sue, at their home in Camden Town, she immediately questioned Sue about their oversize mailbox, which they had installed to accommodate all the bulky post he received in connection with his work, and asked why they'd replaced the original. Patience viewed it as a sign of the excess that she saw everywhere in the city's rapidly gentrifying neighborhoods. "I think she was appalled," said Sue.[6]

Material improvements or progress in the modern sense were invariably viewed as having replaced something of greater value. The gospel of consumerism and convenience, which had extended into every corner of life, she felt was pure nonsense. Ed Behr remembers Patience being equally appalled by the idea of starting polenta in cold water, as it would be an affront to centuries of tradition, whether the practice achieved the desired outcome or not. (In *Honey from a Weed*, Patience has a whole chapter on polenta and memorably describes the act of letting the "deep yellow" cornmeal "fall from your right hand in a fine rain."[7]) Even roasting meat in an oven, she wrote in *Honey from a Weed*, was "a travesty of roasting in its traditional sense," namely on a rotating spit over an open fire.[8] She had a similar attitude toward the use of fiberglass wine barrels in Puglia and most other technological advances. "Science was never going to win out," said Behr.[9]

She could be just as uncompromising when it came to art and literature. Nia Parry recalled being chastised after she sent Patience an English translation of a book by Marguerite Duras, one of Patience's favorite writers. Patience clearly found the notion of reading the book in English offensive. "She had high standards for people around her," said Christine Bullin.[10] Eilidh Brown's daughter, Fiona, said, "I hated the way she could just literally turn her back on someone she judged was not up to her intellectual standards and be so wrong. And yet I admired the things she actually stood for, what she created and her seemingly uncompromising stance."[11]

Over the years Gentleman felt that Patience had become increasingly intolerant, but that it was of a piece with her longstanding antipathy to England and urban life more broadly. "She could be critical of those who submitted to it," he recalled.[12] Gentleman would see Patience one last time when he was staying in Lecce in 1995 or 1996 and drove down for a visit. "It was lovely," he recalled. "There was a feeling as if Patience had never been away. As if we just took up the last time we'd seen each other."[13] Patience maintained that it was "on the periphery where real life happens," as she wrote to one of her granddaughters in 1999.[14]

Patience's appearance could be startling as well. Gentleman remembers being struck by how much she'd aged, her deeply lined and weathered face, her bad teeth. She had long, skinny, "peasant-like arms" and gnarled hands. She often wore long dresses or sheepskin furs draped over her thin frame. "She really did look like a witch," recalled her grand-daughter Rosy.[15] Christine Bullin, who first visited in the early 1970s and remembered her rugged beauty, said that she was "relentlessly natural" and also completely aware of how she'd aged. "She referred to herself, sort of joking, that people might think of her as a ruin," said Bullin.[16]

Though Patience maintained in *Work Adventures Childhood Dreams* that she was "not altogether English," she dutifully kept up with her friends and family and retained fond memories of her life in postwar London.[17] In the preface to the new edition of *Plats du Jour*, she wrote that after going back over the chapter on "Cuts & Joints" she "felt quite nostalgic for English beef as it was then, and for my little kitchen in the converted billiard-room on the heights of Hampstead."[18] The vast archive of letters left behind at Spigolizzi attests to the fact that she never let go of her past life. On the contrary as she got older she sought to preserve her correspondence, asked for letters to be sent back to her, and made tentative plans to pass them on.[19] She cultivated relationships with the children of old friends such as Betty von Fürer-Haimendorf, Alastair Morton, and Alexander Gibson. "To some extent cosmopolitan (or European in outlook) she may have been," says Nick, "but she remained quintessentially English, even somewhat upper-middle-class home-counties blue-stocking Edwardian, specially in her speech."[20]

❦

Norman's last show was in 1991 at a gallery in Cambridge run by Alan Davidson's sister, Rosemary. (He also had a show there in 1989.) At the crowded and animated private view, he saw Ursula for the first time in ages, and, for the last time, his old friend Leopold Kohr. His stepson,

Philip, was also there.[21] On his way back to Italy, he stopped off in Brussels to visit cousins, one of whom was with him in Kleve during the war. Throughout the 1970s and '80s, Norman had exhibited almost exclusively in the Salento, so it was gratifying to return to England for his final show, the traveller returned. After the Whitechapel show in 1975 and his decision to turn down the offer to teach at the Central School of Art in 1977, Norman had worked away in relative isolation. But he was always eager to engage with his peers and discuss his theories and ideas.

In contrast to his previous exhibitions, Philip recalled the works at the Cambridge show as being somewhat unsettling and provocative, something of a departure for Norman. Norman had been painting large brightly colored geometric patterns on Japanese paper in the belief that they had the power to shape human behavior or the "spirit of man." He was known for painting individual *scudi*, "shields," for people, such as the one that graced Rolando's computer, which was designed to offset unhealthy or negative forces emanating from the machine. These scudi were always based on what Norman perceived to be the recipient's individual character and spiritual needs, and his late work was a further elaboration of this idea, though on a much larger scale. Indeed Norman had even placed painted panels, rough-hewn standing stones, and even finished sculptures, which were sometimes buried, in the garden at Spigolizzi to encourage plant growth. The theory, which Norman acknowledged to be entirely speculative, was that the "radiational frequency" of the colors and shapes would somehow interact with various elements—oxygen and nitrogen, for example—that the plants depend on and would therefore concentrate the earth's energy. Norman called it the "ancient science of symbols" and told Derek Cooper that it was "an offshoot of carving."[22] Philip, who found most of the larger paintings in the show a bit too overbearing for a domestic setting, bought several of the smaller pictures, including one showing a pair of black and white figures that he always imagined to be Norman and Patience. "Full of mystery, the figures are depicted in a single wobbly outline using a small paintbrush and Indian ink," he recalled.[23]

By the time of the Cambridge show, Norman had in fact stopped carving altogether due to shoulder pain, the result of a lifetime of sculpting, and was concentrating on painting. He spent more and more time reading the Bible and putting his philosophical speculations down on paper. Aside

from his involvement in environmental campaigns, and in particular studying what he believed to be the negative impact of genetically modified
crops, he devoted much of his time to researching methods of alternative
agriculture. He was a loyal member of the U.K. Soil Association and was
dismayed by the widespread application of pesticides and other industrial
poisons that had become so common. Thus his own garden and field,
planted in a geodetic pattern of expanding circles, reflected his increasingly cosmic vision. In a letter to John Thorne in 1993, Patience wrote,
"Everything is planted in arcs, in curves, and based on the concept of Pi."[24]

Though the Wonderhouse had never materialized, Norman worked
closely with local artists and was a beloved figure in the Salento. He
presided over a lively atmosphere at Spigolizzi with friends and guests
arriving most evenings throughout the summer for wine and conversation. Usually several languages could be heard—a mix of Italian, French,
German, and English. In its own way Spigolizzi had become a cultural
hub and Norman its de facto leader—Patience referred to him as Lord
Spig. "He continued to be first and foremost an artist," said Nick, "his
main preoccupation the importance of art to the world."[25]

Even as Patience and Norman grew older, their way of life—physically
demanding and without the most basic comforts—was largely as it had
been when they arrived in 1970. Maintaining the masseria (the interior was
whitewashed every spring and the exterior treated with a pink lime wash),
tending the fields, making the wine, and harvesting the olives were all ardu-
ous tasks for even the young and able-bodied. Eleven acres of land, including
the olive trees, had to be looked after. They still watered crops by hand with
watering cans filled at the cistern. Weeding was also done by hand or with
a mattock. In 1993 Norman gave in and bought a weed whacker—Patience
called it a "Japanese grass cutting machine"—after an elbow injury made it
impossible for him to scythe. Plowing, done with a heavy diesel cultivator,
was hard work given the stony, unforgiving soil. Of course they enjoyed the
fruits of their labor, but the harvesting, threshing, preserving, and canning
were formidable tasks. In 1995 letter Patience, at the age of seventy-eight,
described "the fruitful glory of spring" marked by "picking peas, beans, *cicoria
asparago* [puntarelle], *broccoletti* [broccoli] and digging out the pea-parasite
la spurchia, and hoeing with Norman the black *ceci* [chickpeas] . . . and many
other labors not to mention cooking."[26] The following year she described

"perishing afternoons in the field planting."[27] By 1997 she said they were largely living on peas and beans, new potatoes or rice, and their own onions supplemented with fish and of course edible wild plants. They'd pretty much given up eating meat, and in *Honey from a Weed* Patience wrote that she was not alone in her conviction "that one should eat less meat." She referred to Pythagoras's address to the people of Crotone, in Ovid's *Metamorphoses*, as the "most moving conjuration in favor of vegetarianism ever written," but admitted to the occasional hankering for beef.[28] In a letter to Ariane she once wrote that vegetarianism "makes you think too much about nutrition, as opposed to having a good appetite. The fact is we are vegetarians . . . aren't you? Only, from time to time we eat fish or meat."[29] Salvatore continued to help with agricultural tasks—together they planted more than 200 pounds of potatoes in 1994—and Norman occasionally hired additional help, but they remained intimately involved in every aspect of cultivating the land.

Winemaking, though always done with the help of friends and neighbors, was also demanding. The whole affair usually involved several days of hard labor: a day or two to prep the winery and clean the barrels; at least one day of picking and crushing the grapes and another day devoted to pressing and filling the large wooden barrels. In advance of the vendemmia, the 54-liter demijohns had to be moved from storage into the garden and cleaned out. The 220-liter barrels, weighing about 90 pounds each, were swilled with a mixture of herbs from the macchia boiled in water and wine. (In *Honey from a Weed*, Norman wrote that one must treat the barrels "like the best of friends."[30]) On day one the grapes were harvested by hand and then transported in the Land Rover back to Spigolizzi, unloaded, broken and stripped from their stems with a hand-wound machine (the *pigiatrice*), and then crushed underfoot. Initial fermentation usually lasted 24 hours (occasionally up to three days, though Norman favored a lighter wine), with the crust forming on the *mosto* having to be regularly pushed down. Norman would get up twice in the night to perform this task.

On the following day the mosto was drained into an underground cistern, and the remaining solids pressed again. Finally the mosto was carried in large galvanized wine jugs to the cantina and poured into the barrels, which were plugged with bunches of winter thyme to keep the fruit flies out. On the last night of the vendemmia, Patience always prepared a meal for the group of workers, sometimes more than a dozen people. "It reminded me of my childhood," said Aldo Magagnino.[31]

After several weeks of fermentation, the barrels were topped up with mosto that had been set aside for the purpose, and, when Norman was sure the wine was no longer "singing" (actively fermenting), were sealed shut. A second feast was held some two months after the vendemmia, on St. Martin's Day, when the new wine is traditionally tasted.

The olive harvest involved several weeks of hard labor, depending on the state of the crop and the autumn weather. Patience and Norman had forty-five trees (over time they planted twenty-four more) spread around much of their 11 acres, and the earth around each one had to be cleared of weeds, shrubs, and large stones in advance. After sweeping up and discarding the olives that had fallen on their own, large plastic nets were laid under the trees. The trees were then climbed and stripped of their fruit by hand or with the use of a small plastic rake. The women gathered the olives and put them in plastic crates or sacks, which were then carried up to the masseria and shaken in a primitive *cernatrice* (sieving machine) to separate out any leaves, branches, stones, acorns, snails, or earth. The aim then was to get 250 or 300 kilograms of olives to the *frantoio* (oil mill) as fast as possible for immediate milling and pressing. "In a very good year," said Nick, "Patience and Norman got one tonne (10 quintali, four pressings) of olives from their trees, and this made a little over 150 kilograms of excellent characterful green extra-virgin oil."[32] In 1994 Norman fell off the olive ladder and hit his head on a rock, foreshadowing the injury that would lead to his death six years later.

The last harvest before his death in 2000, however, was particularly abundant. "Never before have the trees been so generous," Patience wrote.[33] The vendemmia had been equally bountiful, and the grapes yielded the highest ever sugar content they'd recorded, producing potent wines with an alcohol content of more than 15 percent.

In their last years together, they'd faced encroaching old age with remarkable and uncomplaining fortitude. In addition to the various agricultural activities, there was the daily cooking, washing, and cleaning, nearly all of which Patience did. The laundry was done by hand in a bucket with cold water. Dishes were washed with water heated in the kettle. "Norman who was brought up with Flemish charladies sees me as one of them," Patience once remarked in a letter to Nick.[34] As Spigolizzi became known as a cultural lighthouse, the number of visitors only continued to increase. In 1992, the same year they were featured in a spread in *Casa Vogue*, Patience recorded more than five hundred visitors and said that the high volume had "cracked the bentwood chairs."[35]

Well into her eighties Patience continued to pick fungi and gather edible wild plants. Two years before her eightieth birthday, she referred to the appearance of "newly born mushrooms" in mid-January as a "local miracle, in spite of everything these shining objects in the mud."[36] Around the same time, she wrote to John Thorne that she couldn't "resist dashing out with the dog to gather mushrooms in the wild." She was especially struck by the "sumptuous agarics" gleaming like "giant pearls." In October 2000 she helped a friend studying herbal remedies identify and establish the Latin names of a couple of mildly toxic plants and fungi used in very small doses for their beneficial effects. "Both have got muddled up throughout the last 1,000 years by botanists," Patience wrote.[37] Bill McAlister, who visited Patience in 2004, about a year before she died, recalled her delight in showing him the vast collection of arrowheads they'd amassed over the years at Spigolizzi.

With the help of friends and some hired labor, they kept up with the never-ending labors. Winters however had become increasingly difficult to endure. Fending off the cold and damp was nearly impossible. They burned wood, but it was in an open fireplace located in a far corner of the masseria and not designed to heat the stone structure. "I remember your *focolare* [hearth] that heated nothing," Nicole Fenosa wrote in 1995, wondering how they survived the winters.[38] Still wood had to be split, stacked, and then hauled indoors morning and evening to keep the fire burning. Kindling had to be gathered, most of it from the olive and fruit trees, and chopped up with an axe. During her first visit to Spigolizzi in December 1981, Maggie Armstrong, Nick's partner, recalled never having been so cold in her life. Norman, who suffered from acute bronchitis, often sat in front of one of the paraffin or gas stoves that they used to take the chill off their studios to warm himself. Patience took to sleeping in the alcove by the fireplace, wrapped in woolly sheepskins, "just like an animal."[39]

They still relied on oil lamps for light and would often write to Nicolas or Klaus and Ulrike for new wicks or mantles. Patience wrote all of her letters on a typewriter until about 2000, when the shop that serviced her Olivetti got into the business of selling and repairing computers instead.

They did make one small concession to modern life, however, and agreed to the acquisition of a mobile phone in spring 1996. They could receive calls from anywhere in Europe and make calls within Italy. Patience, wary of its usefulness, turned it on only between 6 and 7 p.m. "A little step forward," she wrote, "I wait to be convinced of its utility."[40]

※※※※※※

Perhaps not surprisingly, given their aversion to technology and what they saw as the misapplications of science, Patience and Norman had grave doubts about the wisdom and efficacy of modern medicine. Patience was essentially opposed to all medical intervention, and though she was registered with a doctor in Salve, she never consulted him. The only time she agreed to see a doctor (a friend, not her physician) was after she broke her hip in 2002. (She'd also gone to a hospital in Chelsea during her visit to London in 1990 after she fell on a sidewalk and split her lip open.) She believed in natural cures and above all in the healing power of the herbs of the macchia. *Honey from a Weed* is full of notes and digressions on the various uses of herbs and plants for medicinal purposes, and Patience took them seriously. Toward the end of her life, when she had a weak heart valve that could have been remedied with a stent, she refused treatment. Her approach was to let nature take its course. At one time she'd even talked of wandering off into the macchia to die like a sick animal when she felt her time had come.[41]

In 1997 Norman was diagnosed with intestinal cancer and confronted with the prospect of chemotherapy. He'd become weak and jaundiced, and after several visits to different doctors, they discovered a tumor. He had an internal blockage of his duodenum and needed an emergency operation. The operation was successful, and one year later, after a checkup, Patience wrote that he was "declared free of the enemy."[42] But he still needed treatment and opted for a course of homeopathic measures rather than chemotherapy. Through it all they continued to cultivate the land and carry on as best they could. In 1999 they planted hundreds of tomato plants and "an amphitheater of edible vegetables."[43] However Norman never fully recovered. He had struggled with periodic depression in the past and the bout with cancer seemed to slow him down considerably. Ada Martella, who was living at Spigolizzi during Norman's illness and drove him to his appointments, said that he became increasingly withdrawn. He spent more and more time in the small stone structure built by Salvatore, originally used to keep the chickens. Norman Janis, who visited in 1999, remembers him retiring there after breakfast to sit in the sun and read the Bible. Though he was still producing works of art, his output had slowed considerably. "Norman before he died was removing himself," said Janis.[44]

One morning in late January 2000, just after getting over the flu, Norman fell off the concrete steps that led from the bedroom above the cantina—it had no railing—and suffered a severe head injury. Patience was able to help him get to the fireplace and cover him with a blanket. She called Mirjam Steffens, a friend and neighbor. They both felt that because of the bitter cold it would be better to let him rest by the fire than call an ambulance. That first night Patience slept next to Norman on a camp bed near the fire. The following day Norman was still having trouble speaking, and they called Patience's friend Dr. Daniela, who had him rushed to the hospital in Tricase, about thirty minutes away. As a result of the fall, he had suffered some internal bleeding and developed a cerebral hemorrhage. He was transferred to a hospital in Taranto, which had the capacity to treat traumatic brain injuries, and where the neurologist knew and admired Norman. His bronchitis and the lingering effects of the flu complicated matters, and he remained in the hospital for over a week.

All the while Patience stayed behind at Spigolizzi and kept a diary in the form of a letter addressed to Norman. As it became clear that the recovery and convalescence would be long, Patience called Nick and Maggie, who left their 40-meter barge on the Canal de la Marne à la Saône at Vitry-le-François—they were about to start work on a dredging contract—and took a 24-hour train journey to Presicce via Dijon, Bologna, and Lecce.

The head of the neurology department in Taranto, Enrico Pierangeli, was the brother-in-law of a friend. Norman had now developed a large blood clot in his frontal lobe and was moved to intensive care, where Enrico deemed the only chance to save his life was to operate. Nick had already arrived, and they informed him that their only option was to remove part of the frontal lobe. The relatives were given until midday to decide. Nick was adamant and told the doctors that Norman was an artist and a thinker and that such an operation would be absolutely unspeakable. But the decision was not his to make. He had to call Patience. There was a phone on the wall inside but it wasn't working, and use of mobile phones in the intensive care department was not permitted. Standing outside on the fire escape in the howling wind, he called Patience from his French mobile, and she agreed without hesitation not to give permission for the operation. But she had to sign in person, so Nick and Maggie drove back to Spigolizzi in the Land Rover to fetch her. They had already whitewashed the front room of the masseria, and Norman came home on February 7, nearly two weeks after his fall. That evening Salve's priest, Don Lorenzo, came and read the last rites. Norman died the next day.[45]

⊹≪≪≪⋘⋇⊹

Patience was five years older than Norman and had not envisioned outliving him. Even during his final days in the hospital, she was being given what sadly turned out to be misleadingly optimistic assessments of his condition; friends who visited him reported hopefully that he was "getting better." That nearly two-week period in his absence, receiving updates from Rolando, was harrowing. After her friend Betty Haimendorf died, Patience corresponded with her husband, Christoph, who wondered whether he would ever get over the shock of her death. "If only we had died together," he wrote.[46] Patience and Norman had expressed a similar desire and had more than once talked about walking into the sea together to be enveloped by the waves.

Patience's own health was already somewhat precarious—she was quite frail and weak—and in the year after Norman's death, she aged considerably. In April 2001 Oliver Bernard was traveling in Italy and went to Puglia to stay with Patience. Oliver had written Norman's obituary in the *Independent* as well as a poem for a commemorative book that Patience later assembled. It rained during much of his stay, and he recalled Spigolizzi being wet, dark, and rather melancholy. He stayed in the guest room in the tower and spent much of his time reading volume after volume of Rex Stout's crime novels. "Patience had not long before been bereaved of Norman and was I think aged by her loss, as I was by the loss of my brother," he wrote. "Patience's kitchen, where we always breakfasted, was a little dark place at one end of the gorgeously decorated dining room, behind which Patience had taken to sleeping, beyond the fireplace in a sort of cave. . . . She had now become almost severe when she was not being charming; almost morose when she was not entertaining her friends."[47] (Oliver's brother, the writer Bruce Bernard, had died the previous spring, as had Patience's sister Tania. Tania died on April 23, 2000, shortly after returning from a trip to Mexico.)

What Oliver called a cave was the inglenook fireplace accessible through a low arch. By the fire was a stone bench not long enough to stretch out on full length. Patience slept here with her feet on the ground, and this exacerbated existing circulation problems and led to severely swollen legs. However Patience refused to put her feet up and rejected any kind of medical treatment. In November 2000 she was bitten on the leg by a feral cat that she was feeding, and the wound eventually turned septic. By late 2001 Nick and Maggie, who had come from France to take care of Patience, feared that it would have to be amputated or she would die. As Patience and Norman had done for Arno, he decided to call a rabbi. In this case though the rabbi was her good friend Norman Janis, who'd been ordained in 1999. "The end looked inevitable, and sometime that winter, I called Rabbi Norman to say he should come if he wanted to see Patience alive," Nick recalled. Norman Janis was somewhat skeptical but agreed to come. He flew over in early 2002 and spent several days at her bedside singing—Neapolitan folk songs and opera arias—and talking. She listened acutely, sometimes offering mild criticism and occasional praise.

"She had a very deep understanding of lyrical music," he said. "When I was singing to her she knew just what I was doing."[48]

During his visit they arranged for a heart specialist to come and take a look at Patience, and Janis managed to persuade her to move to a bed in the front room, put her feet up, and begin taking some basic medicine—belladonna and aspirin—to alleviate the swelling. Her health improved markedly—the swelling and abscesses were cured—and she lived for another three years. She continued to write, publish, and receive visitors, even doing an interview with Simon Parkes for the BBC *Food Programme* in 2002.[49]

In 1999 Prospect Books had published a paperback edition of Irving's *Catalan Cookbook* with the unfinished memoir that he'd given to Patience. In early 2000, just after Norman's death, *Work Adventures Childhood Dreams* was finally printed. Norman, who was intimately involved in the book's production, had at least been able to see the advance proofs.

Despite its unconventional approach and being published by an unknown press in southern Italy, the book was reviewed in the *Guardian*, *Financial Times*, and the *Spectator* and was nominated for the PEN Ackerley Prize. Patience sought to find an American publisher for the book and wrote to Elisabeth Sifton of Farrar, Straus and Giroux, whom John Thorne had put her in touch with. "Should you wish to publish *Work Adventures Childhood Dreams* I would not want an advance, but only royalties on sales," she wrote. "Our aim was to make a beautiful book."[50] Tom Jaine visited Patience in 2002 and learned of the manual for cooks aboard the Blue Funnel Line that she had written on Naxos. *The Centaur's Kitchen*, with Miranda's illustrations, appeared shortly after Patience's death in 2005. (Persephone Books also published a new edition of *Plats du Jour* in 2006.) In those final years she no longer used her beloved workroom but spent most of her time on the bed in the front room surrounded by cardboard boxes overflowing with letters, papers, and photos. She continued to write her own letters in a slanting spidery scrawl.

Patience and Alan Davidson had corresponded for more than two decades and his death in December 2003 was especially jarring. (Salvatore died the same year.) In one of his last letters to Patience, he recalled the editing of *Honey from a Weed* and the "unforgettable week" he spent with Patience and Norman at Spigolizzi. He described *Honey from a Weed* as Prospect Books' "finest achievement" and said he "always knew that it would find its place as a classic and that its fame would spread ever wider as the decades roll by."[51] Indeed it has had great staying power. In 1997 Nigel Slater discussed it in an essay on the art of recipe writing and said, "There is no food book that appeals to me more, satisfying both the reader and the cook in me."[52] Leila McAlister, the owner of a highly regarded food shop and café in London and a friend of the family said, "I meet people for whom *Honey from a Weed* was a life changing book. It means a lot."[53] Stevie Parle, a chef and food writer, was one of them. He says that *Honey from a Weed* "changed the way I thought about cooking and food."[54] Jacob Kenedy, the chef-owner of Bocca di Lupo in London, says it was "one of the first books that hooked me as a cook."[55] "What amazes me is that people don't sing its praises all day long," says Ed Behr. "They sing the praises of Elizabeth David so much more than Patience Gray but Elizabeth David is not an exciting writer by comparison."[56] Alan had finally published his own magnum opus,

The Oxford Companion to Food, in 1999 and was later awarded the prestigious Erasmus Prize for his contributions to "food culture." After his death Patience sent his longtime assistant and collaborator, Helen Saberi, a letter and a check for £200 and told her to fill her house with flowers.

The last few years of Patience's life were marked by periods of delirium and confusion as well as inevitable physical decline. To some she seemed to exist in a kind of dream world in which the past and present had merged. She could be uncompromisingly cruel to her caregivers, usually family (one grandchild described her as "behaving like a panther with a thorn in her paw"), and just as charming and kind to visitors.[57] Yet she remained feisty, resolute, and capable of great lucidity right up until the end. Simon Parkes remembers her being "sharply witted" and offering a stinging retort to his comment that "peasant cooking" had become trendy in London. "How on earth can you have peasant cooking without a peasantry?" she told him.[58] Bill McAlister, who visited in spring 2004, said it didn't take much to raise her ire and that she became quite animated and prickly when the conversation turned to America. "It was wonderful to meet someone who was that full of character," he said.[59] After Norman Janis's last visit in spring 2004, Patience wrote to say, "Your voice has never been better," and added, "Separate and together we were close to heaven on music's wing."[60]

One year later, on March 10, 2005, Patience died at Spigolizzi after suffering a stroke. Friends and family had gathered in the front room, where Patience lay in a bed lined with mimosa flowers and wild purple and black irises gathered from the hillside. There were candles burning. Teresa had placed a rosary between her fingers. After she died the windows were thrown open wide to let the soul depart, as is the custom in the Salento.

Despite Patience's remove from the modern world and fear that her work would be misunderstood and even mocked, readers and cooks alike have returned to *Honey from a Weed* precisely because it offers a kind of antidote to the often overwhelming speed, mechanization, and numbing effects of modern life. As Patience told the BBC in her last recorded interview, her raspy voice crackling over the airwaves, "Life has become burdensome, in a way, in its demands on people. And I can lead them a bit to daydreaming, which is rather out of fashion now, isn't it? You could say that I have sort of responded against the present time where I feel that nothing is sacred. It's a counterpoint to that. Because things are sacred. That's what I feel."

ACKNOWLEDGMENTS

Many people assisted me on this book, but I owe a special debt of gratitude to Nicolas Gray and Miranda Armour-Brown. When I first contacted Nicolas in 2006, he wrote to inform me that Patience's literary remains were in a state of "horrendous chaos" and that he expected me to take one look at the closet full of letters and to "hightail it over the horizon to find a saintly monk in a bare cell to write about." My reaction was precisely the opposite, and on that first visit to Puglia in the fall of 2006, I stayed for more than two months, helping in the olive harvest and reading through a small fraction of the letters and papers Patience left behind. Nicolas and Miranda were not only indispensable sources of information but also deeply interested and engaged in the project up until the very end. This book would not have come to be without their gracious support and encouragement. I must also give special thanks to Maggie Armstrong, who has helped to create a first-class archive of Patience's correspondence and unpublished papers that will undoubtedly be of use to future researchers and writers. Along with her own insights, Maggie provided numerous translations of letters and articles from French and Italian, for which I am grateful.

A number of other people were extraordinarily generous with their time and privately held archival material. A series of autobiographical letters and reminiscences that Patience wrote for Ulrike Voswinckel, many of them dealing with her childhood, were crucial in reconstructing Patience's early years. I am grateful to Ulrike for sharing these. Philip Trevelyan provided additional letters and important background on Norman Mommens's life in the 1950s. Caroline Davidson went out of her way to make arrangements for me to consult her father's archive, stored in a barn in Northumberland, on a trip to England in 2014. The two days I spent reading through Alan Davidson and Patience's letters in the back room of a realtor's office in Corbridge were delightful and illuminating. I first had the pleasure of meeting David Gentleman in 2010, when he showed me the sketchbooks he'd taken with him to Italy in 1954 and which formed the basis of his illustrations for *Plats du Jour*. David and his wife, Sue, were always lovely hosts, insisting that I have dinner with them, and I'm grateful to David for letting me use the previously unpublished woodcut of the cottage in Rogate where Patience lived from 1943 to 1947.

A number of librarians and archivists in England and the United States were tireless in answering queries and helping me locate important source material. Neil Parkinson, archives and collections manager at the Royal College of Art, and Robert Winckworth of the University College London Records Office were especially helpful. Sue Breakall, an archivist and senior research fellow at the University of Brighton, provided key documents from the F. H. K. Henrion Archive and Research Library. I also received assistance from Eltham College, the Museum of English Rural Life, the Archives of the Royal Botanic Gardens, Kew, the Penguin Archive at the University of Bristol, the Haslemere Educational Museum, the Royal Navy Research Archive, the Victoria and Albert Museum's Theatre and Performance collections, the University of Sussex Library, the Schlesinger Library at Harvard University's Radcliffe Institute for Advanced Study, the Rare Book and Manuscript Library at Columbia University, and Davis Family Library at Middlebury College, where most of this book was written.

Numerous individuals agreed to be interviewed for this book or to share correspondence with me. Their insights and contributions have improved it greatly. They are: Emmanuel Anati, Colman Andrews, Enzo Apicella, Ashlyn Armour-Brown, Lisa Armour-Brown, Diana Athill, Richard Bawden, Ed Behr, Oliver Bernard, Julia Black, Jane Bown, Candida Brazil, Fiona Clai Brown, Christine Bullin, Ariane Castaing, Rolando Civilla, Conrad Clark, Sandra Close, Joanna da Cruz, Alvin Curran, Sandy Daley, Rosemary Davidson, Marushka Delabre, Vanessa Denza, Grace DiNapoli, Christine Dirnaichner, Helmut Dirnaichner, Annabel Downs, Julia Farrington, Nicole Fenosa, Gerda Flöckinger, Richard Gibson, Henry Gray, Rosy Gray, Skye Gyngell, Nicholas von Fürer-Haimendorf, Carol Hall, Vanessa Harrison, John Hendy, Emma Henrion, Max Henrion, Paul Henrion, Lesley Jackson, Tom Jaine, Norman Janis, Nancy Harmon

Jenkins, Deborah Kaplinsky, Jacob Kenedy, Tyl Kennedy, Corby Kummer, Paul Levy, Antonio Lupo, Aldo Magagnino, Ada Martella, Bill McAlister, Leila McAlister, Harold McGee, Jonathan Meades, Teresa de Mira, Alison Morton, Isabella Morton-Smith, Nancy Newhouse, Jill Norman, Simon Parkes, Stevie Parle, Eugenia Parry, Trevor Pinnock, Marina Pizzolante, Nicholas Quennell, Francesco Radino, A. J. Rathbun, Sarah Reamer, Mario and Ada Ricchiuto, Gillian Riley, Peter Rockwell, Duane Roller, Leticia Roller, Eira and Andrea Sbarro, Helen Saberi, Corinna Sargood, Ruscha Schorr-Kon, Eric Scigliano, Paul Shepheard, Jean Southon, Louis Stettner, John Thorne, Klaus Voswinckel, and Tico Wolff.

I have also benefited from conversations and correspondence with Jeremy Lewis, Andrew Kidd, William Leach, Jojo Tulloh, and Thomas Penn. Erin Edmison, Nicolas Gray, Tom Jaine, and Kathryn Joyce read portions of the manuscript and provided invaluable feedback for which I am grateful.

My parents, Jay and Dorothy Federman, in addition to their unwavering love and support, carried out an important reconnaissance mission to the British Library in search of issues of *House and Garden* and *Harper's Bazaar* from the 1950s. It makes complete sense that I found a copy of *Honey from a Weed* on their bookcase, and I've little doubt that their love of food and cooking is in some way responsible for this book. Andrew Federman and Sara Federman Ames have been great sources of strength and I owe them more than words can possibly convey.

I'm ever thankful to Margo Baldwin of Chelsea Green, who contacted me out of the blue in 2014 and breathed new life into this project just as I was beginning to think it had no future. My editor, Ben Watson, provided wise counsel and a steady hand throughout the book's final stages.

My lovely daughters, Sofia and Lola, have made the last few years some of the most rewarding of my life. Finally I want to thank Sarah Trouslard, who often had more faith in this book than I did, and whose keen observations have undoubtedly made it stronger.

NOTES

I have used the following abbreviations to refer to frequently cited archives and texts:

Archive Masseria Spigolizzi: AMS
Victoria and Albert Museum's Theater and Performance collections:
    Victoria and Albert
Honey from a Weed: HFAW (First US edition, published in 1987)
Ring Doves and Snakes: RDS
Work Adventures Childhood Dreams: WACD

INTRODUCTION

1. Alan Davidson, "The Prospect Behind Us," *Petits Propos Culinaires* 47 (1994).
2. Leo Lerman, "The Cookbook Shelf," *Gourmet*, November 1987; Thorne, *Outlaw Cook*, 332.
3. Judith Jones to Alan Davidson, November 4, 1986, private collection.
4. Jim Harrison, *The Raw and the Cooked: Adventures of a Roving Gourmand* (New York: Grove Press, 2001), 19.
5. Ruscha Schorr-Kon in discussion with the author, telephone interview, April 2016.
6. Ulrike Voswinckel, email message to author, May 2016.
7. Ed Behr, "An Exceptional New Book," *The Art of Eating* 5 (December 1987): 6–7.
8. Levi, *Christ Stopped at Eboli: The Story of a Year*, 4.
9. Gray, *HFAW*, 13.
10. Simon Parkes, BBC Radio 4, *Woman's Hour*, November 16, 2005.

CHAPTER ONE: BEGINNINGS

1. Gray, *HFAW*, 265.
2. Ibid., 200.
3. Patience Gray to Wolfe Aylward, April 10, 1981, AMS.

4. Patience Gray, interview by Derek Cooper, BBC Radio 4, *The Food Programme*, August 11, 1988.
5. Patience Gray to Ariane Castaing, June 1, 1984, AMS.
6. Gray, *HFAW*, 18.
7. Ibid., 346.
8. Gray, *WACD*, 324.
9. *Hampshire Chronicle, Southampton and Isle of Wight Courier*, August 26, 1865, 5; Paul Isidor J. Warschawski, *Progressive Hebrew Course and Music of the Bible* (London: Longmans, Green, Reader, and Dyer, 1870).
10. Gray, *WACD*, 316.
11. Stephanie Fierz to Gray, July 19, 1991, AMS.
12. Gray, *WACD*, 305.
13. Patience Gray to Ulrike Voswinckel, undated, AMS.
14. Patience Gray, "The Free Highway," *The Observer*, April 3, 1960.
15. Though Betty was not trained as an anthropologist, she was closely involved in Christoph's fieldwork and co-wrote several books with him. In his account of their work in Nepal, *Life among Indian Tribes*, Christoph quotes extensively from Betty's diaries.
16. Patience Gray to Ulrike Voswinckel, undated, AMS.
17. Gray, *WACD*, 309.
18. Miranda Armour-Brown in discussion with the author, Cambridge, July 2010.
19. Gray, *WACD*, 327.
20. "Death of Colonel H. S. Stanham," *Hastings and St. Leonards Observer*, October 5, 1935.
21. Gray, *WACD*, 321.
22. Ibid., 337.
23. J. H. P., "Obituary," *British Medical Journal*, July 29, 1967, 313–314.
24. Gray, *WACD*, 337–338.
25. Miranda Armour-Brown in discussion with the author, Cambridge, July 2010.
26. Stephanie Fierz to Patience Gray, July 19, 1991, AMS.
27. Gray, *WACD*, 340.
28. Ibid., 338.
29. Kaye, *A History of Queen's College*, 165.
30. Gray, *WACD*, 338–339.
31. Kaye, *A History of Queen's College*, 155–156.
32. Patience Gray to Wolfe Aylward, March 5, 1971, AMS.
33. Gwendoline Holloway to Edith Goodyear, February 6, 1935, AMS.
34. Gray, *WACD*, 344.

35. Patience Gray to Ulrike Voswinckel, undated, AMS.

36. Hanako Murata, "Material Forms in Nature: The Photographs of Karl Blossfeldt." In Mitra Abbaspour, Lee Ann Daffner, and Maria Morris Hambourg, eds., *Object:Photo: Modern Photographs—The Thomas Walther Collection 1909–1949*, 2.

37. Patience Gray to Ulrike Voswinckel, November 17, 1985, AMS.

38. The description of Barny comes from Christoph von Fürer-Haimendorf's *Life among Indian Tribes*. Christoph had met Betty at a dinner party in Vienna in 1932 but only started courting her when he was in London on a scholarship in 1935 to 1936, which overlapped with Patience's first term at the London School of Economics. "If I had wanted to learn about the atmosphere among the British in India I could not have done better than to have gained an acceptance by the Barnardo family," he wrote.

39. Barnardo, *An Active Life*, 181.

40. Patience Gray to Ulrike Voswinckel, undated, AMS.

41. The National Archives (TNA): KV 2/2936. Between 1947 and 1951 MI5 intercepted several phone calls between Patience and Barbara in which they discussed things like going to the opera, "matrimony," and Patience's "latest boyfriends." According to the files, the Barbara and her husband also sometimes received letters that were then sent on to Otto Hamburger, the brother of Rudolf Hamburger, who was Ursula Kuczynski's first husband and also a Soviet agent. Some of these letters were apparently written by Patience though it appears she did not know Otto Hamburger herself.

42. Patience Gray to Ulrike Voswinckel, undated, AMS.

43. Patience Gray to Ulrike Voswinckel, undated, AMS.

44. Patience Gray to Tom Jaine, October 29, 1993, AMS.

45. Patience Gray to Ulrike Voswinckel, undated, AMS.

46. Patience Gray to Ulrike Voswinckel, undated, AMS.

47. Patience Gray to Kazuo Ishiguro, May 3, 1990, AMS.

48. Gray, *WACD*, 341.

49. Patience Gray to Ulrike Voswinckel, undated, AMS.

50. Patience Gray to Olive Stanham, July 11, 1939, AMS.

51. Patience Gray to Ulrike Voswinckel, undated, AMS.

52. Patience Gray to Olive Stanham, July 11, 1939, AMS.

53. Patience Gray to Olive Stanham, August 4, 1939, AMS.

54. According to one of Barbara Kuczynski's files, KV 2/2935, Patience was indeed of interest to MI5 in 1939. The file includes a memo about a letter from Patience Stanham to Mrs. H. S. Stanham that was "dropped" by Patience in August 1939 "during the period she was under observation." The memo

also suggests that Patience had her own personal file at the time but attempts to locate that file have been unsuccessful. Davenport was well acquainted with Brigadier Jasper Harker, second in command at MI5, who used Hinton Manor as a secure meeting place after the agency's office at Wormwood Scrubs was bombed. In his memoir Davenport writes, "The remoteness and secrecy of Hinton Manor doubtless appealed to an officer in charge of MI5."
55. Patience Gray to Ulrike Voswinckel, undated, AMS.
56. Patience Gray to Ulrike Voswinckel, undated, AMS.

CHAPTER TWO: THOMAS GRAY

1. Royal Navy Command Secretariat 4: JX310097.
2. Miranda Armour-Brown in discussion with the author, Cambridge, November 2014.
3. Milner Gray to Miranda Armour-Brown, November 12, 1978, private collection.
4. Patience Gray to Nicolas Gray, January 14, 1967, AMS.
5. Margaret Gray to Miranda Armour-Brown, May 3, 1991, private collection.
6. Ibid.
7. Margaret Gray to Miranda Armour-Brown, May 17, 1991, private collection.
8. Giles Playfair, chairman of the provisional committee, outline of speech, 1939, Victoria and Albert, London.
9. Patience Gray to Olive Stanham, October 22, 1939, AMS.
10. Memo from R. Wood, November 20, 1939, Victoria and Albert.
11. R. Wood to G. W. Rumble, November 18, 1939, Victoria and Albert.
12. M. C. Glasgow to H. F. Rossetti, July 30, 1940, Victoria and Albert.
13. Thomas Gray to Eilidh Armour-Brown, May 21, 1940, private collection.
14. Patience Gray to Olive Stanham, October 22, 1939, AMS.
15. Patience Gray to Ulrike Voswinckel, undated, AMS.
16. Panter-Downes, *London War Notes: 1939–1945*, 98.
17. Patience Gray to Ulrike Voswinckel, undated, AMS.
18. George Orwell, *George Orwell Diaries*, ed. Peter Davison (New York: W. W. Norton, 2012), 317. In the same entry, written on September 21, 1940, Orwell pointed out that he'd been forced to discontinue his diary for several days because the three or four stationers' shops in his neighborhood had been cordoned off due to the presence of unexploded bombs.
19. The National Archive: HO 250/11/455.
20. Patience Gray to Nicolas Gray, January 23, 1991, AMS.
21. Ibid.

22. Margaret Gray to Miranda Armour-Brown, May 3, 1991, private collection.

23. Patience Gray to Ulrike Voswinckel, undated, AMS.

24. Miranda Armour-Brown in discussion with the author, Cambridge, November 2014.

25. Patience Gray to Ulrike Voswinckel, undated, AMS.

26. Patience Gray to Eilidh Armour-Brown, January 23, 1967, AMS.

27. *The London Gazette*, January 17, 1941, 376.

28. Patience Gray to Wolfe Aylward, undated, AMS.

29. Royal Navy Command Secretariat 4: JX310097.

30. Milner Gray to Miranda Armour-Brown, November 12, 1978, private collection.

31. Patience Gray to Tania Midgley, undated, AMS.

32. Miranda Armour-Brown in discussion with the author, Puglia, June 2011.

CHAPTER THREE: THE EDGE OF AN ABYSS

1. Patience Gray to Norman Mommens, undated, AMS.

2. Patience Gray to Olive Stanham, undated, private collection.

3. Indeed Patience maintained throughout the 1940s and '50s that she had married Thomas Gray. In Barbara Kuczyinski's MI5 file there's reference to a conversation between the two in which they discussed "Patience's ex-husband, Thomas." Even as late as 1987, a profile of Patience in the *Telegraph* referred to "her first marriage and the birth of two children." In her memoir, *Instead of a Letter*, Diana Athill, who was the same age as Patience, recounts her visit to a social worker while contemplating whether to terminate a pregnancy. Athill was told, "There are plenty of war widows about. You can change your job and wear a wedding ring, and no one will suspect a thing."

4. Isabella Morton-Smith in discussion with the author, West Sussex, November 2014.

5. Alvin Curran in discussion with the author, telephone interview, June 2015.

6. Isabella Morton-Smith in discussion with the author, West Sussex, November 2014.

7. Ibid.

8. Nicolas Gray, email message to author, August 2015.

9. Patience Gray to Ulrike Voswinckel, undated, AMS.

10. Miranda Armour-Brown, email message to author, June 2011.

11. Ernest William Brockton Swanton, *A List of the Fungi (Basidiomycetes) of the Haslemere District Including the Forests of Woolmer, Verdley, Charlton, and Singleton* (Haslemere Natural History Society, 1934), 5.

12. Just as the push to develop penicillin led to a greater investment in mycological research during the war, the effort to utilize plants and herbs for medicinal purposes also led to closer scrutiny of Britain's native flora. The Vegetable Drugs Committee spearheaded efforts to collect everything from red seaweed and rose hips to nettles and a host of medicinal plants such as foxglove, belladonna, and valerian.

13. George Smith, "Mycology and the War," *Transactions of the British Mycological Society* 29 (1946): 1–10. Smith also wrote a paper titled "Moulds and Tropical Warfare," in 1946. In 1942 John Ramsbottom delivered a paper before the South-Eastern Union of Scientific Societies on the subject of "Fungi and the Biology of War."

14. Smith, "Mycology and the War."

15. E. W. Swanton, *A Country Museum: The Rise and Progress of Sir Jonathan Hutchinson's Educational Museum at Haslemere* (Haslemere: Educational Museum, 1947), 105–106.

16. Ramsbottom, *Edible Fungi*, 2. The Ministry of Agriculture and Fisheries bulletin on edible and poisonous fungi published in 1945—the previous edition was destroyed by enemy fire—also referred to the increase in "demand for information on the subject of fungi" brought about by the "influx of refugees and armed forces of all the Allied Nations" eagerly collecting toadstools, coupled with "the desire for variety in the restricted war-time diet." In her 1954 book, *The Observer's Book of Common Fungi*, E. M. Wakefield wrote, "Interest in fungi was stimulated during the last war by the realisation, due to the example of some of our allies, that here might be a source of delicious food to supplement the monotony of [a] rationed diet."

17. Miranda Armour-Brown in discussion with the author, Cambridge, November 2014.

18. The book was given to Patience by Philip Thornton, a travel writer and amateur ethnographer who wrote two books: *The Voice of Atlas: In Search of Music in Morocco*; and *Dead Puppets Dance*, a study of the musical traditions of Balkan peasants.

19. Oddy, *From Plain Fare to Fusion Food*, 154.

20. Patience Gray, interview by Simon Parkes, BBC Radio 4, *The Food Programme*, August 11, 2002.

21. Gray, *WACD*, 315.

22. Meynell, *Sussex*, 253.

23. Patience Gray to Ulrike Voswinckel, undated, AMS.

24. Gray, *WACD*, 337.

25. Nicolas Gray, email message to author, September 2014.

26. Patience Gray to Norman Mommens, undated, AMS.

27. Patience Gray to Ulrike Voswinckel, undated, AMS.

28. These quotes come from Patience's author bio on the jacket flap of *Ring Doves and Snakes,* published in 1989.

29. Patience Gray to Ulrike Voswinckel, undated, AMS.

30. Patience Gray to Olive Stanham, undated, AMS.

CHAPTER FOUR: HAMPSTEAD

1. Patience Gray to Ulrike Voswinckel, undated, AMS.

2. Brown, *The English Garden in Our Time,* 204.

3. Patience Gray to Ariane Castaing, undated, AMS.

4. Richard Guyatt, "Head, Heart and Hand," *RCA Papers No. 2* (London: Royal College of Art, 1977), 4.

5. Julia Black in discussion with the author, London, November 2014.

6. Patience Gray to Ulrike Voswinckel, undated, AMS.

7. Cohen, *All We Know,* 200–201.

8. Patience Gray in the exhibition catalogue *Henrion: Designing Things and Symbols* (London: Institute of Contemporary Arts, 1960). Patience also wrote about the exhibit in February 1960 for the *Observer* in an article titled "The Designer at Work in Industry."

9. F. M. L. Thompson, *Hampstead: Building a Borough, 1650–1964* (London: Routledge and Kegan Paul, 1974), 431.

10. Cohen, *All We Know,* 206.

11. Maud Murdoch to Patience Gray, October 12, 1990, AMS.

12. Patience Gray, afterword to Uhlman, *A Moroccan Diary,* 31–32.

13. Patience Gray to Ulrike Voswinckel, undated, AMS.

14. Patience Gray to Ulrike Voswinckel, undated, AMS.

15. Alec Hill to Patience Gray, undated, AMS. Most of the letters between Patience and Hill were written in 1947 and 1948.

16. Alec Hill to Patience Gray, undated, AMS.

17. Patience Gray, "I live in a billiardroom," undated, AMS.

18. Patience Gray to Norman Mommens, undated, AMS.

19. Ibid.

20. Ibid.

21. Ibid.

22. Patrick Kemmis to Patience Gray, undated, AMS.

23. Kynaston, *Family Britain: 1951–1957,* 558.

24. Ariane Castaing in discussion with the author, Vendôme, France, July 2010.

25. Harries and Harries, *A Pilgrim Soul*, 114.

26. Nicolas Gray in discussion with the author, Puglia, June 2011.

27. Patience Gray to Peter Heyworth, 1989, AMS. Patience wrote to Heyworth after reading a review of Meirion and Susie Harries's biography of Elisabeth Lutyens.

28. Nicolas Gray in discussion with the author, Puglia, June 2011.

29. Rick Poynor, "The Useful Art of Graphic Design," in Octavia Reeve, ed., *The Perfect Place to Grow: 175 Years of the Royal College of Art* (London: Royal College of Art, 2012), 107.

30. John Brinkley to Patience Gray, undated, AMS.

31. Dick Guyatt to Patience Gray, April 2, 1955, AMS.

32. David Gentleman in discussion with the author, London, July 2010.

33. On Robin Darwin's attitude to women, see Henrietta Goodden's engaging and sympathetic biography, *Robin Darwin: Visionary Educator and Painter*, 133–134.

34. Susan Jellicoe, *Photographs of Landscape: Private Gardens* (undated: 1950s to 1970s), P JEL PH 2/L/12, Susan Jellicoe Photographic Collection, The Museum of English Rural Life. The collection, which consists of 334 prints, also features the gardens of Patience's neighbors Barbara Jones and architect Leonard Manasseh as well as several gardens designed by landscape architect Brenda Colvin.

35. Patience Gray, "A Room Outdoors," *The Observer*, May 1, 1960.

36. The phrase "all wastes and solitary places" comes from Percy Bysshe Shelley's poem "Julian and Maddalo," which Patience quoted frequently, including in the entry for wild asparagus in *Honey from a Weed*.

37. Miranda Armour-Brown, email message to author, October 2014.

38. Ibid.

39. Clark and Jones, *Indoor Plants and Gardens*, 20. The book was illustrated by Gordon Cullen, an assistant editor of *Architectural Review* and a leading proponent of the Townscape movement.

40. Chloe Bennett, "Frank Clark—His Legacy" (Edinburgh: Urbanism and Landscape Conference, April 2011). See also Brown, *The English Garden in Our Time*, 195–205.

41. Shepheard, *Modern Gardens*, 18.

42. Patience Gray to Alan Davidson, September 10, 1986, private collection.

43. For more on Stearn and his remarkable career, see S. M. Walters, "W. T. Stearn: The Complete Naturalist," *Botanical Journal of the Linnean Society* 109, no. 4 (August 1992): 437–442, doi:10.1111/j.1095-8339.1992.tb0 1442.x.

44. Clark and Jones, *Indoor Plants and Gardens*, 10.

45. John Claudius Loudon, *An Encyclopedia of Gardening* (London: A. & R. Spottiswoode, 1824), 681.
46. The *Encyclopedia* underwent substantial revisions and was republished numerous times throughout the nineteenth century.
47. Loudon, *An Encyclopedia of Gardening*, 606.
48. Gray and Boyd, *Plats du Jour*, 35.

CHAPTER FIVE: *PLATS DU JOUR*

1. The synopsis of the book from Primrose Boyd and Patience Gray was sent to Eunice Frost on November 16, 1953. However they first contacted Allen Lane about a book on "European cookery" in October.
2. Gray, preface to *Plats du Jour* (Devon, England: Prospect Books, 1990), xi.
3. Eunice Frost to Patience Gray, April 5, 1954, Penguin Archive.
4. Cooper, *Writing at the Kitchen Table*, 181.
5. Eunice Frost to Patience Gray, September 27, 1955, Penguin Archive.
6. Gaby Wood, "A Touch of Frost: The Story of Penguin's Secret Editor," *Telegraph*, August 5, 2010.
7. Eunice Frost to Primrose Boyd, February 24, 1954, Penguin Archive.
8. Patience Gray to Eunice Frost, March 24, 1954, Penguin Archive.
9. David, *A Book of Mediterranean Food*.
10. Gray and Boyd, *Plats du Jour*, 26.
11. Ibid., 10 and 61.
12. Patience Gray, "Pots, Pans and Performance," *The Observer*, March 5, 1961.
13. Patience Gray to Candida Brazil, October 16, 1985, AMS.
14. Trevor Pinnock in discussion with the author, telephone interview, September 2015.
15. Miranda Gray in discussion with the author, Cambridge, November 2014.
16. Patience Gray, "Modest Conversions," *The Observer*, October 18, 1959.
17. Ariane Castaing in discussion with the author, Vendôme, France, July 2010.
18. Miranda Armour-Brown in discussion with the author, Cambridge, July 2010.
19. Gray, preface to *Plats du Jour* (Devon, England: Prospect Books, 1990), xii.
20. Gray and Boyd, *Plats du Jour*, 10.
21. Gray, preface to *Plats du Jour* (Devon, England: Prospect Books, 1990), xii.
22. Gray and Boyd, *Plats du Jour*, 175–176.
23. Carolyn M. King, *Katherine Watson: A Life of Poetry, Faith, and Love* (Hamilton, New Zealand: Walrus Books, 2011), 170–171.
24. Gray, *WACD*, 237.
25. Ibid., 243.

26. Gray and Boyd, *Plats du Jour*, 9.

27. Ibid., 249.

28. Daphne Henrion to Patience Gray, April 2, 1989, AMS.

29. Gray, preface to *Plats du Jour* (Devon, England: Prospect Books, 1990), xi–xii.

30. Patience Gray to Clare Ajenusi, October 16, 1987, AMS.

31. Miranda Armour-Brown in discussion with the author, Cambridge, July 2010.

32. Patience Gray to Allen Lane, July 25, 1958, Penguin Archive.

33. Patience Gray to Eunice Frost, May 27, 1954, Penguin Archive.

34. Ibid.

35. Eunice Frost to Patience Gray, July 13, 1954, Penguin Archive.

36. Julian Bell, "David Gentleman: images of postwar Britain," *Guardian*, April 16, 2010.

37. David Gentleman in discussion with the author, London, November 2014.

38. Hans Schmoller to David Gentleman, December 13, 1955, Penguin Archive.

39. David Gentleman in discussion with the author, London, July 2010.

40. Ibid.

41. Gray, preface to *Plats du Jour* (Devon, England: Prospect Books, 1990), xi.

42. Gray, *HFAW*, 209.

43. Patience Gray to Eunice Frost, January 7, 1955, Penguin Archive.

44. Patience Gray to Eunice Frost, October 26, 1954, Penguin Archive.

45. Elsie M. Wakefield, *The Observer's Book of Common Fungi* (London: Frederick Warne, 1954), ix. In her 1950 book, *Common British Fungi*, Wakefield, who served as president of the British Mycological Society in 1929, observed, "There is at present no critical British fungus flora, and most of the existing works of any value are out of print and almost unobtainable, except at prices which most people find prohibitive."

46. Patience Gray to Ariane Castaing, undated, AMS.

47. Patience Gray to Olive Stanham, October 22, 1939, AMS.

48. Shepheard, *Modern Gardens*, 18.

49. Paul Shepheard, email message to author, June 2011.

50. Gray, afterword to *A Moroccan Diary*, 35.

51. Miranda Armour-Brown in discussion with the author, Puglia, June 2011.

52. Peter Shepheard to Patience Gray, April 7, 1952, AMS.

53. Lawrence Halprin, foreword to Downs, *Peter Shepheard*, 7–8.

54. Shepheard, *Modern Gardens*, 20. Notably Shepheard included weeds as part of the "living pattern." In a talk on indoor gardening delivered in 1952, Shepheard said, "I am extremely fond of growing weeds. Anyone who has seen my gardens at the Festival will know that I like weeds."

55. Indeed Loudon was also an enormously gifted illustrator and draftsman who pioneered the use of wood engravings to illustrate his books.

56. Primrose Boyd and Patience Gray to Eunice Frost, March 30, 1955, Penguin Archive.

57. Eunice Frost to Patience Gray, September 27, 1955, Penguin Archive.

58. Elizabeth David to Eunice Frost, June 6, 1955, Penguin Archive.

59. Eunice Frost to Patience Gray, September 27, 1955, Penguin Archive.

60. Irving Davis to Elizabeth David, March 21, 1961, Elizabeth David Papers, Schlesinger Library, Radcliffe Institute for Advanced Study at Harvard University.

61. Patience Gray to John Thorne, August 14, 1998, AMS.

62. Jonathan Meades, email message to author, July 2015.

63. Patience Gray to Ariane Castaing, undated, AMS.

64. Elizabeth David to Patience Gray, March 22, 1987, AMS.

65. Patience Gray to Christopher Driver, undated, AMS.

66. Elizabeth David to Eunice Frost, June 6, 1955, Penguin Archive.

67. Elizabeth David's report on *Plats du Jour* was included in her June 6, 1955, letter to Eunice Frost.

68. Thornton quoted in Cooper, *Writing at the Kitchen Table*, 158.

69. Gray and Boyd, *Plats du Jour*, 253.

70. Patience Gray to Wolfe Aylward, April 10, 1981, AMS.

71. Elizabeth David to Eunice Frost, May 10, 1957, Penguin Archive.

72. Judith Watson to Penguin Books, July 21, 1967, Penguin Archive.

73. Rosemary Hume to Jill Norman, November 29, 1964, Penguin Archive.

74. Angela Carter, "Wolfing It," *London Review of Books* 9, no. 14 (July 23, 1987): 15–16.

75. Elisabeth Sifton to Patience Gray, July 18, 2000, AMS.

76. June Owen, "Food News: Cookbooks," *New York Times*, June 25, 1957.

77. Patience Gray to Eunice Frost, March 7, 1957, Penguin Archive.

78. Patience Gray to Pat Siddall, September 26, 1960, Penguin Archive.

79. Patience Gray to Ulrike Voswinckel, November 1988, AMS.

80. Terence Conran, "Obituary: Michael Wickham," *The Independent*, February 6, 1995.

81. The articles, published between May and December 1958, were titled "New Approach to Kitchens," "Summer Party Magic," "Picnics," "Ices," and "Buffet Parties."

82. Fred Tomlinson to Patience Gray, April 29, 1958, AMS.

83. Patience Gray to Alison Settle, undated, AMS. It's unclear if this letter was ever sent.

84. Patience Gray to Brian Batsford, March 12, 1958, AMS.

CHAPTER SIX: THE EUROPEAN SCENE

1. Gray, *HFAW*, 109.

2. Davis, *A Catalan Cookery Book*, 98.

3. Oliver Bernard in discussion with the author, Kenninghall, England, July 2010.

4. John Irving Davis, *A Beginners Guide to Wines and Spirits* (London: Stanley Nott, 1934).

5. Patience wrote one article for the journal, titled "Decorated Food," a firsthand account of a lavish hotel and catering exhibition at the Olympia published in the winter 1958 issue. After viewing tables laden with sculpted hams, chocolate monuments—including a renaissance temple of the Virgin "executed with a stone-mason's precision"—and elaborately arrayed salmon and turbot, she wrote, "One ceases to wonder if the dishes are edible."

6. Gray, *HFAW*, 109.

7. Gray, *WACD*, 402.

8. Patience Gray to Agnes Greenhall, 1990, AMS.

9. Davis, *A Catalan Cookery Book*, 107.

10. Richard Aldington, *Pinorman: Personal Recollections of Norman Douglas, Pino Orioli and Charles Prentice* (London: William Heinemann, 1954), 39.

11. Ianthe Carswell to Patience Gray, September 16, 1998, AMS.

12. Davis, *A Catalan Cookery Book*, 103.

13. Patience Gray, "Fragmentary Account of a Journey in Calabria, Apulia, and Basilicata," June 1958, AMS.

14. Ibid.

15. Patience Gray to Olive Stanham, July 21, 1968, AMS.

16. Irving Davis to Patience Gray, July 30, 1959, AMS.

17. Patience Gray, "Christmas Joie de Vivre," *The Observer*, December 7, 1958. Patience's very first article for the paper, "Nothing to Declare," published on August 17, 1958, also drew on her travels to France and Italy. In this piece she gave a brief introduction to some of her favorite shops and markets in Paris and Florence. "You'll need a sharp eye to isolate the object from the surrounding dazzle," she wrote, "presence of mind to pounce *au moment juste*. Whatever the spoil it must have intrinsic merit, not just nostalgia value. Even if it is 'nothing to declare' it still has to stand the test—use, amusement, beauty—once you have carted it home."

18. Patience Gray to Wolfe Aylward, undated, AMS.
19. In fact, after her trip with Irving, Patience wrote an article on eating in Paris for *The Observer* that was never published. "The best places aren't always listed," she wrote. "Often you can't even find them in the telephone book. You have to seek a solid Frenchman's advice." Upon returning to London, she wrote in her memoir, "No sooner had my piece been typeset than members of the printing room, abandoning their posts, headed helter-skelter for Paris to put my claims to the proof." Indeed in the article she described some lovely sounding dishes, including fried smelts that "tasted like violets"; scallops fried in butter with garlic and *gros sel*, "quite the best method of preparing them"; and *Pocheuse bourguignonne*, a dish of river fish and eels cooked with salt pork.
20. Gray, *HFAW*, 111.
21. Leona Rostenberg and Madeleine B. Stern, *Old and Rare: Forty Years in the Book Business* (Santa Monica: Modoc Press, 1988), 131.
22. Patience Gray, "Christmas Joie de Vivre," *The Observer*, December 7, 1958.
23. There are several books on the antiquarian book trade that mention Irving Davis and his status as a legendary collector. He's described as "fey and eerie" and as a "literary hobgoblin" in Leona Rostenberg and Madeleine B. Stern's *Old and Rare: Forty Years in the Book Business*. George Sims in *The Rare Book Game* (Philadelphia: Holmes Publishing, 1985) calls him "an extremely shrewd, scholarly dealer." H. A. Feisenberger, a junior partner in Davis and Orioli's bookshop, who went on to become an associate director at Sotheby's, remembered his friend and colleague as "one of the most remarkable bibliophiles of our time."
24. Bernard, *Getting Over It*, 97.
25. Harriet Wilson in discussion with the author, London, July 2010.
26. Ariane Castaing in discussion with the author, Vendôme, France, June 2010.
27. Paul Shepheard, email message to author, June 2011.
28. Conrad Clark, email message to author, May 2016.
29. Serena Allott, "Wild about Creation," *Telegraph*, November 14, 1987.
30. Gray, *WACD*, 37–46. The essay is titled "At Twenty-Two Tudor Street."
31. Patience Gray, "Crafts from Obscurity," *The Observer*, June 26, 1960.
32. Enzo Apicella, email message to author, May 2015.
33. Ibid.
34. Humble, *Culinary Pleasures*, 167.
35. Julia Child to Mrs. Solon Robinson, March 10, 1981, Papers of Julia Child, Schlesinger Library, Radcliffe Institute for Advanced Study at Harvard University.

36. Montagné, *Larousse Gastronomique*, 5.
37. Ibid.
38. Patience Gray to Alan Davidson, August 26, 1984, private collection.
39. Syllabub, "A Book to Banish the Cookery Bull," *The Observer*, April 1, 1962.
40. Gray, *WACD*, 39.
41. Ibid., 40.
42. Patience Gray, "The Designer at Work in Industry," *The Observer*, February 7, 1960.
43. Patience Gray, "A Pleasure to Make," *The Observer*, March 20, 1960.
44. Patience Gray, "Movement and Design," *The Observer*, May 24, 1959.
45. Patience Gray, "The Space-Makers," *The Observer*, April 9, 1961.
46. Patience Gray to Ulrike Voswinckel, November 1998, AMS.
47. Patience Gray, "Wanted: Just a Touch of Barbarism," *The Observer*, October 8, 1961.
48. Ibid.
49. Gerda Flöckinger in discussion with the author, London, November 2014.
50. This article, titled "Battle-Axe or Doormat," appeared in the April 19, 1959, issue of *The Observer*. Notably the banner at the top of the page, which typically read "A Woman's Perspective," was changed to "Modern Woman Goes on Record."
51. Gray, *WACD*, 344.
52. Eugenia Parry in conversation with the author, telephone interview, March 2015.
53. Gray, *WACD*, 38.
54. Astor's feelings about women and the atmosphere at *The Observer* in the late 1950s and early 1960s are elucidated in Jeremy Lewis's excellent new biography, *David Astor: A Life in Print*. I've also relied on Richard Cockett's earlier biography, *David Astor and the Observer*.
55. Gray, *WACD*, 39.
56. Jean Southon in discussion with the author, telephone interview, February 2012.
57. Jane Bown in discussion with the author, telephone interview, March 2012.
58. Carol Hall in discussion with the author, telephone interview, March 2012.
59. Lewis, *David Astor: A Life in Print*.
60. Patience Gray to Peter Heyworth, December 1989, AMS.
61. David Gentleman in discussion with the author, London, July 2010.
62. Gray, *WACD*, 45.
63. Patience Gray to Nicolas Gray, November 26, 1993, AMS.
64. Trant, *Art for Life: The Story of Peggy Angus*.

65. Miranda Armour-Brown, email message to author, September 2014.

66. Patience Gray to Ariane Castaing, April 12, 1977, AMS.

67. Patience Gray to Norman Mommens, undated, AMS.

68. Ravilious quoted in Russell, *Peggy Angus*, 49.

69. Tyl Kennedy in discussion with the author, telephone interview, April 2016.

70. Ruscha Schorr-Kon in discussion with the author, telephone interview, April 2016.

CHAPTER SEVEN: DEPARTURES

1. Norman Mommens to Patience Gray, undated, AMS.

2. Norman Mommens to Muriel Mommens, March 28, 1960, AMS.

3. Miranda Armour-Brown, email message to author, September 2015.

4. Nicolas Gray in discussion with the author, Puglia, July 2011.

5. Patience Gray to Norman Mommens, undated, AMS.

6. Nicolas Gray, email message to author, August 2015.

7. Richard Gibson in discussion with the author, telephone interview, July 2015.

8. Patience Gray to Ariane Castaing, July 21, 1976, AMS.

9. Norman Mommens to Patience Gray, undated, AMS.

10. Miranda Armour-Brown in discussion with the author, Cambridge, July 2010.

11. Patience Gray to Ulrike Voswinckel, undated, AMS.

12. Patience Gray to Norman Mommens, undated, AMS.

13. Ibid.

14. Patience Gray to Norman Mommens, undated, AMS.

15. Norman Mommens: autobiographical notes. October 1973, AMS.

16. Miranda Armour-Brown, email message to author, November 2016.

17. Norman Mommens: autobiographical notes. October 1973, AMS.

18. Patience Gray to Tania Midgley, undated, AMS.

19. I'm indebted to Nicolas Gray for his research into the life of Joseph Beuys in Kleve.

20. Norman Mommens: autobiographical notes. October 1973, AMS.

21. Patience Gray to Muriel Mommens, undated, AMS.

22. Norman Mommens to Jan and Leonore Hubrecht, October 16, 1962, AMS.

23. Norman Mommens to Muriel Mommens, July 17, 1965, AMS.

24. Philip Trevelyan, email message to author, May 2015.

25. Gwen Raverat, *Period Piece* (Ann Arbor: University of Michigan Press, 1991), 104.

26. Norman Mommens to Muriel Mommens, December 1959, AMS.

27. Ibid.
28. Norman Mommens to Leonard Woolf, June 6, 1957, Leonard Woolf Archive, University of Sussex Library Special Collections.
29. Philip Trevelyan, email message to author, May 2015.
30. Norman Mommens to Patience Gray, October 1961, AMS.
31. Philip Trevelyan, email message to author, June 2015.
32. Norman Mommens to Muriel Mommens, February 6, 1962.
33. Gray, *WACD*, 157.
34. Gerda Flöckinger in discussion with the author, London, November 2014.
35. Patience Gray to Norman Mommens, undated, AMS.
36. The piece is owned by Lesley Jackson, Alastair Morton's biographer and a historian of twentieth-century British art and design.
37. Jackson, *Alastair Morton and Edinburgh Weavers*, 278.
38. Ibid.
39. Patience Gray to Olive Stanham, July 1963, AMS.
40. Patience Gray to Ulrike Voswinckel, undated, AMS.
41. Patience Gray to Norman Mommens, undated, AMS.
42. Gray, *WACD*, 46.
43. Patience Gray to Norman Mommens, undated, AMS.
44. Norman Mommens to Patience Gray, undated, AMS.
45. Philip Trevelyan, email message to author, May 2015.
46. Joanna da Cruz, email message to author, October 2014.
47. Patience Gray, "Picnics," *Harper's Bazaar*, June 1958.
48. Patience's piece for the *Observer*, "Paris from an Attic," published in January 1961, was written after visiting Wolfe in his tiny fifth-floor apartment on the Rue de Buci.
49. Joanna da Cruz in discussion with the author, Brighton, July 2010.
50. Nicolas Gray in discussion with the author, Puglia, June 2011.
51. Norman Mommens to Patience Gray, undated, AMS.
52. Ibid.
53. Scigliano, *Michelangelo's Mountain*, 88.
54. Ibid., 140–141.
55. Blessington quoted in Gray, *HFAW*, 155.
56. Gray, *HFAW*, 186.
57. Patience Gray to Olive Stanham, May 14, 1962, AMS.
58. Gray, *HFAW*, 194.
59. Ibid., 293.
60. Ibid., 292.
61. Ibid., 27.

62. Patience Gray to Olive Stanham, June 1962, AMS.

63. Norman Mommens to Leonore Hubrecht, August 4, 1962, AMS.

64. Patience Gray to Olive Stanham, undated, AMS.

65. Gray, *HFAW*, 79.

66. Norman Mommens to Leonore Hubrecht, August 4, 1962, AMS.

67. Details on Fenosa's life come from Nicole Fenosa's essay in *Apel-les Fenosa: Catalogue raisonné de l'oeuvre sculpté* (Barcelona: Ediciones Polígrafa, 2002).

68. Ibid.

69. Patience Gray, *Cantarem la vida*, in *Fenosa ou le Limon Ailé* (Cognac: Le temps qu'il fait, 1997). *Cantarem la vida* (We sing for life) is the title of a ballad sung by the Spanish singer Raimon that Norman loved to play on his guitar.

70. Irving Davis to Patience Gray, July 14, 1963, AMS.

71. Gray, introduction to *A Catalan Cookery Book*, 9.

72. Nicole Fenosa in discussion with the author, Paris, July 2010.

73. Norman Mommens to Patience Gray, 1961, AMS.

74. Nicolas Gray, email message to author, January 2015.

75. Norman Mommens to Jan and Leonore Hubrecht, October 16, 1962, AMS.

76. Ibid.

CHAPTER EIGHT: BEYOND AND AWAY

1. Patience Gray, "Milk-Maid Madonnas and Sugar-Loaf Saints," *The Observer*, August 5, 1962.

2. Norman Mommens to Jan and Leonore Hubrecht, October 16, 1962, AMS.

3. Gray, *RDS*, 3.

4. Ibid.

5. Ibid., 4.

6. Ibid.

7. Ibid., 3.

8. Karl Heller, *Antonio Vivaldi: The Red Priest of Venice* (Portland, OR: Amadeus Press, 1997), 37–38.

9. Gray, *RDS*, 4.

10. Ibid., 6.

11. Patience Gray to Olive Stanham, July 3, 1963, AMS.

12. Norman Mommens to Muriel Mommens, June 23, 1963, AMS.

13. Gray, *RDS*, 40.

14. Norman Mommens to Muriel Mommens, June 23, 1963, AMS.

15. Gray, *RDS*, 3.

16. Patience Gray to Olive Stanham, July 3, 1963, AMS.

17. Gray, *RDS*, xi.

18. Norman Mommens to Muriel Mommens, December 6, 1963, AMS.

19. Norman Mommens to Muriel Mommens, June 23, 1963, AMS.

20. Patience Gray to Nicolas Gray, July 1963, AMS.

21. Gray, *RDS*, 37–39.

22. Ibid., 119–120.

23. Ibid., 60.

24. Nicolas Gray in discussion with the author, Puglia, June 2011.

25. Norman Janis in discussion with the author, New York, August 2012.

26. Gray, *RDS*, 22–24.

27. Ibid., 26.

28. Patience Gray to Nicolas Gray and Corinna Sargood, January 19, 1969, AMS.

29. Gray, *RDS*, 189.

30. Stavros Papastavrou to Patience Gray and Norman Mommens, July 19, 1963, AMS.

31. Patience Gray to Muriel Mommens, September 24, 1963, AMS.

32. Gray, *RDS*, 23.

33. Judith Butcher to Patience Gray, June 20, 1963, Penguin Archive.

34. Patience Gray to Judith Butcher, July 16, 1963, Penguin Archive.

35. Ibid.

36. Jill Norman, email message to author, October 2015.

37. Ibid.

38. Patience Gray to Muriel Mommens, February 23, 1964, AMS.

39. Gray, *RDS*, 108–110.

40. Ibid., 43.

41. Ibid., 44.

42. Norman was working on a children's book called *Baldoer the Car Basher*, which was published in Dutch in 1963.

43. The tenant was landscape architect Nicholas Quennell and his partner, Sandy Daley. Quennell was introduced to Patience through his neighbor, the influential architect and town planner Elizabeth Chesterton.

44. Patience Gray to Olive Stanham, July 1963, AMS.

45. Ibid.

46. Patience Gray to Muriel Mommens, December 1963, AMS.

47. Ibid.

48. Gray, *RDS*, 78.

49. Ibid., 79.

50. Ibid., 84.

51. Patience Gray to Olive Stanham, December 1964, AMS.

52. Patrick Leigh Fermor, "Kevin Andrews: Scholar Gypsy," *The Athenian*, October 1989.

53. Ibid.

54. Patience Gray to Olive Stanham, undated, AMS.

55. Patience Gray to Ariane Castaing, 1963, AMS.

56. Jinkinson, *American Ikaros*, 21.

57. Andrews, *The Flight of Ikaros*.

58. Kevin Andrews to Patience Gray, June 6, 1989, AMS.

59. Kevin Andrews to Norman Mommens and Patience Gray, March 12, 1964, AMS.

60. Patience Gray to Olive Stanham, March 22, 1964, AMS.

61. Gray, *RDS*, 115. The quote comes from a chapter called "Weeds and Obsessions."

62. It was not the only care package they received on Naxos. Norman's sister Ruscha had also sent them a package containing salami, ham, and milk in November.

63. Gray, *RDS*, 129.

64. Norman Mommens to Lena Mommens, April 1964, AMS.

65. Patience Gray to Tania Midgley, March 27, 1964, AMS.

66. Patience Gray to Tania Midgley, April 1964, AMS.

67. Louis Stettner in discussion with the author, telephone interview, January 2015.

68. Patience Gray to Muriel Mommens, May 2, 1964, AMS.

69. Gray, *RDS*, 137.

70. Nicholas Stampolidis and Peggy Sotirakopoulou, *Aegean Waves: Artworks of the Early Cycladic Culture in the Museum of Cycladic Art* (Skira: Museum of Cycladic Art, 2008), 41. See also David W. J. Gill and Christopher Chippindale, "Material and Intellectual Consequences of Esteem for Cycladic Figures," *American Journal of Archaeology* 97, no. 4 (October 1993), 601–659, for a detailed discussion of the illegal trade in Cycladic works in the 1960s. Charles Stewart, who has written one of the only English-language studies of religious life and customs on Naxos, *Demons and the Devil: Moral Imagination in Modern Greek Culture*, lived in the village of Apeíranthos, about 12 miles south of Apollonas, from March 1983 to October 1984. In his book he says he was viewed as either a CIA operative or someone involved in the illegal trade of antiquities.

71. Norman Janis in discussion with the author, New York, August 2012.

72. Gray, *RDS*, 167.

73. Norman Janis in discussion with the author, New York, August 2012.
74. Patience's brother-in-law, John Midgley, had given them the phone number of Spyros Markezinis, a longtime member of the Greek parliament who served briefly as prime minister in 1973.
75. Gray, *RDS*, 156.
76. Ibid., 175.
77. Miranda Armour-Brown in discussion with the author, Cambridge, November 2014.
78. Norman Mommens to Muriel Mommens, May 20, 1964, AMS.
79. Norman Mommens to Leonard Woolf, June 3, 1964, Leonard Woolf Archive, University of Sussex Library Special Collections.
80. Norman Janis in discussion with the author, Puglia, February 2015.
81. Eugenia Parry in discussion with the author, telephone interview, March 2015.
82. Gray, *RDS*, xi.
83. Miranda Armour-Brown in discussion with the author, Cambridge, November 2014.

CHAPTER NINE: TO WORK IS TO LIVE

1. Patience Gray, "Impossible Business," September 1964, AMS.
2. Patience Gray, "Design with Everything," *The Economist*, March 30, 1963; Gray, "Design in Transit," *The Economist*, March 28, 1964. The first piece looked at the growing British obsession with principles of Scandinavian design. In the second article Patience examined the impact of industrial design on Italy's urban centers, particularly Milan.
3. Norman Mommens to Leonard Woolf, April 23, 1965, Leonard Woolf Archive, University of Sussex Library Special Collections.
4. Ibid.
5. Norman Mommens to Lena Mommens, undated, AMS.
6. Patience Gray to Muriel Mommens, August 31, 1964, AMS.
7. Patience Gray to Pat Siddall, June 8, 1964, Penguin Archive.
8. Pat Siddall to Patience Gray, July 29, 1964, Penguin Archive.
9. Primrose Boyd to Patience Gray, July 7, 1964, Penguin Archive.
10. Primrose Boyd to Pat Siddall, August 29, 1964, Penguin Archive.
11. Alan Davidson to Kyle Cathie, April 23, 1987, private collection.
12. Patience Gray to Judith Butcher, July 18, 1963, Penguin Archive.
13. Patience Gray to Jenny Dereham, October 1980, AMS.
14. Patience Gray to Alan Davidson, February 13, 1989, private collection.
15. Patience Gray to Alan Davidson, April 19, 1986, private collection.

16. Patience Gray to Muriel Mommens, August 31, 1964, AMS.
17. Patience Gray to Muriel Mommens, May 3, 1965, AMS.
18. Patience Gray to Olive Stanham, undated, AMS.
19. Gray, *HFAW*, 27.
20. Patience Gray to Wolfe Aylward, March 14, 1987, AMS.
21. Patience Gray to Olive Stanham, 1965, AMS.
22. Peter Rockwell in discussion with the author, telephone interview, April 2015.
23. Patience Gray, "Sculptors El Dorado," *Architectural Review* (June 1966).
24. Ibid.
25. Ibid. In *Honey from a Weed* Patience devotes an entire chapter to the anarchic spirit of the Carrarese, which she attributes to the nature of the marble quarrying work itself relying as it does on a combination of "individualism and human brotherhood." Anarchism was the political philosophy Patience most closely identified with.
26. Carlo Nicoli in discussion with the author, Carrara, September 2006.
27. Gray, *WACD*, 154.
28. Patience Gray to Wolfe Aylward, undated, AMS.
29. Patience Gray to Ariane Castaing, July 21, 1976, AMS.
30. Alvin Curran in discussion with the author, telephone interview, June 2015.
31. Gray, *WACD*, 97.
32. Alvin Curran in discussion with the author, telephone interview, June 2015.
33. Gray, *HFAW*, 190.
34. Patience Gray to Tania Midgley, April 10, 1967, AMS.
35. Gray, *HFAW*, 157.
36. Ibid., 205.
37. Patience often took her recipes from innkeepers or cooks. Her recipe for *zuppa di datteri*, or date-shell soup, was taken "word for word" from the cook at a restaurant in Fiumaretta, and her recipe for braised wild boar from a cook in Provence. Instructions on preparing and cooking a fox, featured in *Honey from a Weed*, were given to her by "an old anarchist."
38. Gray, *HFAW*, 206–207.
39. Patience Gray to Olive Stanham, July 21, 1968, AMS.
40. Norman Mommens to Muriel Mommens, October 7, 1965, AMS.
41. Patience Gray to Olive Stanham, October 30, 1966, AMS.
42. Ibid.
43. Patience Gray to Muriel Mommens, October 28, 1966, AMS.
44. Patience Gray to Olive Stanham, October 30, 1966, AMS.
45. Isabella Morton-Smith in discussion with the author, West Sussex, November 2014.

46. Patience Gray to Wolfe Aylward, November 2, 1966, AMS.

47. Patience Gray to Ulrike Voswinckel, undated, AMS.

48. Miranda Armour Brown, email message to author, November 2015.

49. Patience Gray to Olive Stanham, December 26, 1966, AMS.

50. Peter Brown to Patience Gray, December 20, 1966, AMS.

51. Eilidh Armour-Brown to Patience Gray, January 12, 1967, AMS.

52. Patience Gray to Eilidh Armour-Brown, January 23, 1967, AMS.

53. Miranda Armour-Brown, email message to author, November 2015.

54. Patience Gray to Nicolas Gray, January 14, 1967, AMS.

55. Patience Gray to Ariane Castaing, undated, AMS.

56. Patience Gray to Ianthe Carswell, undated, AMS.

57. Patience Gray to Ariane Castaing, undated, AMS.

58. Alan Lomax's *Folk Music and Song of Italy* was recorded in 1954 and first issued by Tradition Records in 1958. Rounder Records issued a new edition in 1999.

59. D. H. Lawrence, *D. H. Lawrence and Italy* (London: Penguin, 2007), 79.

60. Patience Gray to Olive Stanham, July 21, 1968, AMS.

CHAPTER TEN: *FIN DU MONDE*

1. Patience Gray to Tania Midgley, July 26, 1967, AMS.

2. One evening while Patience and Norman were visiting Sven and Romaine, John Berger came to dinner with a "Russian princess" and, according to Patience, got rather drunk and attacked them for being middle class. In a letter to Alan Davidson many years later, she wrote that Berger began "throwing mud at us for 'living with peasants' in Carrara."

3. Patience Gray to Olive Stanham, July 14, 1967, AMS.

4. Crawford, *C. R. Ashbee*, 197.

5. Felicity Ashbee, "Obituary: Helen Ashbee," *The Independent*, July 2, 1996.

6. Patience Gray to Wolfe Aylward, June 21, 1966, AMS.

7. Ibid.

8. Hendrikus Theodorus Wijdeveld to Norman Mommens, March 16, 1969, AMS.

9. Serena Allott, "Wild about Creation," *Telegraph*, November 14, 1987.

10. Patience Gray to Olive Stanham, July 21, 1968, AMS.

11. Harriet Wilson in discussion with the author, London, July 2010.

12. Patience Gray to Olive Stanham, March 16, 1969, AMS.

13. Patience Gray to Ianthe Carswell, undated, AMS.

14. Patience Gray to Ariane Castaing, undated, AMS.

15. April Bloomfield cited this recipe as a reason why she considers *Honey from a Weed* one of her favorite cookbooks.

16. David, *Italian Food*, xxv.

17. Patience Gray to Ariane Castaing, undated, AMS.

18. Patience Gray to Wolfe Aylward, undated, AMS.

19. Patience Gray to Ariane Castaing, 1968, AMS.

20. Ibid.

21. Humble, *Culinary Pleasures*, 206–208.

22. Elizabeth David to Eunice Frost, February 1963, Penguin Archive.

23. Harriet Wilson in discussion with the author, London, July 2010.

24. Colman Andrews in discussion with the author, telephone interview, March 2016.

25. One of the more remarkable recipes included in *Honey from a Weed* is for Catalan vineyard snails (152), which are starved for several days—the equivalent of a gastronomic cleanse—before being piled together on a mass of straw. "The straw is set alight and the snails are retrieved from the ashes by jabbing them with sharply pointed sticks, and at once dipped into a *vinagretes endimoniades* . . . , eaten with bread and washed down with wine," Patience writes.

26. Jeremiah Tower, *California Dish: What I Saw (and Cooked) at the American Culinary Revolution* (New York: Free Press, 2003), 288.

27. Patience Gray to Ariane Castaing, undated, AMS.

28. Ibid.

29. Patience Gray to Ariane Castaing, undated, AMS.

30. Patience Gray to Ariane Castaing, undated, AMS.

31. Norman Mommens to Muriel Mommens, July 21, 1968, AMS.

32. Patience Gray to Ariane Castaing, August 13, 1968, AMS.

33. Norman Mommens to Muriel Mommens, July 21, 1968, AMS. The letter was written from Ronchi, Italy, while they were staying with Helen and Arno.

34. "La biennale internazionale del gioiello d'arte a Marina," *La Nazione*, August 18, 1968.

35. Norman Mommens to Muriel Mommens, September 22, 1968, AMS.

36. Ibid.

37. Patience Gray to Olive Stanham, July 21, 1968, AMS.

38. Felicity Ashbee, *The Independent*, July 2, 1996.

39. Patience Gray to Ariane Castaing, October 15, 1968, AMS.

40. Patience Gray to Olive Stanham, undated, AMS.

41. Ibid.

42. Ibid.

43. Patience Gray to Olive Stanham, November 10, 1968, AMS.

44. Patience Gray to Olive Stanham, January 19, 1969, AMS.

45. Gray, *HFAW*, 237.

46. Patience Gray to Olive Stanham, December 23, 1968, AMS.

47. Patience Gray to Tessa Sayle, October 2, 1971, AMS.

48. Patience Gray to Muriel Mommens, May 13, 1969, AMS.

49. Patience Gray to Olive Stanham, November 10, 1968, AMS.

50. Patience Gray to Olive Stanham, March 16, 1968, AMS.

51. Patience Gray to Muriel Mommens, May 13, 1969, AMS.

52. Patience Gray to Ariane Castaing, undated, AMS.

53. Norman Mommens to Muriel Mommens, April 23, 1969, AMS.

54. Patience Gray to Muriel Mommens, July 14, 1969, AMS.

55. Patience Gray to Olive Stanham, July 24, 1969, AMS.

56. Patience Gray to Muriel Mommens, August 20, 1969, AMS.

57. Norman Mommens to Muriel Mommens, September 6, 1969, AMS.

58. Ibid.

59. Patience Gray to Wolfe Aylward, undated, AMS.

60. Patience Gray to Wolfe Aylward, September 10, 1969, AMS.

61. Patience Gray to Wolfe Aylward, September 20, 1969, AMS.

62. Patience Gray to Olive Stanham, May 10, 1970, AMS.

CHAPTER ELEVEN: A NEW LIFE

1. Patience Gray to Ariane Castaing, undated, AMS.

2. Patience Gray to Wolfe Aylward, undated, AMS.

3. Patience Gray to Wolfe Aylward, 1983, AMS.

4. David Gentleman in discussion with the author, London, July 2010.

5. Lisa Armour-Brown in discussion with the author, Northumberland, November 2014.

6. Marushka Delabre, email message to author, March 2015.

7. Patience Gray to Olive Stanham, undated, AMS.

8. Oliver Bernard, "Obituary: Norman Mommens," *The Independent*, March 2, 2000.

9. See Vincent Crapanzano's illuminating introduction to Ernesto De Martino's ethnography, *The Land of Remorse: A Study of Southern Italian Tarantism*. The book was originally published in Italian in 1961. Incidentally some of De Martino's musical recordings were included in Alan Lomax's 1958 compilation.

10. Patience Gray to Olive Stanham, July 13, 1970, AMS.

11. Patience Gray to Olive Stanham, May 10, 1970, AMS.
12. Norman Mommens to Muriel Mommens, May 10, 1970, AMS.
13. Patience Gray to Olive Stanham, May 10, 1970, AMS.
14. Patience Gray to Wolfe Aylward, June 10, 1970, AMS.
15. Norman Mommens to Muriel Mommens, May 10, 1970, AMS.
16. Patience Gray to Muriel Mommens, July 7, 1970, AMS.
17. Peggy Angus to Patience Gray and Norman Mommens, December 19, 1971, AMS.
18. Patience Gray to Muriel Mommens, undated, AMS.
19. Norman Mommens to Muriel Mommens, August 21, 1970, AMS.
20. Norman Mommens to Muriel Mommens, July 30, 1970, AMS.
21. Patience Gray to Olive Stanham, October 4, 1970, AMS.
22. Norman Mommens to Muriel Mommens, June 22, 1970, AMS.
23. Patience Gray to Olive Stanham, August 14, 1970, AMS.
24. Patience Gray to Wolfe Aylward, undated, AMS.
25. Salvatore de Mira's wife Teresa in discussion with the author, Salve, Italy, June 2010.
26. Patience Gray to Olive Stanham, April 30, 1981, AMS.
27. Miranda Armour-Brown, email message to author, December 2015.
28. Nicolas Gray, email message to author, December 2015.
29. Patience Gray to Olive Stanham, August 11, 1970, AMS.
30. Norman Mommens to Muriel Mommens, July 30, 1970, AMS.
31. Patience Gray to Olive Stanham, undated, AMS.
32. Patience Gray to Olive Stanham, February 4, 1978, AMS.
33. Patience Gray to Olive Stanham, July 1982, AMS.
34. Patience Gray to Olive Stanham, October 1983, AMS.
35. Patience Gray to Olive Stanham, November 25, 1982, AMS.
36. Deborah Rogers to Alan Davidson, July 13, 1984, private collection.
37. Diana Athill to Patience Gray, June 16, 1970, AMS.
38. Deborah Rogers to Alan Davidson, July 13, 1984, private collection.
39. Judith Jones to Alan Davidson, November 4, 1986, private collection.
40. Patience Gray to Tessa Sayle, October 2, 1971, AMS. The old friend was Peggy Secord, the wife of Campbell Secord, who had been one of Patience's tutors at the London School of Economics.
41. Patience Gray to Olive Stanham, June 3, 1976, AMS.
42. Patience Gray to Nicolas Gray, December 16, 1984, AMS.
43. Patience Gray to Corinna Sargood, March 1972, AMS.
44. Patience Gray to Ariane Castaing, January 24, 1976, AMS.
45. Patience Gray to Olive Stanham, June 3, 1976, AMS.

46. Patience Gray to Ariane Castaing, November 18, 1970, AMS.

47. Ibid.

48. Ibid.

49. Ibid.

50. Hendrikus Theodorus Wijdeveld to Patience Gray and Norman Mommens, May 1, 1971, AMS.

51. Ibid.

52. Patience Gray to Muriel Mommens, April 1976, AMS.

53. Patience Gray to Olive Stanham, June 3, 1975, AMS.

54. Patience Gray to Olive Stanham, undated, AMS.

55. Patience Gray to Nicolas Gray, February 19, 1972, AMS.

56. Helen Ashbee, "Discussion of My Sculptures and of an Artists' Community in Italy," *Leonardo* 11, no. 4 (Autumn 1978). I am also indebted to Klaus and Ulrike Voswinckel for sharing their early memories of the Bufalaria.

57. Patience Gray to Olive Stanham, August 14, 1970, AMS.

58. Philip Trevelyan, email message to author, June 2015.

59. The trip, in a Spanish sailing vessel built in 1915, covered more than 7,500 miles and was described as "a journey outwards from the center to the periphery."

60. In his collection of essays, *The Artful Eater*, Behr writes, "I arrived here [in Vermont] in 1973 as part of a wave of idealistic newcomers. I began to write about food in the mid-1980s, when it was still possible to feel close to that back-to-the-land movement . . ."

61. Gray, *HFAW*, 11.

62. Eda Lord is quoted in Luke Barr's *Provence, 1970: M. F. K. Fisher, Julia Child, James Beard, and the Reinvention of American Taste* (New York: Clarkson Potter, 2013), 108.

63. Patience Gray to Philip Trevelyan, undated, private collection.

CHAPTER TWELVE: AN IMAGE OF WILDERNESS

1. Patience Gray to Muriel Mommens, April 1976, AMS.

2. Patience Gray to Ariane Castaing, December 20, 1974, AMS.

3. A reader for Viking Penguin, in a lengthy memo about the book, wrote that she had "never seen so much cooking lore in one place. . . . It is a fascinating book, but Gray makes Elizabeth David look like *The Joy of Cooking* in simplicity. How she knows what she knows is beyond me. But the editing and publishing of the book would be a massive undertaking and chances are that it would find a small but utterly devoted audience."

4. Patience Gray to Ariane Castaing, May 11, 1976, AMS.

5. Patience Gray to Ariane Castaing, October 22, 1975, AMS.

6. Ariane Castaing in discussion with the author, Vendôme, France, June 2010.

7. Jane Grigson to Patience Gray, October 27, 1976, AMS.

8. Patience Gray to Ariane Castaing, undated, AMS. In that same letter Patience wrote, "It would be so wonderful if you could come. We would just take the scissors and then see what is left."

9. Ariane Castaing in discussion with the author, Vendôme, France, June 2010.

10. Patience Gray to Ariane Castaing, November 1, 1975, AMS.

11. Miranda Armour-Brown in discussion with the author, Cambridge, November 2014.

12. Patience Gray to Ariane Castaing, August 29, 1976, AMS.

13. Patience Gray to Tessa Sayle, September 4, 1976, AMS.

14. Julia Farrington in discussion with the author, London, November 2014.

15. Ibid.

16. Patience Gray to Olive Stanham, June 9, 1972, AMS.

17. Patience Gray to Olive Stanham, June 19, 1973, AMS.

18. Christine Bullin in discussion with the author, telephone interview, December 2014.

19. Norman Janis in discussion with the author, New York, August 2012.

20. Christine Bullin in discussion with the author, telephone interview, December 2014.

21. Philip Trevelyan, email message to author, June 2015.

22. Christine Bullin in discussion with the author, telephone interview, December 2014.

23. Leila McAlister in discussion with the author, London, November 2014.

24. Patience Gray to Nicolas Gray, August 14, 1984, AMS.

25. Patience Gray to Muriel Mommens, January 17, 1976, AMS.

26. Norman Mommens to Muriel Mommens, February 6, 1962, AMS.

27. Norman Mommens to Muriel Mommens, July 23, 1972, AMS.

28. Patience Gray to Muriel Mommens, February 12, 1973, AMS.

29. Norman Mommens to Muriel Mommens, December 6, 1975, AMS.

30. Norman Mommens to Patrick Reyntiens, December 22, 1976, AMS.

31. Norman Mommens to Muriel Mommens, February 22, 1977, AMS.

32. Norman Mommens to Patrick Reyntiens, February 8, 1977, AMS.

33. Norman Mommens to Cecil Collins, undated, AMS. It is unclear if this letter was ever sent.

34. Patience Gray to Ariane Castaing, February 14, 1977, AMS.

35. Patience Gray to Muriel Mommens, July 7, 1970, AMS.

36. Patience Gray to Wolfe Aylward, January 21, 1971, AMS.

37. Patience Gray to Wolfe Aylward, May 19, 1971, AMS.

38. Patience Gray to Olive Stanham, May 13, 1977, AMS.

39. Miranda Armour-Brown, email message to author, January 2016.

40. Patience Gray to Olive Stanham, March 15, 1980, AMS.

41. Lisa Armour-Brown in dicussion with the author, Northumberland, November 2014.

42. Patience Gray to Olive Stanham, May 13, 1977, AMS.

43. Patience Gray to Wolfe Aylward, February 27, 1984, AMS.

44. Patience Gray to Edith Schloss, February 5, 1984, Edith Schloss Burckhardt Papers, Rare Book and Manuscript Library, Columbia University.

45. Aldo Magagnino, "The Rabbi Came . . . ," *The Italian Translator*, October 10, 2012, https://theitaliantranslator.wordpress.com/2012/10/10/153.

46. Ken Matthews to Patience Gray, July 3, 1983, AMS.

47. Patience Gray to Olive Stanham, April 30, 1981, AMS.

48. Patience Gray, interview by Derek Cooper, BBC Radio 4, *The Food Programme*, August 11, 1988.

49. Patience Gray to Nicolas Gray, December 21, 1985, AMS.

50. Patience Gray to Olive Stanham, undated, AMS.

51. Patience Gray to Alan Davidson, March 10, 1986, private collection.

52. Ada Ricchiuto in discussion with the author, Puglia, June 2011.

53. Patience Gray to Ariane Castaing, undated, AMS.

54. Emmanuel Anati in discussion with the author, telephone interview, June 2015.

55. Patience Gray to Nicolas Gray, January 10, 1985, AMS.

56. Gray, *HFAW*, 153–154.

57. Patience Gray to Emmanuel Anati, November 5, 1989, AMS.

58. In the late 1980s an Australian archaeological team, led by Ted Robinson, conducted work in the region. Their first preliminary report was published in 1989. They published a second report with Jean Paul Descoeudres, *The "Chiusa" at the "Masseria del Fano" in Salento*, in 1993. A version of this also appeared in the journal *Mediterranean Archaeology* 9, no. 10 (1996/7): 207–231. Duane Roller's *An Archaeological Survey in the Heel of Italy: The Work of the Southern Messapia Survey, 1989–1997* was published in 2002.

59. Duane Roller in conversation with the author, telephone interview, January 2016.

60. Patience Gray to Nicolas Gray, January 16, 1984, AMS.

CHAPTER THIRTEEN: *HONEY FROM A WEED*

1. Gwenda David to Patience Gray, April 9, 1980, AMS.
2. Deborah Rogers to Patience Gray, April 5, 1984, AMS.
3. Nicola Tyrer, "Fish Man's Tale," *Daily Mail*, 1988.
4. Elizabeth David, *An Omelette and a Glass of Wine* (London: Grub Street, 2009). The article was titled "If You Care to Eat Shark."
5. Elizabeth David to Alan Davidson, June 10, 1963, Papers of Elizabeth David, Schlesinger Library, Radcliffe Institute for Advanced Study at Harvard University.
6. Patience Gray, "Just in Case You Want to Know How to Make Coppa," *American Institute of Wine and Food Newsletter* 2, no. 4 (April 1983) and no. 5 (May 1983).
7. Patience Gray to Alan Davidson, November 17, 1983, private collection.
8. Tyrer, "Fish Man's Tale."
9. Alan Davidson to Patience Gray, August 14, 1984, private collection.
10. Alan Davidson to Patience Gray, July 23, 1985, private collection.
11. Patience Gray to Alan Davidson, August 26, 1985, private collection.
12. Rosemary Davidson in discussion with the author, Cambridge, June 2010.
13. Alan Davidson, "The Prospect Behind Us," *Petits Propos Culinaires* 47 (1994).
14. Helen Saberi, "A Life in the Day of Alan Davidson," *Petits Propos Culinaires* 100 (2014).
15. Caroline Davidson in discussion with the author, telephone interview, January 2015.
16. Patience Gray to Alan Davidson, October 1, 1984, private collection.
17. Ibid.
18. Patience Gray to Alan Davidson, November 25, 1989, private collection.
19. Caroline Davidson in discussion with the author, telephone interview, January 2015.
20. Rosemary Davidson in discussion with the author, Cambridge, June 2010.
21. Alan Davidson to Corinna Sargood, November 11, 1985, private collection.
22. Patience Gray to Candida Brazil, October 16, 1985, private collection.
23. Candida Brazil in discussion with the author, telephone interview, February 2015.
24. Helen Saberi in discussion with the author, London, November 2014.
25. Candida Brazil in discussion with the author, telephone interview, February 2015.
26. Alan Davidson to Patience Gray, November 5, 1985, private collection.
27. Ibid.

28. Patience Gray to Alan Davidson, November 11, 1985, private collection.
29. Gray, *HFAW*, 50.
30. Patience Gray to Alan Davidson, December 27, 1985, private collection.
31. David Gentleman in discussion with the author, London, July 2010.
32. Patience Gray to Alan Davidson, August 26, 1984, private collection.
33. Patience Gray to Alan Davidson, February 19, 1985, private collection.
34. Patience Gray to Alan Davidson, February 13, 1987, private collection.
35. Gray, *HFAW*, 353.
36. Colman Andrews, *Catalan Cuisine*, 94.
37. Valerie Miles, "The Weather Men: The Life, Times, and Meteorological Theories of Josep Pla," *The Paris Review*, March 25, 2014, http://www.the parisreview.org/blog/2014/03/25/the-weather-men. Only two of Pla's books, *The Gray Notebook* and *Life Embitters*, have been translated into English.
38. Patience Gray to Ulrike Voswinckel, undated, AMS.
39. Patience Gray to Alan Davidson, September 10, 1986, private collection.
40. Patience Gray to Alan Davison, September 14, 1985, private collection.
41. Caroline Davidson in discussion with the author, telephone interview, January 2015.
42. Ibid.
43. Patience Gray to Nicolas Gray, December 21, 1985, AMS.
44. Caroline Davidson in discussion with the author, telephone interview, January 2015.
45. Sue Fox, "How We Met: Paul Levy and Alan Davidson," *The Independent*, December 14, 1996.
46. Ada Martella in discussion with the author, Puglia, February 2015.
47. Lisa Armour-Brown in discussion with the author, Northumberland, November 2014.
48. Patience Gray to Nicolas Gray, December 21, 1985, AMS.
49. Alan Davidson to Patience Gray, May 17, 1987, private collection.
50. Ibid.
51. Patience Gray to Alan Davidson, May 28, 1987, private collection.
52. Alan Davidson to Patience Gray, December 16, 1985, private collection.
53. Jane Davidson to Patience Gray, December 29, 1985, private collection.
54. Mary Blume, "A Bohemian's Recipes for Life at Sea," *New York Times*, August 26, 2005.
55. Alan Davidson, "The Prospect Behind Us," *Petits Propos Culinaires* 47 (1994); Caroline Davidson, email message to author, January 2015.
56. Gray, *HFAW*, 193.
57. Patience Gray to Alan Davidson, October 1, 1984, private collection.

58. Derek Cooper, "Food," *The Listener*, September 1, 1988.

59. Patience Gray to Alan Davidson, October 1, 1984, private collection.

60. Gray, *HFAW*, 326.

61. Ibid.

62. Ibid.

63. Marina Pizzolante, email message to author, May 2015.

64. Ada Martella in discussion with the author, Puglia, February 2015.

65. Nicolas Gray, email message to author, August 2016.

66. Gray, *HFAW*, 269.

67. Patience Gray to John Thorne, July 27, 1998, private collection.

68. Patience Gray to Corby Kummer, April 5, 1992, AMS.

69. Patience Gray to Alan Davidson, September 10, 1986, private collection.

70. Alan Davidson to Judith Jones, August 20, 1986, private collection.

71. Harold McGee in discussion with the author, telephone interview, September 2014.

72. Alan Davidson to Patience Gray, October 27, 1986, private collection.

CHAPTER FOURTEEN: DISCOVERING THE SALENTO

1. Jeremy Round, "High Priestess of Cooking," *The Independent*, November 7, 1986.

2. Theodora FitzGibbon, "A Cook's Best Friend," January 17, 1987.

3. Christopher Driver, "Recipes from the Sunny Side of the Ice Age," *Guardian*, March 20, 1987.

4. Angela Carter, "Wolfing It," *London Review of Books* 9, no. 14 (July 23, 1987): 15–16.

5. Fiona MacCarthy's review appeared in the *Sunday Times* on January 1, 1987, under the headline, "Food and the Passionate Englishwoman." In an email message to the author, MacCarthy wrote, "She [Patience] was a remarkable woman and we much admired her."

6. Patience Gray to Alan Davidson, January 15, 1987, private collection.

7. Candida Brazil in discussion with the author, telephone interview, February 2015.

8. Rosemary Davidson in discussion with the author, Cambridge, July 2010.

9. Patience Gray to Ariane Castaing, undated, AMS.

10. Harold McGee in discussion with the author, telephone interview, September 2014.

11. Patience Gray to Alan Davidson, March 29/30, 1987, private collection. She also said there were aspects of their life that might be reminiscent of the 1932

novel *Cold Comfort Farm*, a parody of the back-to-the-land movement in Britain in the 1930s. The book has been adapted for television and radio several times.

12. Patience Gray to Paul Levy, June 8, 1987, AMS.
13. Paul Levy to Patience Gray, June 18, 1987, AMS.
14. Paul Levy, email message to author, February 2016.
15. Patience Gray to Alan Davidson, July 29, 1987, private collection; Patience Gray to Ariane Castaing, July 29, 1987, AMS.
16. Patience Gray to Nicolas Gray, August 11, 1987, AMS.
17. Ibid.
18. The *Observer* article titled "The Virtue of Being Patience" appeared on October 18, 1987. The *Wall Street Journal* version, "From London to Apulia, a Life with Recipes," was published on December 17, 1987.
19. Corby Kummer in discussion with the author, telephone interview, March 2016.
20. Paul Levy to Patience Gray, August 12, 1987, AMS.
21. "Mommens e Gray," *Notiziario Arte Contemporanea* 6–7 (June/July 1973) 19–20.
22. Patience Gray to Wolfe Aylward, 1973, AMS.
23. *Sonne, Mond*, directed by Klaus and Ulrike Voswinckel, 1983.
24. Patience Gray to Alan Davidson, November 22, 1985, private collection.
25. Julia Farrington in discussion with the author, London, November 2014.
26. Patience Gray to Alan Davidson, November 22, 1985, private collection.
27. Patience Gray to Nicolas Gray, December 16, 1984, AMS.
28. Patience Gray to Nicolas Gray, July 7, 1999, AMS.
29. John Thorne, email message to author, August 27, 2014.
30. Ed Behr in discussion with the author, Vermont, September 2014.
31. Corby Kummer to Patience Gray, January 20, 1988, AMS.
32. Ibid.
33. Patience Gray to Corby Kummer, undated, AMS.
34. Patience Gray to Alan Davidson, April 12, 1988, private collection.
35. Vanessa Harrison, email message to author, January 2015.
36. Patience Gray, interview by Derek Cooper, BBC Radio 4, *The Food Programme*, August 11, 1988, and August 13, 1988. The program was part of a series on the politics of food called "Prophets Returned."
37. Derek Cooper, "Food," *The Listener*, September 1988.
38. Alan Davidson to Pat Brown, July 31, 1987, private collection.
39. Patience Gray to David Gentleman, October 23, 1987, AMS.
40. Patience Gray, *RDS*, xiv.
41. Patience Gray to Nicolas Gray, September 19, 1988, AMS.

42. Patience Gray, interview by Melvyn Bragg, BBC Radio 4, *Start the Week*, February 1989.

43. Elizabeth Herring, "Seasons of Culture Shock," *Times Literary Supplement*, July 7–13, 1989.

44. Elizabeth Herring, email message to author, February 2016.

45. Kevin Andrews to Patience Gray, June 6, 1989, AMS.

46. Eugenia Parry in discussion with the author, telephone interview, March 2015.

47. Nancy Andrews to Patience Gray, June 10, 1991, AMS.

48. Patience Gray to Alan Davidson, January 10, 1986, private collection.

49. Patience Gray to Harlan Walker, February 18, 1993, private collection. Patience was of course recalling her essay on decorated food for André Simon's *Wine and Food* in 1958.

50. Alan Davidson to Patience Gray, undated, private collection.

51. Patience Gray to John Thorne, November 19, 1990, private collection.

52. Patience Gray to Caroline Davidson, April 11, 1989, private collection. There were others like Felici who carried out important, site-specific field-work in the sixteenth century. Gherardo Cibo, a gentleman-scholar, did not publish anything in his lifetime but collected and illustrated thousands of plants. Francesco Calzolari, an apothecary without a university degree, was highly regarded for his knowledge of the plants of Northern Italy. In her book *Possessing Nature*, Paula Findlen writes of this period that "Experience now played a greater role in the constitution of scientific authority, and the naturalists who claimed the greatest level of 'experience' subsequently came to possess the highest degree of knowledge."

53. Patience Gray to Alan Davidson, April 12, 1989, private collection.

54. Gillian Riley, email message to author, February 2016.

55. Patience Gray to Alan Davidson, May 25, 1989, private collection.

56. Patience's notion that plants are living forms, capable of communicating and even feeling, has only recently been taken seriously by the scientific community. Patience once wrote that "plants actually speak," only people have stopped hearing them. She also said that "flowers long for recognition," which she felt was her role in the wilderness. In his 2013 *New Yorker* article, "The Intelligent Plant," Michael Pollan explores new research into what some scientists have called "plant neurobiology."

57. Patience Gray to Nicolas Gray, November 22, 1992, AMS.

58. Patience Gray to Nicolas Gray, January 22, 1991, AMS.

59. In a letter to Patience, Alan said he was embarrassed and felt badly about using the title *Fasting and Feasting* after having discouraged Patience from

doing the same. Patience said she did not mind and that it was rather like "keeping it in the family."

60. She encouraged John Thorne to examine the cooking of Fritz Brenner and suggested that it be "accompanied by a text on personal liberty, the fundament of Rex Stout's writing."

61. Patience Gray to Glenfiddich Awards Committee, undated, AMS. Gray closed the letter by saying, "Good food writing is an extremely rare 'commodity.'"

62. Patience Gray to Ulrike Voswinckel, undated, AMS.

63. Alan Davidson to Patience Gray, March 30, 1988, private collection.

64. Patience's friend the painter Edith Schloss also told the story of buying a copy of *Honey from a Weed* at St. Mark's Bookshop in New York. When she went to pay for it, the cashier said, "Do you realize what a wonderful book you are buying?" Schloss told him that she knew the author and that she was in fact wearing a ring made by her. To which he said, "May I touch it?"

65. Patience Gray to Alan Davidson, 1990, private collection.

66. Patience Gray, "South to the Salento," *The Sophisticated Traveler*, March 3, 1991.

67. Ibid.

68. Ibid.

69. Gray, *HFAW*, 289.

70. Patience Gray, "South to the Salento," *The Sophisticated Traveler*, March 3, 1991.

71. Gray, *HFAW*, 12.

72. Jeremy Round, "High Priestess of Cooking," *The Independent*, November 7, 1986.

73. Patience Gray to John Thorne, July 27, 1998, private collection.

74. Patience Gray to Alan Davidson, August 1986, private collection.

75. In November 1990, Penelope Green, then the food editor of the *New York Times*, wrote to Patience, "As far as I'm concerned you could write for me anything you pleased, however arcane be it on horsemeat, or homemade pasta, or whatever."

CHAPTER FIFTEEN: REFLECTIONS

1. Patience Gray to Alan Davidson, August 23, 1986, private collection.

2. Patience Gray to Nicolas Gray, September 28, 1999, AMS.

3. Patience Gray to Nicolas Gray, January 2, 1996, AMS.

4. Ada Martella in discussion with the author, Puglia, February 2015.

5. Patience Gray to Olive Stanham, undated, AMS.

6. Patience Gray to Miranda Armour-Brown, November 17, 1992, AMS.

7. Giovene, *The Book of Sansevero*, 176.

8. Patience Gray to Muriel Mommens, November 10, 1974, AMS.

9. Giovene, *The Third Day*, trans. by Patience Gray.

10. Andrea Giovene, *Lirica dell'Insonnia* (Presicce, Italy: Levante Arti Grafiche, 1992). Indeed Patience had Ada Martella, who was then living in Chieti, deliver a selection of Don Andrea's books and some of his poems to the Italian publisher Sellerio. Ada, who had been corresponding with Patience about Don Andrea, met with the company's founder, Elvira Sellerio, and presented her with not only the parcel but also some of her own letters in which she discussed Giovene's work. Elvira said publishing some of Don Andrea's books might be interesting but that it was Ada's letters she was really drawn to. Ada told Patience she was somewhat disappointed with this outcome, to which Patience replied, "Oh, no, darling this is the important thing." According to Ada this is when she realized she wanted to be a writer and not an architect.

11. Rolando Civilla in discussion with the author, Puglia, February 2015.

12. Leandro's remarkable sculpture garden (in San Cesario di Lecce), *Il Santuario della Pazienza*, completed in 1975, is regrettably neglected but subject to plans for restoration and regular opening as a museum.

13. Rolando Civilla in discussion with the author, Puglia, February 2015.

14. Patience Gray to Nicolas Gray, undated, AMS.

15. Patience Gray to Marushka Delabre, undated, AMS.

16. Gray, *HFAW*, 281.

17. Gray, *WACD*, 9.

18. Tom Jaine to Patience Gray, September 25, 1997, AMS.

19. Vera Rule, "A Woman for All Seasons," *Guardian*, July 28, 2000.

20. John de Falbe, "A Jeweller's Treasure Chest," *The Spectator*, August 18, 2000.

21. However outlandish this notion may have been, Patience seemed to take it somewhat seriously. After Norman's death in 2000, she used to say that he too was still present in the form of a praying mantis. According to Patience's granddaughter Rosy, during a visit in 2003 a praying mantis landed on top of her cane during breakfast. When she got up to leave the table, she turned to the emerald-green insect and said, "Come on, Norman." Another friend, Marina Pizzolante, said the last time she saw Patience, not long before her death in 2005, there was a praying mantis perched on the rim of the glass next to her bed.

22. Gray, *WACD*, 304.

23. Ibid., 335.

24. Ibid., 343.

25. Margaret Gray to Miranda Armour-Brown, May 3, 1991, AMS.

26. Miranda Armour-Brown to Nicolas Gray, January 21, 1991, AMS.

27. Patience Gray to Nicolas Gray, June 4, 1991, AMS.

28. Gray, *WACD*, 170.

29. Ibid.

30. Rosy Gray in discussion with the author, telephone interview, March 2015.

31. Miranda Armour-Brown in dicussion with the author, Cambridge, July 2010.

32. Ruscha Schorr-Kon in discussion with the author, telephone interview, April 2016.

33. *To My Darling*, a film directed by Rossella Piccinno and Tommaso Del Signore, is a strikingly beautiful introduction to the birthday books.

34. Patience Gray to Wolfe Aylward, February 3, 1994, AMS.

35. Patience Gray to Wolfe Aylward, February 10, 1994, AMS.

36. Patience Gray to Wolfe Aylward, March 2, 1993, AMS.

37. Patience Gray to Wolfe Aylward, July 1986, AMS.

38. Julia Farrington in discussion with the author, London, November 2014.

39. Wolfe Aylward to Patience Gray, March 25, 1994, AMS. He was referring to Alain-Fournier's novel of adolescence, longing, and unrequited love published in 1913.

40. Nancy Harmon Jenkins in discussion with the author, telephone interview, April 2015.

41. Patience Gray to Wolfe Aylward, undated, AMS.

42. Ed Behr in discussion with the author, Vermont, September 2014.

43. R. W. Apple Jr. wrote about Puglia for the *New York Times* in 1985, in a piece titled "Apulia: An Ancient, Rugged Land," and described the region as "a touristic backwater." Nancy Harmon Jenkins said it was very difficult to impress R. W. Apple Jr., who had wined and dined with Europe's best chefs, but that he was incredibly keen to meet Patience.

44. Ed Behr, "Patience Gray," *The Art of Eating* 69 (2005).

45. Patience Gray to Wolfe Aylward, undated, AMS.

46. Corby Kummer in discussion with the author, telephone interview, March 2016.

47. Patience Gray to Wolfe Aylward, undated, AMS.

48. Patience Gray to Corby Kummer, April 5, 1992, AMS.

49. Harold McGee to Patience Gray, June 25, 1992, AMS.

50. Patience Gray to John Thorne, August 7, 1992, private collection.

51. Harold McGee in discussion with the author, telephone interview, September 2014.

52. Ibid.

53. Patience once sent Miranda a letter with a list of her favorite books, nearly all of which were Russian. Among her favorites were Lermontov's *A Hero of Our Time*, Dostoyevsky's *The Gambler*, and Maxim Gorky's three-volume autobiography.
54. Nicolas Gray in discussion with the author, Puglia, February 2015.
55. Corby Kummer to Patience Gray, December 4, 1993, AMS.
56. John Thorne, email message to author, August 2014.
57. Bruce Gollan to Patience Gray, July 31, 1990, AMS.
58. Patience Gray to Ulrike Voswinckel, undated, AMS.
59. Alan Davidson to Patience Gray, March 12, 1987, private collection.
60. Patience Gray to Nicolas Gray, May 23, 1995, AMS.
61. According to Patience, Wolfert approached her on the terrace of the restaurant and said, "I have read all your books. Have you read mine?" To which Patience replied, "No, but I have read about you." In a letter to John Thorne, Patience wrote, "The absent outlaw cook couldn't have been more present."
62. Patience Gray to Corby Kummer, June 1, 1995, AMS.
63. In 2007 the *New York Times* food critic Frank Bruni wrote a long feature on Puglia titled "The Heel Is Rising." That same year *Gourmet* published an article on the region titled "Pure Puglia." *Bon Appetit* ran a piece on the food of Puglia in May 2010. In the last several years, the *New York Times Style Magazine*, *Condé Nast Traveller*, *New York Post*, *Telegraph*, and *Guardian* have all devoted features to Puglia, one of the "hottest holiday destinations," according to *Luxury Travel Magazine*.

CHAPTER SIXTEEN: THINGS ARE SACRED

1. Patience Gray to Alan Davidson, September 14, 1990, private collection. Patience was also delighted to have had another excursion in the Bentley. "I would have been glad of at least one traffic jam," she wrote.
2. Betty died suddenly of a heart attack in 1987, just after attending a conference on tribal issues and forest management in Hyderabad, India. Her ashes were buried in the Gond village of Marlavai in Adilabad district, where she and Christoph had conducted research in the early 1940s.
3. Vanessa Harrison, email message to author, January 2015.
4. Maud Murdoch to Patience Gray, October 12, 1990, AMS. As a sign of the times, in the late 1980s Boy George purchased part of The Logs for an undisclosed sum and caused a mild uproar when he threatened to turn the garden into a swimming pool. According to Trevor Pinnock, Boy George invited all of his neighbors to tea and proved to be a "very nice chap."

5. Patience Gray, interview by Melvyn Bragg, BBC Radio 4, *Start the Week*, February 1989.
6. Sue Gentleman in discussion with the author, London, July 2010.
7. Gray, *HFAW*, 226.
8. Ibid., 245. The quote comes from a section titled "How to Cook Birds without an Oven."
9. Ed Behr in discussion with the author, Vermont, September 2014.
10. Christine Bullin in discussion with the author, telephone interview, December 2014.
11. Fiona Clai Brown in correspondence with the author, March 2016.
12. David Gentleman in discussion with the author, London, November 2014.
13. Ibid.
14. Patience Gray to Marushka Delabre, Februrary 1999, AMS.
15. Rosy Gray in discussion with the author, telephone interview, March 2015.
16. Christine Bullin in discussion with the author, telephone interview, December 2014.
17. Gray, *WACD*, 284.
18. Gray, *Plats du Jour* (Devon, England: Prospect Books, 1990), xiv.
19. In 2000 Patience asked Ulrike Voswinckel if she still wished to "inherit" her letters. At the time Ulrike was entertaining the idea of producing a radio program on Patience.
20. Nicolas Gray, email message to author, December 2015.
21. Philip would see Norman and Patience one last time in November 1992, when he and Nelly traveled to Puglia, and he described it as a "lovely reunion."
22. Norman Mommens, interview by Derek Cooper, BBC Radio 4, *The Food Programme*, January 13, 1989, and January 16, 1989. The interview was conducted during Cooper's visit to Puglia in July 1988. Other guests on the program included an analytical chemist from the University of Surrey, professors at a biodynamic farm at Emerson College in East Sussex, and a member of the Soil Association.
23. Philip Trevelyan, email message to author, March 2016.
24. Patience Gray to John Thorne, May 29, 1993, private collection.
25. Nicolas Gray, email message to author, March 2016.
26. Patience Gray to Nicolas Gray, May 2, 1995, AMS.
27. Patience Gray to Nicolas Gray, March 2, 1996, AMS.
28. Gray, *HFAW*, 269.
29. Patience Gray to Ariane Castaing, undated, AMS.
30. Norman Mommens in *HFAW*, 315.
31. Aldo Magagnino in discussion with the author, Puglia, February 2015.

32. Nicolas Gray, email message to author, October 2016.

33. Patience Gray to Nicolas Gray, November 13, 1999, AMS. When he first read *Honey from a Weed*, Ed Behr remembers being astonished at the quantity of olive oil consumed in the Salento.

34. Patience Gray to Nicolas Gray, May 23, 1987, AMS.

35. The piece in *Vogue*, "La Masseria Decorata," appeared in the July/August 1992 issue. Written by an acquaintance, Cinzi Ruggeri, it featured several well-lit photographs of the interior of the masseria and described Patience and Norman as "nomads in flight." The reference to "cracked bentwood chairs" is in a letter from Patience to Nicolas, October 5, 1992, AMS.

36. Patience Gray to Nicolas Gray, January 17, 1995, AMS.

37. Patience Gray to Ulrike Voswinckel, October 28, 2000, AMS.

38. Nicole Fenosa to Patience Gray, February 4, 1995, AMS.

39. Bill McAlister in discussion with the author, telephone interview, January 2015.

40. Patience Gray to Nicolas Gray, April 11, 1996, AMS. In 2003, several years after Norman's death, Nicolas had electricity and a small fridge installed. Patience seemed not to acknowledge the fridge for several days but then one afternoon shuffled past it, looked up, and said to Nick, "You have ruined my kitchen!"

41. Nicolas Gray, email message to author, March 2016.

42. Patience Gray to Nicolas Gray, March 25, 1998, AMS.

43. Patience Gray to Edith Schloss, April 24, 1999, Edith Schloss Burckhardt Papers, Rare Book and Manuscript Library, Columbia University.

44. Norman Janis in discussion with the author, Puglia, February 2015.

45. The response to Norman's death was overwhelming and the procession in Salve on foot from the church to the cemetery drew hundreds of mourners.

46. Christoph von Fürer-Haimendorf to Patience Gray, July 14, 1987, AMS.

47. Oliver Bernard in correspondence with the author, April 10, 2012.

48. Norman Janis in discussion with the author, Puglia, February 2015.

49. Patience Gray, interview by Simon Parkes, BBC Radio 4, *The Food Programme*, August 11, 2002.

50. Patience Gray to Elisabeth Sifton, June 18, 2000, AMS.

51. Alan Davidson to Patience Gray, undated, private collection.

52. The essay appeared in *W*, a small trade publication distributed by the bookseller Waterstones to their customers.

53. Leila McAlister in discussion with the author, London, November 2014.

54. Stevie Parle in discussion with the author, telephone interview, April 2015. Parle was introduced to *Honey from a Weed* by Skye Gyngell, a former food editor of *Vogue* and the chef-owner of Spring restaurant in London.

Parle says he regularly gives copies of *Honey from a Weed* to his cooks as a Christmas present.

55. Jacob Kenedy in discussion with the author, telephone interview, January 2015.

56. Ed Behr in discussion with the author, Vermont, September 2014.

57. Lisa Armour-Brown to Edith Schloss, February 3, 2002, Edith Schloss Burckhardt Papers, Rare Book and Manuscript Library, Columbia University.

58. Simon Parkes in discussion with the author, telephone interview, December 2015.

59. Bill McAlister in discussion with the author, telephone interview, January 2015.

60. Patience Gray to Norman Janis, 2004, private collection.

Selected Bibliography

Allen, *David* Elliston. *The Naturalist in Britain: A Social History*. Princeton, NJ: Princeton University Press, 1994.

Andrews, Kevin. *The Flight of Ikaros: A Journey into Greece*. Boston: Houghton Mifflin, 1959.

Athill, Diana. *Instead of a Memoir*. London: W. W. Norton & Company, 1962.

Atkins, Harriet. *The Festival of Britain: A Land and Its People*. London: I. B. Tauris, 2012.

Andrews, Colman. *Catalan Cuisine: Europe's Last Great Culinary Secret*. New York: Macmillan Publishing, 1988.

Artmonsky, Ruth, and Brian Webb. *FHK Henrion: Design*. Woodbridge: Antique Collectors' Club, 2011.

Barnardo, Frederick. *An Active Life*. London: Bodley Head, 1963.

Bernard, Oliver. *Getting Over It: An Autobiography*. London: Peter Owen, 1992.

Blake, Avril. *Misha Black*. London: The Design Council, 1984.

Blossfeldt, Karl. *Art Forms in Nature: Examples from the Plant World Photographed Direct from Nature*. New York: E. Weyhe, 1929.

Brown, Dona. *Back to the Land: The Enduring Dream of Self-Sufficiency in Modern America*. Madison: University of Wisconsin Press, 2011.

Brown, Jane. *The English Garden in Our Time: From Gertrude Jekyll to Geoffrey Jellicoe*. Woodbridge: Antique Collectors' Club, 1987.

Buchan, Ursula. *A Green and Pleasant Land: How England's Gardeners Fought the Second World War*. London: Hutchinson, 2013.

Castelvetro, Giacomo. *The Fruit, Herbs & Vegetables of Italy: An Offering to Lucy, Countess of Bedford*. Translated by Gillian Riley. London: Viking, 1989.

Chaney, Lisa. *Elizabeth David: A Biography*. London: Macmillan Publishing, 1998.

Cockett, Richard. *David Astor and the Observer*. London: André Deutsch, 1991.

Cohen, Lisa. *All We Know: Three Lives*. New York: Farrar, Straus and Giroux, 2012.

Collingham, Lizzie. *The Taste of War: World War Two and the Battle for Food*. New York: Penguin Books, 2011.

Cooke, Rachel. *Her Brilliant Career: Ten Extraordinary Women of the Fifties*. London: Virago, 2013.

Cooper, Artemis. *Writing at the Kitchen Table: The Authorized Biography of Elizabeth David*. New York: Ecco Press, 2000.

Crawford, Alan. *C. R. Ashbee: Architect, Designer and Romantic Socialist*. 2nd ed. New Haven: Yale University Press, 2005.

Davenport, Nicholas. *Memoirs of a City Radical*. London: Weidenfeld and Nicolson, 1974.

David, Elizabeth. *A Book of Mediterranean Food*. Harmondsworth, England: Penguin Books, 1955.

———. *Italian Food*. London: Penguin Books, 1989.

Davidson, Alan. *Mediterranean Seafood: A Comprehensive Guide with Recipes*. Berkeley: Ten Speed Press, 2002.

Davis, Irving. *A Catalan Cookery Book: A Collection of Impossible Recipes*. Edited by Patience Gray. Devon, England: Prospect Books, 1999.

De Martino, Ernesto. *The Land of Remorse: A Study of Southern Italian Tarantism*. Translated by Dorothy Louise Zinn. London: Free Association Books, 2005.

Downs, Annabel, ed. *Peter Shepheard*. Redhill, England: Landscape Design Trust, 2004.

Driver, Christopher. *The British at Table, 1940–1980*. London: Chatto and Windus, 1983.

Findlen, Paula. *Possessing Nature: Museums, Collecting, and Scientific Culture in Early Modern Italy*. Berkeley: University of California Press, 1994.

Fleming, Fergus. *Amaryllis Fleming*. London: Methuen, 1994.

Giovene, Andrea. *The Book of Sansevero*. Translated by Marguerite Waldman. Boston: Houghton Mifflin, 1970.

———. *The Third Day*. Translated by Patience Gray. Presicce, Italy: Levante Arti Grafiche, 1996.

Goodden, Henrietta. *Robin Darwin: Visionary Educator and Painter*. London: Unicorn Press, 2015.

Gray, Patience, *Honey from a Weed: Fasting and Feasting in Tuscany, Catalonia, the Cyclades, and Apulia*. New York: Harper and Row, 1987. First published 1986 by Prospect Books.

———. *Ring Doves and Snakes*. London: Macmillan Publishing, 1989.

———. *The Centaur's Kitchen: A Book of French, Italian, Greek and Catalan Dishes for Ships' Cooks on the Blue Funnel Line*. Totnes, England: Prospect Books, 2005.

———. *Work Adventures Childhood Dreams*. Presicce, Italy: Levante Arti Grafiche, 1999.

Gray, Patience, and Primrose Boyd. *Plats du Jour*. London: Persephone Books, 2006. First published 1957 by Penguin Books.

Harries, Meirion, and Susie Harries. *A Pilgrim Soul: The Life and Work of Elisabeth Lutyens*. London: Michael Joseph, 1989.

Harris, Alexandra. *Romantic Moderns: English Writers, Artists and the Imagination from Virginia Woolf to John Piper.* New York: Thames and Hudson, 2010.

Humble, Nicola. *Culinary Pleasures: Cookbooks and the Transformation of British Food.* London: Faber and Faber, 2005.

Jackson, Lesley. *Alastair Morton and Edinburgh Weavers: Visionary Textiles and Modern Art.* London: Victoria and Albert Publishing, 2012.

Jinkinson, Roger. *American Ikaros: The Search for Kevin Andrews.* London: Racing House Press, 2010.

Jones, Margaret E., and H. F. Clark. *Indoor Plants and Gardens.* Edited by Patience Gray. London: Architectural Press, 1952.

Kaye, Elaine. *A History of Queen's College, London 1848–1972.* London: Chatto and Windus, 1972.

Kynaston, David. *Austerity Britain: 1945–1951.* New York: Walker and Company, 2008.

———. *Family Britain: 1951–1957.* New York: Walker and Company, 2009.

Levi, Carlo. *Christ Stopped at Eboli: The Story of a Year.* Translated by Frances Frenaye. New York: Farrar, Straus and Giroux, 2006.

Lewis, Jeremy. *David Astor: A Life in Print.* London: Jonathan Cape, 2016.

MacDougall, Elisabeth B., ed. *John Claudius Loudon and the Early Nineteenth Century in Great Britain.* Washington, DC: Dumbarton Oaks, 1980.

MacCarthy, Fiona. *The Simple Life: C. R. Ashbee in the Cotswolds.* Berkeley: University of California Press, 1981.

Marsh, Jan. *Back to the Land: The Pastoral Impulse in England, from 1880 to 1914.* London: Quartet Books, 1982.

Reed, Matthew. *Rebels for the Soil: The Rise of the Global Organic Food and Farming Movement.* Washington, DC: Earthscan, 2010.

Meynell, Esther. *Sussex.* London: Robert Hale, 1947.

Mommens, Norman. *Remembering Man.* Presicce, Italy: Levante Arti Grafiche, 1991.

Montagné, Prosper. *Larousse Gastronomique: The Encyclopedia of Food, Wine and Cookery.* Edited by Charlotte Turgeon and Nina Froud. Translated by Nina Froud et al. New York: Crown Publishers, 1961.

Oddy, Derek J. *From Plain Fare to Fusion Food: British Diet from the 1890s to the 1990s.* Woodbridge: Boydell Press, 2003.

Panter-Downes, Mollie. *London War Notes, 1939–1945.* New York: Farrar, Straus and Giroux, 1971.

Ramsbottom, John. *Edible Fungi.* London: King Penguin, 1943.

Russell, James. *Peggy Angus: Designer, Teacher, Painter.* Woodbridge: Antique Collectors' Club, 2014.

Scigliano, Eric. *Michelangelo's Mountain: The Quest for Perfection in the Marble Quarries of Carrara*. New York: Free Press, 2005.

Shepheard, Peter F. *Modern Gardens*. London: Architectural Press, 1953.

Sheridan, Dorothy, ed. *Wartime Women: A Mass-Observation Anthology, 1937–45*. London: Phoenix Press, 2000.

Spalding, Frances. *John Minton: Dance till the Stars Come Down*. Aldershot, England: Lund Humphries, 2005.

Spoerri, Daniel. *The Mythological Travels of a Modern Sir John Mandeville, Being an Account of the Magic, Meatballs and Other Monkey Business Peculiar to the Sojourn of Daniel Spoerri upon the Isle of Symi, Together with Divers Speculations Thereon*. Translated by Emmett Williams. New York: Something Else Press, 1970.

Stewart, Charles. *Demons and the Devil: Moral Imagination in Modern Greek Culture*. Princeton, NJ: Princeton University Press, 1991.

Thorne, John. *Outlaw Cook*. New York: Farrar, Straus and Giroux, 1992.

Trant, Carolyn. *Art for Life: The Story of Peggy Angus*. Oldham, England: Incline Press, 2005.

Uhlman, Fred. *A Moroccan Diary*. Presicce, Italy: Levante Arti Grafiche, 1995.

von Fürer-Haimendorf, Christoph. *Life among Indian Tribes: The Autobiography of an Anthropologist*. New York: Oxford University Press, 1990.

INDEX

Note: Page numbers preceded by *ci* refer to the color insert section. The following abbreviations are used in the index:

PG = Patience Gray
NM = Norman Mommens
OS = Olive Stanham
TG = Thomas Gray

ABOUT THE AUTHOR

ADAM FEDERMAN is a reporting fellow with the Investigative Fund of the Nation Institute covering energy and the environment. He has written for *The Nation* magazine, the *Guardian, Columbia Journalism Review, Gastronomica, Petits Propos Culinaires, Earth Island Journal, Adirondack Life,* and other publications. He has been a Russia Fulbright Fellow, a Middlebury Fellow in Environmental Journalism, and the recipient of a Polk grant for investigative reporting. A former line cook, bread baker, and pastry chef, he lives in Vermont.

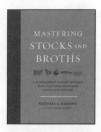

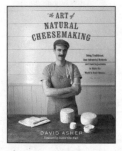
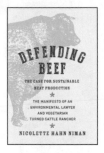